Displacement Risks in Africa

Displacement Risks in Africa

Edited by
Itaru Ohta
and
Yntiso D. Gebre

Kyoto University Press

TRANS PACIFIC PRESS

First published in 2005 jointly by:

Kyoto University Press
Kyodai Kaikan
15-9 Yoshida Kawara-cho
Sakyo-ku, Kyoto 606-8305, Japan
Telephone: +81-75-761-6182
Fax: +81-75-761-6190
Email: sales@kyoto-up.gr.jp
Web: http://www.kyoto-up.gr.jp

Trans Pacific Press
PO Box 120, Rosanna, Melbourne
Victoria 3084, Australia
Telephone: +61 3 9459 3021
Fax: +61 3 9457 5923
Email: info@transpacificpress.com
Web: http://www.transpacificpress.com

Distributors

Australia
Bushbooks
PO Box 1958, Gosford, NSW 2250
Telephone: (02) 4323-3274
Fax: (02) 4323-3223
Email: bushbook@ozemail.com.au

USA and Canada
International Specialized Book
Services (ISBS)
920 NE 58th Avenue, Suite 300
Portland, Oregon 97213-3786
USA
Telephone: (800) 944-6190
Fax: (503) 280-8832
Email: orders@isbs.com
Web: http://www.isbs.com

UK and Europe
Asian Studies Book Services
Franseweg 55B, 3921 DE Elst, Utrecht
The Netherlands
Telephone: +31 318 470 030
Fax: +31 318 470 073
Email: info@asianstudiesbooks.com
Web: http://www.asianstudiesbooks.com

Japan
Kyoto University Press
Kyodai Kaikan
15-9 Yoshida Kawara-cho
Sakyo-ku, Kyoto 606-8305
Telephone: (075) 761-6182
Fax: (075) 761-6190
Email: sales@kyoto-up.gr.jp
Web: http://www.kyoto-up.gr.jp

Japan, Asia and the Pacific
Kinokuniya Company Ltd.
Head office:
38-1 Sakuragaoka 5-chome
Setagaya-ku, Tokyo 156-8691
Japan
Phone: +81 (0)3 3439 0161
Fax: +81 (0)3 3439 0839
Email: bkimp@kinokuniya.co.jp
Web: www.kinokuniya.co.jp
Asia-Pacific office:
Kinokuniya Book Stores of Singapore Pte., Ltd.
391B Orchard Road #13-06/07/08
Ngee Ann City Tower B
Singapore 238874
Tel: +65 6276 5558
Fax: +65 6276 5570
Email: SSO@kinokuniya.co.jp

ISBN 978-1-920901-09-7

Contents

List of Tables

List of Figures

Contributors

Michael M. Cernea is Research Professor of Anthropology and International Affairs, George Washington University, USA. As the World Bank's Senior Adviser for Social Policy and Sociology, he was the main author of the resettlement policy adopted by the World Bank (1980) and by OECD countries' aid agencies (1991), has contributed to defining many other development and cultural policies, strategies, and programs of the World Bank, and has elaborated the Impoverishment Risks and Reconstruction (IRR) model for resettling displaced populations. For his scholarly work, he received the *Solon T. Kimball Award for Public Policy* from the AAA, and the *Bronislaw Malinowski Prize* awarded by the SfAA. He is also an elected Member Cor. of Romania's Academy of Sciences. He has provided advisory work on social policies in development to ADB, OECD, UNDP, CGIAR, FAO, and many governments (For publications, see bibliography of his study in this book). E-mail: mcernea@worldbank.org.

Jeff Crisp is currently Director of Policy and Research with the Global Commission on International Migration. He has worked with the British Refugee Council, the Independent Commission on International Humanitarian Issues, and UNHCR, where he has held the positions of public information officer, senior evaluation officer, and senior policy research officer. He has published widely on refugee, humanitarian, and development issues, as well as African affairs.

Chris de Wet is Professor of Anthropology at Rhodes University in South Africa. He has done research on development-induced displacement and resettlement issues in South Africa and India, and has consulted, *inter alia* for the World Commission on Dams. He is the author of a monograph entitled: *Moving Together, Drifting Apart: The Dynamics of Villagisation in a South African Homeland* (1995), and the editor of several books on resettlement-related issues.

Art Hansen is Associate Professor at the Department of International Affairs and Development, Clark Atlanta University (Atlanta, Georgia USA). He has 13 years of research and consulting experience on development, forced migration, and post-conflict reintegration in Sub-

Saharan Africa and Latin America, chairs the Georgia (USA) Advisory
Council on Refugee Resettlement, is a member of the international
editorial advisory board for the Journal of Refugee Studies, and is the
past president of the International Association for the Study of Forced
Migration.

Gaim Kibreab is a Reader in Sociology (Associate Professor) and Course
Director in Refugee Studies at London South Bank University, Faculty
of Arts and Human Sciences. He has published widely on population
displacement and development. Author of *People on the Edge in the
Horn: Land Use Environment and Displacement* (Oxford: James Currey
Publishers, 1996), *State Intervention and the Environment in Sudan,
1889-1989: The Demise of Communal Resource Management* (Lewiston
Queenston Lampeter: The Edwin Mellen Press, 2002) and many journal
articles and chapters in edited volumes. Currently, he is working on civil
society and democracy in post-independence Eritrea.

Eisei Kurimoto is Professor of Anthropology at the Graduate School of
Human Sciences, Osaka University. He has carried out fieldwork among
the Pari in South Sudan and the Anywaa (Anuak) in Ethiopia. His major
publications include *People Living through Ethnic Conflict* (1996 in
Japanese) and *Primitive and Modern Wars* (1999 in Japanese). He has also
edited *Rewriting Africa* (2001), and co-edited *Conflict, Age and Power in
North East Africa: Age Systems in Transition* (1998), *Colonial Experience:
Anthropological and Historical Approaches* (1999 in Japanese), and
Remapping Africa: Socialism and After (2002).

Jean Marara is Researcher at Institut Rwandais de Recherche Scientifique
et Technologique (I.R.S.T. / Butare, Rwanda). His main research interest
is in the transformation of the rural economy in post-conflict Rwanda. He
has published many reports from I.R.S.T.; one of his most recent works
is 'Conditions de développement de l'habitat groupé au Rwanda: Aspects
psychosociaux et économiques' (2004, co-authored with Mukarubibi
Dancille and Gahongayire Liberata).

Itaru Ohta is Professor at the Graduate School of Asian and African Area
Studies, Kyoto University. He has carried out anthropological research
among the Turkana in Kenya and the Himba in Namibia. He has co-edited
An Anthropological Study of Nature-dependent Societies: Part 2 (1996 in

Japanese), and *The Nomads* (2004 in Japanese) and published a number of articles on the subjects.

Kai Schmidt-Soltau (PhD Sociology at University of Münster/Germany) is presently working as consultant with the World Bank Group, GTZ, KfW, etc., serves on the board of directors of the International Network on Displacement and Resettlement (INDR) (http://www.displacement.net) and is coordinating for IUCN-CEESP a global assessment on conservation induced displacement (http://www.social-impact-of-conservation.net). He has published widely on the subject (http://www.schmidt-soltau.de).

Shin'ichi Takeuchi is Research Fellow at the Institute of Developing Economies (IDE-JETRO, Tokyo). He has carried out researches on political economy in French speaking Central African countries. He edited two books on conflict problem: *Conflict in Africa: History and Subject* (2000 in Japanese), and *State, Violence and Politics: Conflicts in Asia and Africa* (2003 in Japanese).

Roos Willems is currently affiliated to the Catholic University of Leuven (Belgium) as a Research Associate. She did her anthropological PhD research (University of Florida, 2003) on social networking strategies among urban refugees from Congolese, Burundi and Rwandan origin in Dar es Salaam, Tanzania. In publication are articles such as 'Gender and forced migration,' 'Methodological considerations for research among undocumented populations,' and 'Clandestine lives: Freedom of movement and national refugee policies.'

Yntiso D. Gebre is Assistant Professor at the Department of Sociology and Social Anthropology, Addis Ababa University, Ethiopia. He has carried out research among the Ari of southwest Ethiopia and among the Metekel Gumz of northwest Ethiopia. He has years of experience in consultancy research on development issues. Gebre has published numerous articles and book chapters on displacement, resettlement, agricultural production, rotating labor groups, etc. Currently, he is the Chairman of the Department of Sociology and Social Anthropology at Addis Ababa University and the Deputy President of the Ethiopian Society of Sociologists, Social Workers, and Anthropologists.

Preface

Most of the studies included in this volume were initially presented to a symposium on the 'Multidimensionality of Displacement Risks in Africa,' held in Kyoto, Japan, from 2–3 November 2002. This symposium was organized by the Center for African Area Studies at Kyoto University and the COE (Center of Excellence) Program, 'Making Regions: Proto-Areas, Transformations and New Formations in Asia and Africa,' which was sponsored by the Japanese Ministry of Education, Culture, Sports, Science and Technology.

The idea for this symposium on displacement in Africa began to evolve in 2001 when Yntiso Gebre and I met in Kyoto. Gebre spent two years at the Center for African Area Studies, Kyoto University, between 2001 and 2003 as a visiting scholar. He has been conducting anthropological research on resettlement programs in Ethiopia, focusing on the resettlement process and the hard experiences of both those being resettled and their host population. My own research has been among the Turkana pastoralists in northwestern Kenya, although I was not a specialist on population displacement. The catalyst for my interest in population displacement was the establishment of a refugee camp in 1992 at Kakuma, just next to the village of my host family. I started to examine the profound influences exerted on the life of the local Turkana by the camp, with more than 80,000 refugees. Thus, Gebre and I discovered a common interest in the local relationships between resettlers (refugees) and host populations, as well as in the global conditions that lead to the displacement of people.

We discussed the idea of holding an international symposium in Kyoto and chose population displacement as the theme of the symposium in order to understand its implications for Africa. We planned to include all types of displacement—that is, conflict-generated, development-induced, and conservation-related dislocations. We decided to invite not only scholars, but also those with various experiences of working in international agencies, such as the UNHCR, the World Bank, and US Aid. Ultimately, thirteen scholars participated in the symposium and presented papers: four from Japan and nine from abroad. To the best of my knowledge, this was the first international symposium in Japan focusing on displacement in Africa. Unfortunately, we were not able to include in this volume the papers of Della McMillan, Etsuko Chida, Samwel Maghimbi and Shi Guoqing. We have also added contributions by Chris de Wet and Roos Willems to cover topics not addressed by papers at the symposium.

The symposium and the publication of this volume have been possible thanks to various sources of support and assistance. The staff of the Center for African Area Studies, and students of the Graduate School of Asian and African Area Studies, Kyoto University, made tireless efforts to make the symposium possible and successful. We are grateful, among others, to Dr. Masayoshi Shigeta who willingly undertook the considerable variety of tasks necessary to the success of the symposium. Apart from the COE program mentioned above, we received financial support from the Japan Association of African Studies, the Japan Association of Nilo-Ethiopian Studies, and the Toyota Foundation (Research Grant No. D-01B2-020). A Grant-in-Aid for Publication of Scientific Research Results, from the Japan Society for the Promotion of Science (No. 165316), enabled the publication of this book. Mr. Toshiie Ono, chief editor of Kyoto University Press, worked tirelessly towards its publication. Mr. Karl Smith, editor at Trans Pacific Press, gave us editorial assistance with great care and attention to detail.

We gratefully acknowledge the assistance of these individuals and institutions.

Itaru Ohta

Kyoto

December 2004

Introduction:
Displacement in Africa—Conceptual and Practical Concerns

Yntiso D. Gebre and Itaru Ohta

This book is a result of extensive research and professional experiences in Africa. The authors represent academics, researchers, planners, and practitioners, who belong to the different sub-fields of displacement and who share common interests. The contributors hope to accomplish two objectives. The first one is to analyze the underlying causes of population displacements in Africa, identify the various risk groups, explore the types of risks involved, and discuss the strategies for countering the imminent challenges. The second goal is to explore the commonalities and differences in displacement experiences. The identification of common interest is important for developing a broad conceptual framework and/or suggesting justified comprehensive policy treatments. It is hoped that the book will make a valuable contribution to the rapidly evolving literature on population displacement. Moreover, African planners and policy makers, who would certainly encounter the displacement challenges of the 21ˢᵗ century, will find the insights and analyses quite useful.

Displacement as a key concept

There is a growing dissatisfaction with rather superficial distinctions drawn among refugees, internal displacees, economic migrants, and other displaced people. However, there is no consensus among scholars and practitioners on a terminology that would integrate the various aspects and processes of displacement. Some writers suggested migration as a key concept capable of capturing the experiences of people leaving their places of origin voluntarily or forcibly (Hansen and Oliver-Smith 1982; Pankhurst and Piguet 2004).

We believe that the concept of displacement is more holistic and integrative than most other terms. It captures all forms of disruptions due to forced uprooting of people from their physical, economic, social, cultural, and psychological placement. Unlike such concepts as migration, resettlement, dislocation, and relocation, it does not necessarily imply geographical movement. Communities hosting new settlers and villagers residing in and around protected areas experience disruption while being in their homes and/or familiar environments. This suggests that migration to a distant or different location is an aspect of displacement rather than its pre-requisite. The concept 'displaced population', therefore, refers to a wide range of people uprooted from their familiar environment, not only physically but also emotionally, psychologically, economically, etc.

In Africa, the common causal factors of displacement include natural disasters (flood, drought, epidemics, etc.), development projects (dams, roads, irrigation, urban renewal, etc.), conservation and preservation activities (national parks, game reserves, other protected areas, etc.), planned resettlement programs, and violence and conflict (wars, civil unrest, ethnic clashes, religious persecution, etc.). Despite the clear differences in the casual factors, it has been recognized that there are important similarities between the various processes in terms of the consequences for the affected people. Cernea (2000: 17) wrote, 'both involuntary resettlers...and refugees...confront many strikingly similar social and economic problems.' Gebre (2003) argued that displacement has the capacity to disrupt the lives of host populations, and thus the analytical models and tools used to explain the experiences of settlers could be used for those of hosts. Similar arguments have been advanced in this volume by Schmidt-Soltau that conservation programs often displace local residents. Whatever the case, all processes of involuntary displacement disrupt the basic livelihoods of people, or make them prone to risks of impoverishment. This is a common denominator that intersects all the sub-fields dealing with displaced populations.

Is displacement imminent in Africa?

Involuntary population displacement has become a global problem, as it entails social disorder, political instability, and economic impoverish-ment. In Africa, displacement is a serious matter of current as well as future concern. In 2002, between 32 and 37 million people (excluding the Palestinian refugees and development-induced displacees) were estimated to be living in a state of displacement worldwide. Development programs that are supposed to improve the living conditions of people continue to cause the displacement and impoverishment of millions every year. Africa's share of displaced people has been exceptionally high. Jeff Crisp

(2002: 1) wrote, 'While Africans constitute only 13 percent of the global population, around 30 percent of the world's refugees and 60 percent of the world's internally displaced persons (IDPs) are to be found in Africa'. The author further stated that, of the 20 top countries 'producing refugees' around the world, nine were to be found in Africa, a continent that also provides 10 of the 20 countries with the largest internally displaced populations (Crisp 2002).

In addition to those less predictable but quite frequent events such as internal conflicts and natural disasters, numerous predictable occurrences are expected to uproot millions of Africans in the future. As elaborated below, some of the imminent displacement challenges awaiting Africa include the implementation of development projects, the establishment of parks or protected areas, and urban development.

First, after decades of sluggish performance, the continent's development is being stimulated by private sector investments and increased capital flows in the form of foreign aid and official loans. This suggests a return to large-scale development projects. In other words, the construction of dams for power generation, agricultural development through irrigation schemes, and the construction of roads will be top development strategies for decades to come. The irony is that the projects designed to benefit national economies are likely to cause painful displacement disasters, and from history it is evident that the powerless are disproportionately hurt by development projects. A significant percentage of people who confront the challenges of development-induced displacement often come from the most disadvantaged sectors of society. The urban poor, marginal groups in remote locations, ethnic minorities, and indigenous communities are the most vulnerable groups, and are least heard in national political and economic discourse. Their powerlessness and voicelessness increase the attractiveness of their resources (e.g., land) to those who intend to establish claims. Policy makers often try to justify such development injustice by invoking the notion of the greater good for the greater numbers. Africa should pursue development endeavors that would ensure the sharing of both gains and pains equitably.

Second, in many parts of Africa the establishment of national parks and other conservation-related activities are alienating local residents from resources that they rely on for their livelihoods. Some countries in southern Africa have developed norms that would integrate local people and game reserves, thereby facilitating conditions for participatory wildlife management. On the contrary, most countries in eastern, central and western Africa do not seem to have participatory park management standards. The growing increase in the value of establishing national parks and other protected areas throughout the continent warrants the need for developing appropriate norms that would avoid displacement and foster local participation.

Third, at the moment, the overwhelming majority of Africans are living in the countryside, although urban centers are mushrooming and swelling very fast across the continent. In the decades to come, farmland shortage, lack of alternative employment opportunities, poor education and health services, and generally failing livelihoods are expected to trigger rural exodus. Rapid population growth and unplanned settlements in urban centers would lead to crises in living conditions, unemployment, lack of social services, and housing problems. Moreover, urban renewal programs (e.g., slum clearance) and major private as well as public investments in productive and service sectors are likely to target and displace the poor and the most vulnerable people in slums. Likewise, nearby villages and farming communities will undoubtedly be displaced by the expansion of towns and cities.

Beyond the directly or indirectly affected people, displacement may have a further impact on ecology. The concentration of displaced people (e.g., refugees, settlers, or returnees) in specific areas may lead to disruption of host people's livelihoods, conflict over resources, and irreversible environmental damage. The ecological risks associated with displacement may be explained in relation to the influx of people that exceed the carrying capacity of areas, decline of local resource management practices, lack of commitment on the part of the newcomers to long-term conservation, and lack of or inability to enforce resource management/use regulations.

Human rights protection and humanitarian assistance

The question of forced displacement relates to the protection of human rights and provision of humanitarian assistance. Involuntary displacement represents, among other things, denial of people's freedom of movement and choice of residence, which are recognized in Article 13(1) of the Universal Declaration of Human Rights and Article 12(1) of the Covenant on Civil and Political Rights (see Cohen and Deng 1998: 87). In an attempt to address refugee problems, the former Organization of African Unity (OAU) adopted the 1969 Convention to expand the definition of refugees and key refugee protection standards, such as the principles of non-refoulement and voluntary repatriation. Africa's commitment to protect general human rights (and the rights of displaced people in particular) was further manifested through the adoption of the 1981 African Charter on Human and People's Rights and the establishment in 1987 of the African Commission on Human and People's Rights to oversee the Charter. In principle, these legal instruments are supposed to safeguard the rights of individuals and groups, including the right to remain in their homes, on their lands, and in their countries. Consistent with these instruments, States retain the right to prescribe specific laws that may favor limited forced relocation/resettlement for permissible reasons. In practice, however, the rights of displaced people such as freedom of movement and residence are not respected in Africa, as governments continue to impose unjustified restrictions. Monette Zard and colleagues (2003: 33) noted:

> On paper, African refugees benefit from one of the world's most progressive protection regimes. In reality, however, they face endless human rights hurdles involving forced return, discrimination, arbitrary arrest and detention, restricted freedom of movement and expression, and violations of social and economic rights.

The UNHCR has the mandate to provide protection, care, and maintenance to the refugees. Hence, the lives of refugees even in protracted situations may not be at risk. However, living in a prolonged and intractable state of limbo involves such consequences as material deprivation, psychological problems, violence, sexual exploitation, exploitative employment, and resort to negative coping mechanisms (Jamal 2003: 4–5; also see Crisp in this volume).

The situation of IDPs[1] can be imagined to be worse, as they remain without legal or institutional bases for receiving protection from the international community. Nor do they receive the direct humanitarian assistance that is needed to maintain a minimum standard of living. The provision of humanitarian assistance is the responsibility of individual governments. Internally displaced persons receive external humanitarian relief only when their governments acknowledge that the crisis exceeded local capabilities to provide protection and assistance. Except for certain disasters such as those caused by drought and flood, African governments seem to be generally reluctant to admit and publicize the problems of IDPs, including returnees and development-induced displacees.

What should be done when a government is unable or unwilling to help the IDPs and when it fails to request, or rejects, an offer of humanitarian relief? Resolutions 43/131 and 45/100 of the General Assembly of the United Nations provide that the abandoning of victims of natural disasters and similar emergencies 'constitutes a threat to human life and an offence to human dignity'(Cohen and Deng 1998: 114). The global provisions state that it is the responsibility and obligation of States to provide life-sustaining assistance, if necessary by securing international support. On the other hand, Resolution 46/182 declares that external humanitarian assistance should be provided with the consent of the affected country, and in a manner that respects the country's sovereignty, territorial integrity, and national unity (Cohen and Deng 1998: 115).

In Africa, the question of sovereignty is a sensitive issue. Uninvited offers to assist victims of emergencies in a particular country may be construed as unlawful interference in internal affairs. Consequently, the regional organization (the former OAU, the current AU) and the member states often remain spectators of unprecedented human atrocities. Cohen and Deng (1998: 214–15) described the dilemma that rendered the continental body and its member states inactive and inefficient as follows.

> Because one of its founding purposes was to promote respect for the sovereignty of African states, its members have been reluctant to take actions that can be construed as interfering in domestic affairs. Still, the limitations that these restrictions impose have become increasingly evident as massive killings, genocide and deliberate starvation have overcome countries and spilled over borders. Noninterference in internal affairs, observed OAU Secretary-General Salim Ahmed Salim, has been carried to "absurd proportions" in Africa.

Although the need for greater involvement of the continental organization in addressing forced displacement has long been felt, the policy action in the direction of this expectation is slow and disappointing. Africa has not yet assumed full responsibility for its displacement problems. The recent deployment of an African peace keeping force in the Darfur region of the Sudan and the peacekeeping initiatives of the ECOWAS (Economic Community of West African States) in Liberia[2] and other West African countries are encouraging signs that deserve mention. To date, the limited involvement of the regional and sub-regional organizations is restricted to conflict-induced displacements. The flight of people displaced due to other causes such as development projects and environmental conservation are not addressed.

The problems of refugees and IDPs do not end with repatriation of people to their places of origin. There are reports that returnees continue to face formidable challenges in the process of reestablishment and reintegration (see Hansen, Kibreab, and Takeuchi and Marara in this volume), as most of them receive inadequate cooperation and support from humanitarian organizations, their own governments, and local residents. Kamila Carvalho (2003: 31) wrote: 'Far from reducing the humanitarian problems faced by IDPs in Angola, the end of the war has brought out the stark reality of their plight. Of the many challenges facing Angola none is greater than that of reintegration and resettlement of IDPs'.

In many parts of the world (Africa included), indigenous peoples do not enjoy the same basic human rights as other members of the national societies. In 1989, the International Labor Organization (ILO) adopted Convention No. 169, which contains a number of provisions designed to protect the rights of indigenous peoples. Land and its natural resources are the principal sources of livelihood, social and cultural cohesion, and spiritual welfare of these peoples. Because of this, the Convention requires governments to recognize and guarantee effective protection of the rights of ownership and possession over the lands which they traditionally occupy, use, and/or claim to have access to. The Convention also provides that indigenous peoples shall not be removed from the lands they occupy/use without their free and informed consent, and without appropriate procedures established by national laws. None of the African nations ratified Convention No. 169 despite the presence of numerous indigenous peoples in their territories. Most African countries do not seem to have clear national regulations pertaining to involuntary relocation of people.

To conclude, the challenge facing African refugees and IDPs has to do with failure of implementation of the existing laws/conventions, lack of national protection instruments, and inability or unwillingness to take pro-active measures to stop displacement from occurring in the first place. First, the implementation problems may be explained in terms of the lack of a meaningful system of supervision to make sure that states remain committed to the laws they have ratified or adopted. Unless effectively and decisively enforced, making laws alone cannot be expected to serve any purpose. Second, lack of national level protection instruments would undoubtedly handicap the implementation of regional and/or international provisions. For example, most of the African countries that have signed both the 1951 UN Convention and the 1969 OAU Convention do not have national laws or policies on refugees. The UNHCR, despite lack of jurisdiction over the states, has taken responsibility for the determination of the legal status of refugees, and for making other arrangements such as resettlement or repatriation. Finally, almost all displacement-related discourses and instruments focus on the treatment of effects rather than causes of human uprooting. The ideal solution to prevent displacement is to adopt justified norms that would allow pre-emptive actions.

Towards integration of displacement studies

Displacement studies have made remarkable achievements in recording and documenting the experiences of displaced people, developing conceptual models to explain their behaviors, and influencing policies that affect their lives. Over the years, specialized sub-fields of displacement (e.g., refugee studies, disaster studies, and resettlement research) assumed independent forms and greatly contributed to these intellectual advances and disciplinary maturity. At the same time, the compartmentalization of sub-fields prevented cross-boundary communication and knowledge sharing. The strict territorialization of the sub-fields of displacement may be explained in relation to two main factors: conceptual demarcation by scholars in their pursuit of excellence and specialization, and institutional practices of the major international agencies (e.g., World Bank and UNHCR) that maintain separate principles, bureaucracies, and goals.

Some scholars have tried to justify the need for bridging this conceptual and policy separation. Michael Cernea (2000: 17), for example, presented the advantages of linkages and knowledge sharing between refugee studies and development-induced resettlement research as follows: *'Empirically*, the two bodies of research could enrich each other by comparing their factual findings. *Theoretically*, they could broaden their conceptualization by exploring links and similarities between their sets of variables. *Methodologically*, they could sharpen their inquiry by borrowing and exchanging research techniques. And *politically*, they could influence the public arena more strongly by mutually reinforcing their policy advocacy and operational recommendations.'

Of the numerous excellent volumes and articles published on displacement issues in the last three decades, only two works deserve mention for their efforts to breakdown the wall separating related sub-fields. The first book, titled *Involuntary Migration and Resettlement: The problems and Responses of Dislocated People*, was published in 1982, edited by Art Hansen and Anthony Oliver-Smith. It systematically explored differences and similarities among three categories of migrants: refugees, development-induced displacees, and disaster-caused relocatees. The editors rightly stated that although there are excellent studies of specific instances of forced migration, their book is the first to address the broad scope of issues and the wide variety of contexts in which migration and resettlement schemes occurred. The most widely cited resettlement model (commonly called the Scudder-Colson stage or stress model) appeared in this volume.

The second book, *Risks and Reconstruction: Experiences of Resettlers and Refugees*, came out in 2000, edited by Michael Cernea and Christopher McDowell. It focused on two categories of displaced populations: refugees and development-induced resettlers. The editors, who acknowledged that their volume is a logical continuation of prior research, described their book as having dual purposes: 'first, to explore the possible synergies between the two fields—refugee research and resettlement research; second, to focus on the *reconstruction segment* of the displacement–relocation continuum, usually less examined in the scholarly literature' (Cernea and McDowell 2000: 4). Most of the chapters were organized along the terrain of the impoverishment risks and reconstruction (IRR) model. This model significantly influenced displacement research in Africa as evidenced by the extensive and diversed use of the framework. The model, originally developed by Michael Cernea to study development-induced displacees, has proved its potential utility for analyzing the situation of people displaced by conflicts, disasters, conservation programs, and influx of migrants into inhabited areas.

The two major works, however, only partially accomplished the task of integrating the wide variety of displacement experiences, as certain key processes remain unexplored. Building on and benefiting from these two previous books and other related works, the current book provides new dimensions to displacement studies. This book, though geographically confined to Africa, conceptually qualifies to be considered as the third and more broadly conceived approach to promote comparative analysis of displacement experiences. Besides exploring the situation of refugees and development-induced resettlers, the book addresses the concerns of other categories of displaced people, whose flights have been largely underestimated or neglected by donors, mainstream displacement researchers, and policy makers. These other groups include host populations, returnees, child soldiers, and people displaced by conservation projects.

Organization of the book

This book, which consists of eleven chapters, is divided into three major parts: Refugees and Reintegration of Returnees, Development- and Conservation-induced Displacement, and Implication of In-migration for Host Populations. Jeff Crisp states that a large proportion of Africa's refugees find themselves trapped in a protracted situation, with no solution to their plight in sight. Although the international community has devoted considerable attention to the problem of refugee emergencies and their mass repatriation, Crisp argues, it has also disguised the protracted refugee situations in Africa. The author believes that the declining commitment of African states to the local settlement and integration of refugees and the international community's preference for refugee problems to be resolved by means of repatriation has contributed to the problem of long-term refugee situations. Crisp suggests that humanitarian and development agencies, refugee-hosting countries, donor states, and refugees themselves should make efforts to end armed conflicts, maintain the voluntary nature of repatriation, explore the potential of local integration, and promote self-reliance pending their return.

Ross Willems analyses the importance of social networks for the survival of the Congolese, Burundian, and Rwandan refugees in Dar es Salaam, Tanzania. Willems argues that because of a high level of insecurity and dehumanizing living conditions in the camps, increasing numbers of refugees either self-settled among co-ethnics living across the border or headed for the urban centers. In Tanzania, according to the author, humanitarian assistance is provided only to those refugees residing in designated camps. Willems' paper examines the ways that forced migrants in Dar es Salaam depend on social networks in the absence of any possibility of humanitarian aid.

Art Hansen states that the conventional approach to the study of refugees and IDPs overlooks the fact that many other people are also uprooted or displaced from their society in a variety of ways. His paper focuses on the social displacement and reintegration of demobilized child soldiers in Africa and the uncertainties surrounding their lives. The author observes that children who are first socialized and integrated into civil society, enter and become members of military society, and then attempt to re-enter and re-establish membership in civil society. He claims that the reintegration of this militarized population requires special attention as part of the process of ending war, reducing the size of the armed forces, and establishing a sustainable peace. Hansen outlines various strategies for successful reintegration of demobilized soldiers.

Gaim Kibreab addresses the concepts of home and belongingness in the light of two theoretical frameworks: the theory of nationalism and liberal theory. He presents the debate on the relationship between people and particular places, and asks whether the decision of people to return to their homeland is necessarily motivated by their desire to belong to the particular places and communities from which they were displaced. Kibreab elaborates the concept of territorial belonging based on the experience of the 1980s resettlers in Ethiopia. Moreover, he discusses the factors that influenced the choice of destination of Eritrean returnees from Sudan and the meanings that they ascribe to the concept of home. Kibreab points out that the meanings are ambiguous and continuously shifting depending on certain goals the returnees want to realize, and that 'belonging to a group/land' does not have an intrinsic value of its own, but is utilized as an instrument to realize the goals.

Refugee problems in Rwanda attracted international attention, but after the cease-fire, the challenges of reintegrating returnees remained unnoticed. Takeuchi and Marara focus on serious land problems and new conflicts triggered by postwar population movements. When the war ended, the new 'government of national unity' invited all Rwandan refugees to return to their home country. Based on their intensive fieldwork, the authors demonstrate that returnees who arrived early acquired land, which had belonged to somebody else who fled the area because of the civil war. This process of land acquisition was recommended and enforced by the Rwandan Patriotic Front Government to bring political order. However, the authors argue that the invocation of the state power in the land problems became ineffective as it sparked serious conflicts between refugees who claim rights over land invoking prewar occupancy and those who acquired land through postwar policy.

Michael Cernea argues that development-induced forced displacements and conflict-caused forced displacements share profound similarities, as well as important differences. Based on a broad analysis of recent studies on a vast range of individual cases of displacement in Africa, Cernea states that the continent has been experiencing both types of population displacements. His examination of impoverishment risks associated with different types of forced displacements in the region indicates that besides the existing 'old' poverty (e.g., caused by war), there is 'new' poverty generated by development programs. The author holds that the social science knowledge that has been accumulated on specific risks of development-caused displacement could be used to develop strategies capable of preempting or reducing impoverishment.

Chris de Wet asks why attempts to counter the negative effects of resettlement in Africa continue to meet limited success. He explained the puzzle by distinguishing between two levels of risks: the resettlement project level and the national level that impact upon the resettlement process. At the local level, it is often assumed that resettlement would succeed if there were the necessary legal framework, policy, planning, finance, monitoring, political will, etc. The author argues that in overcoming the troublesome complexity of resettlement, these conditions, though necessary, are not sufficient for successful resettlement. At the national level, bureaucrats and policy makers not only simplify the complexities of resettlement procedures and local people's everyday lives but also impose their own alien complexities. According to de Wet, resettlement could succeed when this 'clash of complexities' is averted by formulating policy that allows for a more open-ended, flexible, and participatory approach to planning and decision-making.

Kai Schmidt-Soltau focuses on the social impact of protected areas, specifically the physical and/or economic displacement from the national parks. The protection of unmodified natural communities through the creation of parks all over the world is still seen as an effective conservation method. In Central-Africa, Schmidt-Soltau writes, the 1999 Yaoundé summit declared the creation of more national parks to be a necessity for the survival of mankind. Through a survey of national parks in several African countries, the author claims to have learnt that all protected areas and conservation programs displaced indigenous communities. Schmidt-Soltau proposes several research-based recommendations—guidelines for livelihood restoration and impact mitigation.

Itaru Ohta describes how the Turkana, a pastoral people and the original inhabitants in northwestern Kenya, coped with the establishment of the Kakuma refugee camp. He explores how they perceived their situation and tried to modify their social environments to improve their lives. Ohta examines the specific relationships and interactions between the Turkana pastorals and the refugee population. He discusses how both the hosts and the guests try to take full advantage of the resources and opportunities available to them. The author asserts that in taking advantage of opportunities, they improvised conditions spontaneously in a manner that humanitarian interventions never envisaged.

Eisei Kurimoto examines the impacts of refugees and resettlers in Gambela region of western Ethiopia, where more than 60,000 resettlers were brought by the government's programs, and about 250,000 refugees arrived from the neighboring southern Sudan. The local people felt that their homelands were being alienated and they were being dominated by outsiders, while their basically subsistence oriented economy virtually collapsed. When the Socialist government of Ethiopia was overturned in May 1991, all the refugees and SPLA officers fled back to the Sudanese territories, and under the new government, the resettlers were granted freedom of movement. Kurimoto reveals the profound consequences, both intended and unintended, of the refugee and resettlement policies on the host region and community.

Yntiso Gebre compares the implications of the 1980s resettlement program in Metekel, northwest Ethiopia, for the resettlers and the host people. Based on empirical data, he states that resettlement has the potential to cause considerable harm to hosts the way it does to relocatees. He argues that some of the analytical models developed to analyze the situation of displacees can be employed to examine those of hosts. Unfortunately, the author states, policymakers, donors, and researchers continue to underestimate the risks encountered by host people. This chapter provides a detailed description of what happened to the new comers and the original inhabitants because of the resettlement program.

Notes

1   In the literature, for reasons that are not obvious, people displaced by development projects are hardly considered as IDPs. We define IDPs as people who are displaced within the boundary of their own country due to internal conflict, development projects, systematic violation of human rights, natural disasters, etc.

2   The ECOMOG (Economic Community of West African Monitoring Group or the military wing of ECOWAS) soldiers mistreated displaced persons and civilians by engaging in rampant looting and assaults, including rape (Cohen and Deng 1998: 220).

References

Carvalho, Kamila (2003) 'IDP protection in Angola: Has the momentum been lost?', *Forced Migration Review*, 16, pp. 31–2.

Cernea, Michael M. (2000) 'Risk, safeguards and reconstruction: A model for population displacement and resettlement', in M. M. Cernea and C. McDowell (eds), *Risk and Reconstruction: Experiences of Resettlers and Refugees*. Washington: Word Bank, pp. 11–55.

Cernea, Michael M. and Christopher McDowell (eds) (2000) *Risk and Reconstruction: Experiences of Resettlers and Refugees*. Washington: Word Bank.

Cohen, Robert and Francis M. Deng (1998) *Masses in Flight: Global Crisis of Internal Displacement*. Washington: The Brookings Institution.

Crisp, J. (2002) *Protracted Refugee Situations: Some Frequently Asked Questions*. Geneva: Evaluation and Policy Analysis Unit, UNHCR.

Gebre, Yntiso (2003) 'Resettlement and the unnoticed losers: Impoverishment disasters among the Gumz hosts in Ethiopia', *Human Organization* 62(1), pp. 50–61.

Hansen, A. and Anthony Oliver-Smith (eds) (1982) *Involuntary Migration and Resettlement: The Problems and Responses of Dislocated People*. Boulder: Westview Press.

Jamal, Arafat (2003) 'Camps and freedoms: Long-term refugee situations in Africa', *Forced Migration Review*, 16, pp. 4–6.

Pankhurst, A. and Francois Piguet (2004) 'Summary and conclusion: Migration, relocation and coexistence in Ethiopia', in Alula Pankhurst and Francois Piguet (eds), *People, Space and the State: Migration, Resettlement and Displacement in Ethiopia*. Addis Ababa: Ethiopian Society of Sociologists, Social Workers and Anthropologists, pp. 657–88.

Zard, Monette (in collaboration with Chaloka Beyani and Chidi Anselm Odinkalu) (2003) 'Refugees and African commission on human and people's rights', *Forced Migration Review*, 16, pp. 33–5.

Part 1
Refugees and Reintegration of Returnees

1
No Solutions in Sight: The Problem of Protracted Refugee Situations in Africa

Jeff Crisp

Introduction

While the notion of protracted refugee situations is now commonly used by UNHCR and other humanitarian actors the concept has never been formally defined or elaborated. For the purposes of this chapter, refugees can be regarded as being in a protracted situation when they have lived in exile for more than five years, and when they still have no immediate prospect of finding a durable solution to their plight by means of voluntary repatriation, local integration, or resettlement.[1]

In simpler terms, refugees in protracted situations find themselves trapped in a state of limbo: they cannot go back to their homeland, in most cases because it is not safe for them to do so; they are unable to settle permanently in their country of first asylum, because the host state does not want them to remain indefinitely on its territory; and they do not have the option of moving on, as no third country has agreed to admit them and provide permanent residency rights.

This chapter, it should be noted, confines its definition to those situations in which refugees are living in camps, organized settlements and in designated geographical zones. It does not examine the circumstances of those long-term refugees who have settled independently in rural or urban areas, and who in general receive little or no assistance from UNHCR or any other humanitarian organization.

Africa's long-term refugees

Protracted refugee situations exist in most parts of the world, with the general exception of Central and South America. But by far the majority of these situations are found in Africa.

While it is difficult to provide definitive figures on this matter, it would appear that some three million African refugees found themselves in such circumstances at the beginning of 2002, when UNHCR published its last set of global refugee statistics. These included:

- 400,000 Angolan refugees in Zambia and the Democratic Republic of Congo (DRC)
- 520,000 Burundi refugees in Tanzania
- 275,000 DRC refugees in Angola, Congo-Brazzaville, Tanzania and Zambia
- 325,000 Eritrean refugees in Sudan
- 210,000 Liberian refugees in Côte d'Ivoire, Ghana, Guinea and Sierra Leone
- 165,000 Sahrawi refugees in Algeria
- 150,000 Sierra Leonean refugees in Guinea and Liberia
- 300,000 Somali refugees in Djibouti, Ethiopia, Kenya and Yemen
- 450,000 Sudanese refugees in Central African Republic (CAR), Chad, DRC, Ethiopia, Kenya and Uganda

It would be misleading to give the impression that the problem of protracted refugee situations is entirely new. Indeed, some 17 years ago, the Refugee Policy Group produced an extensive report titled 'Older refugee settlements in Africa', which underlined the fact that many of the continent's refugees had lived in exile for many years (Refugee Policy Group 1985). It is the contention of this chapter, however, that the circumstances and conditions of Africa's long-term refugees have changed significantly—and in almost every respect changed for the worse—over the past two decades.

Causes of protracted refugee situations

Why have so many refugee situations in Africa persisted for such long periods of time, leaving millions of uprooted people without any immediate prospect of a solution to their plight? The answer to this question can be found in a number of different, but interrelated factors.

Conflict and non-intervention
First and most obviously, a large proportion of Africa's refugee situations have become protracted because the armed conflicts which originally forced people to leave their own country have dragged on for so many years, making it impossible for them to return to their homeland.

In this respect, it should be recalled that almost all of the wars that have affected the continent in recent years—Angola, Burundi, DRC,

Liberia, Rwanda, Sierra Leone and Somalia, for example—have been characterized by intense ethnic and communal antagonisms, high levels of organized violence and destruction, as well as the deliberate targeting and displacement of civilian populations. In many of these armed conflicts, moreover, the fighting has been sustained by the fact that various actors—politicians, the military, warlords, militia groups, local entrepreneurs and international business concerns—have a vested economic interest in the continuation of armed conflict.

Wars, human rights abuses and protracted refugee situations have also become endemic in parts of Africa because of the international community's failure to bring them to an end. In this respect, an instructive comparison can be made with Northern Iraq, Bosnia, Kosovo and East Timor—four armed conflicts which produced (eventually) a decisive response from the world's more prosperous states, enabling large-scale and relatively speedy repatriation movements to take place.

In each of these situations, the US and its allies had strategic interests to defend, not least a desire to avert the destabilizing consequences of mass population displacements. In Africa, however, the geopolitical and economic stakes have generally been much lower for the industrialized states, with the result that armed conflicts—and the refugee situations created by those conflicts—have been allowed to persist for years on end.

Repatriation and integration

The presence of so many protracted refugee situations in Africa can be linked to the fact that countries of asylum, donor states, UNHCR and other actors have given so little attention to the solution of local integration during the past 15 years. Indeed, from the mid-1980s onwards, a consensus was forged around the notion that repatriation—normally but not necessarily on a voluntary basis—was the only viable solution to refugee problems in Africa and other low-income regions.

Why exactly did repatriation emerge as the preferred solution to Africa's refugee problems in the 1980s and 1990s? And why did the alternative approaches of local integration and local settlement disappear from the agenda? Such issues have been examined in detail elsewhere, and do not warrant an extensive discussion in this paper.[2] Suffice it to say that the 'repatriation rather than integration' approach assumed dominance for a variety of reasons:

  • because earlier efforts to promote local settlement and self-reliance
    in Africa's rural refugee settlements had achieved very limited
    results;

- because refugees were increasingly regarded as an economic and environmental burden on the countries which hosted them;
- because African countries with large refugee populations felt that the burden they had accepted was not being adequately shared by the world's more prosperous states;
- because many refugee-hosting countries in Africa had declining economies, growing populations and were themselves affected by conflict and instability;
- because refugees came to be regarded (especially after the Great Lakes crisis) as a threat to local, national and even regional security, especially in situations where they were mixed with armed and criminal elements; and,
- because the post-Cold War democratization process in some African states meant that politicians had an interest in mobilizing electoral support on the basis of xenophobic and anti-refugee sentiments.

In combination, the variables listed above contrived to bring about a situation where very few refugees in Africa (especially those in organized camps and settlements) were given any encouragement to remain and settle in their country of asylum. And yet it was precisely at this time that the changing nature of conflict in the continent made speedy and voluntary repatriation an increasingly elusive solution for so many refugees.[3]

Rather than responding to this impasse in innovative ways, the principal members of the international refugee regime (host and donor countries, UNHCR and NGOs) chose to implement long-term 'care-and-maintenance' programmes which did little or nothing to promote self-reliance amongst refugees or to facilitate positive interactions between the exiled and local populations. According to some critics, this was partly because UNHCR, as well as governmental and non-governmental refugee agencies, had a vested interest in perpetuating the 'relief model' of refugee assistance, which entailed the establishment of large, highly visible and internationally funded camps, administered entirely separately from the surrounding area and population (Harrell-Bond 2002).

'Residual caseloads'
Some of the people who find themselves in protracted refugee situations are members of 'residual caseloads'—those who decide to remain in exile when other members of the same population have been able to repatriate, resettle or become locally integrated in their country of asylum.

To give just one example of this phenomenon, large numbers of Liberian refugees returned to their own country at the end of the 1990s, when a new government had been elected and the country was relatively peaceful. Nevertheless, sizeable numbers of Liberian refugees have chosen to remain in countries of asylum such as Côte d'Ivoire, Ghana and Guinea.

Why do some refugees choose not to go home, even when conditions in their country of origin appear to have stabilized? This phenomenon is again a result of several different factors:

- because 'residual caseload' refugees have a continuing and legitimate fear of persecution in their own country, or because they come from minority groups which are at risk of other forms of harassment and discrimination;
- because the degree of destruction in the refugees' place of origin is so great that the people concerned do not feel that they will be able to survive at home;
- because the circumstances which originally forced people to become refugees were so traumatic that they cannot return to their country of origin, even if they would not be at risk if they were to repatriate;
- because they lack the capital required to make the journey home and to make ends meet during the initial process of reintegration;
- because the 'residual caseload' refugees are too old, too young or too sick to embark upon what will inevitably be a very arduous repatriation and reintegration process;
- because the refugees have close ethnic, linguistic, social or economic links with the local population and the country of asylum;
- because refugees who remain in a country of asylum may enjoy better access to education, health services and resettlement opportunities than those who return to their country of origin;[4] and,
- because certain refugee groups may choose to remain in exile and to pursue their political objectives from the country which has granted them asylum.

Political hostages

In some parts of Africa, the search for durable solutions to refugee problems has been complicated and delayed by the political, military and economic interests of key actors.

Analyzing the situation of Sahrawi refugees in Algeria, for example, Van Bruaene argues that Tindouf region, where the refugee camps are to be found, 'was obviously selected for political and military, rather than humanitarian reasons.' 'In some protracted situations,' he suggests, 'elderly charismatic and historical leaderships tend to embody rigid political agenda, needlessly detrimental to the well-being of their own vulnerable refugee population.' 'A good example,' he continues, 'is that although Tindouf is totally unsuitable for supporting a refugee population of 165,000, any idea of temporary scattering to more fertile areas is unmentionable' (Van Bruaene 2001: 17).

The large numbers of Eritrean refugees who remained in Sudan after their country of origin became independent in 1992 provides another example of the way in which refugees can become hostages to fortune. Initially, large-scale repatriation was delayed by the scale of the devastation that had taken place in Eritrea, the refugees' caution in returning to such conditions, and the need for discussions with the new government concerning the repatriation and reintegration effort. According to some commentators, the new government was concerned that the mainly Muslim refugees, many of whom had been exposed to Islamic fundamentalism in Sudan, might have a destabilizing effect on the country.

In 1993, after some very difficult negotiations, the Eritrean authorities and the United Nations agreed upon a $260 million repatriation and reintegration programme for refugees in Sudan, and in November 1994, UNHCR launched a six-month pilot project involving the return of 25,000 Eritreans. While the pilot project is generally considered to have been a success, the organized repatriation movement quickly became stalled, largely as a result of two factors: the deteriorating relationship between the Sudanese and Eritrean governments, which eventually led to a rupture of diplomatic relations; and growing insecurity in the border area, resulting from clashes between the Sudanese armed forces and a rebel group.

Characteristics of protracted refugee situations in Africa

One must be cautious in making generalizations about protracted refugee situations in Africa, as each of these situations has its own history, dynamics and peculiarities. Nevertheless, it is possible to identify some features which are common to many of the continent's protracted refugee situations.

Geographical location
One of the most evident characteristics of Africa's protracted refugee situations is that refugees are usually to be found in peripheral border areas of asylum countries: places which are insecure, where the climatic conditions are harsh, which are not a high priority for the central

government and for development actors, and which are consequently very poor.

The areas which accommodate the continent's Sudanese refugees are typical in this respect. Mboki in the Central African Republic, for example, is about 1,300 kilometres by road from the capital city of Bangui—four days drive in the dry season. When a UNHCR mission visited the area in April 2002, it found that the local hospital had closed down, other regular health services had ceased to function, and the schools were now closed. The mission was only allowed to visit the area after lengthy discussions in Bangui and on condition that it was continually accompanied by two armed escorts (Ketel 2002: 2).

According to Merkx, the part of northern Uganda where Sudanese refugees have been accommodated 'has a history of economic under-development. There is hardly any socio-economic infrastructure, markets are isolated and large investments are scarce. The local economy has been hampered by lack of relations with the centre... Transport is unreliable and often interrupted by insecurity and bad roads' (Merkx 2000: 9). Substantiating this statement, in August and September 2002, the Lords Resistance Army (LRA), a rebel group based in southern Sudan and northern Uganda, launched four attacks on the Sudanese camps, displacing some 30,000 refugees.

In Kenya, the situation is little different. As the author of this paper has written elsewhere, the Kakuma and Dadaab refugee camps

> are both located in remote and semi-arid areas, sparsely populated by desperately poor nomadic pastoralists. They are almost totally devoid of any investment or development activity... The border areas of north-west and north-east Kenya have always been insecure and weakly governed, characterized by banditry, cattle rustling and insurgency, as well as violent clashes between the Kenyan army and local armed groups (Crisp 2000: 618).

It is not just the Sudanese refugees who experience such conditions. Van Bruaene (2001: 7), for examples, writes that in the Sahrawi refugee camps of Tindouf, Algeria,

> temperatures are extreme, the ground is made of dust and rocks, almost completely barren, and mostly unfit for crops or fodder. Sand storms are frequent. All mechanical equipment and spare parts have to be brought in from Algiers or Oran, 1,600 kilometres away. The sad reality is that the

area of Tindouf is totally unsuitable for supporting a refugee population of 165,000.

A final example of this phenomenon can be found in Yemen, which has accommodated a substantial population of Somali refugees since the early 1990s. According to Jawahir Adam (2002: 5–6), who visited the camps on behalf of UNHCR:

> If one could choose the worst location for a refugee camp in the world, Kharaz camp definitely qualifies. It is in one of the hottest areas in Yemen, with a temperature varying from 20 to over 45 degrees centigrade. The camp is approximately 102 kilometres from Aden and takes about three hours to reach. The road is rough and can be treacherous. Security is unpredictable and an armed escort is imperative to and from the camp. The camp is so isolated that it is extremely difficult for refugees to socialise with others or to seek employment opportunities.[5]

Demographic structure

A second characteristic of Africa's long-term refugee camps and settlements is that they tend to be populated by a large proportion of people with special needs, such as children and adolescents, women, and the elderly.

The Nakivale refugee camp in Uganda, for example, currently accommodates around 15,000 refugees (mainly from Rwanda and the DRC), of whom 10,000 are under the age of 14 (Jones 2002: 18). In Kenya's Kakuma and Dadaab refugee camps, just over half of the population are aged below 18, while the figure stands at some 58 percent in the older settlements for Burundian refugees in Tanzania (Economic Research Bureau 2001: 5). In Algeria, the Tindouf refugee camps 'have always been inhabited almost exclusively by vulnerable refugees: women, children, and the elderly. They are almost entirely devoid of adult male population' (Van Bruaene 2001: 7).

Why do longstanding refugee camps and settlements accommodate a preponderance of people with 'special needs'? On one hand, this situation should not come as a surprise: because all populations in developing countries are comprised primarily (i.e. numerically) of women, children, adolescents, the elderly and disabled.

At the same time, however, there are reasons to believe that in protracted refugee situations, refugees with special needs are generally 'over-represented':

- because able-bodied men are most likely to leave a camp and to look for work elsewhere in order to support themselves and their family;
- because the strongest members of a refugee population are usually the first to repatriate, leaving the weaker members behind;
- because refugees who are able to survive without assistance may not choose to live in a camp but will prefer to be 'spontaneously settled' in their country of asylum;
- because some refugee households and communities choose to disperse in different locations (camps, villages and cities) in order to minimize risk and maximize opportunities; and,
- because the birth rate of populations caught up in humanitarian emergencies (and consequently the number of children) is often substantially higher than that of the local population.[6]

An important but neglected issue associated with this demographic analysis concerns the situation of refugee children and adolescents. While it has again not been possible to establish any precise statistics, it is clear that a very substantial proportion of Africa's long-term refugees have been born and brought up in exile, and have never even seen the 'homeland' to which they are eventually expected to return.

Finally, it should be noted that Africa's long-term refugee camps and settlement area are almost invariably also areas of substantial demographic growth. This is partly because refugee numbers often increase, either as a result of new influxes, or as a result of natural growth. But it is also because many host-country nationals are attracted to the economic and employment opportunities to be found in refugee-populated areas. Landau (2001: 18), for example, states that

> Kasulu, an area that was once designated as a labour reserve, has now become a major destination for Tanzanians from all over the country seeking waged employment with the international and non-governmental organizations...New houses and newly improved houses are conspicuous additions to the villages' architectural landscape.

According to Jamal (2000: 28), Kakuma town (in contrast to the camp) increased in size from 5,000 in 1990 to 40,000 in 2000. This rapid rate of growth occurred because Kenyans from other parts of the division, district and country were attracted by the services (health and education), the job opportunities (with international and national NGOs) and trading opportunities (firewood, charcoal, building materials and consumer goods) which became available with the establishment of the refugee camp.

The consistent tendency for Africa's refugee-populated areas to attract citizens of the host country casts some doubt upon persistent governmental claims that refugees have an invariably and exclusively negative impact on local economies.

Indeed, the case studies reviewed in the preparation of this paper suggest that the situation is much more complex: refugees can certainly have a disruptive effect on host communities, especially in the early days of an influx. In the longer-term, however, the presence of refugees and humanitarian agencies would appear to have a catalytic impact on local trade, business, transport and agricultural production.[7] If that were not the case, why would so many host country nationals migrate to the areas where refugees have settled?

Declining international attention

In recent years, UNHCR, donor states and other international actors have tended to focus their attention and resources on high-profile crises in which people are either fleeing in large numbers to countries of asylum or repatriating in large numbers to their country of origin. Protracted situations, which drag on for years and where there is no immediate prospect of a durable solution for the refugees concerned, have consequently been neglected. As a result, and as the following examples indicate, assistance programmes have been deprived of funds.

Reporting from Guinea, Kaiser (2001: 21) writes that

> moving around the camps, one routinely hears complaints that the quality and quantity of food assistance has declined. When the 'old' refugees first arrived, they received up to 12 items in the food basket. Today, they receive only three. In addition, there are widespread complaints that the food ration is insufficient in terms of quantity and does not last the 45 days it is provided for. Decisions about when to cut food rations seem to have been triggered by WFP announcements that not enough food is available for the whole population, rather than on the basis of any actual reduction in need.

Describing the situation in Ngara, Tanzania, Kigaru (2002: 7) tells a similar story.

> Basic assistance in food, non-food items and services such as education, health, water and sanitation are provided in the camps. Budgetary constraints, however,

have curtailed the provision of adequate assistance in most of the areas...For example, the last half of 2000 registered drastic food cuts of up to 40 per cent. Self-reliance and income generating activities are next to nil.

Addressing the situation in Kenya, a senior staff member of the International Rescue Committee (IRC) observes that

> one of the most striking features of Kakuma refugee camp is the extent to which after more than 10 years of existence, it remains almost entirely dependent on international assistance for all aspects of its operations...Donor fatigue, as manifested by stagnant and reduced funding levels, despite increases in population and continued failures to meet minimum international humanitarian standards of service provision, is part of the operating environment for agencies such as IRC, working in a protracted refugee setting (Phillips 2002: 4).

A final example of this phenomenon can be found in the Tindouf region of Algeria:

> The inordinately low visibility and high donor weariness has produced a major funding shortfall, not only for self-reliance and development projects, but even for essential relief items (food, shelter) which reasonably should have been secured after 25 years of continuous crisis...The main priority of the refugees is still centred on emergency food supplies. The first UN common objective of ensuring food security and, subsequently, sound nutritional status is far from being achieved. Essential self-reliance projects and life sustaining activities...are heavily threatened by UNHCR budget constraints, and by the simple lack of basic food...The bare minimum of essential structures for the refugee population were built with light materials between 1978 and 1988. In most cases, this infrastructure has seen neither rehabilitation nor serious maintenance since its construction (Van Bruaene 2001: 7–8).

Restricted refugee rights

A final characteristic that is common to many protracted refugee situations in Africa is the inability of exiled populations to avail themselves of basic human rights—including those rights to which refugees are entitled under the provisions of the 1951 Refugee Convention and other international instruments.[8]

In the words of Jamal, Africa's long-term refugees have been provided with a very conditional form of asylum. They are generally (but not always) spared the threat of *refoulement* (involuntary return to a country where their life and liberty would be at risk). But the right to life has been bought at the cost of almost every other right.

> At Kakuma camp today, some 65,000 individuals enjoy safety from violence and persecution in their respective countries of origin. On Kenyan soil, they benefit from being allowed to remain there, and to not be forcibly sent back to their home countries... The importance of this state of affairs should not be understated. Sudanese, Somalis, Ethiopians and others in Kakuma have all benefited from this particular element of international law, that allows them to cross a border and thereby enjoy protection. Inside Kenya, however, the 65,000 Kakuma refugees (and a further 126,000 in Dadaab), enjoy neither basic freedoms available to nationals nor the somewhat restricted but still generous rights enshrined in the 1951 Convention. Their right to asylum in the country is, implicitly but emphatically, premised upon their complying with certain restrictive conditions (Jamal 2000: 7).

These 'restrictive conditions', which are common to many of the protracted situations in Africa, include the following:
- limited physical security: refugees are at risk of attack and abuse by soldiers, militia forces, rebel groups and bandits, based both in the country of asylum and in the refugees' country of origin;
- limited freedom of movement: refugees are confined to camps or designated areas and can only leave them with special permission; they may be subject to fines and penal sentences if they fail to comply with these regulations;[9]
- limited civil and political rights: refugees may be barred from engaging in any kind of political activity, from holding mass meetings, from establishing their own associations and organizations;
- limited legal rights: refugees in many of Africa's protracted refugee situations do not have a clearly defined legal status, do not have residence rights, and have no prospect of seeking naturalization in their country of asylum. Their children may be effectively stateless; and,
- limited freedom of choice: as indicated earlier, refugees in protracted refugee situations may fall under the control of authoritarian political and military leaders within their community, a situation which further limits their ability to exercise basic human rights, including the right to return voluntarily to their country of origin.

A final right denied to many of Africa's long-term refugees is the ability to engage in agricultural, wage-earning and income-generating opportunities. In some countries of asylum, refugees are confronted with legal constraints on their economic activities: they do not have access to land, they are not allowed to enter the labour market, they cannot take out commercial loans, and restrictions on their freedom of movement make it difficult for them to engage in trade.

Even in situations where host governments have pursued more liberal policies, and have made agricultural land available to refugees, it is becoming increasingly difficult for exiled populations to exercise their rights in an effective manner.

At the Oruchinga camp for Rwandan refugees in Uganda, for example, one finds that 'the land size allocated is inadequate, the soil is not very fertile and there is a lack of fertilisers. This results in low yields, which means that there is not enough produce left over to sell' (Jones 2002: 28).

In the Kyangwali settlement, which has been described as 'one of the few settlements in Uganda that can reasonably claim a high level of self sufficiency,' the primarily Congolese refugee population is nevertheless confronted with a range of economic constraints, including geographical isolation, the limited size of the local market, high transportation costs, a lack of information about market conditions, poor terms of trade and the imposition of taxes on economic activities inside the settlement (Werker 2002: 9–14).

In Guinea,

> there is some evidence that refugees are finding it more difficult to gain access to land than they were even two or three years ago...Refugees say that they were once able to negotiate informal leases with land owners (albeit at a price), but that in some places this is now more difficult as Guineans are less willing to allow them to use it. They admit that this is because the land is becoming exhausted, systems of crop rotation and fallow land having been largely abandoned during the stay of the refugees (Kaiser 2001: 13).

A similar pattern can be observed in Sudan, where large-scale agricultural settlements for refugees have been in existence for several decades.

> In Sudan the government had allocated between five and 10 acres of land for refugee use in settlements. However, except in the six settlements in the Qala en Nahal area, the rest of the land allocated to refugees is located in low rainfall areas. As a result, the refugees in these settlements commonly experience crop failure. In fact, most of them do not even bother to cultivate the land because the return they expect to get is often below the cost of production. Even the refugees

around Qala en Nahal have been facing problems of considerable yield decline because of the depletion of soil nutrients and heavy weed infestation caused by over-cultivation. The refugees are legally prohibited from bringing new cultivable land outside the designated areas into the production process...No additional allocations were made by the government during the last three decades and a half, and the consequence has been over-fragmentation of farms to accommodate the needs of newly established families. Most farmers have been cultivating their plots for over 30 years without fallow periods or fertilizer.[10]

The human consequences

Perhaps the most important element of this analysis is to identify the way in which protracted refugee situations impinge and impact upon the exiled populations themselves. Again, it is difficult to generalize, and one should be careful to avoid an excessive degree of pessimism by identifying only the worst-case scenarios.[11] It must also be acknowledged that refugee populations are generally stratified, with some groups and individuals enjoying better conditions of life than other camp and settlement residents. Even so, the situation of most Africans living in protracted refugee situations would appear to be dismal in a number of respects.

Material deprivation
The case studies reviewed in the preparation of this paper suggest that Africa's long-term refugees take whatever opportunities they can to establish their own livelihoods and to supplement the meagre levels of assistance they receive. As Turner (2001: 161) reports from Tanzania,

> people in Lukole do not sit around with their hands in their laps...Among the most visible signs of this are the various livelihood strategies that they apply in order to improve their material conditions...In the market in Lukole A alone, there were 48 restaurants, 32 bars, 95 shops selling shoes, clothes, batteries, salt, rice etc., 94 *mugorigori* outlets and 116 market stalls selling fresh fruit, vegetables and maize.

Reporting from Kakuma in Kenya, Kurimoto (2001: 5) makes a similar observation:

> What is amazing are the commercial and trade activities carried out at open markets with stalls and at shops. Particularly impressive are 'shopping centres' which stretch for more than one kilometre along two parallel main roads in the

south of the camp. Both sides of the roads are full of kiosks selling a variety of commodities, butcheries, groceries, tea and coffee houses, bars and restaurants, hotels, satellite TV and video theatres, hair salons. There is even a place where international fax and telephone services are available.

While a wide range of economic activities undoubtedly take place in and around Africa's long-term refugee camps, the more visible of those activities—such as the markets in Lukole and Kakuma—would appear to benefit the relatively small number of refugees who have entrepreneurial skills and access to capital. Because of the absence of development and investment in the areas where refugee are accommodated, because of the limited range of rights which they can exercise, and because of the very low levels of assistance they receive, the vast majority of refugees living in protracted situations tend to be very poor. And in some instances they are becoming steadily poorer.

Hermann Ketel (2002: 2), who travelled to the Central African Republic on behalf of UNHCR, writes that

> at the time of the mission, the overall situation in the Mboki refugee area was depressing...The mortality rate was such that during the mission's work in the area there were daily reminders of people's distress in the shape of numerous traditional mourning ceremonies. Great and almost continuous pressure was put on the mission to do what it could to ameliorate these lamentable conditions.

Jones (2002: 28) found a similarly depressing scenario in Uganda.

> All respondents highlighted the major resource that they lacked was sufficient food, and were particularly concerned that the food assistance was decreasing. Originally, refugees were given milk, sugar, salt, peas, beans and tinned fish, but as it is assumed that the refugees can grow enough food, the food assistance has decreased.
>
> ...respondents stated that the majority of their small amount of money was being spent on food to supplement what they grow and the rations from the Red Cross. This is at the detriment to everything else: education, shelter improvements, sanitation, health, etc.

Lawday's review (2001: 3–4) of the protracted refugee situation in Sudan also reaches a gloomy conclusion:

> After years of generous assistance, the refugees were totally dependent on outside assistance. Most projects failed to create self-reliance, leaving refugees

in a precarious economic and social situation, with food security not assured. Land distribution and wage-earning opportunities fell behind refugee needs. A study found that refugees were living in reception centres, nine wage-based settlements and 11 land-based settlements. Only an estimated 16 per cent were able to farm and even fewer kept animals. More than half did wage earning activities, but only seasonally, and could not meet household needs. Food needs remained as before and sometimes even higher.

The failure of Africa's long-term refugees to attain the most basic level of food security has been the subject of some angry commentary by the International Rescue Committee. Describing the situation in Kakuma, Kenya, the IRC reveals that in April 2001, the global malnutrition rate in the camp stood at over 17 percent. 'While alarming in and of itself,' the IRC observes, 'what is more alarming is that global malnutrition rates on Kakuma have not significantly deviated from this level for the last six years. These are rates that one would expect to see in severe nutritional emergencies...What is particularly notable is that this is happening not in an acute emergency setting. But in a care-and-maintenance camp that has been in existence for ten years' (Phillips 2002: 1 and 3).

Psycho-social and gender issues

In recent years, a considerable amount of literature has been published on the psycho-social situation of people who are affected by armed conflicts and other disasters. While relatively little has been written about the psycho-social dimensions of protracted refugee situations, some evidence on this issue can be found in the case studies which form the basis of this paper.

Following a visit to Kenya in 1999, the current author noted that 'reports from medical and social services workers in the camps make frequent reference to the 'nervous depression and dependency' of the refugees, describing them as 'traumatized', 'aggressive', 'highly stressed', and as suffering from 'emotional and behavioural problems'' (Crisp 2000: 624). A year later, Jamal came to similar conclusions. 'The most apparent and prevalent mood in Kakuma camp today,' he wrote, 'is a sense of despair and low self-worth' (Jamal 2000: 17).

In Uganda, Jones found that the refugees he interviewed (primarily Rwandans) were characterized by 'despondency, lethargy, boredom and feelings of inadequacy.' When they were asked to rank the main limitations on their livelihoods, 'certain correspondents felt their own situation so helpless that active participation in such a discussion was useless' (Jones 2002: 36).

In his study of Burundian refugees in Tanzania, Turner nicely captures the social and cultural processes which generate such negative attitudes. Lukole camp, he suggests, is 'an exceptional space':

> Around 100,000 people with very different backgrounds have been crammed into this small area in the Tanzanian bush, where they are taken care of by high-profile international organizations and subjected to a number of extraordinary rules and regulations. They are not allowed to involve themselves in politics, leave the camp, work or (at least formally) barter their food rations. They are given food and water and health care free of charge, irrespective of whether they used to be a minister, a peasant or a street kid in Burundi. In a sense, the camp is like a super-compressed urbanization process.[12]

Turner (2001: 67) goes on to suggest that in this process of social change, the refugees in Lukole have experienced a very specific and concrete sense of loss.

> They have been brutally forced to leave the places that they knew so well and put in a setting that is miles apart from the hilltop where they used to live...They no longer grow the bananas and other crops they used to. They live next door to people whose background they do not know. And they are subjected to strange rules and regulations that are imposed upon them by new and unknown authorities and agencies.

These conditions have had important consequences for relationships within the household and within the population ('community' may not be an appropriate word in this context) as a whole. 'What is perceived to be lost,' Turner suggests, 'is the old social order, and this can be seen in women's lack of respect for men, in children's lack of respect for adults, and in small people's lack of respect for 'big men'' (Turner 2001: 108).

As Turner has pointed out in another paper, protracted refugee situations have some specific implications for male refugees. Employing the notion of 'lost masculinity,' Turner argues that the conditions of life encountered in Lukole represent 'a challenge to the unquestioned authority of the patriarchy.' He goes on to suggest that 'this is most obviously seen by the fact that refugees in Lukole depict UNHCR as the father or husband; it takes the place of the patriarch and it deprives people of any control over their lives' (Turner 1999: 6).

The findings presented in Turner's paper (which bears the self-explanatory title 'Angry young men in camps') find a resonance elsewhere. Describing the situation of Angolan refugees in Zambia, Eruesto points out that adult men 'are no longer perceived as the bearers of wisdom and advice.' In fact, they are perceived to be 'old-fashioned and outdated.' 'Skills that would have been taught to boys are no longer relevant, negating the role of older male members of the family...As people are appointed to lead refugee communities and NGOs focus largely on empowering women, the traditional male role soon disappears and men can start to feel worthless and insignificant' (Eruesto 2002: 14).

Unsurprisingly, such circumstances have a particular impact on adolescent refugee males—teenagers and young men who are unable to assume traditional male roles after puberty, and who have little prospect of establishing a sustainable livelihood. A common finding of recent studies is that males in this age-group are particularly prone to engage in negative coping mechanisms, including various forms of delinquent or anti-social behaviour. Thus in Ghana's Budumbura camp, for example, Dick (2002a: 21) reports:

> A growing problem at the camp are restless youths that have no interest in attending school. One area of the camp, known as The Gap, is particularly notorious...Imitating American-style 'gangsters in the hood', these youths spend their days without much to do and get themselves in trouble from time to time. Some camp residents are concerned that they spoil the reputation of Liberians in Ghana, potentially giving the Ghanaian authorities a good excuse for closing down the camp.

Social tension and violence

Unsurprisingly, given the high levels of material and psycho-social deprivation described above, protracted refugee situations in Africa are generally characterized by high levels of social tension and physical violence.

As the current author has explained elsewhere, the problem of violence is epitomized by the Kakuma and Dadaab refugee camps in Kenya, where 'incidents involving death and serious injury take place on a daily basis,' and where 'outbreaks of violence and unrest occur without warning' (Crisp 2000: 601).

According to the author's study of the two camps, such violence assumes a variety of different forms: domestic and community violence; sexual abuse and violence; armed robbery; violence within national refugee groups; violence between national refugee groups; and violence between refugees and local populations. A recent 'human security analysis' amongst refugees in the Arua District of Uganda yielded similar results (Hovil and Werker 2001).

The roots of such violence, the author's Kenya study suggests, are inherent to the circumstances in which the exiled population is trapped:

> The refugees are obliged to remain in areas which have traditionally been insecure, where the rule of law is weak and where the perpetrators of violence can act with a high degree of impunity. The refugees themselves are obliged to live in very trying circumstances, a factor which increases their propensity and vulnerability to violence. Having fled from countries which have experienced protracted and very brutal forms of armed conflict, they find themselves without freedom of movement, with few economic or educational opportunities, and with almost no immediate prospect of finding a solution to their plight...However well intentioned, and irrespective of their technical proficiency, the security measures introduced by UNHCR and its partners cannot be expected to resolve the problem of violence in Kakuma and Dadaab (Crisp 2000: 631–2).

While Africa has been rightly renowned for its tradition of hospitality to exiled populations, there is considerable evidence to suggest that this welcome has worn very thin in many protracted refugee situations. Indeed, tension and conflict between refugees and local residents would appear to be on the rise.[13] And as Ketel explains in a report on Sudanese refugees in the Central African Republic, those 'local residents' are not necessarily indigenous to the area where the refugees have settled.

> In the early days, the refugees who were settled in Mboki were coming to a generally uninhabited area, to which Central Africans from other parts of the country were later attracted because international development was taking place. Nevertheless, local Central Africans today clearly consider themselves as being the 'permanent' population, whereas they see the refugees as temporary residents. Within this context, friction has arisen from two main issues. One is the degree to which the Central Africans consider that they benefit from projects and services provided to the refugees. Their feeling is that they are being short-changed. The second bone of contention concerns the pressure on natural resources in the area. The host community feels that there is a marked deterioration of a number of resources, most notably land, wood, game and fish. The generally poor social atmosphere in the Mboki area during the time of the mission was further adversely influenced by UNHCR's policy of disengagement from the provision of health care, education, water supplies and social services (Ketel 2002: 4).

Guinea provides another example of a country where relations between refugees and their local hosts have suffered a serious deterioration. When

Tania Kaiser visited Guinea in 2000, she wrote that 'relations between refugee communities and the local population are said to be good.' Nevertheless, the seeds of conflict had already been sown:

> There is a...sense of an increasingly serious situation on the part of the local populations, who in some cases seem to be panicking now about the effects of the refugees on their farming land and on the forest around it. They are relatively resigned to refugees' overuse of the environment, but feel that there are limits...Guinean villagers without exception talked about the desirability of the war in Sierra Leone coming to an end and the repatriation of their refugee guests (Kaiser 2001: 13–14).

Almost immediately after those words were written, the Guinean President made an inflammatory radio broadcast alleging that the Liberian and Sierra Leonean refugees in the country were a source of insecurity and that they should be sent home. According to Studdart, 'literally overnight, the situation in Guinea drastically changed,' with refugees becoming 'the victims of numerous human rights abuses, including arbitrary arrest, harassment, sexual abuse, extortion, eviction and disappearances' (Studdart 2002: 7 and 10).

While this campaign of terror was led by the military, militia groups and civilian vigilantes, it also enjoyed much broader popular support. In the words of Human Rights Watch, there was 'rising hostility among Guineans of all walks of life toward the estimated 300,000 Sierra Leonean and 125,000 Liberian refugees, reversing Guinea's long-standing history of welcoming these refugees over the past decade.'[14]

Survival strategies

Africa's long-term refugees resort to a variety of survival strategies in order to make ends meet and to come to terms with the difficult conditions in which they find themselves.[15] And as the following paragraphs indicate, such strategies often have adverse consequences, both for the refugees and for their local hosts.

Sexual exploitation

Sadly, one of the most frequent means for refugees to survive in a protracted situation is by means of exploitative sexual relationships, either by commercial prostitution or through forms of *concubinage* in which a woman or girl receives goods and gifts from a regular sexual partner. While there is relatively little evidence on this matter, there are some indications that young refugee males might also be the victims of sexually exploitative relationships.

As Dick points out in her case study of Ghana, sexual exploitation is often self-reinforcing.

> Refugee women are particularly susceptible to dependency on relationships with men as a way to sustain themselves financially and to access luxury items that they value. As a result, teen pregnancy is common at the camp, giving many young women the added burden of providing for a child, thus perpetuating the need to be dependent on a boyfriend (Dick 2002: 21).

Exploitative employment
Another way for Africa's long-term refugees to make ends meet is to work for minimal rewards, whether for members of the local population, for more prosperous refugees, or for aid organizations. In some situations, refugee girls may be sent to work as domestic labourers in other households, a situation that evidently increases the risk that they will be subjected to sexual exploitation and abuse.

While little data is available on the income earned by refugees, it is evident that a large-scale refugee presence in a situation where there are few income-earning opportunities has the effect of driving down wages. According to one Guinean businessman, refugees were employed at 1,500 francs a day in 1990. It has now dropped to 500 francs a day, while the purchasing power of the currency has declined significantly during the same period (Kaiser 2001: 14).

In northern Uganda, Sudanese refugees have little option but to engage in an exploitative form of piecework known as *lejaleja*. 'Payment is usually very small and can be made in kind rather than cash.' 'For individuals who have no other source of income,' says Kaiser, 'it represents the only way of contributing to the household' (Kaiser 2000: 19).

Illegal and unsustainable farming
Finding themselves in a situation of having no or very limited access to land, some long-term refugees try to engage in agriculture by encroaching on land which they have no right to use. In Tanzania, for example, researchers found that 'with long-time usage, most of the farm plots are now recording low and declining productivity...This factor, together with the increased number of people has led to increased demand for land. Incidents of refugees expanding beyond the boundaries of settlements are becoming a serious problem' (Economic Research Bureau 2001: 5).

More generally, there is evidence to suggest that refugees may resort to unsustainable or 'anarchic' farming practices in an attempt to make ends meet. According to environmental expert Hermann Ketel, such practices include non-selective tree-felling and indiscriminate land clearance, as well as shifting cultivation without a sustainable rotation strategy (Ketel 2002: 5 and 7).

Another environmental specialist, Matthew Owen, concurs with Ketel.

> A basic contradiction arises in promoting sound environmental management in land-based refugee settlements, when refugees lack formal ownership rights but are expected to live off the land in a sustainable manner. They will tend to take a short-term perspective to meeting their food security needs, and not consider the longer-term implications of their practices for the well-being of the land (Owen 2001: 15).

Manipulating and maximizing assistance

Humanitarian personnel in Africa's longstanding refugee camps often complain that they spend much of their time trying to prevent beneficiaries from 'cheating the system'. That such manipulation takes place is beyond dispute. And in some instances, those engaged in such manipulation may also be amongst the most powerful and prosperous members of the refugee population.

At the same time, it is important to recognize that other refugees—those without a privileged social or political status—may also take steps to maximize the assistance they receive, so as to support themselves and their households. These may include:

- recycling (leaving a camp, returning and re-registering for assistance);
- splitting households into smaller groups, so as to qualify for additional rations;
- ration card fraud and sales;
- obstructing re-registration exercises that might lead to a reduction of relief entitlements; and,
- keeping children deliberately undernourished so they qualify for special feeding programmes.

Negative coping mechanisms

In addition to the survival strategies identified above, refugees in protracted refugee situations engage in a variety of more directly negative coping mechanisms in order to survive or to come to terms with their difficult conditions of life.

Such mechanisms include the theft of crops, cattle and other assets (whether from other refugees, the local population or from humanitarian agencies); the sale of vital assets (including grain stocks or domestic items such as clothes and blankets); the collection (which is often illegal) of natural resources that can be sold or bartered; the use of income-generating loans for the purpose of everyday consumption; engaging in substance abuse; repatriating prematurely to countries where conditions remain unsafe; or simply going hungry and foraging for whatever foodstuffs can be collected in the wild—including some which may prove to be poisonous.

As the IRC has explained, such strategies often reinforce the social tensions that are to be found in and around long-term refugee settlement areas.

> The evidence shows that under worsening conditions, there are...coping strategies that refugees can, and will resort to when all others are exhausted. These include theft, banditry, and violent conflict with neighbours in order to access food... They will steal from neighbours, they will pursue the possession of additional ration cards more aggressively; they will engage in fraud and misrepresentation (Phillips 2002: 5).

Needless to say, while such strategies may represent a short-term solution to the inadequacies of international assistance, they ultimately expose those people to even greater risk and hardship. And in this respect, women are especially vulnerable. As Davey (2002: para56) explains in the case of Kenya:

> The poor food basket provision (by WFP) is undoubtedly having an effect on the necessity of refugees to use other resources to acquire food and some degree of a balanced diet. While many rely on remittances of money from friends and relatives elsewhere, others have little choice but to use the local environment to generate income—collecting and selling firewood, building poles and grass. Mostly it is women who are collecting these materials. Those engaged in this activity are vulnerable to sexual and gender-based violence. The diminished food basket is, at present, one of the key factors putting these women at risk.

Remittances

There is evidence to suggest that refugees in protracted situations are becoming increasingly reliant upon remittances sent to them by family members who have succeeded in moving to another part of the world. This is especially the case with regard to refugees who form part of large diaspora communities.

Liberian refugees in Côte d'Ivoire and Ghana, for example, receive remittances through Western Union, which has established offices in both countries for this specific purpose. The Somalis, on the other hand, transfer money to refugees in Kenya and other countries through the indigenous *hawilaad* network, which has been described as 'an informal system of value transfer that operates in almost every part of the world' (Horst and Van Hear 2002: 32). According to Horst and Van Hear (2002: 32):

> The *hawilaad* system has been of great importance in the lives of many Somalis, including refugees. For those in the three camps around Dadaab in north-eastern Kenya, survival is a daily struggle in an arid environment. The international community hands out rations of maize and flour or beans every 15 days, but these last only about ten days. Firewood is distributed a couple of times a year as well, but amounts are far from sufficient. Besides, people have other needs that are not catered for through handouts. It is very difficult to find additional sources of income in the area.

They continue:

> Receiving a monthly allowance of $100 from a relative in Toronto or Nairobi therefore makes an immense difference to refugees in Dadaab…Beyond helping Somalis to survive, the remittances transferred give people a choice. The money can be invested in business, or used to assist others or for children's education. The recipient can use it to move away: away from insecure areas, towards economic opportunities, towards a better life or family members elsewhere in the world.

From the limited evidence available, one can conclude that remittances benefit refugee populations as a whole, and not simply those individuals and households who receive the cash. According to Dick (2002a: 2), for example,

> with limited and dwindling assistance from UNHCR, remittances have proved crucial in enabling refugees to survive in Ghana. Their effect is felt beyond their immediate recipients. Many refugees have invested remittance money in small businesses, thus fuelling the camp economy. And those without access

to remittances depend on the generosity of friends and family who share their resources.

Similarly, Horst and Van Hear suggest that even though the proportion of refugees who receive remittances may be only 10 to 15 percent, of the populations, others benefit indirectly.

At the same time, the receipt of remittances might also have the effect of increasing the socio-economic inequalities to be found in a refugee population, thereby increasing the potential for tension and social conflict between the 'haves' and 'have-nots'. Additional research is required on this issue.

Mobility and migration

As Horst has pointed out, mobility is a well-established means of coping with insecurity in Africa, especially amongst pastoralist populations whose ability to survive in harsh circumstances is predicated on the assumption of regular movement (Horst 2002).

Trapped as they are in a state of limbo, it is hardly surprising that many of Africa's long-term refugees try to find their own solution by this means of mobility and migration.

This may involve leaving a camp and moving to a town to look for work (an act which is often illegal, which separates family members, and which often exposes refugees to new forms of exploitation and insecurity). It might also entail moving to a refugee camp in another country; Burundian refugees are known to move from Tanzania to Uganda, for example, because the conditions of life and the policies of the host government are thought to be more favourable in the latter than the former. In addition, it can mean that refugees try to move on from their country of first asylum to other parts of the world—a decision which is increasingly likely to put them into the hands of unscrupulous human smugglers and traffickers.

Finally, there is considerable evidence to suggest that the poor quality of life in many of Africa's protracted refugee situations has led a growing number of exiles to regard resettlement as the only way out of their difficult situation. In fact, as Horst explains, Somali refugees in Kenya have a word (buufis) to describe this syndrome, which essentially means 'extreme hope for resettlement' (Horst 2002a). With the development of this syndrome, resettlement has become an increasingly competitive process, a source of tension within and between refugee communities, and a serious source of corruption.

Responding to protracted refugee situations

It would be highly misleading to suggest that there are any quick or easy solutions to the problem of protracted refugee situations in Africa. Indeed, some of the proposals currently made in relation to such situations—including the notion of linking refugee aid to development programmes that also involve and bring benefits to the host population—have been tried in the past with relatively little success.[16]

Other suggestions—such as the 'rights-based' proposal that long-term refugees should not be confined to camps but should be allowed to settle wherever they wish in their country of asylum—would not appear to be politically feasible in many refugee-hosting countries. Indeed, it is clear that many refugees in Africa would be at risk of early refoulement if UNHCR were to advocate such an approach. While it is difficult to be at all optimistic, a number of proposals might warrant additional consideration if the problem of Africa's protracted refugee situations is to be effectively addressed.

Ending armed conflicts

First, the international community as a whole must give greater attention to resolving the conflicts that are at the root of most protracted refugee situations. In too many situations, longstanding conflicts have been allowed to fester for years, to gain their own momentum and to pass unresolved from one generation to another.

What does this mean in practice? It is difficult to think of any entirely new initiatives, but these measures should evidently include more intensive mediation, peacekeeping, peacemaking and peacebuilding efforts, undertaken by the United Nations, by regional and sub-regional organizations such as the African Union, and by states which have an economic and political influence in the countries where conflicts are taking place.

In some situations, more robust forms of intervention may also be required, involving regional and/or international forces. But the limitations of this approach should be recognized. For experience in Africa and other parts of the world has shown that intervention forces can themselves become a source of instability and human rights violations.

Promoting voluntary repatriation

Second, the international community must maintain and promote the principle of voluntary repatriation. With so many refugees trapped in protracted situations, and with refugee-hosting countries expressing growing reluctance to accommodate exiled populations on their territory, there has been a tendency in some quarters to challenge the principle of voluntary repatriation. As long as conditions in the country of origin appear safe, it has been argued, why not simply tell the refugees to go home—and oblige them to do so if they refuse?

A number of different arguments can be made against this position:

- it is contrary to international and African refugee law;
- it ignores the fact that there is a well-established mechanism—the cessation clause of the 1951 Convention—that can be invoked to terminate refugee status when the reasons for flight have been resolved;
- it will inevitably jeopardize the safety and security of some refugees, who may have good reason not to return to their homeland, even if conditions there appear to have improved; and,
- it is likely to lead to further instability in the country of origin; how better to destabilize a country which is recovering from a period of violence and destruction than to send large numbers of people back there against their will, and to areas which are unable to absorb them?

While insisting on the principle of voluntary repatriation, every effort must be made to promoting this solution to long-term refugee situations. As proposed in the preceding section of this paper, this means bringing an end to those wars and communal conflicts that have forced people to abandon their homeland. But it also requires the rehabilitation and reconstruction of countries where the fighting has come to an end or significantly diminished in intensity.

Exploring alternative solutions

Third, the international community should explore alternative solutions to protracted refugee problems. In this respect, some realism is required. Very few of Africa's long-term refugees are likely to be accepted for resettlement, which is in any case a relatively complex and costly way of finding solutions to refugee problems. Similarly, local integration is not a solution that is available or feasible for a large proportion of Africa's refugees—either because their country of asylum does not want them to settle permanently, or because the refugees themselves would prefer to return to their homeland.

In certain protracted refugee situations, however, the potential for local integration may exist:

- when refugees have moved into an area which is populated by people of the same ethnic origin;

• when refugees have moved into an area where there is a surplus of
agricultural land or where other economic opportunities exist;
• when refugees have been able to establish sustainable livelihoods but
where their legal status and residence rights remain unresolved; and,
• when a 'residual caseload' of refugees has established strong social
and economic links to their country of asylum.

In many parts of Africa, large numbers of refugees have settled 'spontaneously' amongst their local hosts, and have managed to support themselves
without international assistance. This suggests that the potential for local
integration is somewhat greater than is often assumed.

Promoting self-reliance pending voluntary return

Fourth, the international community should promote the principle of
refugee self-reliance, pending the time when voluntary repatriation (or,
in a much smaller number of cases, local integration or resettlement)
becomes possible.[17]

The notion of 'self-reliance pending return' has advantages for all
of the stakeholders in a protracted refugee situation. It would improve
the quality of life for refugees, giving them a new degree of dignity and
security. It would enable refugees to make a contribution to the economy
of the host country and thereby make their presence a boon, rather than a
burden, to the local population. And it would enable UNHCR, its donors
and implementing partners to withdraw from costly and complicated 'care-
and-maintenance' programmes which only enable refugees to survive at
the level of basic subsistence.

Such a policy will not necessarily be welcomed by many refugee-hosting
countries, which claim that refugees who develop a degree of self-sufficiency and who become 'comfortable' in their country of asylum will
never want to go home. But this need not be the case. In fact, experience
shows that refugees who have led a productive life in exile, received an
education, developed practical skills, and accumulated some resources may
actually be better prepared and equipped to go home and contribute to the
reconstruction of their country than those who have languished in camps
for years, surviving on minimal levels of humanitarian assistance.[18]

But (and it is a very big but) what can be done to realize the principle
of self-reliance pending return? There would appear to be several
requirements.

Rights and the rule of law

As argued earlier in this paper, many refugees in protracted situations
are unable to escape from poverty because they live in conditions of

insecurity and because they are unable to exercise the basic rights which would enable them to be productive. A first step in the direction of 'self-reliance pending return' must therefore be the restoration of the rights and security to which refugees are entitled under international law. In this respect, the 'Agenda for Protection', a global programme of action that has been endorsed by UNHCR's Executive Committee, provides an important starting point.

Education

It is taken for granted in most countries that a society's level of economic growth and prosperity is intimately linked to the quality of education and training that its citizens receive. Refugees also appear to recognize this fact, and generally place an enormous importance on the education of their children.

Unfortunately, the international community as a whole does not seem to have adopted the same position. Indeed, with assistance budgets under pressure, the quantity and quality of education available to refugees in many parts of Africa appears to have declined. This trend must be reversed.

As Sperl has argued, 'there is a profound difference between camps conceived merely as holding centres for survival and camps which provide their residents with the means to acquire knowledge and skills which will help them to rebuild their lives.' 'Residence in refugee camps,' he continues, 'undesirable as such, should be treated as an opportunity to provide the residents with new or upgraded skills so as to help them reconstruct their livelihood when the opportunity arises. To this effect, education, training and literacy programmes aimed at all sectors of the population should not, as so often, be seen as ancillary but as vital, primary and no less important than the provision of food and health care' (Sperl 2000: 11).

International resources

Promoting self-reliance amongst Africa's long-term refugee populations will not be a cost-free undertaking, especially in the short-term. As earlier sections of this paper have explained, many refugees remain poor because the land they have been given is unproductive; because they have access to inadequate medical services and water supplies, and are consequently in bad health; and because the infrastructure in their camps and settlement areas is in an advanced state of disrepair. Without addressing these issues—and without mobilizing the resources required for these issues to be addressed—the goal of 'self-reliance pending return' is unlikely to be attained.

Expertise

Given the limited resources at their disposal and the difficult environments in which they have to work, humanitarian agencies are struggling to ensure that even the most minimum of standards are maintained in Africa's protracted refugee situations. Those agencies are even less well equipped for the task of promoting self-reliance in refugee-populated areas, pending the time when repatriation becomes possible.

UNHCR, for example, has relatively little expertise (and probably has less expertise than it had a decade or two ago) in areas such as agricultural extension, micro-finance and income-generating activities. UNHCR and its humanitarian partners are also unable to address the macro-economic factors that place such a severe constraint on the promotion of self-reliance in refugee-populated areas. In such circumstances, the involvement of development actors—national, regional and international—is a necessary condition for the pursuit of the approach proposed in this paper.

A longer-term and more ambitious approach

Last but by no means least, humanitarian actors must learn from experience. And experience suggests that in Africa, refugee situations are far more likely to persist for long periods of time than they are to be resolved in a matter of weeks or months. Nevertheless, UNHCR and its donors have continued to administer what are essentially emergency relief operations for periods of five, ten or fifteen years. As Dick has argued, a longer-term perspective is required:

> It would be useful to assume that refugees will stay for a few years and to make plans to utilise their presence. If this assumption proves false and refugees return home in a matter of days or months, nothing has been lost. But if refugees do stay on, community development efforts would be a better alternative to repeating the same scenario of funding years of relief that only perpetuate refugee dependency (Dick 2002b: 28).

Jamal makes a similar point. In protracted refugee situations, he argues, UNHCR operates long-term care-and-maintenance programmes which are essentially static, which take no account of the evolving needs of a refugee population (or their local hosts), and which are geared towards the maintenance of minimum, emergency-oriented standards in the face of declining resources (Jamal 2000: 32). Jamal provides a three-part prescription for this situation.

First, he argues that UNHCR and other actors, including host governments, local populations, development agencies and the private sector, should collectively develop a far more ambitious vision with regard to the management of protracted refugee situations.

Second, Jamal proposes the adoption of a 'segmented and targeted approach,' recognizing that long-term refugee populations are not an undifferentiated mass, but that they comprise different groups of people with various needs, abilities and aspirations. In this respect, much greater efforts could be made to understand and develop the skills profiles of Africa's refugee populations, rather than working on the outdated assumption that the continent's displaced people are invariably farmers. Indeed, with so many children growing up in camps where they have no access to land, such assumptions must be radically revised.

Third, Jamal (like Dick) argues that efforts to enhance individual skills and competencies in protracted refugee situations should be matched by efforts to develop community structures and systems of self-governance. Recognizing the city-like nature of many large refugee camps, he also suggests that useful lessons might be learned from participatory municipal management and urban planning techniques. 'A durable solution may be out of reach,' Jamal concludes, 'but human capacities can be worked upon at any point...A programme for a protracted refugee situation could concentrate on developing refugee communities and the individuals that comprise them, both for their current well-being, and in preparation for a future durable solution' (Jamal 2000: 35).

Finally, if the more ambitious approach proposed by this paper is to gain any real currency, then the governments and people of Africa must be persuaded that they have an interest in pursuing refugee policies which are amenable to the objective of self-reliance pending return. Simply calling on states to respect international law and to show solidarity with refugees is unlikely to prove very effective, particularly at a time when the world's more prosperous states are closing their doors to asylum seekers. Instead, we must demonstrate that the economy and security of refugee-hosting countries will both be strengthened by means of measures that provide displaced populations with a peaceful and productive life in exile.

Notes

1 The five-year cut-off period is admittedly a somewhat arbitrary one, and is not always easy to apply in practice, given the fluid nature of many refugee situations.

2 See, for example, Chimni (1999), Crisp (2000a), Jacobsen (2001) and Rutinwa (1999).

3 It should also be noted that the other solution to refugee problems—resettlement to a third country—has not been available to significant numbers of African refugees. Between 1992 and 2001, only some 90,000 African refugees were resettled in other parts of the world, a tiny proportion of the continent's refugee population.

4 Sommers (2002), for example, highlights the fact that the educational facilities and opportunities that are available to refugees in Kakuma camp in Kenya are far superior to those available in southern Sudan. Sommers also points out that some of the Sudanese in Kakuma have gone to the camp in order to access such opportunities, rather than to escape from armed conflict. If repatriation to Sudan were to become possible, one could therefore envisage that a proportion of the population in Kakuma would choose to remain in Kenya.

5 While Yemen is not in Africa, it has been included in this review because it accommodates an African (Somali) refugee population.

6 The population growth rate amongst Burundians in Tanzania's older refugee settlements is around 5.0 per cent per annum, which is double the corresponding rate for Tanzanians. Economic Research Bureau (2001: 5).

7 Whitaker (1999), Landau (2001) and IRIN (2002), for example, all provide details of the positive impact of the Burundian refugee presence in western Tanzania.

8 See Kibreab (2001) for a more detailed examination of refugee rights in Africa.

9 As a later section of the paper observes, Africa's long-term refugees remain highly mobile, despite these restrictions.

10 Gaim Kibreab, quoted in Lawday (2001: 3–4).

11 It could be argued that this paper is inherently pessimistic, as it looks only at the situation of refugees in camps and organized settlements. A review of the situation of long-term refugees who have settled outside such camps and settlements would almost certainly be more positive in tone.

12 Perouse de Montclos and Kagwanja (2000) make a similar observation in relation to the urban nature of Kenya's long-term refugee camps.

13 This statement conceals the complex nature of the relationship that often exists between refugees and local populations. See Ohta (in this volume).

14 Human Rights Watch (2001).

15 Horst (2001; 2001a) and Dick (2002) provide particularly illuminating examinations of refugee survival strategies.

16 A detailed analysis of these initiatives is provided in Crisp (2001). The latest variant on this approach, UNHCR's new 'Development through Local Integration' (DLI) strategy, remains to be operationally tested. For an example of this approach, the 'Zambia Initiative', see Marie and Shimo (2002).

17 This approach is explored in UNHCR (2002).

18 This assertion is substantiated by the case of Ukwimi camp for Mozambican refugees in Zambia. While the refugees were able to attain a high degree of self-reliance in the camp, they returned to their own country almost immediately, once it became safe to do so. See Lin (2001).

References

Adam, Jawahir (2002) *Assessment of the Situation of the Somali and Ethiopian Refugees in Kharaz Camp, Yemen.* Geneva: Regional Bureau for Africa, UNHCR.

Chimni, B. S. (1999) *From Resettlement to Involuntary Repatriation: Towards a Critical History of Durable Solutions. New Issues in Refugee Research,* No. 2. Geneva: Evaluation and Policy Analysis Unit, UNHCR.

Crisp, Jeff (2000) 'A state of insecurity: The political economy of violence in Kenya's refugee camps', *African Affairs,* 99.

———(2000a) 'Africa's refugees: Patterns, problems and policy challenges', *Journal of Contemporary African Studies,* 18(3).

——— (2001) 'Mind the gap! Humanitarian assistance, the development process and UNHCR', *International Migration Review,* 35(133).

Davey, Christopher (2002) *Review of Environment-Related Activities Supported by UNHCR Kenya.* Geneva: Engineering and Environmental Services Section, UNHCR.

Dick, Shelly (2002) *Liberians in Ghana: Living without Humanitarian Assistance. New Issues in Refugee Research,* No. 57. Geneva: Evaluation and Policy Analysis Unit, UNHCR

———(2002a) *Responding to Protracted Refugee Situations: A Case Study of Liberian Refugees in Ghana.* Geneva: Evaluation and Policy Analysis Unit, UNHCR.

———(2002b) *Review of CORD Community Services for Congolese Refugees in Kigoma Region, Tanzania.* Geneva: Evaluation and Policy Analysis Unit, UNHCR.

Economic Research Bureau (2001) *Study on Burundian Refugees in Settlements in Tanzania.* Dar es Salaam: University of Dar es Salaam.

Eruesto, Jose (2002) 'The breakdown of cultures in refugee camps', *Forced Migration Review*, 14.

Harrell-Bond, Barbara (2002) *Towards the Economic and Social Integration of Refugee Populations in Host Countries in Africa.* Paper prepared for a Stanley Foundation conference on refugee protection in Africa, Entebbe.

Horst, Cindy (2001) *Vital Links in Social Security: Somali Refugees in the Dadaab Camps, Kenya. New Issues in Refugee Research*, No. 38. Geneva: Evaluation and Policy Analysis Unit, UNHCR.

——— (2002) *A Nomadic Heritage: Understanding Ways of Coping with Insecurity.* Unpublished paper, University of Amsterdam.

——— (2002a) *Buufis: Imagining or Realizing Migration to the West.* Unpublished paper, University of Amsterdam.

Horst, Cindy and Nick Van Hear (2002) *Counting the Cost: Refugees, Remittances and the War on Terrorism. Forced Migration Review*, No. 14. Geneva: Evaluation and Policy Analysis Unit, UNHCR.

Hovil, Lucy and Eric Werker (2001) *Refugees in Arua District: A Human Security Analysis. Refugee Law Project Working Paper*, No. 3. Kampala, Uganda: Makerere University.

Human Rights Watch (2001) 'Guinea: Refugees subject to serious abuse', press release, 5 July.

IRIN (2002) *Burundi-DRC-Tanzania: Focus on Positive Aspects of Refugee Crisis.* Kibondo: Integrated Regional Information Network.

Jacobsen, Karen (2001) *The Forgotten Solution: Local Integration for Refugees in Developing Countries. New Issues in Refugee Research*, No. 45. Geneva: Evaluation and Policy Analysis Unit, UNHCR.

Jamal, Arafat (2000) *Minimum Standards and Essential Needs in a Protracted Refugee Situation: A Review of the UNHCR Programme in Kakuma, Kenya.* Geneva: Evaluation and Policy Analysis Unit, UNHCR.

Jones, Richard (2002) *Participatory Poverty Assessment of Nakivale and Oruchinga Refugee Camps in Southern Uganda: Livelihood Characteristics, Economic Constraints and Recommendations for Change.* York: Post-War Reconstruction and Development Unit, University of York.

Kaiser, Tania (2000) *UNHCR's Withdrawal from Kiryandongo: Anatomy of a Handover. New Issues in Refugee Research*, No. 32. Geneva: Evaluation and Policy Analysis Unit, UNHCR.

———(2001) *A Beneficiary-Based Evaluation of the UNHCR Programme in Guinea.* Geneva: Evaluation and Policy Analysis Unit, UNHCR.

Ketel, Hermann (2002) *Central African Republic: Towards Environmental Management in Refugee-Hosting Areas.* Geneva: Engineering and Environmental Services Section, UNHCR.

Kibreab, Gaim (2001) *Displacement, Loss and Constraints on (Re)construction of Sustainable Livelihoods.* Paper prepared for a workshop on displacement, impoverishment and development processes, Cornell University.

Kigaru, Esther (2002) *Protection Briefing and Hand-Over Notes.* Ngara: UNHCR.

Kuhlman, Tom (2002) *Responding to Protracted Refugee Situations: A Case Study of Liberian Refugees in Côte d'Ivoire.* Geneva: Evaluation and Policy Analysis Unit, UNHCR.

Kurimoto, Eisei (2001) *Changing Identifications among the Pari Refugees in Kakuma.* Paper prepared for a conference on changing identifications and alliances in north-eastern Africa, Max Planck Institute for Social Anthropology, Halle, Germany.

Lawday, Andrew (2001) *Lessons from a Protracted Refugee Situation: UNHCR and Eritreans in Sudan.* Geneva: Evaluation and Policy Analysis Unit, UNHCR.

Landau, Lauren (2001) *The Humanitarian Hangover: Transnationalization of Governmental Practice in Tanzania's Refugee-Populated Areas. New Issues in Refugee Research*, No. 40. Geneva: Evaluation and Policy Analysis Unit, UNHCR.

Lin, Christine (2001) *Ukwimi, Zambia: The History of a Successful Refugee Settlement.* Geneva: Evaluation and Policy Analysis Unit, UNHCR.

Marie, Delphine and Kelvin Shimo (2002) 'The Zambia Initiative', *Conflict Trends*, 2.

Merkx, Jozef (2000) *Refugee Identities and Relief in an African Borderland: A Study of Northern Uganda and Southern Sudan. New Issues in Refugee Research*, No. 19. Geneva: Evaluation and Policy Analysis Unit, UNHCR.

Owen, Matthew (2001) *Evaluation of BMZ-Supported Environmental Activities in Refugee-Hosting Areas of Northern Uganda.* Geneva: Engineering and Environmental Services Section, UNHCR.

Perouse de Montclos, Marc-Antoine and Peter Mwangi Kagwanja (2000) 'Refugee camps or cities? The socio-economics of the Dadaab and Kakuma camps in northern Kenya', *Journal of Refugee Studies*, 13(4).

Phillips, Jason (2002) *Testimony before US Senate Subcommittee on Oversight of Government Management*. New York: International Rescue Committee.

Refugee Policy Group (1985) *Older Refugee Settlements in Africa*. Washington DC.

Rutinwa, Bonaventure (1999) *The End of Asylum? The Changing Nature of Refugee Policies in Africa*. New Issues in Refugee Research, No. 5. Geneva: Evaluation and Policy Analysis Unit, UNHCR.

Sommers, Marc (2002) *Trip Report: The First of Two Planned Assessment Trips Concerning the Impact of a New Teacher Training Center in the Kakuma Refugee Camps, Kenya*. Boston.

Sperl, Stefan (2000) *International Refugee Aid and Social Change in Northern Mali*. New Issues in Refugee Research, No. 22. Geneva: Evaluation and Policy Analysis Unit, UNHCR.

Studdart, Kaysie (2002) *Perceived National Security Threats and the Erosion of Refugee Protection in Guinea: A Mano River Region Crisis*. M.Sc. dissertation, Refugee Studies Centre, University of Oxford.

Turner, Simon (1999) *Angry Young Men in Camps: Gender, Age and Class Relations among Burundian Refugees in Tanzania*. New Issues in Refugee Research, No. 9. Geneva: Evaluation and Policy Analysis Unit, UNHCR.

—— (2001) *The Barriers of Innocence: Humanitarian Intervention and Political Imagination in a Refugee Camp for Burundians in Tanzania*. PhD dissertation, Roskilde University.

UNHCR (2002) *Local Integration*. Geneva: Global Consultations on International Protection, document EC/GC/02/6.

Van Bruaene, Michael (2001) *Tindouf as a Protracted Refugee Situation*. Geneva: Evaluation and Policy Analysis Unit, UNHCR.

Werker, Eric (2002) *Refugees in Kyangwali Settlement: Constraints on Economic Freedom*. Refugee Law Project Working Paper, No. 7. Kampala, Uganda: Makerere University.

Whitaker, Beth (1999) *Changing Opportunities: Refugees and Host Communities in Western Tanzania*. New Issues in Refugee Research, No. 11. Geneva: Evaluation and Policy Analysis Unit, UNHCR.

2
Coping with Displacement: Social Networking among Urban Refugees in an East African Context

Roos Willems

Introduction

Despite (the recent recognition of) ever increasing urban refugee populations on the African continent (Rogge 1986; Kibreab 1996), there remain significant 'lacunae in knowledge about African urban refugees' (Kibreab 2002: 328) resulting in 'a dearth of data on their demographic structure, socio-economic background, treatment and survival strategies' (1996: 132).[1] Many of the findings of this research project are compatible with the data generated from the research done on Ethiopian and Eritrean urban refugees in Khartoum, Sudan, in the 1980s and 1990s (Kibreab 1996; Goitom 1987; Karadawi 1987), such as the urban background of the majority of urban refugees; the diversity of reasons to flee the home country; the bypassing of border towns or refugee camps in heading straight for Dar es Salaam (or Khartoum); the on average higher education levels and the proliferation of urban-based, professional skills, etc. (Kibreab 1996; Willems 2003).

The particular focus of this chapter, however, is the analysis of refugees' social networks as a coping strategy. The existence of social networks and their importance to the survival strategies of forced migrants have been mentioned by only a few researchers. Outside of Tanzania, there have been a few small-scale projects looking into the role of social networks in a refugee situation (e.g., Koser 1997; Williams 1993). Williams, for example, found, in her small-scale study among Angolan self-settled refugees in rural Zambia, that the refugees formed social relationships with non-kin individuals, Zambian or Angolan, to a much larger extent than was previously assumed. In addition, she discovered that those social networks were the channels par excellence through which the refugees were able to rebuild their livelihoods in a new and unfamiliar environment. With regard to urban refugee populations in Tanzania, one researcher remarked that the Burundi urban refugees in Kigoma (Tanzania) in the late 1980s 'relied on networks of their own making' (Malkki 1995: 46), without, however, undertaking any systematic analysis of these networks, while another noticed how the group of Burundi refugees in Dar es Salaam in the early 1990s, were able to obtain employment through networks, yet again, no further analysis was ventured (Sommers 2001; 1994).

Before embarking on the process of collecting the social network data, it is essential to have a closer look at the term 'social relationships'. According to one of the pioneers in social network theory, a relationship (or relation) may be conceptualized as the social process that ultimately links one with his/her social network members (Mitchell 1969). As such, potential network members are that category of people who 'in terms of the general norms or values of the community might be expected to provide [one] with some type of service or support,' while potential relationships become a link in the personal network when 'some social exchange or transaction...converts the possible into an actual social linkage' (Mitchell 1969: 43). Applying this principle to this research project, I conceptualized a social relationship to consist of the actual provision of some type of support (whether material or immaterial) to the urban refugees in the wake of their situation of forced migration.

The body of research on support networks of the past two decades—none of which took place in a situation of displacement or forced migration, and few outside the Western hemisphere—uncovered a number of common patterns. A first finding was that strong ties or ties between individuals with common characteristics (also called homophilous ties) are more important conduits of social support than weak ties or those between individuals with dissimilar characteristics (also called heterophilous ties) (Wellman and Wortley 1990; Lin, et al. 1985). Secondly, kin appeared as a primary source of support while residential proximity proved essential in support transactions involving material aid (Fischer 1982; Antonucci and Akiyama 1987; Wellman and Wortley 1990). Lastly, at the network structure level, it seemed that individuals who are embedded in dense, homogeneous networks receive more social support in emergency situations than do individuals in wide-ranging networks (Marsden 1988; Smith-Lovin and McPherson 1993; Beggs, et al. 1996). The following analysis of the social networks of Congolese, Burundi and Rwandan refugees in Dar es Salaam, Tanzania, evaluates some of these patterns in an East-African context of forced migration in an urban setting.

Research setting and sample population

In the wake of the violent events of the 1990s in the Great Lakes region in Central Africa,[2] hundreds of thousands of men and women from (Eastern) Congo, Burundi and Rwanda sought a safe haven in neighboring Tanzania. At the time of research (2001–02),[3] over half-a-million officially registered refugees resided in Western Tanzania's 'designated areas' (i.e., refugee camps), the overwhelming majority (99%) of which originated from the Great Lakes region: 69% from Burundi, 25% from (Eastern) Congo and 5% from Rwanda.[4] The total refugee population in the country, however, was estimated by the Tanzanian authorities to be over one million. Because of a persistently high level of insecurity and dehumanizing living conditions in the refugee camps, increasing numbers of men and women resisted the official Tanzanian policy (prescribing all refugees to reside in the 'designated areas') and either self-settled among co-ethnics living across the border, or, in increasing numbers, headed for one of Tanzania's urban centers.

In Tanzania, refugees who do not reside in one of the refugee camp areas and who do not have a permit allowing them to reside outside of the 'designated areas' are considered illegal immigrants under the 1995 Immigration Act, and risk much heavier penalties and sanctions than those prescribed in the 1998 Refugee Act. In addition to facing the daily fear of being denounced to the immigration authorities and possibly face *refoulement* to their respective country of origin, self settled refugees in Tanzania can also not count on any type of humanitarian assistance which, under the 1998 Refugee Act, is to be provided only to those refugees residing in one of the designated areas in the Western part of the country.[5] Hence, in the absence of any possibility of humanitarian aid, Dar es Salaam's forced migrants necessarily depend on themselves and their social network members to make ends meet.

Because of its focus on the reconstruction of individuals' personal social networks in the wake of their forced migration, only respondents with a maximum of ten years, yet a minimum of one year of residence in Dar es Salaam were included in the research sample.[6] This selection criterion thus excluded those Congolese, Burundi and Rwandan who sought refuge in Dar es Salaam in the 1960s and 1970s, quite a few of whom are now Tanzanian nationals, particularly among the Rwandan. Secondly, respondents were to have recollections of life at home as an adult, i.e., older than fifteen years of age at the time of leaving home, and these recollections should be no older than ten years in order for the individuals to be able to compare social relations at home and in the country of asylum. This second criteria excluded many Burundi refugees who spent over twenty years, sometimes thirty years, in exile in (then) Zaire, and who came to Tanzania only because of the 1996 and 1998 wars in the Eastern part of the Democratic Republic of Congo. The third selection criteria pertained to the motive for leaving the home country, and relates to the principle of forced migration. In addition to persons deciding to leave home for political reasons or the dangers of war, the sample equally includes individuals who came to Dar es Salaam for lack of economic opportunities at home as a result of the political situation in the Great Lakes region.[7]

It is impossible to estimate the configuration by nationality or by place of residence of these self-settled refugees in Tanzania, who, for lack of any legal status and/or residence permits, are forced to live a clandestine life. Because of their overwhelmingly illegal status,[8] and subsequent lack of statistical information on their composition or whereabouts, respondents could be located through snowball sampling only. In order to deal with possible biases related to this method and with a comparative objective in mind, I set out to locate one hundred respondents of each of the three nationalities, each group gender balanced and representative of different age categories.[9] The final sample of three hundred refugee men and women from the Great Lakes region surveyed (see Table 2-1) was located through multiple points of entry into the refugee community, such as the United Nations High Commissioner for Refugees (UNHCR office), Umati,[10] the University of Dar es Salaam, the French Cultural Center, the Congolese school (*Groupe Interscolaire des Grand Lacs*), etc, but above all through personal contacts.

The Congolese, Burundi and Rwandan forced migrants in Dar es Salaam show a high rate of urbanization, namely three times the respective national averages. Whereas, for example, the national urbanization rate for Congo was 30% in the year 2000 (UNDP 2001), nine in ten Congolese refugee respondents reported being prior inhabitants of one of the three major urban centers in Eastern Congo (Uvira, Bukavu and Goma). A similar trend was observed in both Burundi and Rwanda. Even as only 8% of the Burundi population is urbanized (ibid.), 39% of the Burundi respondents in the sample resided in the capital Bujumbura before the flight.[11] The same holds true for the Rwandan respondents, among whom 34% originate from the capital Kigali, compared to a national urbanization rate of only 6% (ibid.). As urbanites, the refugees in Dar es Salaam are also considerably more educated than their compatriots in the refugee camps: barely 1% of the camp refugees has a university degree, compared to between 8% of the Burundi and 18% of the Congolese urban refugees.[12] In addition, close

Table 2-1. Composition of final sample by gender, nationality, and age group

Nationality and gender	Age group				Total
	20–25 years	26–35 years	36–45 years	≥ 46 years	
Congolese					
Women	14	15	14	7	50
Men	14	17	15	4	50
Burundi					
Women	14	16	13	7	50
Men	16	17	14	3	50
Rwandan					
Women	15	15	15	5	50
Men	15	15	15	5	50
Total	88	95	86	31	300

Source: Willems 2003.

to nine out of ten respondents (88%) arrived in Dar es Salaam less than five years before the time of research, i.e., from 1996 onward, a trend indicative of the recent sharp increase in the numbers of refugees heading for Tanzania's urban centers.

Fending for oneself

When solicited to explain why they had decided to avoid the refugee camps where all the humanitarian assistance is provided, more than half of all respondents (55%) mentioned (having heard of) intolerable living conditions in the refugee camps, such as insufficient food rations, the prevalence of illnesses, or the general perception of camp life as miserable. While many refugees based their decision to avoid the refugee camps on the hearsay and testimonies of fellow refugees, others had had first hand experience. One Congolese informant, for instance, recounted that during his 1996–1998 stay in a Western Tanzania camp, one of his children had died, in his opinion, 'due to lack of medical attention' from the camp's infrastructure. This person, together with his family members, had repatriated to Congo in 1998, when after a few months the Rwandan/Ugandan invasion took place, prompting them to leave their home again. This time, however, husband and wife and three children headed straight for Dar es Salaam, determined never to set foot in the refugee camps again.

Security concerns for politico-ethnic reasons was the second major motivation cited by one in three respondents (31%) to avoid the refugee camp.[13] Only those refugees whose security concerns are considered 'genuine' or 'serious enough' by UNHCR are eligible for a permit to reside in Dar es Salaam and a monthly living allowance. Many however, find their concerns not taken seriously by the refugee agency and are told to go to one of the refugee camps when turning to the UNHCR office for assistance.

> In Dar es Salaam...I first went to the UN. UN [UNHCR] told me to go to the Ministry [of Home Affairs]. At the Ministry they gave me forms to fill...and the UN decided to provide assistance for the next six months...After that, they decided that I should go to the camp...But I refused to go...I wasn't going to live there with these people, because you can never be sure that there is no infiltration...That is why I refused to go. But the UNHCR didn't accept my refusal and cut the assistance I was receiving. They told me to go fend for myself, and so I did...

Fending for oneself in a situation of forced migration, particularly where the refugee lacks any type of legal documentation or entitlement to human-itarian assistance, is quite a challenge. While, in general, one's educational level is often indicative of one's occupation, in a situation of forced mi-gration, this direct link is blurred by the lack of employment opportuni-ties as a result of the restrictive refugee policies of the asylum country. The occupations held by respondents at home, *before* coming to Dar es Salaam, were, in order of importance: students (36%), trade (18%), paid employment (16%), and self-employment (12%). Compared to the profes-sional occupations held by respondents *after* coming to Dar es Salaam, the proportion of self-employed tripled (39%) to become the most important one, while roughly the same number of people as before engaged in trade activities (20%). Two-thirds of the self-employed respondents were en-gaged in only two types of activities: hairdressing and the braiding of hair (exercised by 16% of all respondents, mostly female), and *mission towns* (10%). *Mission town*[14] is a typical Dar es Salaam term, translatable to 'mid-dleman' in English. They are persons, usually young men, who basically bring sellers and buyers of any type of goods or services (e.g., landlords and tenants) together and make a living from the commission. Whereas this activity does not require a start up capital (contrary to trade), the person intending to become a *mission town* needs excellent communication skills and the ability to make personal connections easily. The remaining third of self-employed respondents earned a living as tailors, carpenters, mechanics, plumbers, etc. Not allowed to start up their own workshop for lack of the necessary legal documents, self-employed refugees (except for the *mission towns* whose 'office' consists solely of a cell phone) needed to locate a Tanzanian-owned shop in their area of expertise, and to agree with the owner to work on commission rather than receiving a fixed salary at the end of each month. Other respondents, mostly older women, managed to make a living by preparing *mandazi* or *chapatis*, which are local types of pastry, or other food items, such as smoked fish, which they subsequently sell to passersby in the street. A few respondents self-defined as photographers, preachers or prostitutes. *Trading activities*, on the other hand, included the buying and selling of any type of goods, from precious stones and African art objects (e.g., Central African masks are popular with tourists) to women's wear, including the West and Central African fabrics (such as the *basin* or the *superwax*) which are very different in quality, fashion and price range from the ones produced locally in Tanzania (such as the *kitenge* and the *kanga*). Under *paid employment*, self-reported by one in twelve respondents as their main means of survival, were included not only jobs in the formal sector (e.g., pharmacist, shop attendant, school teacher or receptionist) but any type of activity for which a respondent receives some type of salary: e.g., housegirls, private teachers, drivers, and even a football trainer.

Throughout people's testimonies on their coping strategies to make ends meet, it became increasingly clear that a certain level of cooperation, albeit friendship, develops with Dar es Salaam's Tanzanian residents at the individual and personal level. Many of the urban refugees in Dar es Salaam were able to circumvent the officially required work permits or business licenses by making arrangements with established Tanzanian businesses or workshops and working on commission. At other times, Tanzanian friends offered a place to live, introduced refugees to church communities or assisted them in acquiring new professional skills. In trading activities as well, Tanzanian contacts appeared indispensable. In addition, the refugees often depended on material as well as immaterial support in the form of companionship or advice from friends or other social network members—whether Tanzanian, compatriots or fellow refugees—to bridge them over occasional particularly harsh periods.

Social networks

The social network data of the three hundred respondents were elicited through the following question: 'Could you give me the names of ten persons who have helped you from the time you left your home as well as during your stay in Dar es Salaam? They may include persons from any nationality, men and women, no matter where they live, and who have helped you in any way, be it financially, emotionally, information-wise, socially, neighbourly, or otherwise'.[15] The formulation of the name generator did not mean to suggest that the respondents only *received* support, and that they did not *provide* any support to others. As it appeared from the data, a substantial amount of the assistance provided to ego[16] came from fellow-refugees, implying that ego him/herself equally supported his/her alters whenever and however possible. In social network analysis terms, the name generator contained a numerical limit ('names of ten persons'), a time frame ('since the time you left your home'), and was content-based ('persons who provided support both material as well as immaterial'). No spatial boundaries nor affective specifications were included in the name generator.

The survey resulted in a database of the attributes and other particulars of a total of 2921 individuals who were quoted by the three hundred respondents to be their most important supportive social network members since their displacement from home. The data show that the urban refugees in Dar es Salaam on average count more men than women among their social network members, 58 versus 42% respectively (see Table 2-2). Bearing in mind that a sample of three hundred respondents generates a margin of error of 6%, we may state with 95% confidence that between 52 and 64% (58+/-6) of all alters providing or having provided some type of support to the refugees in Dar es Salaam since the time they left their respective home countries are men. When disaggregating the data between alters that ego knew *before* and *after* arriving in Dar es Salaam,[17] the proportion of women providing some type of support becomes significantly larger among alters s/he met after arrival in Dar es Salaam (48%) than among those known from before (33%).

With regard to nationality, roughly one out of every three alters is of Tanzanian nationality (35%), the second is Congolese (27%), while the third originates from either Burundi (20%) or Rwanda (16%). These proportions change considerably when disaggregated by the moment/place of establishing the relationship. Whereas only 8% of the alters ego has known since before arriving in Dar es Salaam are Tanzanians, this percentage increases to 54% of all alters whom were met after arrival. Not surprisingly, the proportion of alters originating from the Great Lakes region evolves in the opposite direction: 89% (33, 30 and 26% respectively

Table 2-2. Social network members by gender, nationality and age (in %)

Demographics of alters whom ego met	Before arrival in Dar es Salaam n=1228	After arrival in Dar es Salaam n=1693	Average N=2921
Gender			
Female	33	48	42
Male	67	52	58
Total	100	100	100
Nationality			
Tanzanian	8	54	35
Congolese	33	23	27
Burundi	30	13	20
Rwandan	26	9	16
Other nationality	3	1	2
(Same nationality as ego)	(77)	(31)	(49)
Total	100	100	100
Age			
≤ 25 years	10	12	11
26–35 years	35	34	34
36–45 years	31	21	26
≥ 46 years	19	15	17
Don't know	5	18	12
Total	100	100	100

Source: Willems 2003.

for Congolese, Burundi and Rwandan) before versus 45% (23, 13 and 9% respectively) after arrival in Dar es Salaam.

The 2% or 60 alters not of Tanzanian, Congolese, Burundi or Rwandan origin are of the following nationalities: Belgians (12), Kenyans (11), French (9), Ugandans (4), Zambians (3), Cameroonians (3), US Americans (3) and 15 more nationals from Brazil, Canada, Ethiopia, Ghana, Iran, Lebanon, Liberia, Mali, the Netherlands and the UK. Close to one in two alters in the average network are of the same nationality as ego (49%). Yet again, this proportion changes when disaggregating the average network across alters met before and after arriving in Dar es Salaam to 77 and 31% respectively.

On average, three out of every five persons providing some type of support to the refugees are between 26 and 45 years of age (34 and 26% respectively). Comparing before and after, data show that—while the proportion of alters younger than 35 years of age remains more or less

the same—the proportion of persons older than 35 years of age decreases
from 50 to 36%. At the same time, however, the percentage of alters whose
age ego does not know increases from 5 to 18%, thus rendering difficult an
in-depth comparison of the proportion of the different age groups among
alters met before and after arriving in Dar es Salaam.

Ways of meeting alters and support received

The five most important ways through which ego met his/her supportive
social network members are: the neighbourhood (22%), through a mutual
friend (19%), as a relative or in-law (18%), through a religious congregation
(10%) and through one's daily activities, such as work or school (9%) (see
Table 2-3). Comparing between alters met before and after arriving in
Dar es Salaam, significant changes in importance appear among four of
the above ways of meeting people. Whereas relatives make up 40% of the
supportive pre-Dar es Salaam alters, they represent only 3% of the alters
met after.[18] On the other hand, the neighbourhood, mutual friends and the
church or mosque gain in importance as ways to meet people and establish
new relationships in the situation of forced migration. The neighbourhood
generates more than twice as many alters for ego in Dar es Salaam compared to before (29 instead of 13%), and so do mutual friends (25 instead
of 10%) and especially the church and mosque (14 instead of 3%). Together,
these three avenues of meeting people generate more than two thirds (68%)
of all of ego's relationships established in Dar es Salaam, compared to only
26% in the pre-Dar es Salaam era.

When asked the question 'In what respect did this person help you?', not
seldom did respondents give multiple answers. For example, a neighbour
can provide ego not only with friendship and advice but with material
assistance as well, such as water and cooking oil. Multiple answers with
regard to the type of support received were given for 24% of the alters
listed. On average, ego receives friendship, advice, companionship and
emotional support from two thirds of all his/her alters (66%), and some
type of material assistance such as money (21%), food (11%), accommodation (8%), clothes (3%), or other items (2%) like household articles, medicines, merchandise, etc. from close to half of all his/her alters (47%).

Among 'a specific deed' (6%) were categorized instances such as when
an alter helped ego to find a relative residing in Dar es Salaam, or when a
network member drove ego's sick child to the hospital. Among the alters
known before arriving in Dar es Salaam, there are military officers who

Table 2-3. Ways of meeting network members and types of support received (in %)

Relationship attributes of alters whom ego met	Before arrival in Dar es Salaam n=1228	After arrival in Dar es Salaam n=1693	Average N=2921
How did you meet this person?			
Was/is my neighbour	13	29	22
Through a mutual friend	10	25	19
Is a relative[a]	40	3	18
In church/the mosque	3	14	10
Through my work/school	9	10	9
Through a family member	8	6	7
In his/her official capacity	5	5	5
Other	12	8	10
Total	100	100	100
In what respect did this person help you?[b]			
Emotional support, friendship, advice	56	73	66
Financial support	34	15	21
Food	10	13	11
Accommodation	8	7	8
A specific deed	7	4	6
Clothes	4	2	3
News from home	6	1	3
Helped me find a job/work	2	3	2
Other material help	2	2	2

a = Includes family-in-law.
b = Multiple answers possible.

Source: Willems 2003.

smuggled ego out of the home country, while other alters are currently guarding ego's personal properties (e.g., house, car, fields) left behind. 'Providing news from home' is equally appreciated by the respondents as a type of support, in that it helps alleviate to a certain extent the worries about relatives and friends that remained behind. Mainly pre-Dar es Salaam alters bring news from home (6%). Only a small percentage of alters was reportedly instrumental to ego in finding a job or establishing self-employment, whether among alters met before (2%) or after arrival in Dar es Salaam (3%).

From the analysis, it appeared that women play an important role as providers of support to Dar es Salaam's refugees. While male network members were found to be instrumental in providing financial assistance, female network members were twice as likely to provide respondents with food, clothes and/or accommodation in Dar es Salaam. This finding is compatible with the fact that women are the ones in charge of domestic matters rather than men in the regional socio-cultural context, while men have more access to financial means, hence in a better position to provide financial support.[19]

Out of every three social network members providing ego with food, clothes and/or accommodation, two are Tanzanian friends with whom a relationship already existed before arrival in Dar es Salaam. From the interviews, it emerged that these, more often than not, were traders plying their merchandise in the countries of the Great Lakes region, or others who had resided in the Great Lakes region for a number of years before the conflicts. Often, these Tanzanian nationals had fled to their home country together with the very persons who had helped them integrate (whether in Congo, Burundi or Rwanda) and to whom they were happy to extend the same level of hospitality.

Supportive ties and homophilous relationships

Homophilous relationships are ties in which ego and alter may share common characteristics such as, for example, gender, age, nationality, marital status, child status, religion, professional activity, etc. (McAllister and Fischer 1983: 83). As mentioned earlier, studies have shown that in view of the fact that homophilous relationships are indicative of strong ties, they represent more important conduits of social support than ties between people with dissimilar characteristics (e.g., Haines et al. 1996: 254; Lin et al. 1985: 249; Beggs et al. 1996: 217; Marsden 1988: 58). The analysis of the social network data collected among the refugees in Dar es Salaam suggests that sharing the same gender as well as sharing the same nationality plays an important role in their networking strategies.

Reconfiguring gender?
The centrality of gender as an organizing principle of human societies has been profusely documented during the past decades. However, gender constructs are not only 'constituted in the culturally patterned rhythms of everyday life', but, as any other cultural categories, they will be influenced by historical events and altered material circumstances (Grosz-Ngaté 1989: 168). In other words, constructs of gender, of what it means to be a woman or a man, change across space and across time. With respect to the establishing of new ties by Dar es Salaam's refugees, the research findings suggest that local cultural perceptions of gender, of what it implies to be a man or a woman in the regional context, constitute

an essential element in the process of reconstructing social networks in exile. At the same time, the very situation of forced migration appears to exert a certain influence on the gender dynamics between refugee men and women.

On average, respondents share their gender with 64% of their alters, and this proportion does not change when considering separately social network members met before or after arriving in Dar es Salaam. This finding is very similar to the 62% homophilous rate for gender arrived at in a study based on the 1985 U.S. General Social Survey, which analyzed social networks in a context unrelated to a situation of forced migration (Marsden 1988). However, when comparing networks of men versus women respondents, female refugees appear to count fewer women among their supportive alters (55%) than male refugees do men (71%). Further disaggregating for the moment of establishing the relationship by comparing rates among pre- and post-Dar es Salaam alters, the data show that men in particular establish a proportionally larger number of relationships with persons of the opposite sex in the situation of forced migration, thereby reducing their initial high rate of homophily. The opposite pattern emerges among women who count more alters of the same sex among post-Dar es Salaam alters than among their pre-Dar es Salaam alters, thereby increasing their initially lower homophilous rates. The proportion of female alters of women respondents *increases* from 47 to 62%, that of men's male alters *decreases* from 79 to 67% when comparing relationships established before and after arrival in Dar es Salaam. In other words, both refugee women *and* men have established an increasing number of ties with female social network members after arriving in Dar es Salaam.

It is my suggestion that the local cultural perception of women as 'apolitical'[20] has facilitated the increased number of contacts between the urban refugees and the women they established ties with *after* arrival in Dar es Salaam. Despite more education and growing economic autonomy resulting from increasing entrance to important positions in the private as well as the public sector, women remain subjugated to men at the decision-making level in the East African cultural context. The often heard expression 'she is a woman who takes decisions like a man' illustrates the cultural norm that women should never aspire to exercise the same level of self-determination as men.[21] In other words, economic independence does not translate into political autonomy, whether in the public or private domain.[22]

In view of the fact that (often national) politics are at the basis of a refugee's decision to leave home and seek asylum, it is not surprising that politics and political perceptions continue to play an important role in his/her life in exile. Whether it regards Tanzanian officials, compatriots or fellow refugees, men are considered to be more politicized than women. Considered as the political representatives of their respective nationalities or political affiliations, men are therefore much more likely to raise suspicion among persons of other nationalities or opposite political affiliations. This situation impedes the easy establishment of new relationships between refugee men and women with men unknown from before the flight, for lack of its basic ingredient, 'trust'.

Ultimately, the fact that women's social networks consist of an increased number of strong, homophilous ties in the situation of forced migration decreases their level of dependency on men, whether with regard to material or immaterial support. At the same time, the decreasing number of strong, homophilous ties of refugee men attributes to their increasing level of dependence on women when compared to the pre-flight situation. As Turshen and Twagiramariya (1998: 20) point out: 'War also destroys the pat-riarchal structures of society that confine and degrade women. In the very breakdown of morals, traditions, customs, and community, war also opens up and creates new beginnings'. In the recomposition of their social networks during exile in Dar es Salaam, refugee women demonstrate an increased level of independence from men, whereas refugee men experience an increased level of dependence on the support provided by female network members. The new situation does not constitute a reversal of roles—men continue to make up the majority of supportive alters—however it does entail a reconfiguration of gender (Hodgson and McCurdy 2001) in that the power dynamics and relations between men and women are affected.

Social networking as a way of life

In the literature, African identity has traditionally been closely linked to ethnicity rather than nationality. Nevertheless, from independence onward, integrationist policies aimed at overcoming ethnic differences and oppositions at the national level—such as, for example, Mobutu's *retour à l'autenticité* during the 1970s—generally succeeded at creating a national identity without excluding the ethnic one. These national projects allowed 'the idea of a *cultural* community to emerge' (Palmer 1998: 180, italics added) in which 'an historically transmitted pattern of meanings [is] embodied in symbols, a system of inherited conceptions expressed in symbolic forms, by means of which men communicate, perpetuate, and develop their knowledge about and attitudes to life' (Geertz 1973: 89). As social constructs, cultural conceptions are embedded in the historical, economic and political structures of the cultural community. Based on this definition, nationals of each of the three refugee-producing countries under study are expected to dispose of similar patterns of meanings and conceptions about life on the basis of being a member of their respective nations of origin, where they shared a common history and dealt with the same economic, political and social structures and infrastructures as their fellow country men and women.[23]

The data show that some nationalities enjoy more homophilous relationships in Dar es Salaam than others, indicating stronger and more supportive networks. Whereas close to one out of every two social network members of Congolese respondents is of Congolese origin him/herself, Burundi respondents share their nationality with only one out of three of their social network members. Among Rwandan refugees, the rate of homophilous relationships for nationality is even lower as only one in four of their alters are reported to be Rwandan. I suggest that these coping strategies are embedded in the economic histories of the respective home countries of the refugees. History shows that the trajectory of the economic system of the past decades in Eastern Congo is very different from the one followed in either Burundi or Rwanda.

From the early 1970s onward, the Zairian (now Democratic Republic of Congo) central government in Kinshasa, for political reasons had done nothing in the way of public spending in its eastern provinces, especially the Kivu region, from where the overwhelming majority of Congolese refugees in Dar es Salaam originate. The Zairian state all but completely withdrew from the region, leaving the *Kivusiens* to 'fend for themselves'. Over the past few decades, private initiatives from individual men and women organized in extensive social networks have reinvigorated a state-less economy while dealing with the complete breakdown in public health services and public education through private projects. 'Traders, petty producers, truckers, and retailers have elaborated ties of clientage into networks, extending sometimes over enormous distances, to organize unofficial systems of distribution and marketing that, in large measure, provide the food supply for cities and towns' (MacGaffey 1992: 254).

The situation in Burundi over the past decades has been very different. Its economy is dominated by an elite for whom 'the control of the public sector as a source of accumulation, the army as the guarantor of this control and the education sector as a means of accessing it are crucial factors' (Ngaruko and Nkurunziza 2000: 384). Not only does 'public employment represent 80% of full-time employment in the modern sector' (p. 388), in addition, wages are relatively high when compared to the average Burundi salary. While the agricultural sector, the backbone of the nation and source of income to the majority of the Burundi people, hardly receives much needed financial government resources, 'almost all large private firms belong to former high-ranking civil servants' (p. 387). The situation in Rwanda is similar to the one in Burundi, its state system having been described by analysts as one where 'those in power try to control and direct from above many (or all) aspects of political and social activity' and 'where the president and other powerful actors use offices and material rewards to build a dominant coalition of supporters' (Newbury 1992: 199).

From the above, it emerges that the economic vacuum left by the Congolese state ultimately gave rise to a booming second economy[24] built on the existence of informal trade networks as well as the 'nurturing of social networks for mutual support' (Newbury 1986: 100). In Burundi's and Rwanda's state-led systems, on the other hand, there was no economic space in which individual or private initiatives could develop or flourish due to the suffocating hold on the economy of a bureaucratic elite bent on keeping total control of the state at all costs. These situations have been in existence for decades and have given rise to different coping strategies among Burundi and Rwandan nationals. In contrast, the average Congolese in Eastern Congo was never able to rely on formal government structures, and instead has developed the art of nurturing strong, large personal social networks that function as safety nets in case of unpredictable or crisis situations and social networking became a way of life.

Hence, in a situation of forced migration this way of life became the backbone of Congolese informal systems of support, while Burundi and Rwandan refugees are inclined to rely on assistance and support from formal structures instead. For example, whereas barely one in ten of the Congolese respondents passed through one of the refugee camps in Western Tanzania before heading for Dar es Salaam, as many as one in four Burundi and almost one out of every two Rwandan respondents did. In addition, Beggs et al. (1996) have argued that individuals embedded in more homogenous networks are less likely to seek formal support than those in more diversified networks, because of higher access to informal sources of support through their personal social networks. Their thesis is confirmed by the data with regard to the proportion of respondents that have sought assistance from UNHCR across nationalities: only one in five Congolese respondents had registered with the international refugee agency compared to one in three Burundi and one out of every two Rwandans.

Policy reflections and recommendations

Conversations with UNHCR officials and other staff members of the UNHCR branch office in Dar es Salaam were all too often replete with elements of a discourse portraying urban refugees as 'demanding' and 'too expensive'. The general perception is that

> there is a growing tendency whereby refugees prefer to reside in the urban areas than going to camp [sic]. The obvious reason is that life in town, especially when paid for is better and easier than camp life (UNHCR 2001a: 2).

And yet, the refugees who decided to come to Dar es Salaam despite the official refugee policy, are overwhelmingly well aware of the fact that material or financial assistance is generally not obtainable from the UNHCR office in Dar es Salaam. Instead of material assistance, informants expressed their need for the UNHCR office to provide them with protection as is stipulated in the first paragraph of chapter one of the 1950 *Statute of the Office of the United Nations High Commissioner for Refugees*, namely that the UNHCR shall first and foremost 'assume the function of providing international protection[25]...to refugees' (UNHCR 2000: 41). Providing protection usually (but not exclusively) takes the form of a so-called 'Protection Letter', confirming one's status as an asylum seeker or refugee. Its function is to protect the bearer from being arrested by the Tanzanian authorities as an illegal alien and facing possible forced repatriation. This letter does *not* involve the providing of material assistance, for which separate criteria are used, and as such carries no financial or budgetary implications for UNHCR.

As one among many other informants, this Congolese informant, in Tanzania since 1995, bitterly complains about the way the UNHCR Office in Dar es Salaam has been receiving refugees and asylum seekers that come to seek their protection.

> Going to UNHCR? The reception you get when you go there, they leave you standing outside, and even one time...the police came, they entered into the compound of the UNHCR to arrest people. This was in 1997. That event made us even write to the representative at the time, to say that it was not normal that police officers came, entering the [UNHCR] compound and arresting people inside. This shows that we are not really protected here, we have no protection.

From talking to both refugees and asylum seekers on the one hand, and UNHCR and its implementing partner Umati on the other, I found their interactions to be rife with tensions, misinformation and misunderstandings—mostly from a lack of communication. While the refugee agencies are pre-occupied with budgetary arguments based on the conviction that urban refugees first and foremost seek material assistance, the refugees themselves are concerned by the inability (unwillingness?) of the UNHCR office to issue them legal documents and/or residence permits that would protect them from the Tanzanian police and immigration authorities. The recurrent argument from UNHCR officials that there is insufficient funding to assist urban refugees—whose cost *per capita* exceeds by far that of a refugee in the camp[26]—becomes obsolete in a situation where the large majority of informants emphasized that they are not seeking UNHCR's financial assistance, but are instead relying on the international organization for documents that would legalize their stay in Dar es Salaam and possibly allow them to exercise their profession. In fact, if more self-sufficient urban refugees were to be issued with work permits, there would automatically be fewer requests for financial assistance directed at the refugee organizations.

Ultimately, the decision to allow refugees to reside in urban centers and engage in gainful employment is dependent on the authorities of the country of asylum. The motivation of the Tanzanian government to deny legal residence and the right to work to refugees in Dar es Salaam is based on the assumption that local integration is a disincentive for repatriation. And yet,

> the pattern of repatriation to Rwanda after the genocide in 1994 and to some extent that of South Africans in the early 1990s suggests that educated and economically well-off refugees might be the first to repatriate when conditions allow since they are empowered, and have better prospects of playing a key part in the process of reconstruction and rehabilitation in the country of origin (Rutinwa 2002: 23).

In addition, there have been proposals by the Center for the Study of Forced Migration at the University of Dar es Salaam to the Tanzanian government to issue a separate class of work permits affordable to refugees. Given the policy guidelines, as well as academic arguments, in favor of treating the urban refugees in Dar es Salaam as 'assets' rather than 'the problem' (UNHCR 1997: 17), it is regrettable that UNHCR Dar es Salaam continues to invest so much effort in counseling urban refugees to go to the refugee camps, instead of redirecting their efforts towards lobbying with the Tanzanian government for a change of the national refugee policy. While it is true that UNHCR at the level of the Branch Office in Dar es Salaam have in the recent past undertaken a few modest attempts to sensitize the Tanzanian Refugee Department to the advantages of issuing work permits to urban refugees,[27] I believe that UNHCR, as an international organization could and should make more high level efforts to advocate their policy with the Tanzanian authorities. In view of the fact that in a number of countries—such as India, Egypt, Kenya, Macedonia, Russia, Syria, Yemen and others (UNHCR 2001b: 3)—thousands of refugees are UNHCR registered and, in certain instances, have been allowed to work, it is recommended that expertise gained and arguments collected in the afore-mentioned countries is shared with others, so as to allow for an effective lobbying of a more humane approach to urban refugees in general. Advocating at the level of the Executive Committee that

> employment, educational opportunities and a certain measure of economic and
> social integration in the country of asylum are important for refugees' well-
> being, including their psychological and physical health (UNHCR 1994: 23).

is ineffective, when not accompanied by directives for country offices to advocate among reluctant host countries the right for self-sufficient refugees to legally reside and be gainfully employed in urban centers. Involving the urban refugees in the process, through local refugee committees and elected representatives, would but enhance a worthy and respectful dialogue and exchange of experiences and expectations, and as such, avoid the current, unnecessary misinformation and frustrating gaps of communication, contributing in the end to the development of a more workable urban refugee policy and a more dignified life for Africa's forced migrants.

Notes

1 For the purpose of this chapter the terms 'refugee' and 'forced migrant' will be used interchangeably.
2 The 1993 assassination of the Burundi president Ndadaye, the 1994 assassination of the Rwandan president Habyarimana and the subsequent genocide, and the outburst of armed conflicts in Eastern Congo in 1996 and again in 1998.

3 The nine months of field research was funded by a Field Research Dissertation grant from the Wenner Gren Foundation for Anthropological Research.

4 The remaining 1% consisted of a variety of nationalities, such as Somalis, Ugandans, Ethiopians, Sudanese, etc.

5 Apart from a few dozen high profile politically sensitive individuals and their families, who have the Tanzanian government's permission to live in Dar es Salaam and receive a monthly living allowance from UNHCR.

6 E.g., someone who spent 5 years in a Tanzanian refugee camp, and came to Dar es Salaam only 6 months ago did not fit this criteria.

7 E.g., a Rwandan university lecturer lost his job of many years to a 'returnee' from Uganda who was more closely related to the current regime in Kigali than he was.

8 In all, only one in three respondents (36%) had at one time registered with UNHCR, whether at the camp level or with the UNHCR office in Dar es Salaam.

9 For more details on selection criteria, sample parameters and the methodology used, refer to Willems (2003).

10 A Tanzanian NGO and UNHCR's implementing partner in Dar es Salaam.

11 These data show that the Burundi refugees who arrived in Dar es Salaam over the past 10 years are considerably more urbanized than they may have been in the past. The first—and so far only—research study on Burundi refugees in Dar es Salaam (Sommers 2001) focused solely on the rural-urban migration of the children of the 1972 refugees, who had grown up in the settlements in the 1970s and 1980s, and decided, as young adults to head for Dar es Salaam. The findings of my research project contradict the author's contention that 'nearly all the Burundi youths in Dar es Salaam were raised in the refugee settlements' (p. 348).

12 Based on statistical information from Muyovosi, Mtabila 2, Kanembwa, Karago, Mtendeli, and Nduta camps, representing a total of 95,114 Burundi refugees, and Nyarugusu, Lugufu 1 and Lugufu 2 camps representing a total of 47,332 Congolese refugees. Unfortunately, no similar information for the Rwandan camp refugees was obtainable (Courtesy of UNHCR, Dar es Salaam—Mr. Kwakye, Senior Program Officer).

13 Among young men, so I was told by informants, an additional important motive for avoiding the refugee camps was the fear to be (forcibly) recruited into one of the rebel factions.

14 In French often called *commissionaire*. There exists no Swahili translation for the term.

15 In Swahili, the expression *hali na mali* was used to indicate that the word 'help' was to be interpreted in its material as well as immaterial sense.

16 In social network analysis terms, 'ego' refers to the respondent while 'alter' is the term used to indicate the individual social network members of the respondent.

17 For the sake of brevity, these categories of social network members may be referred to as pre-Dar es Salaam and post-Dar es Salaam alters respectively in the following sections.

18 Spouses as well as members of the family-in-law were categorized as relatives.

19 Other studies in the area of social network support have come to the same conclusion (e.g., Schweizer et al.; Haines et al. 1996; Smith-Lovin and McPherson 1993).

20 This statement is in no way intended to downplay the political roles women played in pre-colonial Africa; many historical studies have documented the detrimental influence of colonialism on the status and role of women in African society. In addition, recent studies have pointed out the active role women play in contemporary political and violent conflicts as perpetrators (e.g., Moser and Clark 2001; African Rights 1995). For the purpose of this chapter, however, I am concerned only with popular gender perceptions.

21 In this respect, most married female informants and respondents had to obtain the permission of their respective husbands in order to participate in the survey or ethnographic interviewing.

22 'African women in many countries still face an uphill battle to...reduce entrenched gender inequities in many aspects of life. The slowness with which discriminatory laws concerning marriage, inheritance, employment, and housing have been reformed bear dramatic evidence of the blurred line between the domestic and the public, turning the household into a political arena' (Hansen 1992: 8).

23 Allowing for degrees in variation due to class, gender and ethnic differences.

24 Following Newbury (1986), defined as extralegal or legal forms of economic production and exchange which do not enter into national statistics.

25 In view of the fact that a refugee can no longer avail upon the legal protection of his own state through one of its embassies.

26 Around $48 per camp refugee annually, or 1% of the annual cost of an urban refugee $4,800 (UNHCR: personal communication).

27 A 1998 letter from the former UNHCR Senior Protection Officer to the

Head of the Refugee Department in the Tanzanian Ministry of Home
Affairs recommended the issuance of work permits to refugees.

References

African Rights (1995) *Rwanda Not So Innocent: When Women Become Killers.*
London: African Rights.

Antonucci, Toni C. and Hiroko Akiyama (1987) 'Social network in adult
life and a preliminary examination of the Convoy Model', *Journal of
Gerontology*, 42(5), pp. 519–27.

Beggs, John J., Valerie A. Haines and Jeanne S. Hurlbert (1996) 'Situational
contingencies surrounding the receipt of informal support', *Social
Forces*, 75(1), pp. 201–22.

Fischer, Claude S. (1982) *To Dwell among Friends: Personal Networks in
Town and City.* Chicago, IL: University of Chicago Press.

Geertz, Clifford (1973) *The Interpretation of Cultures: Selected Essays.* New
York: Basic Books.

Goitom, Eyob (1987) 'Systems of social interaction of refugee adjustment
processes: The case of Eritrean refugees in Khartoum, Sudan', in John
R. Rogge (ed.), *Refugees: A Third World Dilemma.* Totowa, NJ: Rowman
& Littlefield, pp. 130–42.

Grosz-Ngaté, Maria (1989) 'Hidden meanings: Explorations into a Bamanan
construction of gender', *Ethnology*, XXVIII(2), pp. 167–83.

Haines, Valerie A., Jeanne S. Hurlbert and John J. Beggs (1996) 'Exploring
the determinants of support provision: Provider characteristics, personal
networks, community contexts, and support following life events',
Journal of Health and Social Behavior, 37, pp. 252–64.

Hansen, Karen (1992) 'Introduction: Domesticity in Africa', in Karen
Hansen (ed.), *African Encounters with Domesticity.* New Brunswick,
NJ: Rutgers University Press, pp. 1–33.

Hodgson, Dorothy L. and Sheryl A. McCurdy (eds) (2001) *'Wicked'
Women and the Reconfiguration of Gender in Africa.* Portmouth, NH:
Heinemann.

Karadawi, Ahmed (1987) 'The problem of urban refugees in Sudan', in John
R. Rogge (ed.), *Refugees: A Third World Dilemma.* Totowa, NJ: Rowman
& Littlefield, pp. 115–29.

Kibreab, Gaim (1996) 'Eritrean and Ethiopian urban refugees in Khartoum:
What the eye refuses to see', *African Studies Review*, 39(3), pp.
131–78.

——— (2002) *'Review of* "Fear in Bongoland: Burundi Refugees in Urban Tanzania"', *Journal of Refugee Studies,* 15(3), pp. 326–8.

Koser, Khalid (1997) 'Social networks and the asylum cycle: The case of Iranians in the Netherlands', *International Migration Review,* 31 (4), pp. 591–612.

Lin, Nan, Mary W. Woelfel and Stephen C. Light (1985) 'The buffering effect of social support subsequent to an important life event', *Journal of Health and Social Behavior,* 26, pp. 247–63.

Malkki, Liisa H. (1995) *Purity and Exile: Violence, Memory, and National Cosmology among Hutu Refugees in Tanzania.* Chicago, IL: University of Chicago Press.

Marsden, Peter V. (1988) 'Homogeneity in confiding relations', *Social Networks,* 10, pp. 57–76.

McAllister, Lynne and Claude S. Fischer (1983) 'A procedure for surveying personal networks', in Ronald S. Burt and Michael J. Minor (eds), *Applied Network Analysis: A Methodological Introduction.* Beverly Hills: Sage Publications, pp. 75–88.

MacGaffey, Janet (1992) 'Initiatives from below: Zaire's other path to social and economic restructuring', in Goran Hyden and Michael Bratton (eds), *Governance and Politics in Africa.* Boulder, CO: Lynne Riener Publishers, pp. 243–61.

Mitchell, J. Clyde (1969) *Social Networks in Urban Situations.* Manchester: Manchester University Press.

Moser, Caroline O. N. and Fiona C. Clark (eds) (2001) *Victims, Perpetrators or Actors? Gender, Armed Conflict and Political Violence.* New York: Zed Books.

Newbury, Catharine (1986) 'Survival strategies in rural Zaire: Realities of coping with crisis', in Nzongola-Ntalaja (ed.), *The Crisis in Zaire: Myths and Realities.* Trenton, NJ: Africa World Press, pp. 99–112.

——— (1992) 'Rwanda: Recent debates over governance and rural development' in Goran Hyden and Michael Bratton (eds), *Governance and Politics in Africa.* Boulder, CO: Lynne Riener Publishers, pp. 193–219.

Ngaruko, Floribert and Janvier D. Nkurunziza (2000) 'An economic interpretation of the conflict in Burundi', *Journal of African Economics,* 9(3), pp. 370–409.

Palmer, Catherine (1998) 'From theory to practice: Experiencing the nation in everyday life', *Journal of Material Culture,* 3(2), pp. 175–99.

Rogge, John R. (1986) 'Urban refugees in Africa: Some changing dimensions to Africa's refugee problem, with special reference to Sudan', *Migration World,* XIV(4), pp. 7–14.

Rutinwa, Bonaventure (2002) *Prima Facie Status and Refugee Protection: New Issues in Refugee Research*, electronic document, http://www.unhcr.ch, accessed March 10, 2003.

Schweizer, Thomas, Michael Schnegg and Suzanne Berzborn (1998) 'Personal networks and social support in a multiethnic community of Southern California', *Social Networks*, 20, pp. 1–21.

Smith-Lovin, Lynn and J. Miller McPherson (1993) 'You are who you know: A network approach to gender', in Paula England (ed.), *Theory on Gender/Feminism on Theory.* New York: Aldine De Gruyter, pp. 223–51.

Sommers, Marc (1994) *Hiding in Bongoland: Identity Formulations and the Clandestine Life for Burundi Refugees in Urban Tanzania.* PhD thesis, Boston University.

—— (2001) *Fear in Bongoland: Burundi Refugees in Urban Tanzania.* New York: Berghahn Books.

Turshen Meredeth and Clotilde Twagiramariya (eds) (1998) *What Women do in Wartime: Gender and Conflict in Africa.* New York: Zed Books.

United Nations Development Programme (UNDP) (2001) *Human Development Report 2001*, electronic document, http://www.undp.org/hdr2001/back.pdf, accessed November 25, 2002.

United Nations High Commissioner for Refugees (UNHCR) (1994) *Note on International Protection. Executive Committee of the High Commissioner's Programme A/AC.96/830*, electronic document, http://www.unhcr.ch, accessed May 21, 2003.

——— (1997) *UNHCR Comprehensive Policy on Urban Refugees.* Geneva: UNHCR.

———(2000) *International Instruments Relating to Refugees.* Dar es Salaam: UNHCR.

——— (2001a) *Urban Refugees in Tanzania.* Internal document, dated October 15, 2001.

——— (2001b) *Evaluation of the Implementation of UNHCR's Policy on Refugees in Urban Areas. EPAU/2001/01*, electronic document, http://www.unhcr.ch/epau, accessed October 1, 2002.

Wellman, Barry and Scott Wortley (1990) 'Different strokes from different folks: Community ties and social support', *American Journal of Sociology*, 96(3), pp. 558–88.

Willems, Roos (2003) *Embedding the Refugee Experience: Forced Migration and Social Networks in Dar es Salaam, Tanzania.* PhD dissertation, Department of Anthropology, University of Florida. Electronic document, http://purl.fcla.edu/fcla/etd/UFE0002281, accessed August 31, 2004.

Williams, Holly Ann (1993) 'Self-settled refugees in north-western Zambia: Shifting norms of assistance from social networks', in Mary Carol Hopkins and Nancy D. Donnelly (eds), *Selected Papers on Refugee Issues: II*. Arlington, VA: American Anthropological Association, pp. 135–55.

3
The Uncertainties of the Child Soldier Experience and Subsequent Reintegration into Civil Society[1]

Art Hansen

Introduction

Wars and civil conflicts displace many children and adults in different ways. Traditional studies of displacement or forced migration associated with wars and civil conflicts focus on refugees and internally displaced persons (IDPs), who are geographically uprooted and are living in camps and settlement schemes, or in towns and cities as a consequence of the rural-urban migration that often accompanies guerilla warfare. Similarly, the study of post-conflict population movements concentrates on the repatriation of refugees and the impact of decisions by IDPs to return to their pre-conflict home areas or remain in urban areas. This focus on refugees and IDPs overlooks the fact that many other people are also uprooted or displaced from their society in other ways. The wide range of people who are displaced becomes evident when the war ends, or the conflict subsides, and the country begins the complex process of political, social, and economic integration of the fragmented national population and civil society. The national population is composed of all the people who are citizens (whether residing inside or outside of the national territory) as well as resident non-citizens.

Civil and military societies

'Civil society,' on the other hand, is a political or social term, and the concept of civil society is defined in many different ways, depending on the political agenda or theoretical orientation.[2] One definition, associated with the governance and democratization agenda, contrasts civil society with the government, with civil society being the 'arena of private economic and social relations, rather than [the arena] of government' (Walzer 1998: 29). According to this agenda, an organized and mobilized civil society can pressure the state to become more democratic and more accountable to its citizens. Another definition, associated with the economic growth and development agenda, considers civil society to be one of three sectors, with the government (or state) and the economy being the other two. From this perspective, civil society is seen as one of the 'inescapable noneconomic dimensions' affecting economic growth (Rostow cited in Candler 1999). One common element in these definitions is the separation of civil society from the government.

In this chapter, civil society is conceptualized as separate from the government and also as separate from 'military society,' the array of militarized or armed groups ('fighting forces') that include the national military (army, navy, air force, etc.) as well as paramilitaries, militias, guerilla forces, etc. All of the people in the civil and military societies are residents in, and may be citizens of, the country and count as part of the national population. But only those in civil society are considered to be 'civilians,' whereas military society is composed of soldiers, combatants,[3] and others who are 'associated with the fighting forces.'[4] These soldiers and associated people include children and adults who have been abducted as well as those who entered military society voluntarily.

In most civil wars and disturbances, the soldiers and combatants (men, women, and children) who are demobilized from the various armed groups (military society) are an important category of people who need to re-enter, or be reintegrated into, civil society after the war ends, or the conflict subsides. This militarized population is usually targeted for special attention as part of the process of ending the conflict, reducing the size of the fighting forces, and establishing a sustainable peace. The reintegration of ex-soldiers into civil society is the third phase in the normal Disarmament, Demobilization, and Reintegration (DDR) Program that is negotiated during the peacemaking and cease-fire process in war-torn countries.

Purpose and focus of this chapter

This chapter extends the study of the displacement or forced migration associated with wars and civil conflicts to look at the uncertainties associated with the social dynamics of the problematic wartime experience and subsequent, post-conflict reintegration of another subpopulation of displaced persons. This other subpopulation consists of the children, men, and women who leave civil society with its rules and statuses, enter and become members of another (military) society that has intermittent or perhaps continual (frequently violent) interaction with civil society, and then attempt to enter and re-establish membership in civil society again.

The child soldiers who are the center of attention in this chapter go through five phases:

1. They begin their lives and spend years being socialized and integrated into civil society.
2. Then they are displaced from civil society and lose their civilian status by their recruitment (whether forced or voluntary) into various fighting forces.
3. They spend months or years being socialized and integrated into a military society.
4. Then they are demobilized (freed or displaced, depending on the perspective) from their military society and status.
5. They are confronted with the opportunities and challenges of reintegration into civil society and the need to establish a civilian status.

The particular focus of this chapter is on child soldiers (both boys and girls) when they try to re-establish membership and status (reintegrate) in civil society.

This chapter explores another dimension (the division between civil and military) of conflict-induced social fragmentation (or disintegration) and post-conflict reintegration in Africa. The exploration of this civil-military dimension compares and contrasts civil and military societies and how they value and educate their children. This theoretical exploration presents ideal types of these two societies rather than presenting a detailed case study. The ideal types are based on a review of the literature and observations from short-term field research that the author has conducted on soldiers (men, women, and children), demobilization, and post-conflict attempts at reintegration in Angola, the Democratic Republic of Congo (DRC), Eritrea, Liberia, and Sierra Leone (Hansen et al. 2001; 2002; United Nations 1995; Bernard et al. 2003; Hansen 1994). However, the ideal types are not intended to portray conditions in these specific countries, and the conceptual statements about civil and military societies ignore the empirical variability that exists among African military units and among African civil societies.

This chapter also analyzes three critical choices that must be faced by those who design and implement demobilization and reintegration programs for child soldiers. The decisions all revolve around the issue of whether to target and separate child soldiers for special attention and benefits while they reintegrate into civil society. Experience has shown that the process of transition between military and civilian life may be troubled.[5] These reintegration programs focus on the needs and suffering of the ex-soldiers, but tend to minimize the needs and uncertainties of the host communities.

This chapter addresses not only the wartime experience and post-conflict reintegration of child soldiers, but also the uncertainties that confront other social actors who are directly affected by the attempt to reintegrate and reconcile with children who have been soldiers. These other actors include the parents and family members of the demobilized children, as well as other adults and children who live in the communities that are supposed to receive the demobilized child soldiers. Communities may have good cause to resist being selected as hosts to reintegrate their demobilized children or young men.

The rights of children in armed conflict

The recruitment (mobilization), wartime service, demobilization, and reintegration of child soldiers are significant issues for a variety of reasons, but questions about morality are what attract so much passionate global attention. The interest in child soldiers has been driven by humanitarian concerns and debates about human rights. Children's rights have been included or mentioned in a number of general documents on human rights, including the Geneva Conventions (1949), the Additional Protocols to the Geneva Convention (1977), and the Rome Statute of the International Criminal Court (1998). Of particular relevance here is that the Rome Statute defines as a war crime the conscription, enlistment, or use in hostilities of children (defined as persons under 15 years of age) by national armed forces or by armed groups.

In addition to these general documents, other international agreements address the human rights that are specific to children and to the specific threats that confront children in times of armed conflict. The 1989 United Nations *Convention on the Rights of the Child* (hereafter referred to as the UN Convention) is the keystone document. It articulates a full range of children's rights and, of special interest here, commits signatory states to promote the physical and psychosocial recovery and social reintegration of children who have been victims of armed conflict. The UN Convention establishes the now widely-accepted international definition of a child as a person less than 18 years of age, but does not prohibit the recruitment for military service of young people in the 15 to 18 year old age cohort.

Later agreements build upon the widely-circulated 1996 report by Grac'a Machel, who had been appointed by the United Nations (UN) Secretary-General as an independent expert to study the impact of armed conflict on children (United Nations 1996). Following that report, the UN Secretary-General in 1997 appointed a Special Representative for Children and Armed Conflict.

Two of the most important changes since then are the redefinition of the status of child soldier and the redefinition of the legal age of children in terms of their involvement in armed conflict. In terms of the status of child soldier, there had existed some confusion or disagreement over whether all of the children who are 'associated with the fighting forces' qualify as soldiers. Many of these children are not carrying weapons or killing people, but are providing domestic labor, acting as porters or spies, supplying sexual services, etc. The distinction becomes really important in two ways. Armed groups may claim that they are not violating international standards because they are not recruiting children as soldiers, and none of their soldiers are children; the groups are merely employing children as workers or helping them by providing food and shelter. Another way in which the distinction is important is when children leave the armed group. Are they demobilizing, thus qualifying for benefits and services provided to other demobilized soldiers to help them reintegrate? Or are they simply being freed to return unassisted to their families and communities?

In 1997 the *Cape Town Principles and Best Practices on the Prevention of Recruitment of Children into the Armed Forces and Demobilisation and Social Reintegration of Children in Africa* were adopted, and these principles and guidelines are now widely-accepted.[6] The Cape Town Principles establish that any child who is 'associated with the fighting forces' in any way is to be considered a child soldier.

In terms of redefining the legal age of children in armed conflict, the 1999 International Labour Organization (ILO) *Convention (No. 182) on the Elimination of the Worst Forms of Child Labour* is the first international convention to apply the 'less than 18 years of age' definition of childhood to 'forced or compulsory recruitment of children for use in armed conflict.' The 1999 Organization of African Unity (OAU) *African Charter on the Rights and Welfare of the Child* has a similar provision prohibiting the recruitment or participation in hostilities or internal strife of children under 18.

The 2000 UN *Optional Protocol to the Convention on the Rights of the Child on the involvement of children in armed conflict* clearly mandates that signatory states should ensure that 'persons who have not attained the age of 18 years are not compulsorily recruited into their armed forces' and do not participate directly in hostilities. The 2000 Optional Protocol also calls upon signatory states to provide technical cooperation and financial assistance to improve the rehabilitation and social reintegration of former child soldiers.

How many children are soldiers?

The most widely-accepted estimate is that, at any given time during the past decade, approximately 300,000 children were serving as soldiers (Coalition to Stop the Use of Child Soldiers 2001). In Africa during the past decade, children have served as soldiers in the following 14 countries (in alphabetical order)—Algeria, Angola, Burundi, Chad, the Republic of Congo, the Democratic Republic of Congo (DRC), Eritrea, Ethiopia, Liberia, Rwanda, Sierra Leone, Somalia, Sudan and Uganda.

It is impossible to state with precision (the statistics are uncertain) the exact number of child soldiers, but children are estimated to constitute a significant proportion of the soldier population in many of these countries. An August 2001 report by three NGOs stated that more than 15 percent of newly recruited combatants in DRC were children at that time, and many child soldiers were under 12 years of age (Christian Aid et al. 2001). A 2004 report by another NGO noted that about 80 percent of the people associated with the Lord's Resistance Army in Uganda are abducted children, and estimates of the total number of children abducted in Uganda range from 20,000 to 25,000 (Anderson et al. 2004).

Estimates of the numbers of soldiers (including children) in a war-torn country are complicated by several factors. First, armed groups still at war are reluctant to divulge any information about the size and composition of their forces. Second, many of the less formal armed groups probably do not know exactly how many soldiers they control at any given time.[7] Recruitment into many of the fighting forces, whether voluntary or forced, is an ongoing, largely undocumented process that is often under the control of localized, uncoordinated groups. Groups also know that the international community frowns on the recruitment and use of children as soldiers and tend to deny that their forces recruit or contain any children.

Note that until the adoption of the Optional Protocol by the UN General Assembly in 2000, the UN used the 1989 Convention's guidelines and defined as child soldiers only children less than 15 years of age. This affects all of their statistics for the number of child soldiers in previous years. Since the adoption of the Optional Protocol, the UN statistics include as child soldiers all persons younger than 18 years of age who are associated with a fighting force. Statistics for the year 2000 are a watershed, as sometimes they are reporting on the number of child soldiers as of the end of 1999 (using 15 years as the measure), whereas in other cases they are referring to the number in 2000 (using 18 years as the measure).

The author encountered an example of the variance in estimates during his field research in the Democratic Republic of Congo (DRC) in 2001. The most widely-cited estimate (from the UN) stated that there were more than 10,000 (sometimes rephrased as between 10,000 and 15,000) child soldiers in the DRC (United Nations 2000). Later that same year the UN Secretary-General estimated 10,000 to 20,000 child soldiers (United Nations Security Council, 2000).

My research concentrated on only three areas in the west and east of the country:

1. The government-controlled west of the country, including the national capital, Kinshasa.
2. North Kivu Province, with its capital at Goma.
3. South Kivu Province, with its capital at Bukavu.

The two Kivu provinces are located in the rebel-controlled east of the country.

My own estimate of the numbers of child soldiers in the DRC was based on reports from the government for areas it controlled in the west and on reports from the opposition forces and local non-governmental and community-based organizations (NGOs and CBOs) for North and South Kivu. These reports located and described 11 populations of child soldiers in the three focus areas. Based on this information, my estimate was that there were between 15,000 to 25,000 child soldiers in 2001 in only these three areas of the DRC (Hansen et al. 2001). These areas did not include the other populous areas to the north and south that were also embroiled in civil war.

Risk and uncertainty

This chapter draws attention to the uncertainties surrounding the situation of these children during their time in military society and when they re-enter civil society. When economists and anthropologists study decision-making behavior, they sometimes differentiate between risk and uncertainty.[8] Risk exists when there is a known probability of a negative outcome occurring, while uncertainty refers to situations when the probability of a negative outcome is unknown (Roumasset et al. 1979; Ortiz 1980). Given the lack of research and knowledge concerning many dimensions of the child soldier experience and the reintegration process, it seems more appropriate to refer to the uncertainties, rather than the risks, surrounding the displacement, wartime experience, and reintegration of child soldiers.

Very little scientific research has been conducted in Africa on the:

1. Wartime experiences of soldiers (especially of child soldiers) and civilians.
2. Post-conflict processes of societal integration and reconciliation, especially when it includes the reintegration of demobilized soldiers (and the repatriation of refugees).
3. Short-term and longer-term impacts of wartime experiences on children, childhood, and civil society.[9]

Almost all of the existing literature on child soldiers in Africa is advocacy-oriented (such as the reports from the Coalition to Stop the Use of Child Soldiers and various UN and NGO charitable appeals), based on anecdotal descriptions of individuals and specific cases, and/or based on the evaluation of western-funded programs or projects that provide services to children. Thus, the existing literature accurately reflects the western and multinational emphasis on human rights (especially children's rights) and humanitarian assistance, and this literature is valuable for informing the world about the existence of child soldiers and contributing to the global debate about children's rights.

Unfortunately, this literature of anecdotes and individual cases and faces camouflages the relative absence of field research in Africa and research-based findings and recommendations.[10] This means that western and host national observers and the people involved in designing and implementing humanitarian assistance programs and specific projects in Africa now base their actions on their personal idiosyncratic experiences in the field and on many assumptions about the impact of wartime experiences on child soldiers, the trauma that the children have suffered, and the extent to which children's reintegration will occur through family reunification and 'going home.'[11] These assumptions in turn are based on more fundamental assumptions about the universal nature of childhood and the nature and hospitality of traditional African society.

The author's experience and observations question the validity and universality of these (largely western) assumptions. Many questions remain unanswered about the civil-military experience and the lives of these children, now and after they disappear from official attention.

What is the situation that children confront when they become soldiers? What are the differences between the experiences of any child in a wartorn environment and the experiences of a child soldier? How important is the amount of time and opportunity for social learning that children have before being recruited into military society? How does the content and form of social learning change when a society endures warfare for months? For years?

What sorts of changes are African civil societies experiencing because of warfare? How widespread is post-conflict reintegration, or post-conflict continuation of social divisions? What happens to child soldiers when they return to their home communities, and what happens to those children whose home communities refuse to accept them? How do parents, families, and communities cope with the memory that they allowed their children to be abducted or recruited as soldiers? To what extent are there general patterns across African societies and countries as opposed to patterns unique to different communities, societies, and countries?

Due to the absence of research-based findings, it is difficult to question the validity and accuracy of the assumptions that now determine the types and quality of assistance offered to demobilized African child soldiers. Hopefully the discussion generated by this chapter about uncertainties will stimulate more research that will provide answers to these questions.

The education of children in civil and military societies

Social learning

The theoretical orientation in this chapter is the study of social learning. As infants and children grow, they learn about their society and acquire social identities. Social scientists usually refer to this as the process of socialization or enculturation. Socialization is the process of learning the social structure of a particular society—the norms (or rules of behavior), values, statuses, and roles. Enculturation is a term used to describe a similar process of learning a particular culture. The process of enculturation includes the absorption of more information than socialization in that culture (sometimes called the 'way of life' of a people) includes the social rules as well as information about religion and philosophy, cuisine, arts and crafts, etc.

Both of these terms are commonly used to describe what children learn about their home society and culture while growing up. This formulation of social learning represents an ideal formal model and implies the passive reception by a child of a fixed and established set of social rules and cultural content. The assumption is that the child learns, practices what has been learned, and then, as an adult, becomes the 'carrier' of these unchanged rules and cultural content and, in turn, passes them on to his or her children.

Defining education in the broadest sense, social learning is an educational process. Social learning, as defined in this chapter, includes more than socialization and enculturation. To understand, or even to study, the social learning of children who become soldiers in wartime, a framework is needed that will accept:

1. Dramatic changes in the children's social environment (home and civil society) during childhood. The immediate home environment as well as the orientation of civil society may change dramatically.
2. The children's reception of mixed, conflicting, and contradictory messages from adults.
3. The children's observations of behavior (by adults and other children) that offers alternatives to the messages they are taught.
4. The children's agency (their active initiative rather than only passive reception) in synthesizing and selectively incorporating alternatives into their lives.

This chapter explores the content and type of social learning that a child might experience in civil and military societies, how this learning might affect the child, and how this might affect the process and content of demobilization and reintegration programs. This is an exploratory discussion that is intended to stimulate research and outline a potential research agenda. Civil and military societies are presented as ideal types and do not attempt to represent the variability found in different African countries. Several ways to advance this research would be for other researchers to contrast the features of these ideal types with the features of any particular civil or military society, to contrast the idealized social learning presented here with the lessons and process of social learning that occur in any particular society, to contrast this general portrayal of children who are soldiers with the life histories of young Africans who personally have incorporated wartime and peacetime experiences into their lives and personalities, or to study the processes of social integration and reconciliation in African communities that have lived through the incorporation and personal maturation of ex-soldiers.

Childhood formation in civil society

Childhood is understood to be a time of formation, when children have the opportunity to mature and learn how to function as normal adults in their civil society. The process of social learning includes both informal and formal education. Informal education is important in all societies, whether they are rural or urban, pastoral or industrial, literate or based on an unwritten language. Parents and other family members, neighbors, and others in the community teach children the rules and principles of social life, the mores, values, history, and traditions of that particular civil society and culture, and the sanctions (rewards and punishments) that family and society use to enforce their standards of behavior. Children learn, usually by observation, about the roles adults play and how adults earn a living. Children also learn, usually by observation, about contradictions and alternatives practiced by other children and by adults.

Civil society is not homogeneous. There are many differences by gender, ethnicity, age, and temperament. Men and women in the same society transmit some different lessons to children, and boys and girls receive some different lessons and emphases. Children learn that they should respond to different people in different ways. Most lessons about appropriate social behavior are non-verbal, and children learn most of their lessons about how to function as adults by observing the adults around them. Children also learn many lessons from other children. Many lessons concern the etiquette, protocol, and patterns of respect that are found in all societies, and children also learn about inconsistencies, conflicts, and different ways to play the system.

Part of this informal education is vocational training. Children learn many skills informally—how to prepare food, clean clothes, take care of other children, construct buildings, farm, tend livestock, fish, etc. Children also learn from their parents and neighbors the skills of particular trades or professions and become comfortable practicing them, which is part of the reason why so many children end up following the trades or professions of their parents or neighborhood.

Part of this total process of education is psychological because children internalize the information and value systems that they are taught and have observed. Internalizing means that the children accept these lessons (intended and unintended) as part of their own identities and conscience. For example, instead of always having to be told by someone else that some action is 'bad,' the child may learn to think of that action as bad and to avoid it because the child feels bad. Instead of having to be told to work, the child may learn to value work and to feel good because he or she is a good worker. Thus, sanctions become internal as well as external. This is part of the process by which children themselves become the carriers and, eventually, often the guardians of their culture and society, even when their own lives diverge from the rules they were taught.

Literate societies create formal (school) education to supplement informal education. Literacy allows people to accumulate a vast storehouse of information, and formal education is the system that societies use to systematically prepare their children to access and use this storehouse. In the broadest sense, formal education is all of the education occurring in classes with teachers and curricula. Thus, it includes class-based vocational training as well as more academic education. Formal school education prepares children for many future careers and responsibilities. Formal education does not replace informal because informal education is still the primary mechanism for social and moral instruction and for a tremendous amount of practical vocational training.

Therefore, in addition to informal education, childhood is also a time for formal education in schools and, often, for formal religious education or training that introduces or emphasizes moral and epistemological knowledge and values. Another component of every country's formal educational system is citizenship training in which children learn the history of their country, learn about loyalty and patriotism, and learn the importance of bonding with other citizens.

Civil versus military society
The process of adults teaching children about the rules and traditions of their society and culture continues to some extent even in time of war or civil conflict, as many people probably try to maintain many of the routines of peacetime. Depending on the character, ferocity, and immediacy of the war or conflict, the civil society may change in various ways, perhaps becoming more militarized. Children may observe and learn new lessons or priorities and may be taught to behave in ways that would be unacceptable in peacetime.

Although it is uncertain to what extent a particular civil society may be transformed by wartime conditions, civil societies are structured and operate differently than military society, In general, civil society is more complex, less severe, and less rigidly disciplined. Civil society presents a variety of perspectives, including both the masculine and feminine, and permits more independent or individualistic action. Conversely, military society is simpler, more severe, more masculine, more hierarchical, and more disciplined than civil society.

Military society is simpler because it concentrates on fewer domains and presents child soldiers with fewer options and recommended behaviors. Military society is more severe because it focuses on and prepares soldiers for life or death activities and requires soldiers to prepare for and carry out actions that are proscribed by civil society. For instance, in general, civil societies proscribe killing people, except in exceptional circumstances, whereas the military may require that child soldiers are ready to kill people on command. Strictly enforced obedience to commands from superiors in the hierarchy and rigid or severe sanctions are characteristic of military society.

Recruitment or enrollment in the military is part of a social process in which recruits leave civil society and enter military society. At this time the recruit assumes the social status of soldier (or military trainee), which replaces what were his (or her) most important social statuses (son or daughter, student, etc.) in non-military life. Belonging to one social group is often expressed in terms of opposition to another group (the in-group versus the out-group). In the beginning, the new recruit may be forced to undergo initiation rituals or training that emphasize the difference between military expectations and civil society. In the American military this is time for the 'boot camp' that emphasizes in many ways, from haircuts to daily routines, that the new recruit is no longer a civilian.

Other armed groups have more brutal ways of stressing the change, including forcing the new recruit to participate in atrocities that clearly separate him and his new companions from the civilians being tortured. These atrocities may include killing, maiming, raping, and otherwise terrorizing civilians, burning homes, and poisoning wells. The brutality and frequency of atrocities will vary from one individual child to another, and there will be differences from one armed group and country to another. Members of a local militia or self-defense force usually (although this is uncertain) identify with and do not commit atrocities against the local population that they are defending.

Military service is a formative time for these children newly recruited from civil society. During the period of military service, the child soldier is socialized and enculturated with the rules and principles of military life, the mores, values, history, and traditions of that military society, the rewards and punishments (sanctions) that the military society uses to enforce its standards of behavior, the importance of that military group, and loyalty to the other soldiers. Part of this process is psychological in that child soldiers, to varying degrees, internalize these lessons, which become part of their identity.

The recruited child is expected to learn the rules of this new society and become a different person. This is as abrupt a change as if the new recruit had entered a completely different culture in which he was required to rapidly become a 'native'. This transition will be minimized if the military unit is a local militia (or self-defense militia) in which the members are already known and the time spent being active in the militia is sporadic instead of consistent.

Gender and sexual relations in civil and military societies

Civil society relies on the integration of men and women. All civil societies have a division of labor in which each gender performs essential tasks, and both men and women play essential roles in the rearing and formation of children. Sexual or gender tension or opposition is also common in many societies, and there is often some degree of hostility, perhaps portrayed in a joking manner, between the sexes. Regardless of the division and tensions, the complex interdependencies of civil society require that men and women work out normal modes of compromise and respect that follow the society's rules for social interaction. Sexual relations are always important, but they also become part of each society's life cycle patterns for preparing people for marriage, family life, and child-rearing.

Traditionally, military society is primarily or exclusively male. Men are the fighters and leaders and, in a camp composed only of men, perform the domestic tasks (food preparation, cleaning the camp, etc.) that women usually perform in civil society. When soldiers (men) are married, their wives often remain separate from the male military camp, either staying at home or in separate living quarters. Other women and girls (not wives) also might be living with the military men and providing sexual and domestic services.[12]

There are exceptions to this male model, as the modern western military has become more sexually integrated, and the Eritrean military featured fighters of both sexes. However, in general, certainly in reference to most current African situations, military society is exclusively male or dominated by men. (There are some exceptions.)[13] The single-sex basis for traditional military society means that it does not rely on the integration of men and women for the normal functioning of society or need to respect civil society's rules for social and sexual interaction. The sexual opposition and hostility that is modified or controlled to varying degrees in civil society is less controlled.

One result is an increase in male violence (including rape, torture, and murder) against women and girls in civil society. Rape and sexual violence by soldiers becomes a common occurrence in these conflicted regions and times, and many women and girls in Africa today have been abducted (sometimes to become 'bush wives'). These violent acts would be considered abnormal (by the rules of civil society) if they were committed during peacetime. How will the girls and women in the community who were sexually attacked respond to the attempted reintegration of demobilized ex-soldiers?

Another result is the uncertain effect on the male child soldier being socially formed by the military. To what extent does he learn not to respect the complex interweaving of men and women, opposition and interdependence, that he would learn in civil society? Instead, to what extent will he learn to devalue and exploit women, to perceive women and girls as prey rather than as future mates and partners? How will this influence these boys' abilities in the future to form stable social relationships? How will this impact on these boys' future performances as husbands and fathers? The lessons learned during wartime must be addressed later as part of social reintegration.

Girls may confront other problems and be stigmatized, threatened, and even ostracized and considered unmarriageable. In Eritrea, women who had been inducted into military society at an early age learned after demobilization that their entire militarized socialization and meaning of being a woman ran counter to the traditional values of Eritrean civil society. They faced a different world where the social constructs of military society no longer applied and where they were in conflict with the expectations of civil society. In Uganda, when some returned girls attempted to reintegrate, they were threatened by their husbands: 30 percent of these girls were mothers (with children conceived in the bush) who needed additional assistance. Also in Uganda, traditional ceremonies for 'cleansing' a boy or girl ex-soldier provided psychological security for both the child and the community and made it easier for a community to accept and reintegrate the child. Cleansing was especially important for girls who had served as 'bush wives' to improve their chances for post-war marriage. In Sudan, child soldiers who were stigmatized by their communities were more likely to be recruited back into the rebel movement.[14]

Variation among child soldiers

The children who become soldiers are a heterogeneous population of individuals before they enter military society. Most child soldiers spend years in the military, but the social and psychological experiences of different children will vary. Children will have different experiences and memories and will differentially incorporate their military service into their post-service identities. Therefore, the child soldiers who are demobilized and face the challenges and opportunities of reintegration do not form a homogeneous population.

Before children join the military, their temperaments and behaviors may range from the friendly and peaceful to the violent and aggressive. Their home and family situations may vary from the peaceful and loving to the abusive and desperate. Some families are prosperous, while the difficult economic conditions of other families may force them to encourage or force their children to leave home to seek their own livelihood. Many children are forced or abducted to serve as soldiers, and forced recruitment per se is an issue. Many other children volunteer for various motives related to their enduring hunger and poverty, the desperate conditions of a collapsed wartime economy, a desire to protect themselves and their family, or the attraction of being soldiers (Hansen et al. 2001).[15]

During the war, the children confront different situations and commit a variety of acts. However, all of the child soldiers are exposed to violence, and many are trained and become experienced in learning how to hurt and kill people. Many of the current armed struggles are characterized by the commission of atrocities against the civilian population, and child soldiers are sometimes forced to be active participants in these atrocities. In some of these conflicts, children are given or forced to take drugs or alcohol to encourage them to be fearless and to commit acts that the children would otherwise be unwilling to commit. This means that the children being demobilized are accustomed to acts of violence, may be accustomed or addicted to taking drugs or alcohol, and may have committed atrocities, even against their own families or other people in the communities that are expected to serve as hosts and reintegrate the demobilized ex-soldiers.

The adult who enters military service has already passed through the formative period of childhood in civilian society and created a civilian identity for himself. He has already learned how boys and girls interact and has begun to anticipate a future for himself as an adult in civil society. For the adult recruit, to varying degrees the formation and indoctrination of military society adds another layer to an already formed civilian identity, or is incorporated to create a more complex identity.

The children who enter military service are more impressionistic. Depending on age, intelligence, temperament, and home environment, each child was still in the process of learning the principles and practices of civilian life, how adults should behave, how to interact with other children, how children and adults handle disputes and quarrels, how boys and girls interact, and how children move beyond the initial intense dependence on the mother and father to a more independent existence as an adult. The process of learning and internalizing the lessons of civil society was cut short—an incomplete process of formation—and replaced by learning the lessons of military society.

Demobilization and reintegration

It was noted at the beginning of this chapter that the children go through
five phases. Three have been discussed already—social learning in civil
society, followed by recruitment (mobilization) and service in military
society. The chapter now addresses the final two phases—leaving the
military (demobilization) and re-entering civil society (reintegration).
In reality, most African child soldiers go through another, additional
intermediary phase after demobilization and before reintegration. This
is a temporary camp or transit center, where demobilized children stay
before reintegration. During the days, or weeks (sometimes months) the
children are in the transit center, their families are traced and notified
about the location of their children. Sometimes reintegration is a simple
process of arranging for the child to be reunited with his or her family.

Other cases are not as simple. The child has been changed by his or her
life and experiences as a soldier, and the home (family and civil society
itself) has changed because of time and wartime experiences. Family
members and friends probably have died, moved, married, or divorced
in the child's absence, and the child's wartime activities may have
endangered or estranged the rest of his or her family. Thus, the child may
not be welcomed at home by his family, and other community members
may discriminate against this particular child or against all children who
were soldiers.

A case in point concerns Thomas, a young boy whom the author met at
a center for demobilized children in Goma, North Kivu (DRC).[16] Thomas
spoke about his life as a soldier and the people he had killed. Later, the staff
said that the boy had learned that his parents had been arrested, perhaps
because of their son's wartime behavior, and the boy did not think that he
could ever return to them. The fate of this boy was uncertain, and no one
could predict what would happen to him (Hansen et al. 2001).

Social learning, uncertainty and demobilization
When child soldiers demobilize, they leave the status of soldier, leave
behind the prestige, lifestyle and security of carrying a gun, leave the
life with which they have become familiar, and leave the community of
soldiers who have been companions through many experiences. Children
must replace their self-image as soldiers with the uncertain process of
personal and vocational development in civil society. Some children are
reluctant and refuse to leave, or return after having been demobilized.
Staff members of a transit center for demobilized child soldiers in Goma
(DRC) related how many children in the beginning would run away from

the center and return to their military camp. This stopped only when the local military commanders were instructed by their regional commander (these were rebel units) to refuse to permit children to return and to send them back to the center (Hansen et al. 2001).

The period of social learning in military society and forming an identity as a soldier may have been longer than the time in civil society, and the experience of being a soldier may have been the capstone of a childhood. One example was Alex, a boy who was five when the rebels took him from his family in Makeni, Sierra Leone. Shy and soft spoken, he would not give his name, and his older brother, Michael, helped tell his story.[17] Alex lived for ten years as a rebel soldier, and, when he demobilized and returned to reintegrate in his home village, he was not accepted into his home. An uncle brought him to the Sackville neighborhood, just outside Freetown (the capital of Sierra Leone), and enrolled him in a program to reintegrate child soldiers. Having grown up in the bush with the social values brought by the war, Michael's little brother could not comprehend how to function within the bustling civil community of Sackville. Normal values and understandings were lost as he struggled to find a fit in civil society. Fortunately, after a while, Alex understood that he could not go back to the bush, where violence was a way of life. He stopped doing drugs and learned the social implications of violent actions, such as rape, that he had committed as a soldier (Hansen et al. 2002).

The story of Alex shows how many of these children were still in formation, learning what was expected of them as normal adults, before entering the military society. While they were still learning how adult men and women should behave in civil society, these children were taken into and socialized by military society. Social reintegration for many of these children should include their continuing the interrupted process of learning the principles, rules, values, statuses, and expected behaviors of civil society. That learning should stress the principles of the culture of peace and of the human rights of women. Demobilized soldiers need to learn to express themselves non-violently and that rights are balanced with responsibilities.

Many children will be happy to leave the armed group and return to their homes and civil society, and they may not wait for a formal cease-fire and demobilization order. Instead, they demobilize on their own (desertion, in military terms), a practice called 'auto-demobilization' in the DRC. In a neighborhood of Kinshasa (the capital of DRC) the author talked with an 11 year old child soldier who had auto-demobilized. At the age of 9, he left his family and joined the army. Life in the army was very different than he expected, so he left and came home.

When Daddy died, I joined the army. I was hungry, doing nothing in Kinshasa, and living with no money. I had already finished primary school. At nine, I left home and joined the army. They promised to pay $100 a month. The army never paid us properly. I spent one and a half years away. I carried weapons, but was not afraid because my spirit was gone (meaning that he had lost the will to live). Much of the time I was training in training camps. I was eventually sent on a mission. It was then that I fled. But I was afraid to come home, so I stayed in hiding with a group of about 50 other former child soldiers. We ate insects and survived on our wits. We buried our weapons and wore the civilian clothes we had kept. We were attacked in our hideout and faced many hardships. That is when I came home to my mother (Hansen et al. 2001).

He now participates in a project operated by an NGO[18] in an abandoned factory in a poor neighborhood of Kinshasa. The children are involved in rabbit breeding and small garden projects to generate income. 'Now I raise rabbits,' he said. 'With the money I earn, I study electricity and do some work. One day I hope to be an electrical engineer. Maybe one day I'll study abroad and become a real expert.'

Economic needs during reintegration

When asked why he became a soldier, he replied, 'For the money.' This was true for all of the children that were interviewed in that area of Kinshasa. The other children interviewed were older; they had gone to the front lines when they were 14 to 17 years old. They all said that they joined the military because they were promised $100, but some received nothing, and others got only $10. The boys were disappointed when they were underpaid, and they described their lives as soldiers as being hard, a tough lifestyle—hard officers, bad food, and no medicine. Several boys had visible shrapnel wounds on their legs. Fortunately, they had been well received back home. Their families had celebrated when their children came back from the front because many parents had thought that their children were dead.

Economically, the military either provided for the needs of the soldier or allowed the soldier to forage (or take at gunpoint), whereas the non-military economy probably will not be prepared to provide the jobs and services that ex-soldiers (and other civilian youth) will need or want. The story told by another demobilized child soldier (now 18 years old) in Kinshasa notes the lack of opportunities for employment before and after being a soldier.

I was a street child. When I heard (former) President Laurent Kabila was recruiting, I decided to join up. I had no job, and was doing nothing. I had finished primary school. At 16, I went to a training camp to join the 3rd Brigade. I went to the front in Equateur province at Basankusu. I stayed there seven months learning how to use heavy weapons—rocket launchers, mortars, and 60 PCM, as well as light weapons. We had been doing nothing, and the good side was that we made friends and some money. The bad side was the killing. We saw many people die, and we killed many people. I regret this fact, and I'm sorry for the families of these young people. Adults send kids to war. That's the problem. After the battle we returned to Kinshasa ... My dream is to start a metalworking company that will employ others and stop them from going to war. I ask the United States and rich countries to stop making weapons that kill people in Africa. We need to make peace in Congo. Rich countries should send money so that people can go to school instead of going to war. Many foreigners come and take our pictures, but we wonder if they actually do anything for us. We need something practical like money, and a chance to go to school (Hansen et al. 2001).

Some children will have the capacity to re-enter immediately the formal educational track. These will generally be the children who had better academic training before entering the military and who spent fewer years in the military. Other children may require alternative education (sometimes called non-formal or bridging the gap, or, in DRC, *'remise a niveau'*) for months or years, either to replace the formal education for which they are not suited, or to prepare the students to later re-enter the formal educational track. Re-entering formal education will facilitate the children's social formation as well as delay their immediate need for employment. However, formal education will not satisfy the child's need for informal education about moral and social values and responsibilities.

Observers noted in the DRC that, for the most part, child soldiers who averaged between 16 and 17 years of age had lost about two or three years of school, compared with other children who had not entered the military life. The author also noted, while interviewing demobilized child soldiers in the Sackville neighborhood outside of Kinshasa, that the educational status of child soldiers was illustrated by the language they used in the interviews. These children had attended school for years before entering the military and had learned the French language in school. Their French language skills had regressed significantly while in the military, which is why child soldier interviews in Kinshasa (even for those with secondary school education) were conducted only in Lingala, while those in North and South Kivu were conducted only in Swahili (Hansen et al. 2001).

Many reintegrating child soldiers will need some way to earn money. This will be especially true when returning to school would be inappropriate. These children would benefit from vocational training or immediate employment. Few of them had experience earning a living before becoming soldiers. Most were still living with their families. Many were students, and few of them were prepared in terms of training or other resources to become economically independent. Many may have voluntarily joined the military or remained in the military after being drafted because they saw no possibility of employment outside of the military life. If the ex-soldiers come to believe, after a rapid appraisal of the non-military life, that civilian life still offers no hope for the future, then they may choose to try to return to the military economy or to a socially undesirable alternative (street children, gangs, or bandits).

A 2004 story in the *New York Times* about the civil unrest in Côte d'Ivoire notes 'the problem that fueled conflict in the first place, namely a generation of frustrated young men to whom war signals economic opportunity.' The article also refers to the worry that 'veterans' (who would include many children who were soldiers) from the civil wars in Liberia and Sierra Leone may come to Côte d'Ivoire to fight; 'Despite millions invested to demobilize child soldiers in Sierra Leone and Liberia, economic prospects remain dim for young men across the region' (Sengupta 2004).

Girls who demobilize face similar economic problems. The author encountered one group of 30 girls in the DRC who were being helped by an indigenous CBO. All of the girls said that they had been child soldiers, but had been drafted mostly for sexual service. After they deserted and re-entered civil society, the only way they had to earn a living was by working as prostitutes before being discovered and assisted by the CBO (Hansen et al. 2001).

Socio-psychological needs during reintegration

It is uncertain how many ex-soldiers will have socio-psychological needs. The 1994–1997 Liberian experience pointed out the importance of recognizing the individuality of war-affected children and women. Each individual may react and recover differently and have psychological wounds that vary depending on the level of involvement in the conflict, the exposure to and participation in violence, individual temperament and coping mechanisms, and family and community support (Kelly 1998). A report on that experience noted that children may appear to be 'highly

agitated...constantly jumpy and on the move...quick to overreact, often
with violence.' They may demonstrate 'enormously inflated egos...mistrust
of authority...difficulty sleeping, nightmares and flashbacks.' Most of the
children suffered 'deep-seated remorse and guilt...(and) an overwhelming
need to reveal or unburden themselves by confessing to the atrocities they
committed.'

Girls who are being demobilized probably will tend to experience
the same feelings of guilt, remorse, and hopelessness as boys with the
added burden of struggling with their history of sexual abuse, sometimes
complicated by their wartime experiences of bearing, rearing, and perhaps
losing babies. They might have a sense of hopelessness and lack of faith
in the future that is deepened by the knowledge that they face a double
stigma, association with combatants and having been raped.

One of the women interviewed in Sierra Leone ("Ruth') had been
abducted as a child and became a 'bush wife,' which is the term for women
who were abducted and forced into sexual servitude. Their stories of
wartime experiences in the bush are graphic and often horrifying (Hansen
et al. 2002). Unfortunately, their abuse has not ended with the war. Bush
wives are not accepted easily back into civil society because of the stigma
that rape carries. Often they continue to be considered outcasts. Ruth was
afraid to go out in public and was shy in crowds because she felt rejected
and ashamed. This means that these women feel that they cannot escape
their past.

A minority of the children in the earlier Liberian demobilization and
reintegration program did not show remorse. They were usually very
young, had witnessed continual violence for a long time, and had been
socialized into a 'culture of violence' by the adult combatants, who
served as the children's only role models. To these children, 'killing is
normal.' The report noted that, during and after their demobilization
and reintegration, these ex-combatant children (like Alex above) would
have to learn new social rules and values as they were socialized into
civil society. Also, caregivers were advised to be careful because these
children, when confronted with the disparity between society's values
and their past behavior, might develop suicidal tendencies, even though
suicide is rare in Liberian society (Kelly 1998).

Protection needs during reintegration

This indicates that protection may be important, both for the child soldiers
from society and for society (and other children) from the ex-soldiers
who have been socialized to believe that 'killing is normal.' Soldiers
learn violent solutions to problems. Non-violent conflict resolution is an

important component of life in civil society that many demobilized child soldiers will have to learn to appreciate and practice.

A report from a recent (October 2004) trip to observe the reintegration of Liberian child soldiers notes the differences in how ex-soldiers and other children confront daily life, and the subsequent difficulty of deciding whether to house ex-soldiers with other children in the same dormitory (i.e., integrate the ex-soldiers) at this school, or place the ex-soldiers in their own dormitory. The other children reported that a cat had wandered into the dormitory one day, and the ex-soldiers had killed and eaten the cat. The other children felt frightened by this experience and by the ex-soldiers' general attitude and feared living with them.[19]

Protection for the child soldiers from civil society will also be important. The society must come to some resolution that recognizes the past violence as well as recognizing that these were children who were (mis)guided by adults. The community must be educated to appreciate that the children were stunted in their social learning and that, although older than usual, the children are still going through an interrupted process of learning to be normal civilian adults.

The issue of community education and protection is illustrated by what happened in Goma (DRC) when the government and an NGO opened a new transit center for demobilized child soldiers.[20]

This was located in a large building, with a capacity for about 300 children, outside town near a residential neighborhood. This building, owned by a Protestant church, was previously a high school. Just a week after the center had moved to this new location, local residents threw stones at the center, and some of the children and their caregivers were slightly injured. Since a military logistics center was located nearby, the military intervened and restored order to the situation.

After the incident, NGO staff talked with neighbors of the transit center and representatives of the neighborhood and learned that there were grievances and misinformation about the center and its children. The problem was caused by envy, fear, and confusion about the purpose of the center. These interviews determined that:

1. Some people thought the transit center was a re-education camp for captured ex-child soldiers who would be integrated into the government army.
2. Others thought the center was going to be an orphanage sponsored by an international humanitarian NGO.
3. People were angry because the building could have been used as a school for the local community, but was instead used for ex-soldiers.

4. Others complained that children at the center benefited from better treatment (better education, medical care, food, etc.) than their own children, and they wanted the opportunity for their children to benefit from the center.

It became clear that the incident had occurred because the host community was neither informed about the establishment of a transit center nor prepared in advance for the arrival of the children. In order to inform and involve the neighborhood, the NGO organized a meeting with community representatives to explain the demobilization program in general and the work at the transit center. That meeting took place at the transit center to reassure the children that the community accepted them and gave neighbors the opportunity to visit the center. Community representatives prepared and disseminated messages to churches and community organizations to inform community members about the center and their responsibility to protect the children there. Visits and playtime were organized with the children in the neighborhood, which later became an integral part of the transit center activities. People from the community were allowed to visit the transit center and talk with children about different issues.

Important lessons were learned from this incident and its resolution that are applicable to other reintegration programs:

1. It is important to involve the local community in the initial planning and development of any program or strategy that will be housed or operating within their local area. This is a good place to prepare children and community members for the child's reintegration.

2. Opening the transit center or reintegration program to the local community is a way to facilitate the psychosocial rehabilitation of the child soldiers and to involve communities in the protection of these children.

3. Public information and awareness programs are important to keep the local community informed and to communicate the importance of human rights, children's and women's rights, and communal reconciliation. NGOs, community-based organizations (CBOs), and churches may play important roles in disseminating these messages (Hansen et al. 2001).

Three programmatic choices

During the war or conflict the government, the UN, and civil society (usually through NGOs and CBOs) begin to plan for ending the war or conflict and for what should happen after the war or conflict subsides. Here are three critical choices that these planners must face when designing and establishing a program to help reintegrate children into civil society after the war or conflict is over. All of these decisions are inter-related and, to some extent, interdependent:

1. What is the primary purpose of the program? Is the priority ending the war or helping children? This may also be rephrased as a decision about which children the program is trying to help.
2. When does the program start? Does it wait until the cease-fire is signed, and demobilization officially starts?
3. What is the best treatment to rehabilitate and reintegrate these children? Should treatment be based on individual therapy or social insertion into the family and community?

First choice: What is the primary purpose of the program?

End the war?

If the primary purpose is to stop the fighting and end the war, then the goal is to control and eliminate (or reduce the size of) the armed groups and the number of weapons. To accomplish this purpose, the program will target armed soldiers for special benefits because the program wants to encourage soldiers (including child soldiers) to identify themselves and come with their weapons and ammunition to the demobilization camps.[21] Without any special encouragement, soldiers might simply take their weapons (or bury them carefully preserved), change into civilian clothes, and attempt to disappear into civil society. If this happened, the soldiers could easily remobilize at a later date, or embark upon civilian careers as armed bandits.

The encouragement that such a targeted program could offer child (and other) soldiers would probably include giving each soldier some money (either a lump sum or an allowance paid over intervals for six months or a year), the possibility of enrolling in an educational or vocational training program, and material benefits (a tool kit, home-building materials, etc.). To qualify for the program, the soldier has to come to a demobilization site, bringing with him (occasionally her) a weapon or enough ammunition, be identified by a commander as a soldier, and surrender the weapon or ammunition.

Making this choice means establishing a special program for soldiers (including children), especially armed soldiers, who receive special benefits that non-combatants do not receive. Targeting assistance means establishing a segregated program that gives ex-soldiers some special benefits that civilians do not receive. This also means isolating demobilized child soldiers from other children. There are social and psychological reasons for targeting and isolating demobilized child soldiers. They may have participated in killing, mutilating, and torturing people and may be more traumatized than other children. There is also the issue of protection from the child soldiers who express violent behavior and need to learn non-violent conflict resolution procedures as well as the rationale for practicing non-violence. Separate reintegration programs that serve only child soldiers can provide this training while protecting other children, men, and women.

In Sierra Leone the policy decision to provide separate assistance to all ex-soldiers during the early phases of reintegration was effective. The separate program was set up and became operational relatively quickly, which helped keep the ex-soldiers from becoming frustrated at the slowness with which other reintegration programs were being established.

However, there are social consequences for the future when child soldiers receive privileges and benefits (for their education, health, and living) that other children do not receive. This may send the wrong messages about children benefiting from becoming soldiers and whether people should send their children into the army. The next time there is conflict or a war, parents may think that sending their child to the armed forces for a few months or years would ensure that he or she, in the future, would receive support from the UN or an international NGO that would give money, send him or her to school or to a vocational training center, and provide him or her with a starter kit or tool kit for re-entry and self-sufficiency in civil society.[22]

Another social consequence is that demobilization programs that focus on ending the war focus on men (and older boys) with guns and tend to ignore girls. Most of the children who act as actual combatants (carrying and firing weapons) are boys, and girls often constitute a small proportion of the total child soldier population. For example, at the most only three percent of the child soldiers in the DRC appear to be girls, most of whom seem to have been recruited and kept by commanders for sexual purposes (Hansen et al. 2001).

Help children?
If the primary purpose is to help children recover from their wartime experiences, the goal is to rescue children and help them reintegrate into society. Then one question is—which children? Given that programs have limited resources and cannot help everyone, which children will benefit, and which will not benefit? From this perspective, child soldiers (boys and girls) may be only some of the needy children who were directly

affected by the war, and all girls, even those most directly affected by the war, may be ignored. The girls most directly victimized by the war would include those who were combatants, servants, or slaves (often for sexual services) in military camps and girls who were raped, tortured, or sexually violated by soldiers.[23]

Sometimes even the broader category of 'war-affected children' seems too narrow. By 2001 the UN and most NGOs in the DRC had decided to focus their child-welfare programs on an even broader category ('children in particularly difficult circumstances') because the UN and NGOs thought that the terrible impacts on Congolese children of the years of warfare and poverty had essentially eliminated the significance of the distinction between war-inflicted vulnerability and chronic vulnerability.[24] They argued that all children living in desperate situations deserve to be helped, and humanitarian agencies should not turn away desperately needy children just because they did not fit into a targeted category. This more inclusive category includes unaccompanied children and orphans, physically handicapped or chronically ill children, and street children.

Another argument for including more children in programs is based on the belief that child soldiers should be put together with other children as soon as possible—in the transit center, and then in training centers and schools. Rehabilitation of child soldiers and their social reintegration would be facilitated by social interaction with other children, which means that demobilized child soldiers would benefit from being integrated with other children in the same programs. Integration in the program would facilitate reintegration in society. Children ex-soldiers need to learn how to play and learn in company with other children, and that should not wait until the soldiers return to their families and local communities.

A compromise solution was successful in Sierra Leone. Even though the program directed benefits to the child soldiers, the decision was made to open access to the program's health care services to the surrounding community. This gave the entire community a benefit from the presence of child ex-soldiers and was a means by which targeted programs could still benefit a larger community, which was also suffering from the effects of warfare and destruction (Bernard et al. 2003).

Second choice: When does the program start, and why?

When do official demobilization and reintegration start?
If the program targets only child soldiers who are officially demobilized, then the program probably will not start until there is a formal demobilization. Formal demobilization is only part of the process of officially ending

a war or conflict and usually does not occur until two critical preceding events have taken place:
1. Formal peace treaty is agreed and signed.
2. Formal (and effective) cease-fire is agreed and signed.
3. Perhaps even a formal disarmament is completed, although usually this event occurs simultaneously with demobilization as soldiers bring with them their weapons and ammunition to the demobilization sites.

This means that the start of (perhaps even the commitment to and funding for) a program for child soldiers is dependent on the success of other programs. In other words, a formal peace treaty and cease-fire become necessary preconditions that determine the timetable for programs specifically dedicated to demobilizing and reintegrating child soldiers. Given the fact that the other events may be delayed indefinitely (perhaps for years), the programs that target child soldiers also may be indefinitely delayed in their implementation.

Whenever there are children in need (or immediately)?
Programs that work with more types of needy children may start whenever there is funding because there are always children in need. Even if the purpose of the program is to benefit only child soldiers, there are good reasons to start the program and establish centers to work with other needy children before the beginning of official demobilization and reintegration. When the official demobilization begins, the centers would already be operational and functional and could reorient themselves to accept and assist only child soldiers.

A program needs trained staff, which means that staff members need to be recruited and trained. Transition centers need buildings that are equipped with beds (or sleeping mats) and cooking equipment, and food supplies. This means locating and possibly rehabilitating buildings and establishing systems to acquire and distribute food and other supplies. Family reunification programs need to begin gathering information about local communities and communication systems. Public education programs need to start informing and educating communities about the program and the rights of child soldiers (and all children) before the children arrive.

Waiting indefinitely to start a program for child soldiers, and then hurriedly preparing to receive and assist perhaps thousands of children, means that there probably will be chaos and confusion. Beginning these programs before the peace treaty and cease fire are actually signed means that civil society, local communities, and transit centers are prepared, and the staff of transit centers are trained and have learned to work together before being confronted with an influx of child ex-soldiers who are trying to cope with the problematic experience of re-entering civil society.

Third choice: The best way to rehabilitate and reintegrate child soldiers?

Individual therapy?
The modern western perspective on childhood is that all children grow through the same developmental cycle, a unilinear succession of phases with specific neurological, physiological, and psychological characteristics. Childhood is a time of formation and maturation, and children are vulnerable, susceptible, dependent, and need special protection (in the US, for example, protection from statutory rape, pedophilia, and pornography).

The western model of health and healing is individualistic. When someone becomes traumatized, he or she is usually treated as a social isolate. Children are assumed to be 'particularly susceptible to the effects of trauma...(and our)...medicalized model of trauma' (Gibbs 1997: 228–9) calls for individual therapy. This means that child soldiers should remain in separate living facilities for a while (how long?) while they are evaluated and given extensive individual therapy. This is closely related to the question of how long child soldiers should remain in the transit centers before being released. The therapeutic approach calls for an extended stay in the center.

Family and community re-insertion?
The African perspective emphasizes rapid re-insertion of the child soldier into his or her family and home community. Normal social life in civil society is seen as the best treatment. In Mozambique, people said that suffering and healing were similar for children and adults, and 'the process of healing (was) through engaging in the work of building, planting, and producing' (Gibbs 1997: 232). From this perspective the child should remain in the transit center only until the child's family has been traced, and the program staff members learn where the family members are located and whether the child can return to live with them.

This perspective believes that reintegration will not be complete until ex-soldiers learn how to play and learn in company with other children, so demobilized child soldiers should be integrated with other children in the same programs. Educational programs (non-formal as well as vocational), counseling, and games with other children will also help child soldiers recover. In societies that feature traditional healing procedures, including spirit possession ceremonies, holding these ceremonies for returned children who were soldiers may be effective in emphasizing spiritual cleansing and social acceptance.

Regardless of whether the program emphasizes therapy or re-insertion, another issue concerns the level of care and facilities provided for child soldiers. One simple example concerns bedding. Beds with mattresses and blankets seem to be the obvious choice of bedding for the UN and NGOs to provide for children. In Liberia in 1994–1997, UNICEF chose to provide child soldiers with only sleeping mats that lay on the floor, because these were normal and available in most homes and communities. UNICEF wanted to make sure it did not give the impression that child soldiers were being rewarded for fighting by giving them better living conditions than most civilian families. This would breed resentment among civilians and also make it less likely that the former child soldiers would want to return to the lower living conditions of their families (Kelly 1998).

Uncertain reception in the community

Family and community are overwhelmingly important to reintegration programs. In practice, all African child reintegration programs rely much more on family and community resources rather than on individualized therapy. Whatever one's perception of the theoretical utility of individual psychotherapy, there simply are not enough therapists in these African countries to staff a therapy-based program or even to quickly interview all of the demobilizing child soldiers. This means that all programs rely ultimately on the ability and willingness of families and communities to absorb and reintegrate these child ex-soldiers. How certain is that reception?

What are the conditions, expectations, needs, and fears of these families and communities? The focus in this chapter has been on the suffering of the children who became soldiers and their needs upon demobilization. Equally important, and affecting a much larger population, are the suffering and needs of the families and local communities that are called upon to receive and reintegrate demobilized child soldiers as well as a larger number of other reintegrating returnees (repatriating refugees, returning IDPs, adult soldiers, unaccompanied children and orphans, etc.). What about the human rights and needs of the hosts?

These families and local communities are trying to survive and earn a living in a war-desolated economy. They do not usually have many resources and are struggling to feed and support themselves. Why should they welcome, or accept, an additional burden by reintegrating more people? Even though these ex-soldiers are their children, they return with the stigma of having been part of the warfare that devastated the countryside, and many of them return having learned and still practicing social behaviors that are inappropriate in civil society.

These realities explain why successful reintegration programs incorporate community education and community development components. Note the lessons described earlier that were learned from the violent encounter between the transit center and the local community in Goma (DRC). Community education programs concentrate on issues of human rights, the need for reconciliation, and the culture of peace and non-violence. Family and community members need to learn about and discuss how everyone's human rights have been abused, including the rights of these children who became soldiers.

At the same time, the families and local communities need to receive some material assistance. This assistance should be part of a community development program that provides the opportunity for community residents and returning child ex-soldiers to work together to help reconstruct community infrastructure that was destroyed or abandoned during the years of warfare. Working together to rebuild schools and clinics and repair roads gives the returning children a way to visibly benefit the community and to rebuild, simultaneously, more trusting social relationships.

Conclusion

This chapter has extended the study of the displacement and uncertainty associated with wars and civil conflict to include an exploration of the social dynamics of the wartime experience and post-conflict reintegration of child soldiers (both boys and girls). This exploration recognized the uncertainties, concerns, and fears that confront child soldiers and other social actors (families and communities) who are directly affected by the post-conflict attempts to reintegrate and reconcile with children who had been soldiers.

The civil-military dimension of conflict-induced fragmentation of African societies has been explored by comparing and contrasting ideal types of civil and military societies and how they value and educate children. In addition, the chapter addressed three critical choices to be faced when designing and implementing demobilization and reintegration programs for child soldiers. At the heart of these choices was the issue of the costs and benefits of targeting only child soldiers for special attention.

In closing, it is important to note the uncertain reception and future for demobilized child soldiers in Africa. What is and has been happening to child soldiers (both boys and girls) when they return to their home communities? It appears that, at best, they are accepted by family and community and integrated in a civil society and economy devastated by years of conflict. There is little employment, chronic hunger and poverty, usually a non-functional educational system, and a largely destroyed infrastructure. In addition to the children who have been or will be officially demobilized, there are many undocumented child soldiers who have or will demobilize themselves without utilizing any of the facilities provided by the government, the UN, or NGOs.

An undetermined number of demobilized child soldiers do not want or are unable to return to their families and original communities. Their families may have died, may be too poor, or simply may not want the child to return, perhaps due to atrocities or other activities committed by the children during their time in the military. The current situation and future of these children are not known, but an undocumented number have become homeless street children, earning their living as prostitutes, thieves, scavengers, or through other activities in the extended informal economy.

This exploratory study raises more questions than it provides answers. One question concerns the changes (including potential militarization) that occur in civil societies during wartime, or as a consequence of the civil and military social learning experienced by their children and youth. What sorts of changes have African civil societies experienced because of their years of warfare? How do the content, form, and importance of social learning change when a civil society endures warfare for months, or years? To what extent are there general patterns across African societies and countries as opposed to patterns unique to different communities, societies, and countries?

Moving beyond the uncertainties confronted by child soldiers, other children in particularly difficult circumstances, and their host families and communities, this chapter also invites the reader to consider and explore the question of the proper place that children should occupy in society and the uncertainties faced by any society and by the global community when children become warriors. This question is relevant to a world in which there is widespread recruitment and abduction of children to become soldiers and widespread exposure of children to, and their acceptance of, interpersonal violence in reality, interactive games, movies, and television.

Acknowledgements

Funding for the desk review of literature and field research in Angola, the Democratic Republic of Congo, Eritrea, Liberia, and Sierra Leone came from a variety of sources: a faculty research grant awarded by Clark Atlanta University's WEB Dubois Institute (funded by the Andrew W. Mellon Foundation); United States Agency for International Development (USAID)-funded contracts with CARE, Inc., Creative Associates International, and Development Alternatives, Inc.; and contracts with Deutsche Gesellschaft fur Technische Zusammenarbeit (or GTZ, the German foreign aid agency) and the World Bank.

Notes

1 This chapter is a revision of a paper originally entitled 'Social Displacement and Reintegration of African Child Soldiers' that was presented at the November 2–3, 2002 Kyoto Symposium on Multidimensionality of Displacement Risks in Africa at Kyoto University, Japan. The symposium was hosted by the Graduate School of Asian and African Area Studies and the Center for African Area Studies at Kyoto University and sponsored by the Japan Society for the Promotion of Science.
2 See Walzer (1998). Earlier conceptualizations (starting with the ancient Greeks) essentially equated civil society with civilized society and contrasted this with the state of nature. A similar perspective continues today that contrasts 'civil' society with social disorder and the absence of a moral order based on shared values and social solidarity (see Hearn 1997).
3 There are definitional issues with terms such as soldier and military unit, versus combatant and fighting force. The term 'soldier' is sometimes applied only to a person who serves in a formal army (or military unit). This is contrasted with the term 'combatant,' which is applied to a person who serves in a more informal and often less publicly recognized armed group (or fighting force), such as a militia. These distinctions are much less critical to the thesis of this chapter, so the two terms (soldier and combatant) will be used interchangeably in this chapter.

4   This terminology is useful for recognizing the status of people (primarily
    children and women) who might otherwise be ignored when establishing
    who is eligible for services and benefits when fighting forces are
    demobilized.

5   Public awareness of this in the US seems to center on the prevalence of
    the post-traumatic stress syndrome (PTSD) among veterans.

6   UNICEF, 30 April 1997, *Cape Town Principles and Best Practices on
    the Prevention of Recruitment of Children into the Armed Forces and
    Demobilisation and Social Reintegration of Children in Africa.* Adopted
    by the participants in the Symposium on the Prevention of Recruitment
    of Children into the Armed Forces and Demobilisation and Social
    Reintegration of Child Soldiers in Africa that was organized by UNICEF
    in cooperation with the non-governmental organization (NGO) Sub-group
    of the NGO Working Group on the Convention on the Rights of the Child,
    Cape Town, Republic of South Africa.

7   Author's observations based on interviews with government officials and
    officers in various fighting forces in Angola, the Democratic Republic
    of Congo (DRC), Liberia and Sierra Leone.

8   At other times, social scientists use the two terms interchangeably. They
    are distinguished in this chapter to emphasize the extent of our ignorance
    in this arena of children and reintegration.

9   The existence of some studies shows that social scientists are beginning to
    look at this situation. See Anderson et al. 2004; Ball 1997; Boyden 2002;
    Gibbs 1997; and Honwana 2001. Three new PhD dissertations (Finnstrom
    2003; Utas 2003; and Kelley 2004) are good examples of field research in
    the midst of conflict, and the Living Beyond Conflict Seminar at Uppsala
    University (www.antro.uu.se) is stimulating more research in the field.
    Although not specifically addressing child soldiers, a seminal book in
    the study of children and conflict is Apfel and Simon (eds) (1996).

10 See above note for some relevant research.

11 The repatriation of refugees also seems from the outside to be a simple
    matter of 'going home,' but studies of repatriation have revealed that the
    process is much more complicated and difficult.

12 If the wives and other women are adults, they are counted as being
    'associated with the fighting forces' but not as soldiers during a
    demobilization. There is a movement to accord these 'associated'
    women a more formal status, similar to what the Cape Town Principles
    established for children.

13 One vivid exception to this male dominance was the famous woman
    commander the author met in Zwedru, Liberia in 1997. Her nom de

guerre was Attila (as in Attila the Hun) and she was greatly feared as a ferocious fighter.

14 The lessons were noted during the review of field reports cited in Bernard et al. 2003, Sierra Leone report.

15 Private communication from Dr. Priye Chris Torulagha (Florida Memorial College) during a workshop in San Juan, Puerto Rico, in November 2004. Based on his personal experiences as a boy during the Baifran War in Nigeria, he noted that boys wanted to become soldiers because girls liked the soldiers, and because, if a boy did not join the military, the next time he asked something from his family, they would ask, 'Why ask for food? Look at that boy. He joined the army.'

16 All personal names of child soldiers in this chapter are pseudonyms to protect the children's privacy.

17 Again, all personal names of children are pseudonyms for their protection.

18 Paysanat is an indigenous NGO that operates the project, which is funded by Save the Children Foundation-UK.

19 Private communication with Dr. Sayku Waritay (Lincoln University) during a workshop in San Juan, Puerto Rico, in November 2004. He had just returned from visiting a project at Cuttington College in Liberia.

20 A transit center is where demobilized child soldiers stay for a short while until they are able to go to their homes.

21 In this chapter the term soldier includes combatants associated with more informal fighting forces.

22 This argument was made in every country (and region) where the author studied the issue of targeted programs.

23 The number of girls in Africa who have been victimized in these ways is almost impossible to estimate, but, for instance, it is estimated that at least 15,000 to 25,000 girls in DRC were sexually victimized by combatants in the five years after warfare began in 1996 (Hansen et al. 2001). Many of the victims try to hide their misfortune: they are stigmatized because of having been raped, being associated with combatants, or bearing a soldier's child.

24 The UN estimated that at least 50,000 children lived in 'particularly difficult circumstances' in the DRC at the end of 2000.

References

Anderson, Rory E., Fortunate Sewankambo and Kathy Vandergrift (2004)

Pawns of Politics: Children, Conflict and Peace in Northern Uganda. World Vision.

Apfel, Roberta J. and Bennett Simon (eds) (1996) *Minefields in Their Hearts: The Mental Health of Children in War and Communal Violence.* New Haven: Yale University Press.

Ball, Nicole (1997) 'Demobilizing and reintegrating soldiers: Lessons from Africa', in Krishna Kumar (ed.) *Rebuilding Societies after Civil War: Critical Roles for International Assistance.* Boulder, Colorado: Lynne Rienner Publishing, pp. 85–105.

Bernard, Belinda, Brian Brewer, Sahana Dharmapuri, Edwin Dobor, Art Hansen and Sue Nelson (2003) *Assessment of the Situation of Women and Children Combatants in the Liberian Post-Conflict Period and Recommendations for Successful Integration.* Report presented to USAID. Bethesda, Maryland: Development Alternatives, Inc.

Boyden, Jo (2002) *Social Healing in War-Affected and Displaced Children.* Web-based report, http://users.ox.ac.uk/~rspnet/casocialhealing.html.

Candler, Gatlord George (1999) 'Civil society and development', *Policy Studies Journal*, 27.

Christian Aid, Oxfam Great Britain, and Save the Children United Kingdom (2001) *No End in Sight: The Human Tragedy of the Conflict in the Democratic Republic of Congo.*

Coalition to Stop the Use of Child Soldiers (2001) *Child Soldiers, 2001 Global Report.* Web-based report, http://www.child-soldiers.org/report2001/

Finnstrom, Sverker (2003) *Living with Bad Surroundings: War and Existential Uncertainty in Acholiland.* PhD dissertation. Uppsala: Department of Cultural Anthropology and Ethnology, Uppsala University.

Gibbs, Sara (1997) 'Postwar social reconstruction in Mozambique: Reframing children's experiences of trauma and healing', in Krishna Kumar (ed.) *Rebuilding Societies after Civil War: Critical Roles for International Assistance.* Boulder, Colorado: Lynne Rienner Publishing, pp. 227–38.

Hampton, Janie (ed.) (1998) *Internally Displaced People: A Global Survey.* London: Earthscan Publications and the Norwegian Refugee Council.

Hansen, Art (1994) *Final Report from Dr. Art Hansen to the GTZ Integrated Food Security Project Gash-Setit.* Asmara and Tesseney, Eritrea: GTZ.

Hansen, Art, Francine Ahouanmenou-Agueh, Andre Lokisso Lu'Epotu, L. Diane Mull and Kevin Elkins (2001) *Planning Educational Response Strategies for Reintegration of Demobilized Child Soldiers in the Democratic Republic of Congo.* Final report prepared (in English and

French) for the United States Agency for International Development, Washington, DC: Creative Associates International.

Hansen, Art, Julie Nenon, Joy Wolf and Marc Sommers (2002) *Final Evaluation of the Office of Transition Initiatives' Program in Sierra Leone.* Report presented to USAID, Washington, DC: CARE, Inc. and Creative Associates International.

Hearn, Frank (1997) *Moral Order and Social Disorder: The American Search for Civil Society.* New York: Aldine de Gruyter.

Honwana, Alcinda (2001) 'Children of war: Understanding war and war cleansing in Mozambique and Angola', in Simon Chesterman (ed.), *Civilians in War.* Boulder, Colorado: Lynne Rienner Publishing, pp. 123–42.

International Labour Organization (ILO) (1999) *Convention (No. 182) on the Prohibition and Immediate Action for the Elimination of the Worst Forms of Child Labour.*

Kelley, Kathryn A. (2004) *Socialization of Acholi Children and Child Soldiers in Northern Uganda.* PhD dissertation. Atlanta: Department of International Affairs and Development, Clark Atlanta University.

Kelly, David (1998) *The Disarmament, Demobilization and Reintegration of Child Soldiers in Liberia 1994–1997: The Process and Lessons Learned.* UNICEF-Liberia and the US National Committee for UNICEF.

Organization of African Unity (OAU) (1999) *African Charter on the Rights and Welfare of the Child.*

Ortiz, Sutti (1980) 'Forecasts, decisions, and the farmer's response to uncertain environments', in Peggy F. Bartlett (ed.), *Agricultural Decision-Making: Anthropological Contributions to Rural Development.* New York: Academic Press, pp. 177–202.

Roumasset, James A., Jean Marc Broussard and Inderjit Singh (1979) *Risk, Uncertainty and Agricultural Development.* New York: Agricultural Development Council.

Sengupta, Somini (2004) 'Turmoil in Ivory Coast: Once again, things fall apart', *New York Times,* November 15.

United Nations (1989) *Convention on the Rights of the Child.* New York: UN.

———— (1995) *The Identification of Social and Economic Expectations of Soldiers to be Demobilized.* Final report to the Humanitarian Assistance Coordination Unit (UCAH/UN). Luanda, Angola: UN.

———— (1996) *Report of the Independent Expert of the Secretary-General, Ms. Grac'a Machel. Impact of Armed Conflict on Children,* A/51/306. URL: http://www.unicef.org/graca/women.htm.

———(2000) *Optional Protocol to the Convention on the Rights of the Child on the Involvement of Children in Armed Conflict.* General Assembly Resolution A/RES/54/263.

United Nations Security Council (2000) *Report of the Secretary-General on Children and Armed Conflict.* General Assembly, Fifty-Fifth Session, A/55/163–S/2000/712.

Utas, Mats (2003) *Sweet Battlefields: Youth and the Liberian Civil War.* PhD dissertation. Uppsala: Department of Cultural Anthropology and Ethnology, Uppsala University.

Walzer, Michael (1998) *Toward a Global Civil Society.* Providence, Rhode Island: Berghahn Books.

4
Belonging, Displacement, and Repatriation of Refugees: Reflections on the Experiences of Eritrean Returnees

Gaim Kibreab

Introduction

After a brief statement of the problem at hand, this chapter first outlines the conceptualisations of belonging from two theoretical perspectives: the theory of nationalism and liberal theory. Second, it presents a brief discussion of territorial belonging based on the experience of forcibly relocated Ethiopian peasant communities in the 1980s. Third, it critically reviews the debate on the relationship between people, particular places and identity and examines the extent to which, for example, the voluntary repatriation of refugees is motivated by their desire to belong to the particular places and communities from which they were displaced. Fourth, it discusses the ambiguity of the meanings that Eritrean rural communities ascribe to the concept of home and the extent to which its meaning and physical expression is linked to issues of livelihood and survival. Fifth, it describes the repatriation process, donor responses, the risks, opportunities and coping mechanisms adopted by the returnees to avoid or minimise the risk of failure. Sixth, it identifies the factors that influenced the choice of destination of Eritrean returnees from Sudan. Finally, it draws some general conclusions.

Statement of the problem

Proliferation of identity-based conflicts in the post-Cold War period
Identity-based conflicts have become not only the dominant features of the post-Cold War period, but they have also become the major causes of involuntary displacement. As the result of these developments and the globalisation process reflected, *inter alia*, in increasing interconnections

and movement of people, goods, ideas, finance, and technology, the debate on the politics of place (location) and belonging (identity) has assumed unprecedented centrality in the burgeoning literature. One of the controversies that permeate the debate is the relationship between people and particular places (the local) and more specifically whether it is possible to belong to a group that does not have a territorial reference point or whether belonging is necessarily rooted in a territory. Although, as we shall see, there are varied theoretical perspectives on the subject, the answer to this deceptively simple but, in actual fact, highly complex and contested question has some profound implications on displacement, resettlement, and repatriation. The issue is not, however, about mobility or immobility manifested in static attachment to particular places as such. It is not a moot point to state that movement rather than fixed settlement has always been one of the dominant characteristics of human populations, particularly of those who inhabit arid and semi-arid regions such as the Horn of Africa or the Sahel. This was true even before academics became obsessed with global interconnections and movements. In such regions, people have always been moving seasonally or permanently, *inter alia*, to take advantage of the variations in the environment. It must also be recognized, though, that, ironically, during the last three or four decades, these movements (at least the voluntary ones) have been disrupted, particularly in the Horn of Africa due to lack of security and political instability.

As we shall see, how a group becomes deterritorialised will determine whether they belong to a group with a territorial reference point. The issue of whether it is possible to make new homes elsewhere is also relevant. My argument is that if the displacement is involuntary or if the territory (the homeland) in question is lost against the will of the people concerned, the loss will be inexorably conceived in terms of 'uprooting'. This condition consequently engenders a powerful proclivity and resolve to be 're-rooted' in the territory from which one is uprooted. It is also important to understand that the proclivity for being re-rooted in places of origin is even more powerful in the absence of alternative opportunities for developing new roots outside that particular locality or place of origin.

The reality of most refugees in the developing countries—with the exception of those who, using pre-existing ethnic or economic networks, are able to carve out lives outside of the formal power structures, in realms beyond the reach of the nation-state (see e.g., Hansen 1990; 1982; Bakewell 2000)—is characterised by an absolute dearth of such possibilities (see Kibreab 1996a; 1996b; 2000; 2002b; 2003a). In such situations, belonging is necessarily perceived as being rooted in a territory. However, if the movement is voluntary and if, on the one hand, there is an opportunity to develop roots in the new place of abode and, on the other, there is a possibility of returning to the place of origin no matter how impractical and improbable, it is conceivable and possible to belong to deterritorialised groups or homelands. A common scenario in which a diasporic community belongs to an imagined community is when the possibility of returning to the place of origin is impossible or undesirable. A classic case is that of Iraqi Assyrian ethno-religious minority in London and elsewhere who left Iraq with a settler mentality (see Al-Rasheed 1994). Most of the diasporic and transnational groups in the different parts of the world also fit this description. Though it is still important to reject the simplistic view that the revolution in information and communications technology has reduced the world to a single global village (my birth place still remains as disconnected and inaccessible as it was when I was a child, both in terms of information and communication),[1] it is still true that the possibility to belong to non-spatially bounded 'imagined' groups has been enhanced (but not in all places and for all groups) by the profound change in the information and communication technologies.

People, place and identity

Since the changes in the global geo-political milieu that followed the demise of the bipolar world order of the Cold War period, there has been a plethora of writings examining the relationship between people and particular places and the extent to which return movements are related to displaced populations', particularly refugees', attachment to their places of origin. Some argue that belonging to a particular community and to a specific place is *sine qua non* for recognition, understanding, well being, and identity. Forced migration is seen, from this perspective, as the result of a struggle between two mutually exclusive conceptions of belonging: those who are perceived not to belong to the spatially defined community are expelled or regarded as 'Others', notwithstanding the fact that the latter may feel the contested territory belongs to them. For such communities a particular place is a crucial component of their identity and therefore loss of spatial attachment renders their identity incomplete and thus compromises their well-being. The central thrust of Michael Cernea's empirically grounded Impoverishment Risks and Reconstruction Model (IRR) is that in the absence of countervailing remedial measures, impoverishment is intrinsic in forced displacement (1990; 1995). In his recent publication, he states, 'For refugees, homelessness and "placelessness" are intrinsic by definition' (2000: 23) and therefore the risk for impoverishment looms large. The exponents of this perspective argue that attachment to particular places or territorial belonging is equally important in all forms of involuntary displacements (see Coles 1985; Wolff 2001). The corollary of this, as we shall see, is that return movements of involuntarily displaced populations are, *inter alia*, motivated by the need to be re-rooted in their places of origin.

Others argue that not only is belonging to a group possible without a territorial reference point but the conception of displacement as constituting 'uprooting' is also more than anything else a product of the sedentarist assumptions that underpin the idea of country, nation and national identity (Warner 1994; Allen and Turton 1996; Malkki 1995; Robinson 2002; Turton 2002). The central thrust of this perspective is that if it were not on the one hand, for our sedentarist assumptions that tend to naturalise the relations between people and places, and on the other, for the world being divided into nation-states whose *raison d'être* is to protect the rights of their own citizens, migration would be normal and therefore would constitute no 'uprooting' or problem per se. This perspective is underpinned by the assumption that global interconnections and movements that have allegedly become a way of life have reduced the significance of 'the local' in all aspects of social, cultural and economic life bringing to an end the sense of attachment and belonging to particular places. The corollary of this perspective is that not only is it possible to construct imaginary homes 'out of place', but people have no need to belong to particular 'homes' or places and therefore the desire to belong to spatially grounded particular 'homes' or places of origin or communities would play no significant role in motivating refugees to return subsequent to the elimination of the factors that prompt their displacement.

This perspective has some degree of counter-factual element in it. The counter-factual analytical approach has been fruitfully employed in some social science disciplines, for example, in the New American Economic History, intended to fill gaps in existing historical data. Discussion would be an unnecessary digression; suffice it to say that the present world is willy-nilly divided into discontinuous nation-states that are bent on providing all sorts of protections to their own nationals and treat non-nationals (save those whose presence is beneficial to national and societal interests)—particularly asylum seekers, refugees, and illegal immigrants—either with disdain or suspicion. Hence the attitudes of displaced communities towards their places of origin and destination are shaped within such socio-political realities.

I have tried to argue elsewhere that as long as the factors that prompt population displacements persist and asylum seekers and refugees are hosted in the developing countries of Africa, Asia, South and Central America where refugeehood, regardless of its duration, leads to no acquisition of nationality or denizenship rights, the longing and inclination to be re-rooted not in any space but in territorialized places from which one was forcibly uprooted will always loom large (see Kibreab 2002a; 2003a). This reality cannot be wished away by counter-factual assumptions or other means. The distinguished Jewish Italian writer, Primo Levi, was once asked whether he would have still been an eminent writer had it not been for his harrowing experience at Auschwitz. He answered the question in his typically lucid and succinct manner, stating: 'The counter-factual does not exist.'

In what follows, the role of territory or land in theories of nationalism and ethnic conflict, which contrary to the prediction of early twentieth century social theorists still constitute the major causes of involuntary population displacements, will be discussed and an attempt made to see the extent to which longing to belong to spatially grounded communities of origin plays a role in the return movements of involuntarily displaced populations. In the early twentieth century, many social theorists argued that the importance of ethnicity and nationalism would decline and eventually disappear 'as a result of modernization, industrialization, and individualism' (Eriksen 1993: 2). However, history is rarely made to order and as Eriksen argues, 'On the contrary, ethnicity and nationalism have grown in political importance in the world, particularly since the Second World War. Thirty-five of the thirty-seven major armed conflicts in the world in 1991 were internal conflicts, and most of them—from Sri Lanka to Northern Ireland—could plausibly be described as ethnic conflicts' (1993: 2). One may also add that at the heart of all these conflicts has been the desire to belong to a particular territory by excluding the 'Others' who are perceived as being different from oneself.

Territorial belonging in nationalist movements

Since the demise of the former Soviet Union and its satellite states in Eastern Europe and elsewhere, the factors that have been prompting massive population movements are inextricably linked to ethnic and national conflicts. The single most important factor in these rapidly proliferating violent conflicts has been the question of longing to belong or to exclude 'Others' from particular territories. Even though the issue of belonging to particular places based on ethnic, religious, tribal, and clan identities rather than on class interests was underplayed with the triumph of Communism and the non-capitalist road of development in the Third World countries, it is important to recognise that land or territory has always occupied a central position in the theories of nationalism and ethnicity. As Levy states, 'Nationalism celebrates a people's history and culture, but it also celebrates their land. More over it celebrates the link between the two' (2000: 203). For Johan von Herder not only is the link between people and territory critical but the well-being of a people is inseparably bound to a particular territory or country. He states, 'In the first place it is obvious why all sensual people, fashioned to their country, are so much attached to the soil, and so inseparable from it. The constitution of their body, their way of life, the pleasures and occupations to which they have been accustomed from their infancy, and the whole circle of their ideas are climatic. *Deprive them of their country, you deprive them of everything*' (1995: 51, emphasis added). For Guiseppe Manzzini belonging to a spatially bounded territory or country is *sine qua non* not only for social identity but also for the enjoyment of basic, material progress and protection against harm. He states:

> Without Country, you have neither name, token, voice, nor rights, no admission as brothers into the fellowship of the Peoples. You are the bastards of Humanity. Soldiers without a banner, Israelites among the nations, you will find neither faith nor protection; none will be sureties for you. Do not beguile yourselves with the hope of emancipation from unjust social conditions if you do not first conquer a Country for yourselves; where there is no Country there is no common agreement to which you can appeal; the egoism of self-interest rules alone; and he who has the upper hand keeps it, since there is no common safeguard for the interests of all. Do not be led away by the idea of improving your material conditions without first solving the national question...
>
> O my Brothers! Love your Country. Our Country is our home, the home which God has given us, placing therein a numerous family which we love and are loved by, and with which we have more intimate and quicker communion of feeling and thought than with others/ a family which by its concentration upon a given spot, and by the homogenous nature of its elements, is destined for a special kind of activity (Manzzini 1995: 93–4).

The liberal theorist, John Rawls, accentuates the importance of belonging to a spatially bound society and the detrimental consequences that may result from leaving such a place and cultural communities. He states:

Normally leaving one's country is a grave step: it involves leaving the society and culture in which we have been raised, the society and culture whose language we use in speech and thought to express and understand ourselves, our aims, goals, and values; the society and culture whose history, customs, and conventions we depend on to find our place in the social world. In large part, we affirm our society and culture, and have an intimate and inexpressible knowledge of it, even though much of it we may question, if not reject. The government's authority cannot, then, be freely accepted in the sense that the bonds of society and culture, of history and social place of origin, begin so early to shape our life and are normally so strong that the right of emigration (suitably qualified) does not suffice to make accepting its authority free, politically speaking, in the way that liberty of conscience suffices to make accepting ecclesiastical authority free (Rawls 1993: 222).

Nationalism is politically expressed in the call for self-rule—self-determination and self-rule became historically possible because '...men [and women] were willing to die for the *patria*' (Taylor 1993: 41). The demand for self-rule is inconceivable without a claim over a particular place. As Charles Taylor states, 'People can only rule themselves if they are grouped in their *patriae*. Only those who form a *patria* can achieve self-rule, not just any agglomeration of humans who happen to be contiguous with one another' (1993: 42). Though historically those who formed a *patria* and hence entitlement to the right of self-determination were conceived to be homogenous in terms of language, religion, and way of life, this has not been the case in the post-World War II period in which states were established on the basis of the colonial units of administration. Margaret Moore (1998: 136), for example, rightly argues:

Whereas self-determination in the Wilsonian period was conceived of as the political independence of ethnic or national communities, in the post-Second War period, self-determination has been conceived as 'the right of the majority within...a political unit to exercise power' and boundaries have been drawn without regard for the linguistic or cultural composition of the state.

The borders of the ex-colonial states were, for example, drawn on the basis of the previous administrative units without any regard for the cultural or ethnic identities of the peoples that inhabited them (Moore 1998: 138).

Ethnic and indigenous groups and their political movements also express strong attachment to land in which the latter is conceived not only as being a source of livelihood but also as being an integral part of social and cultural life. In many such groups, land is given religious or sacred meaning and consequently its permanent alienation is proscribed or seen as taboo. Rights of access to and use of land are determined on the basis of belonging to a socially recognised group. Those who don't belong to such a group or groups are either completely excluded or need permission from such a group or groups to gain entry. When permission is granted for entry, the founding lineages or customary rights holders define the conditions and the duration. These rights are often governed by intricate institutional rules that constitute an integral part of indigenous peoples' cultures and way of life (see Kibreab 2002b).

It is important to point out, however, that the meaning and significance ascribed to a territory or land in theories of nationalism and ethnicity has also been shifting and changing over time. In what follows the conception of belonging or attachment to a territory in the liberal theory of nationalism and ethnicity is briefly presented.

Belonging and liberal theory

In liberal theory where nationhood and ethnicity are conceived as cultural rather than as political constructs, the importance of attachment to land is acknowledged, but the emphasis is on 'societal culture' which is said to provide members of a given cultural community '...with meaningful ways of life across the full range of human activities, including social, educational, religious, recreational, and economic life, encompassing both public and private spheres. These cultures tend to be territorially concentrated, and based on a shared language' (Kymlicka 1995: 76). According to the liberal perspective, in situations where the boundaries of the nation and the state do not coincide, or when more than one cultural community inhabits the latter, cultural attachments may transcend the boundaries of a state suggesting that the critical attachment is to a cultural rather then a territorial community. Will Kymlicka in his comment on the Rawlian perspective we saw earlier, for example, opines:

> I agree with Rawls's view about the difficulty of leaving one's culture. Yet his argument has implications beyond those which he himself draws. Rawls presents this as an argument about the difficulty of leaving one's political community. But his argument does not rest on the value of specifically political ties (e.g. the bonds to one's government and fellow citizens). Rather it rests on the value of cultural ties (e.g. bonds to one's language and history). *And cultural boundaries*

may not coincide with political boundaries. For example, someone leaving East Germany for West Germany in 1950 would not be breaking the ties of language and culture which Rawls emphasises, even though she would be crossing state borders. But a francophone leaving Quebec City for Toronto, or a Puerto Rican leaving San Juan for Chicago, would be breaking those ties, even though she is remaining within the same country (Kymlicka 1995: 87, emphasis added).

This conceptualisation has fresh and considerable implications on displacement and repatriation, particularly in the African context where the borders of multi-national states were carved out by dismembering and dissecting tens of thousands of cultural communities. If Will Kymlicka's argument holds substance, the thousands of African refugees who have by force of circumstances joined members of their cultural communities across the borders may not feel that they are 'out of place' or de-placed and therefore, *ceteris paribus*, the idea of repatriation may become irrelevant or redundant. This is because displacement does not lead to breaking of language and cultural ties. In fact previously broken cultural ties and language are re-established, ironically because of displacement. For example, the Beni Amer and the Habab of Eritrea were re-united with members of their ethnic groups across the border in Sudan as a result of involuntary displacement. Ironically, sometimes displacement may undo colonial dismemberment. Though this theoretical perspective obviously sounds refreshingly logical, it overlooks the divisive project of the nation-state which unlike people is fixed to particular places and whose *raison d'être* is to fix people to such places by granting them certain rights and by controlling their movements. The fixing of 'nationals' to particular territories is invariably accompanied by exclusion of 'Others', including those who are structurally identical (reflected in dense cultural ties) with the constituencies of the nation-state concerned. The existence of a separate nation-state is legitimised, *inter alia*, by the creation and perpetuation of difference both in terms of people and territory. Thus, the implication of Will Kymlicka's argument on displacement and repatriation under the present dominant form of social organisation is improbable. As David Turton (2002: 22–3) perceptively argues:

> In a world exhaustively divided into nation-states, the individual's rights cannot be upheld and enforced except through his or her membership of a state—but not any state. For the nation-state exists, by definition, to protect the rights only of its own citizens, who are assumed to be members of a single historically continuous and culturally homogenous nation, not a collection of people who just happen to be living within the same territory.

...So the refugee, as a person who is unable or unwilling to obtain the protection of his or her own state, makes visible a contradiction between citizenship as the universal source of all individual rights, and nationhood as an identity ascribed at birth and based on a sentimental attachment to a specific community and territory.

It is in this sense, Howard Adelman (cited in Turton 2002) describes the refugee as the 'Achilles heel of the nation-state system'. However, as we shall see later, though the *raison d'être* of the nation-state has been to create differences by fixing its citizens to particular places (countries) and by excluding those who don't belong to such places, in the context of sub-Saharan Africa, it is wrong to assume that the nation-state has succeeded in creating impervious borders. In most sub-Saharan African countries, the borders still remain without effective boundaries or, in other words, they remain porous in spite of the respective nation-states' desire to exclude those who do not belong to the territory of the nation-state as defined by the colonial power.

In spite of this, however, some liberal theorists even go to the extent of denying the existence of links between land or territory and ethnicity or nationalism in which both are conceptualised in pure deterritorialised cultural terms. Yael Tamir (1993: 86), for example, states:

We still need to clarify the use of the term 'living within one's nation.' This could sound like a territorial claim, suggesting that individuals must live in physical proximity to other members of their group, but in the modern world this is not necessarily the case...As the phenomenon of modern diasporas proves, a national community could in fact have more than one public sphere and need not occupy a continuous territory.

According to this perspective whilst states require land, nations do not. In fact Tamir argues against state-seeking nations on the grounds that there isn't enough space to accommodate all nations with their own states.

The real issue is not, however, about space, it is rather about a particular place or a place of origin to which one attaches special significance. Nationalists or ethnic groups do not fight or shed their blood for any space but for particular places. How is 'ownership' of this 'particular place' to be determined? Among traditional societies where written communal or individual title deeds are unknown, indigenousness or relative time of arrival is the single most important basis of distinctions of hierarchies of claims (Horowitz 1985; Moore 1998). As Levy argues, 'It's not that every nation needs x amount of space, but that every nation wants a very particular place and as often as not, two or more nations want the same very particular place...the concern with a particular place is actually central to nationalism' (2000: 200) or ethnicity.

The loss of such a place and the determination to regain that place by all means, including by violent means, constitutes the *raison d'être* of most nationalist movements and hence a major cause of population displacement. There is no more powerful weapon of political mobilisation than the loss of a 'motherland' or 'fatherland' and a political agenda designed to recoup the loss. The loss of homeland engenders a strong sense of longing of belonging to such homeland expressed in the hope and expectation to return or in the determination to shed one's blood in the fight to regain it. Without such sense of loss and the intense feeling engendered as a result, it would be difficult to recruit thousands or tens of thousands of people who would be willing to sacrifice their lives on the altar of the nationalist cause.

As Anthony Smith states, it would be impossible to '...instil in people a sense of kinship and brotherhood without attaching them to a place that they feel is theirs, a homeland that is theirs by right of history' (quoted in Wolff 2001: 53). Michael Walzer argues, 'Statelessness is a condition of infinite danger' (1983: 32). And since states unlike nations cannot be constructed outside of particular places, the need to belong to spatially bounded geopolitical state entities is considered as an important human need (Berlin in Ignatieff 1993; Coles 1985). The right to self-determination or self-government is derived from this profound principle based on the links between people and particular places or homelands. The right of minority groups to self-government is also derived from this principle.

A few exponents of the liberal theory, however, still regard belonging to a spatially bounded geopolitical state as one of the conditions of human security. For example, Michael Walzer argues that the most important good that people '...distribute to one another is membership in some human community' (1983: 31). Human communities do not exist in a vacuum but in particular territorial places that they currently occupy or aspire to re-occupy if 'Others' have taken them away from them. He further opines, 'The link between people and land is a crucial feature of national identity' (Walzer 1983: 44). However, not only is Walzer almost alone in the liberal school of thought, save John Rawls in the particular case referred to earlier in this regard, but in his recent work he theorises that liberal society is characterised by four mobilities of which geographic and social mobility are linked to the sale of land, without which people are most likely to remain rooted in their places of origin (1993). The assumption underpinning this view is that commodification of land enhances geographic social mobility because people in places where land is indivisible and inalienable are unlikely to relocate by abandoning their key resource—land. The implication of this perspective is that capitalism, or for that matter modernisation, would weaken identification with particular territories or spatially grounded communities—which is analogous to the previously mentioned view of early twentieth century social theorists concerning ethnicity and nationalism.

In mainstream liberalism, land is a commodity with exchange value that can be bought, sold, mortgaged to secure loans, leased, rented, etc. It is seen to be like any other commodity that can be disposed at will. This conception of land is completely different from the meaning nationalists, ethnic groups, tribes, indigenous peoples, and refugees ascribe to it. The significant consequence of this conception of land is the absence of a necessary connection between particular people and particular places. Any person, regardless of her place of origin, race, religion, or ethnicity can buy land anywhere in the world. This may apply even to people who may not be entitled to enter the territories where such land may be located. In liberal theory, land is property, not place (Levy 2000: 207).

According to Gordon Wood, one of the earliest liberal projects was 'the abolition of primogeniture and entail' (in Levy 2000: 207). Levy argues that for Jefferson, Burke, Smith and Mill the fungibility of land and other goods reflected in the ability of new people to buy new pieces of land for new use, as in the case of any other property, was critical to a free society (ibid.). The pre-occupation of liberal theorists with the abolition of primogeniture and entail or feudal inheritance rules was due to the need to promote freedom of movement and residence, as well as occupational mobility in which private land ownership was considered critical. This thinking was underpinned by the assumption that in societies where land is conceived as being the source of identity, and therefore, inalienable rather than a commodity with exchange value, not only would people tend to be rooted to the soil with little or no propensity to move between places or allow others to move into in search of new opportunities, but one of the key resources—land—would remain either wasted or inefficiently utilised. Once land is commodified, it would be allocated to economic activities where returns are highest. Liberal theorists viewed the indivisibility and inalienability of land as being a constraint on the development of a free and modern society because the ideals of freedom and modernity were considered unachievable in the absence of unrestrained movement of the factors of production.

The corollary of conceiving land as any other commodity or property that can be acquired or exchanged for cash or any other good is that land becomes an economic asset and ceases to be a place with which particular groups of people identify themselves and will kill or die for. When land is commodified, not only does it cease being a place, but its location, except to the extent that it impinges on its quality, becomes irrelevant. Not only does this kind of theorisation constitute a diametrical opposite of nationalist or ethnic movements' conceptions of land, but it also denies or grossly understates the importance of the links that exist between particular peoples and particular places, as well as the rights derived thereof.

As mentioned earlier, most of the wars fought since the mid-1980s have been intra-state, caused by disputes over territorial claims derived from the principle of first occupation. In multicultural social and political settings, those who claim to be 'first settlers' often regard their entitlements to the places concerned as being superior to the rights of latecomers. As Horowitz points out, 'Despite the doubtful quality of many claims to indigenousness, relative time of arrival is a common basis of distinctions among people...' (1985: 203). Thus, as pointed out earlier, at the heart of most ethnic conflicts and nationalist movements lies territory and not just any land, as such, but rather 'the historic land, the land of past generations, the land that saw the flowering of the nation's genius...' (Smith 1979, quoted in Wolff 2001). Margaret Moore rightly argues that the issue at the heart of the 1991–95 violent conflicts in former Yugoslavia was that of borders (1998: 138). She also states: 'The claim to territory which flows from indigenousness is primarily a claim to prior, rightful ownership, based on first occupancy. Since the indigenous people are rightful owners of the land, the latter arrivals were engaged in "theft"' (1998: 142).

Local peoples' perspectives on territorial belonging

The following examples show that some local peoples' perspectives on belonging appear to be inconsistent with the liberal perspective. Some governments use population relocations or resettlements as a political weapon to weaken nationalist or ethnic movements. However, there has never been a situation where these policies were embraced voluntarily by those who are ousted or would be ousted from their homelands regardless of how attractive the new location is in terms of economic opportunities and social amenities.

During the thirty years' war of national independence, the Ethiopian government, in an attempt to weaken the armed struggle by depriving it of its rural mass base, considered relocating Eritrean peasants and pastoralists to parts of Ethiopia where land and pasture resources were abundant. These policies were, however, abandoned before they got off the ground because they were unacceptable even to the most zealous pro-Ethiopian politicians of the 1950s and 1960s.

Again in the mid-1980s, the military government in Ethiopia—the Derg—relocated hundreds of thousands of Ethiopians from the poverty stricken areas of Tigray and Wollo to southwestern and southern Ethiopia—namely, Metekel, Metema, Assosa, Gambella and Kefa (Gebre 2002) where land and rainfall were said to be abundant (Rahmato 1989). Initially, the government planned to relocate 300,000 families or 1.5 million individuals. The financial costs and the massive logistics of the operation were beyond the government's capacity. Nevertheless, nearly 600,000 people were trans-ferred within 18 months (see Wolde-Selassie 2000; Gebre 2002). Although officially the aim of the relocation operation was the rehabilitation of the drought victims, there are analysts who argue that the actual *raison d'être* of the operation was politically designed to remove people from insurgency areas and to use the relocatees as a buffer against insurgency (Wolde-Selassie 2000). Yntiso Gebre, argues that though the government's main aim was to avoid the recurrence of famine and to overcome its devastat-ing effects in a lasting manner, '...the government may have planned for collateral advantages of resettlement' (Gebre 2002: 268). This is because 'Four of the five major resettlements were located in regions troubled by insurgent activities. Security advantages may have been factored in, as Metekel resettlement served as a source of militia forces against the guer-rilla fighters of the Ethiopian Peoples Revolutionary Party' (Gebre 2002: 268). According to Wolde-Selassie (2000: 416):

> The controlled resettlement schemes were full of social injustice and human rights violations. Coercion was used during recruitment, and at all times resettlers were heavily guarded to prevent them from escaping. The scheme increased state control over the resettlers...Free travel was absolutely impossible, as resettlers were strictly forbidden to travel out of the area, and village-to-village travel was possible only with pass letters obtained from the village authorities.

The demise of the Derg's regime in May 1991 ushered in a possibility for the relocatees to escape and in one of the resettlement sites—the Beles Valley, the size of the relocatees dropped from 82,000 in 1987 and 1988 to 26,660 in 1993 and 1994 (Wolde-Selassie 2000: 422). This is in spite of the fact that the new area was better endowed with natural resources and rains than the relocatees' places of origin. It is important to recognise, however, that at the initial stage when information was disseminated to the would be relocatees, the fertility of the soil, land availability and the amount of rainfall and its distribution were most probably exaggerated in order to attract willing candidates for the relocation programme. This was what some of Yntiso Gebre's informants suggested (see Gebre 2002: 277). Those who remained behind when the large majority deserted the place were people '…who have no alternative place of settlement either in their area of origin or elsewhere in the country, those who are incapacitated or weak…' (Wolde-Selassie 2000: 416). Gebre's studies show that those who remained behind were not only people who had no where to go or were disabled but also included people who were 'undecided, confused, determined to remain, and those who returned after visiting their homelands' (e-mail communication with Ohta and Gebre July 2004).

Wolde-Selassie's and Gebre's surveys were conducted among those who did not respond to the change of government by 'voting with their feet' homewards. Though Gebre's study suggests that he had visited the areas of return, both authors' data only tell us about those who stayed behind. Without knowing the characteristics of those who left, it is difficult to characterise those who remained behind. The only way valid conclusions could be generated about the characteristics of those who stayed would be by conducting a comparative study of the two population groups—namely, those who stayed put and those who 'voted with their feet' by abandoning the place of relocation. The destination of those who abandoned the place of relocation cannot be taken for granted, either. Some of them, instead of returning to their homes of origin, have probably gone elsewhere in search of sustainable sources of livelihood. For example, some of them (I am not sure about the exact number), instead of returning to Tigray, have crossed to Sudan to join the refugee camps.

Wolde-Selassie's findings suggest that the extent to which the relocatees detested the new location and missed their places of origin, despite economic hardship in the latter, can be understood from what they told him during his fieldwork. '*Agaraachin balten inniwozallen, sawunnetachin muuz yimaslaall; izzih, balten uniwozam, sawunnetaachinim kasal yimaslaal*—At home, even though we ate little, our looks were as smooth and bright as a banana fruit, whereas, here, no matter what we eat, we look like a charcoal' (Wolde-Selassie 2000: 421).

It is possible to interpret the abandonment of the place of relocation by the majority of the Ethiopian relocatees in two different ways. Some analysts may argue that for such groups, belonging to particular places (home) has much broader meaning and value than being a source of bread and butter. The implication of the resettlers' statement is that belonging to one's home is not only a means to an end but may have intrinsic value. They may further argue that if territory (land) were simply an economic asset or a commodity whose value is measured in terms of the quality of its soil (its fertility) and weather conditions, as suggested by the liberal theory, there is no doubt that the new location was far superior to the old farms located in the highly degraded, drought-prone, and overpopulated areas of origin.

The fact that the large majority of the relocatees 'voted with their feet' when the opportunity to do so emerged, in spite of their awareness of the potential economic hardship that awaited them in their areas of origin, such analysts argue, clearly suggests that the meaning and status people ascribe to land is diametrically opposed to the liberal theorists' conception of land or territory. They add further that if land were purely and simply an economic asset and hence divisible and alienable, there was a clear incentive for the Ethiopian peasants to embrace and celebrate the opportunities brought to them by the government's resettlement scheme. The exponents of this view emphasise that this experience shows not only the importance of the link between particular places and particular people, but also that the ability of people to adapt to new places and the decision to stay or return to their homes of origin is to a large extent influenced by attachment to particular places of origin.

Other analysts reject these ostensibly logical arguments on the grounds that, firstly, the reasons for the relocatees abandoning the new locations may have nothing to do with a desire to belong to their places of origin. Their responses might instead have been a reaction to exclusion. The corollary of this is that had the resettlers been recruited voluntarily, had they taken part in the whole process of recruitment, planning, site identification and implementation, as well as having been given the freedom to choose between staying in the resettlement schemes and returning to their places of origin (with assistance provided to facilitate their return), the responses of some, if not all, of the relocatees might have been different. Since none of these took place, however, such arguments build on counterfactuality and are hence not amenable to empirical scrutiny.

The first interpretation, in spite of its ostensible logic and coherence, is based on an unproven assumption. Structurally, in comparison to the relocatees' places of origin such as Tigray and northern Wollo, the places of relocation were probably endowed with more under-utilised natural resources and greater rainfall. However, it is wrong to assume that this would automatically mean that those who are relocated would enjoy more secure lives and livelihood. Security and secure livelihoods are not solely functions of natural resource availability. Resources are necessary but they are not sufficient conditions for secure and sustainable livelihoods. It is important to underscore the fact that this interpretation is underpinned by the assumption that the places of relocation are full of 'bread and honey.'

There is no doubt that life in their places of origin was marked by insurmountable hardship. However, life at the destination was also difficult and insecure. In view of this it is very difficult to say why some left and others remained. Perhaps those who 'voted with their feet' towards their homes of origin or elsewhere were people who failed to 'make it' and those who stayed behind, save the physically disabled and mentally infirm, had somehow 'made it' at the destination; But this cannot be determined *a priori*. It is an empirical question which awaits further evidence. Data produced from comprehensive comparative studies of the two populations—namely, those who stayed put and those who left—may enable us to shed light on the underlying reasons for their respective decisions.

It is tempting to interpret the departure of the majority of the relocatees in response to the opportunities created by changes of government as being centrally motivated by strong yearnings to belong to 'homes and communities of origin'. However, it is important to realise that, being intrinsically risk averse, people in general and poor people in particular are rational decision makers. Their decisions are often a culmination of complex and multiple factors which are not easy to disentangle without an intimate knowledge of their entitlements, resource endowments and survival strategies. There is evidence which suggests that some of the relocatees, if not all, were not better off at the destination than they had been in their places of origin. For example, when Yntiso Gebre talked to people who had never relocated, they told him that those who returned from the places of relocation were not only impoverished, but were left worse off by their relocation than they had previously been. This was confirmed by his own findings on the ground (Gebre 2002: 280). Although, as noted, further evidence is required before we can draw any solid conclusions, it seems less likely that the primary reason for the large majority of the Ethiopian resettlers to have left the places of relocation when the opportunity to do so arose was because of the relocatees' powerful yearning to belong to their particular places and communities of origin, than that life in the new place entailed unbearable economic and physical insecurity. While awaiting further evidence, allow me to tentatively hypothesise that those who 'voted with their feet' were people who failed to make it at the destination and those who stayed put, save those who were physically unable to 'vote with their feet', were those who had somehow made it at the destination.

Repatriation of refugees and belonging

The meaning involuntarily displaced populations ascribe to particular places—homes—and the extent to which, on the one hand, belonging to such particular places constitutes a fundamental human need and, on the other, decisions concerning repatriation of refugees subsequent to the elimination of the factors that prompt displacement are influenced by the need to belong to such particular places, is one of the most sustained controversies in the social sciences. As mentioned, in the past few decades, there has been a surge of academic interest in the relationship between people, particular places, and the significance of these relationships for the return movements of refugees (see Coles 1985; Warner 1994; Allen and Turton 1996; Turton 2002; Stepputat 1994; Malkki 1995. For a critique of this literature see Kibreab 1999a). For Coles, the need for displaced populations to belong to spatially bounded communities is a fundamental human need, 'the satisfaction of which is conducive to individual and social well-being and the denial of which is conducive to suffering and to social disorder' (1985: 185–6). In wartime England Weil wrote, 'To be rooted is perhaps the most important and least recognised need of the human soul' (cited in Malkki 1992: 24). A European refugee once stated:

> ...home is a feeling of contentment and belonging. It is the world of familiar faces, a house, a garden of one's own. It is a spiritual atmosphere to which one belongs, a civilisation whose language, history, traditions have become so much a part of one's personality that one feels...Home is a condition of life, which brings with it a sense of security and protection, as far as one can be secure in this imperfect world. At home a man can go about his business without undue strain, because he moves within a social order which he understands intuitively. *Life here is comparatively easy, for we are part of this order and know that we have a rightful place in it. The displaced person has lost his security* (quoted in Coles 1985: 187, emphasis added).

An Eritrean refugee elder in Dehema refugee settlement (Eastern Sudan) in December 1989 told me:

Home is where you are recognised as a full human being. You know everyone
and they know you. You have certain entitlements that no one can take away
from you. At home, you recognise the diverse plant and animal species—you
are part of them. They are also part of you. People and nature were inseparable
constituents of the landscape. When our enemies forcibly uprooted us from
our country, not only did we lose our loved ones, homes, land, livestock, and
other belongings but also our humanity and dignity. A person forced out of his
place is no longer a complete person. Our land was a source of life, identity,
dignity and belonging. When we lost our roots and left behind the place where
our ancestors and our umbilical chords were buried, we lost our lives, identity
and belonging. We are half human beings. We have not been able to live a full
life because we are in someone else's land against our will. This land does not
belong to us. Nor do we belong to it. We are no longer part of the landscape. We
are foreign bodies and that is how our surroundings view us and treat us. The
land belongs to the Sudanese. We are at their mercy. There is nothing worse than
owing your life and dignity to strangers' mercy. They can withdraw their mercy
at anytime and there is nothing we can do about it except face the consequences.
We are always reminded that we don't belong here. If we don't do as our hosts
tell us, we are threatened that the mercy would be withdrawn from us. We live
under permanent fear of uncertainty and insecurity.

   Whenever we want to visit a relative outside the camp, we have to apply
for a *tesrih* (a travel permit) against payment of fees. Whether we get such a
permit or not depends on the whims of the *modir* (camp manager). He can say
'no' for no reason and there is no redress against his decision. If we complain,
we are reminded that we should not abuse their generosity and hospitality. We
are praying to the Almighty, Allah, to help us recoup our lost lands, our lives,
our freedom, and our dignity (personal communication).

Though this testimony is critically important for understanding the
meanings refugees ascribe to home, exile, and repatriation, most
refugee communities are not homogenous in terms of ethnicity, culture,
political outlook, and interests. Thus, it is important to interpret such
statements cautiously and contextually. Refugees' views on home, exile,
and homecoming are varied, depending on many factors. In fact it is
worth noting here that the attitude of some Eritrean refugee groups in
Sudan towards home, exile, and homecoming have changed dramatically
with the changing political climate in the country. Also as mentioned in
the beginning, once the opportunity to return exists, the urge to return
is no longer experienced as intensely as when it did not exist. Many of
these refugee groups have—in spite of the UNHCR's repeated pleas and

threats of loss of refugee status, and, notwithstanding the fact that the original factors that prompted their displacement had ceased to exist with the country's independence, *de facto*, in May 1991 and, *de jure*, in May 1993—refused to return to Eritrea. In fact all the Eritrean refugees who could not show well-founded reason for not returning, risked losing their refugee status after December 2002. The UNHCR decided to apply the cessation clause as stipulated in the 1951 Convention. This is in spite of the fact that there are still an unknown number—estimated between 125,000 and 150,000—Eritrean refugees in Sudan and reports suggest that there are thousands of youngsters who are fleeing to Sudan to avoid the 'open-ended' national service. This is exacerbated by the fact that, in May 2002, the Eritrean government introduced another burdensome obligation known as the 'Warsai-Yikaalo Development Campaign', in which all men and women aged between 18 and 40 are required to work for the government without remuneration, save minimum pocket money. The duration of this obligation has not been stipulated either, leaving it open-ended. Many of those affected have been fleeing to Sudan to avoid the onerous obligation. In this light, the UNHCR's decision to apply the cessation clause was misplaced.

It is also difficult to determine whether the negative attitudes towards life in exile and the powerful desire to return are the result of the injustices and ill-treatments suffered at the hands of host governments, or such feelings are intrinsic to being involuntarily displaced. If the latter were the case, the feelings of repugnance of life in exile and the desire to return home as expressed by the elder cited above are engendered by powerful proclivity to belong to places of origin. However, if such negative feelings are the consequences of misconceived host government refugee policies and the injustices suffered at the hands of government officials, security forces, employers, local residents, etc., by reversing these policies and practices, it may be possible to reverse refugees' attitudes towards home, exile, homecoming or repatriation. There is ample evidence to suggest that not only is this possible but that is precisely what has been happening in North America, Europe and Australia where the granting of refugee status invariably results[2] in the enjoyment of full citizenship or denizenship[3] rights regardless of naturalisation (see Kibreab 2003a). In such countries repatriation has effectively become redundant, even after the elimination of the factors that prompt population displacement (for detailed comparative study see Kibreab 2003a). This may suggest that the two contending theories presented in the first part of the paper may not be adequate to explain why refugees return home in response to political changes in their countries of origin or stay put in countries of asylum after the factors that prompted displacement have been eliminated. As we shall see, the single most important reason why repatriation to countries of origin is regarded by governments, the UNHCR and the UN system in general as 'the best solution' is because most states in the developing countries conceive asylum as a transient phenomenon in which refugees are received as temporary guests regardless of the duration of their stay in exile (Kibreab 1996d; 1999a).

In most developing societies, nationality is *sine qua non* for the enjoyment of citizenship rights. In contrast, as mentioned, in the North one does not need to be a national to enjoy citizenship rights. Denizens or those who have permanent residence permits have equal access to civil, social and political rights, except for participation in national elections which are typically restricted to nationals. Refugees in the South, however, are invariably received or accepted as temporary guests without any access to civil, political and social citizenship rights (see 1996d; 2002a; 2003a). Although many African refugees manage to self-settle in defiance of the host government's polices (see Hansen 1990; 1982; Bakewell 2000; Wajbrandi 1986), refugee groups are often kept in spatially segregated sites until their repatriation becomes possible (see Kibreab 1987; 1996a).

Ignatieff (1993: 6) argues, 'belonging...is first and foremost protection from violence. Where you belong is where you are safe; and where you are safe is where you belong.' He further argues that belonging also means, 'being recognised and understood.' Though the central thrust of Ignatieff's captivating metaphor is in many cases fundamentally true, it is important to observe that firstly, 'belonging' is not solely a function of safety. History is replete with examples of people who have not been safe, even in societies and places where their belonging has never been contested. Take, for example, the black South Africans under the Apartheid regime;[4] the Eritreans during the period of Ethiopian occupation (1952–1991); members and sympathisers of the opposition in Mugabe's Zimbabwe; the Kurds in Iraq and Turkey; members of the Communist Party in Suharto's Indonesia in the 1960s; the East Timorese under Indonesia, the Oromos of Ethiopia—and the list goes on. In none of these situations was/is the issue of 'belonging' contested by either the victims or the perpetrators. Ironically, it is not uncommon that the perpetrators are the one's who do not belong to the communities and places where they commit atrocities.

Secondly, there have been many examples where people have been safe outside their countries or places of origin, but have neither relinquished

their desire to return nor failed to seize every opportunity to return subsequent to the elimination of the factors that prompted their displacement.
If we reduce the issue of 'belonging' to 'safety' alone, we may be implying
that the solution to the contemporary chronic problem of displacement is
a question of finding new places where people can rebuild their lives in
safety—pure and simple. The assumption underlying such conceptualisation is that once displaced populations find a safe place to live, they will
develop a feeling of belonging to the new place. But then, one must ask,
if it were a question of safety, would the Kurds, Palestinians, the Tamils,
etc. lay down their weapons in return for alternative safe places, e.g. in
the Amazon or elsewhere?

It is probably safe to say that the answer is 'no', but it is important not
to dismiss the question out-of-hand. How the Palestinians, Kurds, Tamils
or any other troubled peoples in the world would react to such a project
cannot be determined *a priori*. Some may even suggest that the number
of refugees from Africa, Asia, Latin America and Eastern Europe who
abandon the idea of voluntary repatriation—even after the elimination of
the factors that prompt their displacement—when they find safe homes in
North America, Europe and Australia indicates the viability of seeking
alternative homes outside of the refugees' countries of origin. However,
the meaning and importance that people attach to particular places (of
origin) vis-à-vis secure livelihood outside such places is so complex that
one could not predict the outcome of any such effort with any acceptable
degree of certainty.

Isaiah Berlin (in Ignatieff 1993: 7) also says that among my own people, 'they understand me, as I understand them, and this understanding
creates within me a sense of being somebody in the world.' In view of the
particular historical injustice suffered by the Jewish peoples, individuals
of such origin may feel more understood and secure among 'their own
people'. Because they were rejected as being non-entities, it is possible
that Berlin experienced 'a sense of being somebody in the world'. This
is only one of many other perspectives and therefore it is important to
guard against generalising from this standpoint. It would be a tragedy of
enormous proportions if we were to feel understood, secure and a sense of
self-worth only among those who are similar to us in race, religion, ethnicity, sex, age, etc. Ironically, it is precisely such perceptions and xenophobic concerns that generate the securitisation of migration (voluntary and
involuntary) issues in nearly all receiving as well as many non-receiving
countries.[5] Nothing can be more divisive and damaging to the international protection regime than the misconceived belief that commonality

of religion, ethnicity, and race are *sine qua non* for harmonious social co-existence. At the same time, to extrapolate any general or universal human condition from this view is clearly not valid: although the Jews of Isaiah Berlin's generation shared a common experience of suffering and deprivation, the Jewish people are not homogenous and it would be mistaken to assume that every Jew regardless of class, ethnicity, region, race and place of origin would feel understood and appreciated simply because they are among Jewish people. This is most probably a function of class, race, ethnicity and political persuasion within the diverse Jewish populations.[6] The experiences of the Ethiopian Felasha who migrated to Israel in the first half of the 1980s and later is the case in point.

Stefan Wolff also argues:

> This fundamental socio-cultural need for recognition and understanding is all the more important in circumstances of forced migration because the sense of belonging, not just to a particular community, but also to a specific place, is brutally disrupted, and the reason for this disruption is often located by the perpetrators of forced migration in the particular community and place. As such, forced migration is the result of the struggle between two mutually exclusive conceptions of belonging: those who are perceived not to belong to the (territorially) defined community are expelled, regardless of whether they feel they belong to the contested piece of land as much as it belongs to them. *Since for most communities place is a crucial component of their identity, the loss of spatial attachment makes their identity incomplete* (2001: 53, emphasis added).

Although the thrust of this conceptualisation of forced migration is fundamentally true, the generalisation is, to a large extent, influenced by the specific tragic experiences of European history of forced migrations where ethnic cleansing, genocide, and population deportations have been the major weapons of assertion and denial of belonging to contested territories and communities. However, note that in situations where the causes of forced migration may be conflicts over the social order rather than disputes over territorial or societal belonging, the impacts of the losses of spatial attachment on identity may be experienced in a similar way. For example, Edward Said (1984: 50) describes exile as '...the unhealable rift forced between the human being and a native place, the self and its true home. The essential sadness of the break can never be surmounted.' Said is not specifically referring to the case of Palestinians where the cause of displacement is over territorial belonging, but is rather generalising to the experience of exile in general. Worby's (2000: 18) study of Guatemalan returnees' 'emotional claims' to the land they occupied before their displacement 'were powerful.' She states, 'Stories abound of elderly men and women who stayed behind to die on their land rather than leave it, and of refugee families who would sneak back to check on their lands and even harvest abandoned crops' (ibid.). Worby's subjects are indigenous peoples whose attachment to particular territories—homelands—is so powerful and mythical that it is not safe to generalise their experience to other populations.

The corollary of this conceptualisation of 'home' or native land and its importance to human well-being and security is that not only is the principal motivation of return movements assumed to be the desire to belong to one's own community and land—the 'motherland' or the 'fatherland'—the 'sacred' place where one's ancestors and one's own parents' or grandparents' are buried, but *for repatriation to be meaningful, it should result in the restitution of refugees' original homes as a requisite for recovery of their dignity, security and wellbeing.* The term to repatriate is originally derived from the Latin word *repatriāre. Patria* as we saw earlier means native land. Though its meaning has been changing over time, originally to *ripatriare* (French) meant to restore a person to his own home (Oxford Dictionary). This is the sense of the term understood by governments, inter-governmental organisations and most academics. This is evident from the dominant terminologies used in the repatriation discourse such as 'reintegration', 'rehabilitation', 'reconstruction', 'readjustment', 'readaptation', 'reassimilation', 're-establishment', 'rebuilding' etc. (for a critique see Hammond 1999). Warner who otherwise is critical to the 'place attachment perspective' argues:

> Voluntary repatriation means return to home, not merely return to country of origin. While the country of origin is a simple, geopolitical concept, the home that the refuges are supposed to return to is more than a territorial place that is associated with a political entity. Voluntary repatriation is more than just return to country of origin; it is return to a home and community.
>
> What is the difference between a territorial place that is the country of origin of refugees and the home and the community? The concept of home and community in the country of origin is most frequently related to two elements. First there is the association of the refugee with those who are similar. A community in this sense is really a homogenous group. Second, there is the association of this group with a specific place (1994: 162).

Again this cannot be generalised to all refugee situations. As we shall see, voluntary repatriation has, for the large majority of Eritrean refugees from Sudan, meant a return to Eritrea—the refugees' country of origin—not to the villages, homes and communities where they had lived prior to being displaced (see Kibreab 2002a). The same was true to a large extent Ethiopian refugees from Tigray who instead of returning to the Tigrayan highlands were resettled through government initiatives in the land-abundant Humera area along the Sudan border. In the case of the refugees from Tigray, the decision to re-settle the returnees was taken by the new government in Ethiopia (see Hammond 1999). However, the returnees did not 'vote with their feet' and abandon the resettlement areas in favour of returning to their villages of origin, as did their compatriots from the Beles Valley as discussed earlier.

As we shall see, the reality of places inhabited by homogenous groups is non-existent because most refugees' places of origin, for example, in Africa, are inhabited by heterogenous groups. Poul Hartling, a former High Commissioner for Refugees, in his opening statement to the 35th EXCOM session (8 October 1984) declared that one of the three most important criteria for any organized movement of repatriation in which the UNHCR may be involved is that returnees should be 'allowed to return to their places of origin—ideally to their former homes, their villages, their land.' Nearly all tripartite agreements signed between the UNHCR, governments in countries of asylum and origin include the right of refugees to return to the actual homes from where they were originally displaced.

The ambiguous meaning of home:
The experience of Eritrean returnees from Sudan

I had to leave that space I called home to move beyond boundaries, yet I also needed to return there…Indeed, the very meaning of home changes with decolonisation, with radicalisation. At times, home is nowhere. At times, one knows only extreme estrangement and alienation. Then home is no longer just one place. It is many locations. Home is that place which enables and promotes varied and ever-changing perspectives, a place where one discovers new ways of seeing reality, frontiers of difference (bell hooks 1991).

The discussion presented in the preceding section indisputably suggests that repatriation does not mean return to country of origin but rather to one's home and community of origin. What does the empirical evidence show? Do refugees return to the particular places where they lived prior to their displacement or do they return to their country of origin? To my knowledge, there are no empirical studies that address this question; the answer, therefore, is unknown. The only exceptions are Hammond's (1999) and Kibreab's (2002a) studies on Ethiopian and Eritrean returnees from Sudan, respectively. One likely reason for this academic indifference may relate to the widespread assumption that refugees return to their former homes of origin and communities and are consequently expected to reintegrate by re-assuming the roles they played before becoming refugees. The process is considered straightforward and non-problematic and therefore generates no research interests. The assumption is that once the factors that prompt flight are removed, refugees return 'home' and once they are at 'home', they 're-integrate' themselves by utilising pre-existing social networks of relationships, statuses, kinship ties, old skills, knowledge, property rights, etc.

Not only does this presuppose a society whose belief systems, values, norms, rituals, occupations and aspirations have remained in stasis; but it also assumes a willingness on the part of the displaced populations to return to the *status quo ante*. This conception, or rather misconception, takes little account of the cultural (material and non-material) and occupational changes that might have been experienced by all actors in the (re)-integration process—namely, returnees, local residents, IDPs, demobilized soldiers and ex-combatants—in societies recovering from protracted and traumatic intra-state or inter-state wars. Another misconception is the assumption that the stayee populations would welcome returnees with open arms as if nothing has changed since their departure and prolonged absence. The actors in the so-called (re)-integration process are conceived as homogenous groups of people all sharing the same interests, visions, goals and opportunities. In most cases, the nature of reception accorded to returnees by stayee populations in areas of return is, to a large extent, a function of the benefits and costs they bring with them—schools (teachers, buildings, furniture, teaching materials, and books) health care (buildings, medicines, beds, doctors, nurses, health care assistants), water, feeder roads, markets, food aid, employment, credit, extension and veterinary services, cultivable and grazing land, fuel wood, etc. (Kibreab 2002a).

One fundamental principle permeating the discourse on repatriation is the assumption that the 'home' refugees 'return to' is their birthplace—the place where their fathers and forefathers lived and were buried. A case study of Eritrean refugees returning from Sudan shows, however, that refugees do not always return to their places of origin or 'homes'. There are many reasons for this. Some refugees might have been living elsewhere outside their 'homelands' as migrants in the immediate pre-flight periods. Though historically the 'homes' of origin of a considerable proportion of the Eritrean refugees in Sudan were the Eritrean Plateau, the eastern escarpments of the country and Senhit (see Kibreab 1987; 1996a), many of the Tigrinya, Saho, and even some of the Tigre speaking groups, e.g. the Maria, Ad Shuma, and Bet Juk lived in the Gash Barka region prior to their displacement—particularly in Um Hajer, Tessenei, Ali Gidir, Koreken, Agordet, Barentu, Haikota, Tokombia, Shilalo, etc. Some also had two or three homes before they became refugees. Thus, the question of what constitutes 'home' to such groups is quite ambiguous. It is also important to point out that the overwhelming majority of those who lived in the Gash Barka area prior to their displacement—both original settlers such as the Nara and the Kunama and the earlier migrants from other parts of Eritrea—have not returned to the villages where they had lived prior to displacement

Is home where their fathers and forefathers lived or is it the place where they had lived themselves at the time of displacement? Some of them had lived in two or three places in the period preceding their displacement. Historically, and this is still the case, though Eritreans have strong attachment to their 'villages of origin', it is important to recognise that Eritrean communities have always been mobile. This mobility was necessitated by the need to take advantage of variations in the environment. The populations that inhabit the different climatic and geographic zones have always been intrinsically interdependent. For example, the Eritrean western lowlands, the eastern escarpment and the highland Plateau constitute symbiotic, complementary and interdependent ecological zones on which the livelihoods of the highlanders and lowlanders mutually depend. Eritrea is neither geographically nor climatically uniform (Kibreab 2001). The highland Plateau and the eastern and western lowlands vary widely in altitude, rainfall patterns, soil types, vegetation, and water supply systems. These differences, and the limitations of each location to provide adequate livelihoods for inhabitants, have historically necessitated the utilisation of resources in different ecological zones. This continuous mobility between different ecological zones to make ends meet in an environment that is not favourably endowed weather wise suggests that the idea of 'home' as an immutable fixed place to which people remain attached as fixtures is meaningless. Inasmuch as people moved between places, it was common for a family to maintain more than one 'home'—one in the place of origin and another in the place where there was bread.

During the British Military Administration (BMA) an attempt was made to establish two systems of administration, one based on territoriality for the 'detribalised sedentary' population and the other, a native administration, for the 'pastoral' or 'tribal' groups (see Kibreab 2001). However, the classification was based on the British colonial policies and practices adopted throughout its Empire rather than on the objective Eritrean context. The classification of Eritreans on the basis of a dyadic mode of existence—sedentary versus nomadic—was misleading. Most Eritreans continuously shifted from one mode of existence to another or moved within the sedentary-pastoral continuum. It was thus difficult to classify them on the basis of livelihood/economic habits or settlement patterns.

In the following, the Eritrean returnees' choice of destination will be discussed. However, before dwelling on this, the process of repatriation and (re)-integration of the former refugees from Sudan, in the areas of return, shall be discussed briefly.

Repatriation of Eritrean refugees:
Donor responses, risks, opportunities and coping strategies

In view of the fact that involuntary displacements are caused by the interplay of political, economic, social, cultural and environmental problems, changes to the political factors that prompted population displacement, though of critical importance, are not a sufficient condition for successful repatriation and reintegration of returnees. Rather, successful repatriation is to a large extent dependent on the reintegration program's effectiveness in addressing the social, economic and environmental problems that contributed to the displacement.

For example, in Eritrea, the root cause of displacement was the denial of the people's right to self-determination and the accompanying persecution and violence. These problems came to an end with the country's independence in May 1993. However, the Eritrean economic and physical infrastructures were devastated by the thirty years war and between a third and a quarter of the country's population was displaced by it. The task of repatriating and (re)-integrating the large number of refugees was therefore beyond the economic and human resources of the newly established Eritrean State and required a concerted international action. Unfortunately, the relationship between the Provisional Government of Eritrea and the UNHCR was from the outset marked by misunderstanding and lack of co-operation, constituting one of the major initial obstacles to organised return operations. Despite the stormy relations between the UNHCR and the Provisional Eritrean government, though, an ambitious and meticulously documented repatriation plan known as the Programme for Refugee Reintegration and the Rehabilitation of Resettlement Areas (PROFERI) was prepared in collaboration with the UN agencies (see Kibreab 1996d).

Nevertheless, notwithstanding the fact that the tenets of PROFERI were consistent—almost identical—with the international donor community's new approach to resolving refugee problems, particularly with regard to the concept of returnee aid and development espoused by the UNHCR at the beginning of the 1990s, the international donor community's response in financial contributions was quite sluggish. The general funding requirements of PROFERI were estimated at US$262.2 million and it was planned to be implemented in three consecutive phases—Phase I US$110.9 million, Phase II US$79.9 million and Phase III US$71.4 million. The aim was to repatriate and reintegrate 430,000 returnees as well as assisting the large number of self-repatriates, IDPs and local residents in the areas of return. Of the first US$110.9 million required, though, only US$32.5 was pledged at a conference organized by the United Nations Department of Humanitarian Affairs (DHA) and the United Nations Development Program (UNDP) for that purpose. The pledging conference was held in Geneva in July 1993, less than two months after the country's independence (Kibreab 1996c).

Following this unfavourable donor response, a decision was taken to scale down the program and initiate a Pilot Project as a precursor to PROFERI Phase I. The PROFERI Pilot Project (PPP) was governed by two bilateral memorandums of understanding signed, on the one hand, between the Government of Eritrea and UNHCR, and on the other, between the Government of Sudan and UNHCR. PROFERI Phase I could not be implemented as planned partly because of insufficient funds but also due to the Government of Sudan's insistence on a tripartite agreement, and the Eritrean Government's forthright rejection of this proposal. Although the latter insisted that there was no need for a new instrument when the bilateral memoranda of understanding were still valid, in fact the relations between the two governments had hit rock-bottom immediately after Eritrea's independence. In December 1994, during the implementation of the PPP, the Eritrean government severed diplomatic relations with Sudan. Though the PPP continued at a very slow pace, the more ambitious plan for three phases of PROFERI was almost declared dead and buried when diplomatic relations between the two countries were severed. The main reasons for the deterioration of relations between the two governments was the alleged political, financial and military support provided to the Eritrean Islamic Jihad Movement by the Islamic National Front, which was the real behind-the-scenes power in Sudan. After 1995, the Eritrean government retaliated by openly supporting Sudanese opposition groups.

When the promised organized repatriation failed, many refugees 'voted with their feet' and returned homewards without any international assistance. This partly explains why 87% of those who returned between 1989 and 1998 organized their own return movements and (re)-integration despite a very high-risk of failure (ERREC 1996; 1997; 1998). Low levels and erratic distribution of rainfall was a major source of risk of impoverishment. This was exacerbated by the lack of draught power and tractors with appropriate attachments; insect, pest and weed infestations; shortages of family labour and the means to hire labour; and food and cash shortages during the hungry season.[7] Shortage of food meant that instead of working their own farms, farmers were forced to work for others in order to meet their families' immediate needs. In other words, the need to salvage the present required sacrificing the future. As a result, most of the returnees who were dependent on crop and livestock production lived with the permanent threat of impoverishment. Land shortage was also a major problem, especially for the few families who settled outside the Gash Setit sub-region.

The question that arises is how the returnee families withstood, coped with, or if afflicted, recovered from the risks of failure or impoverishment. The self-repatriates, as well as those who returned under the PPP, adopted return strategies that were risk averse. Most attempted to avoid subsistence insecurities upon return by adopting a strategy designed to take advantage of the return option without losing the benefits derived from being refugees in the Sudan. This was typically achieved by splitting their families; i.e. some returned to Eritrea while other family members stayed behind (for a detailed discussion see Kibreab 2003c). Those who returned received (re)-integration assistance packages, including land, while those who stayed behind continued to engage in diverse types of economic activities and sent remittances to the family members who had returned—towards building houses and (re)-establishing themselves in the areas of return. Some family members collected rations in the camps and settlements, while others worked as wage labourers or looked after the livestock of the families concerned. In spite of the fact that only 13% of the total number of returnees returned through the organized program, most of the international assistance was directed to them. The remaining

87% shared whatever services and facilities were available in the areas of return. They also tapped into the trans-ethnic and trans-religious social networks that had been created in the refugee camps, settlements and areas of self-settlement for help in coping with adversity (see Kibreab 2002a; 2003b).

These efforts were buttressed by an area-based holistic development approach adopted by the Eritrean Government in the returnee-receiving areas. The government's approach was intended to create social and economic capacities for absorption by simultaneously addressing the social, economic and environmental problems that had contributed to the problem of population displacement. All residents, regardless of their status (whether they were returnees, internally displaced persons, local residents, migrants, or ex-fighters etc.) were expected to benefit from newly created opportunities in the areas of return. The country was in the early stages of recovering from thirty years of devastating war, during which the overwhelming majority of the rural populations had lived near or below the subsistence margin. Where the objective is to provide development assistance, it makes neither moral nor practical sense to discriminate between people on the basis of their status; and hence the Eritrean government's and its partners' approaches were appropriate and worthy of emulation. It is worth noting that the effects of the border war between Eritrea and Ethiopia in May 1998–June 2000, undermined most of these achievements. Not only did the border war create new refugees, but the processes of reconstructing livelihoods and communities in the areas of return were also detrimentally affected. However, after the peace agreement between the Eritrean and the Ethiopian governments was signed in December 2000, all of the refugees produced by this border war have returned through the UNHCR's assistance. 'Since 2000, the UNHCR together with the Eritrean Relief and Refugee Commission (ERREC) have assisted 119,903 people return to Eritrea in safety and dignity' (UN Office for the Co-ordination of Humanitarian Affairs 2004). It is important to note that more than 70,000 of these returnees were pre-independence refugees.

Theoretically, in the reintegration program, relief and development were conceived to be aspects of a single process in which the inputs and technologies employed for rehabilitation were consistent with plans for longer-term undertakings. In line with the Government's policy of National Execution, all line ministries were involved in identification, design, implementation, monitoring and evaluation of the reintegration programs. The concept of National Execution constituted the linchpin of the whole reintegration program. What this meant in theory was that the various line ministries implement most of the program activities in collaboration with regional and local administrations under the co-ordination of the Eritrean Relief and Refugee Commission (ERREC). The policy framework provided that all of the sectoral departments should be directly involved from initiation until the finalization of program design. This was meant to ensure subsequent commitment to program activities by all concerned parties. This was supposed to take place within an overall strategic framework in which departmental responsibilities for every element of the program were clearly defined and agreed upon. Definite and appropriate budgets were also supposed to be allocated, while overall control of the reintegration programs and financial resources were vested in a single agency—the ERREC. Co-ordination mechanisms were also put in place to provide regular feedback on performance and facilitate prompt remedial action. In the PROFERI Pilot Project, very little of this conceptually sound and impressive framework was implemented due to lack of funds and underdeveloped human resources (see Kibreab 1999b)

At a policy level, the reintegration program aimed to maximize community participation, but this was not borne out by the findings of a study conducted by the author in 1997 (see Kibreab 1999b). Although all interviewees saw the processes for distributing resources as being fair and transparent, and reported that returnees participated through their representatives in the Land Allocation and Livestock committees, their roles were limited to contributing labour during its implementation. They could not influence the design or the delivery procedures of the various components of the projects. There was undoubtedly a genuine desire at a policy level to maximize community participation, but in practice, most of the decision-making powers remained beyond the influence of the returnees' representatives (Kibreab 1999b). For example, the restocking assistance package was designed without any involvement or consultation with the returnees' representatives and, not surprisingly, the project failed dismally. Key informants among the returnee communities attributed this failure to the lack of community participation.

The same research found that the restocking project was unsuccessful on the grounds that most of those who received livestock (goats and sheep) through the project soon lost some or all of their animals. The reasons for this were manifold, the most significant of which included: lack of community participation; failure to target beneficiaries on either the basis of need or the greater probability of success; failure to purchase animals from the locality where they were distributed (which led to problems of adaptability and the importation of contagious disease); distribution of animals during the wrong part of the year; and insufficient funds to purchase veterinary drugs after the first year (see Kibreab 1997; 1998). The returnees also experienced crop failures during three consequent years of drought and many families had to sell their animals to make ends meet. initially, free food was distributed to the refugees, but this was interrupted at the end of the first year. This may suggest that a restocking project is unlikely to succeed among food insecure households.

In what follows the Eritrean refugees' choice of destination and the factors that influenced their choices are discussed.

Eritrean returnees' choice of destination

In view of the ambiguous meaning of the concept 'home' in the Eritrean context, it is interesting to see where the majority of the repatriates have settled. Among the 6,386 families who returned under the Programme for Refugee Reintegration and Rehabilitation of Resettlement areas (PROFERI) pilot repatriation scheme, the overwhelming majority (5,173: 81.0%) have settled in the Gash Setit sub-region of Barka, where opportunities for employment and self-employment in the agricultural and the informal urban and peri-urban sectors as well as access to fertile land and grazing resources are greater (see Table 4-1). Of the remainder, nearly 13% (830 families) were resettled in the greater Barka region (ERREC 1996). The majority of the self-repatriates have also settled in the Gash Setit area (ERREC 1997).

Though the data in Table 4-1 show that the overwhelming number of returnees have settled in the Gash Setit sub-region, they do not show the places of origin or the areas where the refugees lived prior to their displacement to Sudan, and thus do not directly indicate what proportion of returnees have returned to or settled outside of their places of origin. However, since the war of independence affected all parts of Eritrea to varying degrees during different periods of the thirty year war, and there was no part of the country that did not produce refugees during those thirty years, the fact that the overwhelming majority of the returnees have settled in the Gash Setit sub-region indicates that most of the returnees have not returned to their villages of origin.

This has been confirmed by a survey conducted by the author in 1998. The results of a survey based on randomly selected representative

Table 4-1. Distribution of returnees by regional destination 2001–2002

Region	Number of households (%)		Number of individuals (%)	
Gash Barka	16,963	(93.2)	49,236	(95.3)
Anseba	380	(2.1)	894	(1.7)
Southern Region	126	(0.7)	256	(0.5)
Southern Red Sea	2	(0.0)	5	(0.0)
Central Region	85	(0.5)	151	(0.3)
Northern Red Sea	644	(3.5)	1,141	(2.2)
Total	18,200	(100.0)	51,683	(100.0)

Source: UNHCR and ERREC, Repatriated Eritrean refugees by destinations (Cumulative Convoys 1–94), Asmara.

samples of 166 self-repatriated returnees from Sudan in Barentu, Goluj, and Tessenei (all in the Gash Setit sub-region) show that 90% of the heads of the respondent households lived elsewhere in Eritrea (both within the Gash Setit sub-region and other regions) prior to their displacement to Sudan. Only 10% of the respondents reported that they were originally from the sites where they lived at the time of the survey. These data clearly show that only 10% of the returnees have returned to what Daniel Warner (1994) refers to as 'a home and community.' The overwhelming majority have constructed new homes and communities outside their places of origin—not necessarily among strangers, but mainly among fellow returnees. As we shall see, the bulk of the constituents of the new homes and communities were underpinned by social relationships and networks developed and consolidated in exile. Hence in the particular experience of Eritrean refugees, voluntary repatriation has not resulted—as the conventional wisdom suggests—in the reconstruction of pre-existing homes and communities. Instead return has led to construction of new homes and communities in places outside the returnees' places of origin but nevertheless within the country of origin.

It is important to guard against interpreting these data to imply that 90% of the returnees who are now settled in Gash Setit were originally from other regions in Eritrea. What the data show is that even those who prior to their displacement lived in the Gash Setit sub-region, instead of returning to the villages of their origin, have chosen different destinations within Gash Setit upon return. In fact the large majority of the returnees were originally from the Gash Setit area. These data clearly show that voluntary repatriation has resulted in the return of the large majority of the refugees

to the country rather than to places of origin. These data clearly contradict
Daniel Warner's assertion that 'voluntary repatriation is not a return to
a country of origin but rather to the particular homes and communities'
where the refugees concerned lived prior to their displacement. An attempt
will be made later to explain this.

The large majority of those who returned between 2001 and 2002 have
also settled in the Gash Barka region. Among the 18,200 households who
returned from Sudan to Eritrea, 93% have settled in the Gash Barka region
with the overwhelming majority settling in the Gash Setit sub–region.
Among the 51,683 individuals, 95% have settled in the same region.

All of the available data indisputably show that the overwhelming
majority of those who returned under government and self-sponsored
repatriations have returned to new places other than their homes of origin.
The Eritrean data indisputably suggest that voluntary repatriation does
not necessarily mean a return to the place of origin. In countries such as
Eritrea, where the cause of displacement was a war of national independence fought against an external enemy, repatriation is conceived to be a
return to the country of origin rather than to a particular place of origin.

Why have the majority opted to settle outside their places of origin?
The results of a series of surveys, personal interviews and focus group
discussions conducted by the author in 1997, 1998, 2000/2001 show that
there are well thought out rationales underlying the returnees' choices
of destination. The most important factors that influenced their choice
of destination are: (i) undesirability and impossibility of returning to
the past; (ii) opportunities for employment and self-employment; (iii)
proximity to the country of asylum; (iv) continuity of the trans-ethnic
and trans-religious social networks established in exile; (v) repugnance
of rural life due to cultural, social and occupational changes experienced
in exile; and (vi) access to schools, health care and water for human and
livestock consumption as well as for rain-fed cultivation and irrigation.

In the following I argue that the reasons for the returnees having
settled outside their places of origin are inextricably linked to the social
changes and transformations that they had undergone in exile. First,
the social changes and transformations effected by exile are briefly
discussed. Second, an attempt is made to examine how the social changes
and transformations the refugees underwent in exile influenced their
decision to settle mainly in urban and peri-urban areas in the Gash Setit
sub-region—such as Tessenei, Goluj, Ali Gidir, Talata Asher, Barentu,
etc—and outside their villages of origin.

Exile, social change, development of co-operative networks and choice of destination

Prior to their return, the Eritrean refugees in Sudan had undergone some fundamental socio-economic changes and transformations in terms of power relations, occupations, gender relations, authority, status, social relations and networks, organisation, participation in regional and international markets, settlement pattern (urbanisation), aspirations and consumption habits (Kibreab 1996a; 1996c; 1999b; 2000; 2002a; 2003b; 2004). Prior to their displacement, the overwhelming majority of the refugees were pastoralists and agro-pastoralists who produced most of their subsistence needs without much reliance on regional or international markets. This all changed in exile. In Sudan, the majority produced for the market as wage labourers, cash crop producers and self-employed in the informal sector (Kibreab 1987; see also Tables 4-2 and 4-3). When they fled their country, they lost all of their possessions, including livestock (Kibreab 1987). The only way to earn a living was by selling their labour. For the overwhelming majority, wage labour and self-employment in the informal sector represented the major sources of livelihoods. The occupational profile of the 40,108 returnee male heads of households who returned between 1989 and 1997, for example, show that only 13.9% and 2.5% were farmers and agro-pastoralists, respectively (Table 4-2). Though data based on total enumeration regarding the refugees' pre-flight occupational profile are lacking, studies conducted by the author in the 1980s show that the large majority were pastoralists, agro-pastoralists and farmers (Kibreab 1987; 1990). The data in Tables 4-2 and 4-3 clearly show that the occupational profile of the heads of the returnee households is not typical of any rural sub-Saharan African standard.

The data show that the returnee households had undergone a considerable degree of occupational transformation in exile, resulting from increased participation in diverse economic activities and the acquisition of new skills. The proportion of skilled individuals such as mechanics, carpenters, drivers, teachers, nurses, medical assistants, laboratory technicians, masons, shoemakers, tailors, electricians, etc. is remarkably high. The data also show that a sizeable proportion of the female household heads participated in economic activities, some of which are not traditionally considered as female occupations, e.g. wage labour and commerce (Table 4-3). Some of the skills were acquired prior to the refugees' displacement, but a large number of the refugees also acquired new skills in exile.

Table 4-2. Occupational profile of returnee male heads of households
         1989/1995–1997

Type of occupation	1989–1995	1996	1997	Total	Percent of total
Farmers	5,379	145	64	5,588	13.9
Agro-pastoralists	968	11	13	992	2.5
Wage-labourers	11,854	874	540	13,268	33.1
Skilled[a]	6,782	1,670	1,128	9,580	23.9
Traders	1,332	306	155	1,793	4.5
Truck owners	75	7	1	83	0.2
Students	4,173	313	54	4,540	11.3
Ex-soldiers	153	8	12	173	0.4
Unemployed	3,431	371	172	3,974	9.9
Seamen	94	23	0	117	0.3
Total	34,241	3728	2139	40,108	100.0

Source: ERREC 1996; 1997; 1998.

a = Some of the skills include mechanics, plumbers, carpenters, drivers, teachers, medical-personnel, pharmacists, masons, shoe-makers, tailors, accountants, computer programmers and technicians, engineers, managers, electricians, agronomists, etc.

Most of the refugees who fled between the 1960s and the mid-1970s were from pastoral camps or small villages that were socially and physically isolated. Displacement brought together different ethnic and kinship groups in the reception centers and border towns of Sudan for the first time. The losses experienced during flight and the early phases of exile weakened the barriers that divided them into different socio-economic categories. Displacement led to breakdown of kinship and clan based communal cohesion. The refugees all considered themselves to be victims of a common enemy whose defeat required concerted action. They felt that they did not receive the treatment accorded them by the international instruments at the hands of Sudanese authorities and NGO staff. This resulted, on the one hand, in the discernible weakening of clan and kinship-based social relationships and, on the other, in the emergence of intra-group social support networks that increased fraternity and social cohesion. The threats (both real and perceived) and the strong desire to return home reinforced the refugees' unity and cohesion, regardless of their ethnic, clan, tribal and religious affiliations. The findings suggest that a returnee identity transcending other forms of associations was in the making in the areas of return.

Table 4-3. Occupational profile of female-headed returnee households
          1989/1995–1997

Type of occupation	1989–1995	1996	1997	Total	Percent of total
Farmers	337	14	0	351	1.4
Agro-pastoralists	86	4	0	90	0.4
Wage-labourers	1,908	204	131	2,243	9.1
Skilled[a]	830	84	75	989	4.0
Traders	321	68	48	437	1.9
Truck owners	1	0	0	1	0.0
Students	2,167	84	56	2,307	9.4
Ex-soldiers	5	0	1	6	0.0
Unemployed	7,829	561	390	8,780	35.8
Housewife	6,651	713	462	7,826	31.9
Domestic servant	1,061	228	204	1,493	6.1
Total	21,196	1,960	1,367	24,523	100.0

Source: ERREC 1996; 1997; 1998.

a = Some of the skills include mechanics, plumbers, carpenters, drivers, teachers, medical-personnel, pharmacists, masons, shoe-makers, tailors, accountants, computer programmers and technicians, engineers, managers, electricians, agronomists, etc.

The refugees were also exposed to modern social services for the first time. Prior to their displacement, those from the rural areas, especially those who had fled from the most neglected parts of Eritrea, such as the western and eastern lowlands and the Sahel, had no access to the most basic services. Those refugees who joined the camps and settlements enjoyed access to basic services such as health care, primary education, water supply, sanitation, etc., provided by the UNHCR and non-governmental organisations. Although those who had self-settled did not have free access to such facilities, many were able to benefit either by paying a fee or from various services provided by NGOs and the government.

The question that arises is: in what way did these changes and trans-formations in occupations, settlement patterns, consumption habits and development of trans-ethnic and trans-religious social relations and net-works influence the refugees' choice of (return) destination? As the data in Table 4-2 and to some extent in Table 4-3 show, the returnees are no longer what they used to be. In view of the social change and transforma-tions they underwent in exile, for the overwhelming majority, settlement in rural Eritrea was not a viable option. The most important factors in their decision, according to data elicited from the returnees, were access to children's education, healthcare, water provision, cultivable land, employment opportunities, desire to join returnee friends, neighbours and relatives and greater opportunities for self-employment. Most of the key informants and members of the focus groups pointed out that proximity to the country of asylum was also a major factor. Cross-border trade and employment are some of the most important economic activities in the border areas and are considered to be crucial. Most of the refugees would have forgone all of these opportunities had they returned to their isolated villages where employment opportunities are non-existent and social services are either completely absent or rudimentary. Rural life was no longer relevant for those who derived their livelihoods from wage labour, employment and self-employment in the urban and semi-urban informal sector. The same was true for the skilled and semi-skilled people. Why, for example, would a mechanic, a plumber, an electrician, a nurse, etc., return to rural Eritrea where not only would the skilled be unable to find jobs, but the likelihood of being de-skilled was also high. For all categories in Tables 4-2 and 4-3, save the small minority of farmers and agro-pastoralists, rural life had lost its meaning. Even for the latter categories, Gash Setit was more attractive, as the availability of cultivable and grazing lands is greater.

Displacement among Eritrean refugees has been a vehicle for the development of trans-ethnic and trans-religious social networks (for an extensive discussion of the extent to which the Eritrean refugees in Sudan formed new communities see Kibreab 2000). Prior to their displacement, the returnees originated from different parts of Eritrea. Return to their respective places of origin would have meant the loss of invaluable social capital, which has proved an indispensable asset for constructing communities and livelihoods (Kibreab 2003b). It is the need, *inter alia*, to maintain this form of social capital that has been pulling the returnees together to share their place of abode upon return rather than scattering themselves to their myriad small villages. Data elicited from different key informants and focus groups show that the social relationships and neighbourhood networks established in exile were more valued than old kinship ties, neighbourhood networks, or attachment to particular places—'homes'. One of the reasons why the returnees opted to settle outside the places from where they had been uprooted was the desire to continue living with friends, neighbours and relatives who lived in Sudan with them. Most of the returnees were reluctant to part from the cohesive trans-ethnic and trans-religious communities they had constructed in exile.

Conclusion

The relationship between people, particular places, a given geopolitical state entity, and identity is complex. Repatriation also means different things to different refugees. Though it is not possible to generalize the findings of this study to all repatriation situations, for the majority of Eritrean refugees returning from Sudan, repatriation has meant a return to the country of origin and not to 'homes' or places of origin. The meaning the returning refugees ascribe to home is also ambiguous and shifting. Though their choice of destination or home making upon return was undoubtedly determined by issues pertaining to livelihoods and the need for continuity of social networks developed in exile, some of the returnees clearly distinguished between places of abode and 'homes' whilst for others 'home' was nothing other than the place of abode.

It is also worth noting that the ambiguity of the meaning of home was not limited to the boundaries of the geopolitical state entities. There are some refugee groups whose perceptions of home transcend the internationally recognized boundaries that separate Eritrea and Sudan. This is particularly true of the Beni Amer and the Habab ethnic groups who straddle the border regions now dissected by boundaries imposed by the colonial powers and enforced by the post-colonial states. The groups that inhabit the border areas have always had borders, but no boundaries.

In the first part of the paper, two contending theories on belonging and their implications on repatriation movements were discussed. The data presented do not fully support or reject either of those theories. Not only have the large majority of the Eritrean refugees not returned to their homes and communities of origin, but it is also doubtful that the decisions of those who returned to Eritrea were primarily motivated by a desire to be re-rooted in the territories of their origin or to belong to their cultural communities, even though during the war, while the opportunity for returning did not exist, the refugees were exceedingly pre-occupied with the dream of re-rooting themselves in their places of origin and communities.

It appears that once the factors that prompted them to flee ceased to exist, the powerful yearnings to 'return' ease considerably, with the decision to return or to stay based on careful calculations of the probable costs and benefits of various options. This was particularly so for those households whose livelihoods hovered around the subsistence margin. People in such socio-economic conditions are intrinsically risk averse, as even a slight miscalculation in such a decision could have detrimental consequences on the well-being and survival of the refugees concerned. Although it has been overlooked in the relevant literature, for poor refugees—and these are usually the large majority—the structural conditions and residency rights in countries of asylum are as, if not more important in determining whether refugees return to their countries of origin or stay put in countries of asylum after the factors that prompted displacement have been eliminated. This may be equally true of populations displaced by development projects and government relocation programs.

Notes

1 I recently returned to the village of my birth, which is located less than 80 kilometers away from Eritrea's capital, Asmara. The place was more accessible thirty years ago than it is now. Then it was possible to access the village by a 4-wheel drive in great difficulty. Thirty years later, the village is completely inaccessible even by the most powerful vehicle because of erosion and land degradation. There is only one transistor radio in the whole village and no resident understands any foreign language. Though there are only a few people and nearly all of them are old and small children, they look much more impoverished now than when I knew them thirty years ago. This is in spite of the fact that some of the families in the village have sons and/or daughters living in London, New York, Stockholm, Berlin, etc. The presence of some of their members in the cosmopolitan cities has not led to greater interconnectedness and social change. My village of origin cannot be the only one that is not globally interconnected. All the neighboring villages seemed to be in a similar state. It is therefore important to guard against overstating the impact of globalization on the everyday life of people living in the remote rural areas of developing societies, particularly in sub-Saharan Africa.

2 In recent years some countries such as Australia have begun to rescind the refugee status granted to some categories of persons. 'The news in Australia this week (Nov. 2004) includes reports that the government is forcibly repatriating large numbers of Kosovars who received 'Temporary Protection Visas' when granted refugee status. Since the late 1990s Australia has granted these TPVs to refugees rather than providing them with permanent residence status.' I am grateful to Karl Smith, the copy-editor of this volume, for pointing this out to me.

3 Denizens are foreign citizens who are entitled to equal treatment in every aspect of life as citizens.

4 In the particular experience of South Africa, even the most zealous exponents of Apartheid never contested the blacks' 'belonging to' the country; but it must also be noted that millions of blacks were nevertheless uprooted from their homes of origin and resettled in the so-called Homelands.

5 I am grateful to Karl Smith for the suggestion that it is not only receiving but also non-receiving countries that securitise migration issues.

6 I am grateful to Karl Smith for this suggestion.

7 The hungry season is the period in which households exhaust their food crops from the previous season's harvest and usually coincides with the period immediately preceding the next harvest.

References

Allen, T. and D. Turton (1996) 'Introduction: In search of cool ground', in T. Allen (ed.), *In Search of Cool Ground: War, Flight and Homecoming in Northeast Africa.* Oxford: James Currey Publishers, pp. 1–22.

Al-Rasheed, M. (1994) 'The myth of return: Iraqi Arab and Assyrian refugees in London', *Journal of Refugee Studies*, 7(2/3), pp. 199–219.

Bakewell, O. (2000) 'Repatriation and self-settled refugees in Zambia: Bringing solutions to the wrong problems', *Journal of Refugee Studies*, 13(4), pp. 356–73.

Cernea, M. M. (1990) *Poverty Risks from Population Displacement in Water Resources Development.* Cambridge, MA: Development Discussion Paper No. 355, Harvard University Institute for International Development.

———— (1995) 'Understanding and preventing impoverishment from displacement', *Journal of Refugee Studies*, 8(3), pp. 245–64.

———— (2000) 'Risks, safeguards, and reconstruction: A model for population displacement and resettlement', in M. M. Cernea and C. McDowell (eds), *Risks and Reconstruction: Experiences of Resettlers and Refugees.* Washington, DC: World Bank, pp. 11–55.

Coles, G. J. L. (1985) A Background Study prepared for the Round Table on Voluntary Repatriation Convened by the Office of the United Nations High Commissioner for Refugees in Co-operation with the International Institute of Humanitarian Law, San Remo, 16–19 July.

Eriksen, T. H. (1993) *Ethnicity and Nationalism: Anthropological Perspectives.* London: Pluto Press.

ERREC (1996) *Synoptic Report on Returnees (Refugees) Information, 1989–End 1995.* Asmara: Data and Statistics Department, Eritrean Relief and Rehabilitation Commission.

——— (1997) *Synoptic Report on Returnees (Refugees) Information, 1996–End 1997.* Asmara: Data and Statistics Department, Eritrean Relief and Rehabilitation Commission.

——— (1998) *Synoptic Report on Returnees (Refugees) Information, 1997–End 1998.* Asmara: Data and Statistics Department, Eritrean Relief and Rehabilitation Commission.

Gebre, Y. D. (2002) 'Contextual determination of migration behaviours: The Ethiopian resettlement in light of conceptual constructs', *Journal of Refugee Studies,* 15(3), pp. 265–82.

Gebre, Y. D. and I. Ohta, Comments on the draft paper (e-mail communication, July 2004).

Hammond, L. (1999) 'Framing the discourse of repatriation: Towards a more proactive theory of return migration', in R. Black and K. Koser (eds), *The End of the Refugee Cycle?* Oxford: Berghahn Books, pp. 227–44.

Hansen, A. (1982) 'Self-settled rural refugees in Africa: The case of Angolans in Zambian villages', in A. Hansen and A. Oliver-Smith (eds), *Involuntary Migration and Resettlement: The Problems and Responses of Displaced People.* Boulder: West View Press.

——— (1990) *Refugee Self-settlement versus Settlement on Government Schemes: The Long-Term Consequences for Security, Integration and Economic Development of Angolan Refugees.* Geneva: UNRISD Discussion Paper 17.

hooks, b. (1991) 'Homeplace: A site of resistance', in *Yearning: Race, Gender and Cultural Politics.* London: Turnaround Books.

Horowitz, D. L. (1985) *Ethnic Groups in Conflict.* Berkley: University of California Press.

Ignatieff, M. (1993) *Blood and Belonging: Journeys into the New Nationalism.* London: Vintage.

Kibreab, G. (1987) *Refugees and Development in Africa: The Case of Eritrea.* Trenton, NJ: The Red Sea Press.

——— (1996a) *People on the Edge in the Horn: Displacement, Land Use and the Environment in the Gedaref Region, Sudan.* Oxford: James Currey Publishers.

——— (1996b) *Ready and Willing ... but Still Waiting: The Dilemma of Return of Eritrean Refugees in the Sudan.* Uppsala: Life and Peace Institute.

———— (1996c) 'Left in limbo: Prospects for repatriation of Eritrean refugees from Sudan and the response of the international donor community', in T. Allen (ed.), *In Search of Cool Ground: Displacement and Home Coming in Northeastern Africa.* London: James Currey Publishers.

———— (1996d) 'Eritrean and Ethiopian refugees in Khartoum: What the eye refuses to see', *African Studies Review,* 39(3), pp. 131–78.

———— (1997) *Evaluation of the Programme for Refugee Reintegration and Rehabilitation of Resettlement Areas in Eritrea (PROFERI).* Asmara: USAID.

———— (1998) *Returning Refugees in Eritrea: Reconstruction of Livelihoods.* London: Research Report, Department for International Development.

———— (1999a) 'Revisiting the debate on people, place, identity and displacement', *Journal of Refugee Studies,* 12(4), pp. 384–421.

———— (1999b) 'The consequences of non-participatory planning: Lessons from a livestock provision project to returnees in Eritrea', *Journal of Refugee Studies,* 12(2), pp. 135–60.

———— (2000) 'Resistance, displacement and identity: The case of Eritrean refugees in Sudan', *Canadian Journal of African Studies,* 37(2), pp. 249–96.

———— (2001) *The Politics of Ethno-Religion, Strategic Interests and British Policy on the Disposal of Eritrea 1941–1952.* Paper prepared for the Eritrean Studies Association Summer 2001 Conference, Asmara.

———— (2002a) 'When refugees come home: The relationship between stayees and returnees in post-conflict Eritrea', *Journal of Contemporary African Studies,* 20(1), pp. 53–80.

———— (2002b) *Common Property Institutions, State Intervention and the Environment in Sudan 1890s–1990s.* Lewiston, Queenston, Lampeter: The Edwin Mellen Press.

———— (2003a) 'Citizenship and repatriation of refugees', *International Migration Review,* 37(1), pp. 25–73.

———— (2003b) 'Displaced communities and reconstruction of livelihoods in Eritrea', in T. Addison (ed.), *From Conflict to Recovery in Africa.* Oxford: Oxford University Press, pp. 73–86.

———— (2003c) 'Rethinking household headship among Eritrean refugees and returnees', *Development and Change,* 34(2), pp. 311–37.

———— (2004) 'Refugeehood, loss and social change: Eritrean refugees and returnees', in P. Essed, G. Frerks and J. Schrijvers (eds), *Refugees and Transformation of Societies: Agency, Policies, Ethics and Politics.* Oxford, New York: Berghahn Books, pp. 19–30.

Kymlicka, W. (1995) *Multicultural Citizenship*. Oxford: Oxford University Press.

Levy, J. (2000) *The Multiculturalism of Fear*. Oxford: Oxford University Press.

Malkki, L. (1992) 'National geographic: The rooting of peoples and the territorialisation of national identity among scholars and refugees', *Cultural Anthropology*, 7(1), pp. 24–44.

———(1995) *Purity and Exile: Violence, Memory and National Cosmology among the Hutu Refugees in Tanzania*. Chicago: Chicago University Press.

Manzzini, G. (1995) 'Duties of man', in Omar Dahbour and Miicheline R. Ishay (eds), *The Nationalism Reader*. New Jersey: Humanities Press, pp. 87–97.

Moore, M. (1998) 'The territorial dimension of self-determination', in Margaret Moore (ed.), *National Self-Determination and Secession*. Oxford: Oxford University Press.

Rahmato, D. (1989) 'Settlement and resettlement in post-revolutionary Ethiopia: Problems and prospects', in *Report of Conferences Proceedings Vol. II, Conference on Population Issues in Ethiopia's National Development*. Addis Ababa.

Rawls, J. (1993) *Political Liberalism*. New York: Columbia University Press.

Robinson, J. (2002) 'Introduction', in J. Robinson (ed.), *Development and Displacement*. Oxford: Oxford University Press, pp. 1–18.

Said, E. (1984) 'The mind of winter: Reflections on life in exile', *Harpers*, September, pp. 49–55.

Stepputat, F. (1994) 'Repatriation and the politics of space: The case of the Mayan diaspora and return movement', *Journal of Refugee Studies*, 7(2/3), pp. 175–98.

Tamir, Yael (1993) *Liberal Nationalism*. Princeton: Princeton University Press.

Taylor, C. (1993) *Reconciling the Solitudes: Essays on Canadian Federalism and Nationalism*. Edited by Guy Leforest, Montreal: McGill-Queens University Press.

Turton, D. (2002), 'Forced displacement and the nation-state', in J. Robinson (ed.), *Development and Displacement*. Oxford: Oxford University Press, pp. 19–76.

United Nations Office for the Co-ordination of Humanitarian Affairs (2004) *Eritrea: Humanitarian Update*. Asmara, 16 July.

von Herder, J. G. (1995) 'Reflections on the philosophy of the history of mankind: National genius and the environment, (Book VII)', in Omar Dahbour and Miicheline R. Ishay (eds), *The Nationalism Reader.* New Jersey: Humanities Press, pp. 48–69.

Wajbrandi, B. (1986) *Organised and Spontaneous Settlement in Eastern Sudan: Two Case Studies on Integration of Rural Refugees.* Free University of Amsterdam, Faculty of Economics.

Walzer, M. (1983) *Spheres of Justice: A Defence of Pluralism and Equality.* Oxford: Martin Roberston.

——— (1990) 'The communitarian critique of liberalism', *Political Theory,* 18, pp. 6–23.

Warner, D. (1994) 'Voluntary repatriation and the meaning of return to home: A critique of liberal mathematics', *Journal of Refugee Studies,* 7(2/3), pp. 160–74.

Wolde-Selassie, A. (2000) 'Social re-articulation after resettlement: Observing the Beles Valley Scheme in Ethiopia', in M. M. Cernea and C. McDowell (eds), *Risks and Reconstruction: Experiences of Resettlers and Refugees.* Washington, DC: World Bank, pp. 412–30.

Wolff, S. (2001) 'German expellee organisations between 'homeland' and 'at home': A case study of the politics of belonging', *Refuge,* 20(1), pp. 52–64.

Worby, P. (2000) 'Security, dignity: Land access and Guatemala's returned refugees', *Refuge,* 19(3), pp. 17–24.

5
Returnees in Their Homelands: Land Problems in Rwanda after the Civil War

Shin'ichi Takeuchi and Jean Marara

Introduction

Refugee problems and armed conflicts are closely related. Although people who are displaced involuntarily by an armed conflict are not considered to be refugees according to the definition of the 1951 UN Refugee Convention,[1] the activities of refugee assistance organizations such as the UNHCR are primarily oriented towards the victims of armed conflict. Despite the definition of international law, most refugee problems are in fact created by armed conflicts.[2]

This is especially true in Africa.[3] To explain the scale of the refugee problem in Africa, Crisp notes that 'while Africans constitute only 12 per cent of the global population, around 28 per cent (i.e. 3.2 million) of the world's 11.5 million refugees and just under 50 per cent (i.e. 9.5 million) of the world's 20 million internally displaced persons are to be found in Africa' (Crisp 2000: 158). In both of the areas he cites as principal sub-regions of displacement—five West African countries around Liberia and Sierra Leone and eleven Central African countries around the Democratic Republic of Congo (ex-Zaire, hereafter DR Congo)—the main factor was armed conflicts. The Organization of African Unity adopted a Refugee Convention in 1969, which defined those who took refuge in foreign countries because of a war or armed rebellion as refugees. This recognizes the fact that refugee problems in Africa have been closely connected to armed conflict since the early post-independence period.

If refugees are mainly created by armed conflict, causes and consequences of the conflicts should be considered in any efforts to deal with refugee problems. This is an important point for refugee policy. The current trend in the international community is to promote voluntary repatriation as a policy solution to refugee problems, but while voluntary repatriation is of course desirable, we should be aware that repatriation does not necessarily mean the end of the matter. On the contrary, it might create new problems. It is crucial to maintain the peace and order of society after the repatriation, which requires careful consideration of the potential problems caused by the repatriation itself. In this context, one of the most intractable problems is land availability. In many developing countries, where agriculture is the most important occupation for nationals, the majority of refugees were previously farmers. As a consequence, when they return to their homelands, they immediately need land to make a living. However, providing land to these returnees often sparks conflict with those who already reside in the place.

The Rwanda case provides substantive support for this argument. The close relationship between armed conflict and refugee problems can be clearly observed in Rwanda and the Great Lakes Region. Many Rwandan (mainly Tutsi) refugees took flight during the turmoil that immediately preceded independence, when the kingdom that had administered the country both before and during the colonial era collapsed. About thirty years later, a civil war broke out with the invasion of the Rwandan Patriotic Front (RPF), which had been formed mostly by second generation Rwandan refugees whose parents had fled to Uganda around the time of independence. In 1994, RPF won the war after ferocious fighting and genocide, and established the new 'government of national unity', which called for national reconciliation and invited all Rwandan refugees to return to their home country.

The mass return of refugees created new problems, among which the issue of land distribution is very serious.[4] Rwanda is one of the most densely populated countries in Africa. In fact, President Habyarimana, who governed the country from 1973 to 1994, had used this as a pretext for not allowing the refugees to return. As soon as the RPF established the new regime, however, a tremendous number of returnees flooded back into Rwanda from neighboring countries. At the time, there was another huge exodus of refugees as well, but the majority of them returned two years later. Post-conflict Rwanda is therefore confronted with the land distribution problems created by two massive influxes of returnees.

Rwanda's refugee problem attracted a lot of attention in the international community (UNHCR 2000). But this attention was primarily focused on refugees while they were residing in neighboring countries; once they returned to Rwanda, the international interest rapidly waned. There have been few attempts to date to study the impact of returnees on a country.[5] This chapter tries to analyze, on the basis of the authors' fieldwork conducted from 1999 to 2003, how post-conflict Rwandan rural society is experiencing and responding to the problem of land distribution. We will present comparative data from two different research sites in Rwanda in order to examine the following questions: how might masses of returnees acquire land in a short period; what was the government's policy for returnees; how was such a policy possible; and what new problems are now emerging. We will see that the post-conflict Rwandan government is indeed faced with new land problems. And although our research is at a relatively small scale, we believe that the results can clarify aspects of the new land problems in Rwanda.

Rwandan political change and refugees

Land problems in Rwanda tend to be explained by its high population density. According to a national census in 2002, its average population density was 322 people per square kilometer (République Rwandaise 2003: 17). This is undoubtedly the highest population density level in Africa, but it is not the only reason for the frequent land disputes in Rwanda. As Adriaenssens (1962) and André and Lavigne Delville (1998) point out, political power has often been a significant factor in land distribution in Rwanda. Even in the traditional context, politically powerful chiefs sometimes, for their own benefit, forced ordinary people to leave their land. In the latter half of the twentieth century, political conflicts repeatedly created refugees, who were obliged to abandon their homeland, sometimes for very long periods. Due to these large movements of people, the land in Rwanda has become highly politicized in its modern history. This politicization of land, and the particular ecological conditions, makes Rwanda's rural society highly susceptible to land disputes. In this section, we summarize Rwanda's political changes and fluxes of refugees during this half-century.

The first big wave of refugees fled Rwanda on the eve of independence. In November 1959, the violence sparked by power struggles between political parties transformed into a conflict between two ethnic groups: Tutsi and Hutu.[6] This was the first large-scale ethnic violence in the history of Rwanda. The turning point was when the colonial government provided political and military assistance to the Hutu elites, causing a revolutionary change to the Tutsi-dominated political system: important administrative posts, monopolized until then by Tutsi elites, were rapidly replaced by the Hutu elites and the monarchy was abolished. During this period, which the Hutu elites called the 'Social Revolution', at least several hundred were killed and a large number of refugees, mainly Tutsi, fled to neighboring countries. Although the refugees attempted to invade Rwanda several times during the early 1960s, each failure brought retaliation and persecution upon the Tutsi still in Rwanda, leading to additional outflow of refugees.[7]

There are several estimates of the size of the refugee outflow during this period.[8] Although the difference among them was considerable, the number around 200,000 (between 150,000–250,000) seems to be the likeliest, if we estimate on the basis of the population before the exodus.[9] Regardless of the precise figure, though, it is quite clear that a great number of refugees fled Rwanda due to the Social Revolution in the early 1960s, and most of them were Tutsi.

No significant research has yet been conducted into how the refugees' property was treated after their departure. It is nevertheless certain that their lands were confiscated by the local administration if no family member could inherit them. The decree of 11 July 1960 classified the land in Rwanda into two different legal categories: areas of customary law and areas of codified law. The decree stipulated that a kinship group, namely a family, was primarily responsible for land allocation in rural areas, which was in principal considered to be the area of customary law. However, the state had superior rights to the land, and the local administration, the 'Commune',[10] was made responsible for managing the communal land, such as grazing areas, vacant land, and wetlands. The 'Commune' was also responsible for allocating these lands to peasants (André and Lavigne Delville 1998: 161). Parcels left by refugees were considered to be vacant lands unless someone residing in the area could inherit them. If declared vacant, the Commune could take control and reallocate them. In the following sections, we will see that those parcels that were transferred by the local administration became the source of many land disputes after the civil war of the early 1990s, as returnees reclaimed them.[11]

This civil war and massacre produced the largest movement of refugees in the history of Rwanda. The civil war broke out in October 1990 when the RPF invaded from Uganda. The hard core of the RPF was the second generation of the refugees who had fled to Uganda to escape the Social Revolution.[12] Although a peace treaty (Arusha peace accord), including agreements on the return of refugees and the power sharing, was concluded in August 1993, it totally collapsed in April 1994, when an airplane crashed with Rwandan President Habyarimana onboard, leading to the outbreak of fighting and a nationwide massacre of Tutsi, as well as Hutu opposed to the regime. The RPF, which finally won the war, established a new government in July, but by then more than 500,000 civilians had been massacred.

A series of incidents created a huge flux of refugees. Following the outbreak of civil war, the Tutsi began to flee Rwanda as the Habyarimana government increased its persecution of them. The outflow was considerably accelerated after the fighting broke out in April 1994; almost all Tutsi who had escaped the massacre fled into neighboring countries. At the same time, many civilians, mainly Hutu, took flight from the area controlled by the RPF, as the political leaders of the regime spread the idea that the RPF would kill them in retaliation. When the RPF brought the capital under control in July, enormous numbers of refugees, comprising the former political leaders and civilians, flowed into neighboring countries. At the same time, a massive flow of returnees poured into Rwanda.

Table 5-1 indicates the number of returnees for the years 1994 to 1999. The returnees are divided into two categories: 'Old Case' and 'New Case'. The Old Case refugees are those who fled the country due to the Social Revolution around independence, and their children. Most are Tutsi, and many returned to Rwanda after the RPF's victory in July 1994. The New Case refugees were mainly Hutu who escaped Rwanda in 1994, after the civil war intensified and the RPF regime was established. Table 5-1 shows the scale of return and the time lag between the two categories of refugee: the return of the Old Case refugees was concentrated in the year of 1994, just after the end of the civil war, while the greatest number of New Case refugees returned in 1996, although they continued to return in 1999. The movement of refugees depicted in Table 5-1 can be explained as follows: on the one hand, the Old Case refugees, who could not return while Hutu elites were in power, began to return to Rwanda just after the RPF's

Table 5-1. Number of returnees and internally displaced persons in Rwanda after the civil war[13]

	1994	1995	1996	1997	1998	1999
Population (millions)	5.22	5.7	6.17	7.67	7.88	8.1
No. of 'Old Case' returnees[d]	900,000[a]	146,476	28,646	19,615	7,723	890
No. of 'New Case' returnees[d]	200,000[a]	79,302	1,271,936	199,183	3,167	19,337
Internally Displaced Persons	1,000,000	n.d.	n.d.	n.d.	720,000[c]	40,000[b]

Source: Office of United Nations Resident Coordinator for Rwanda 2000: 2.

a = Government statistics
b = Figures from UNOCHA
c = New IDP fleeing insurgency in North-West
d = 'old caseload returnees,' and 'new caseload returnees' in the original table.
For the meaning of 'Old Case' and 'New Case' returnees, see the text.

Figure 5-1. Local administration and research sites

victory; on the other hand, the New Case refugees, especially civilians, who were mainly Hutu, were taken to refugee camps by the leaders of the Habyarimana regime, stayed there for a while, and then returned to Rwanda after the civil war broke out in the DR Congo in 1996. The fact that New Case refugees continue to return until this day means that a lot of Rwandan refugees remain living in neighboring countries.

Research method and research sites

Two research sites

The authors conducted socio-economic research from 1999 to 2003 in two rural areas in Rwanda. The research was conducted by interviews with fixed households in Rukara District, Umutara Prefecture and Kibingo District, Butare Prefecture[14] (Figure 5-1). In 1999, we carried out a medium-scale socio-economic survey of 208 rural households, of which half was randomly chosen from a Sector in Rukara and the other half from Kibingo.[15] Among the 104 households of each Sector, we chose 22 rural households in Rukara and 21 in Kibingo as subjects for deeper research into their standard of living. Visiting twice a year since 2000, we talked with them about their means of making a living and their wartime experiences. In addition to the interviews, we measured every parcel of land owned and exploited by each household to record changes to their total landholdings. From the year 2000, we included all of the responsible persons of local administration, namely a Sector-chief (*Conseiller*) and Cell-chiefs (*Responsables*), to our interviewees, so that the number came to 26 in Rukara and 25 in Kibingo. The following analysis is primarily based on these data to discuss land problems in Rwanda after the civil war.

Two research sites were chosen in consideration of their contrasting characteristics. To begin with, the geographic features of Rukara and Kibingo are different. Generally speaking, in Rwanda, the further to the east, the lower the altitude, the warmer the temperature, and the lower the precipitation. Rukara District, being situated in the far eastern part of the country, adjoins Akagera National Park, next to Tanzania. The altitude there is about 1300–1500 meters, annual average temperature about 20–21 degrees centigrade, annual rainfall less than 1,000 mm (Bart 1993: 41). The weather conditions in the eastern part of Rwanda are generally more severe than that of the western and central parts, contributing to the former being less densely populated than the latter. Kibingo District enjoys cooler temperature and more abundant precipitation than Rukara. Because of the good climatic condition and the role of the political center since the era of the traditional Kingdom of Rwanda, the population density of southern Rwanda is very high. Ironically, the region was impoverished through overpopulation, which made the cultivated area per household generally small and fragmentary.

These points can be verified by several statistics. Table 5-2 shows the population and the population density by Prefecture in 2002. The population density of Butare greatly exceeds the national average at nearly 400, in contrast to Umutara Prefecture at 100. Average sizes of land holding in each Prefecture are shown in Table 5-3. Although the table has no data for Umutara prefecture, which was created in the mid 1990s, the figure of Kibungo Prefecture, which has similar geographic condition to Umutara, can be used as a reference. Table 5-3 indicates two clear characteristics: the generally small-size of land holdings and the disparities between Prefectures. On the one hand, the national average parcel of cultivated land was only 0.62 ha. On the other hand, the average in Kibungo (1.00 ha)

Table 5-2. Population and population density by prefecture in Rwanda

Prefecture	Population	Area (km²)	Population density
City of Kigali	608,141	313	1,943
Kigali Ngali	792,542	2,780	285
Gitarama	864,594	2,141	404
Butare	722,616	1,872	386
Gikongoro	492,607	1,974	250
Cyangugu	609,504	1,894	322
Kibuye	467,745	1,748	268
Gisenyi	867,225	2,047	424
Ruhengeri	894,179	1,657	540
Byumba	712,372	1,694	421
Umutara	423,642	4,230	100
Kibungo	707,548	2,964	239
Total	8,162,715	25,314	322

Source: République Rwandaise, Service National de Recensement 2003: 17.

Table 5-3. Land use in each prefecture by household (October 1989–March 1990) (ares)

	Butare	Byumba	Cyangugu	Gikongoro	Gisenyi	Gitarama	Kibungo	Kibuye	Kigali	Ruhengeri	Average
Banana	14.51	19.65	10.13	8.51	9.40	21.50	38.33	5.74	17.34	12.45	16.06
Beans	12.20	21.79	9.05	16.99	9.27	12.84	32.95	17.52	19.13	17.84	16.71
Cereals	2.43	8.26	5.38	4.67	10.27	2.03	6.38	17.10	5.62	16.06	7.44
Root crops	15.55	12.42	16.00	14.62	9.60	20.56	14.08	21.50	12.92	13.40	14.95
Industrial crops	5.40	2.37	9.26	4.10	4.69	5.75	5.88	2.89	6.42	0.92	4.71
Vegetables & fruits	0.92	3.66	0.86	2.18	0.72	2.69	2.37	1.80	3.47	2.85	2.25
Cultivated area	51.01	68.13	50.69	51.06	43.95	65.38	99.99	66.55	64.90	63.52	62.11
Fallow & pasturage	22.40	33.47	8.43	26.51	5.07	24.38	39.33	50.56	23.27	11.55	23.70
Cultivable area	73.41	101.60	59.12	77.57	49.02	89.76	139.32	117.12	88.16	75.07	85.81
Woodland	7.63	9.19	6.03	21.52	4.57	9.12	4.07	47.93	3.37	16.60	11.66
Non-cultivable & housing	2.73	3.22	2.30	3.74	2.36	3.28	5.57	2.62	2.63	3.87	3.19
Total Area	83.77	114.01	67.46	102.84	55.95	102.16	148.97	167.67	94.17	95.54	100.66

Source: République Rwandaise, Ministére de l'Agriculture et de l'Elevage 1992: 46.

was double that in Butare (0.51 ha). Although climatic conditions around Butare are suitable for agriculture, overpopulation and small allotments have considerably reduced its standard of living. According to the large-scale survey on poverty, conducted from 1999 to 2001, the proportion of households living below the poverty line in Butare was 74%, the second highest rate among all Prefectures, after Gikongoro (77%). The proportion in Umutara Prefecture (51%) was the second lowest after the city of Kigali (République Rwandaise 2002: 33).[16]

Different characters of the research sites

The results of our field survey confirm that the standard of living is generally lower in Butare than in Umutara. Tables 5-4 and 5-5 indicate the structure of land tenure of the canvassed households from 1999 to

Table 5-4. Land holdings of canvassed households in Kibingo (m²)

	1999	2000	2001	2002	2003
Average exploited land	5,191	4,679	4,787	4,468	4,472
Maximum	21,858	16,779	18,114	17,852	17,357
Minimum	519	0	0	0	0
Standard deviation	4,883.0	4,085.4	4,302.6	4,363.4	4,372.1
Gini coefficient	0.46	0.45	0.45	0.49	0.50
Average owned land	6,236	5,767	5,598	5,477	5,886
Maximum	32,118	32,118	32,831	32,831	40,892
Minimum	399	399	399	399	399
Standard deviation	7,943.6	7,303.3	7,438.8	7,484.7	8,920.8
Gini coefficient	0.57	0.56	0.56	0.58	0.60

Source: Survey data.
Note: N = 21.

Table 5-5. Land holdings of canvassed households in Rukara (m²)

	1999	2000	2001	2002	2003
Average exploited land	9,049	10,112	10,803	10,402	10,633
Maximum	19,079	19,079	21,718	21,718	37,254
Minimum	2,608	2,654	1,859	0	0
Standard deviation	4,131.1	4,076.1	4,828.3	5,226.4	7,887.8
Gini coefficient	0.30	0.27	0.30	0.33	0.43
Average owned land	7,781	8,497	8,552	8,500	9,753
Maximum	19,079	19,079	19,079	19,079	37,254
Minimum	300	2,015	288	288	928
Standard deviation	4,349.7	4,098.2	4,868.0	4,836.1	7,796.8
Gini coefficient	0.36	0.32	0.37	0.37	0.44

Source: Survey data.
Note: N = 22.

2003.[17] Here, 'owned land' is defined as the sum of parcels over which a household considers that it has the first and strongest rights. It comprises parcels acquired by any of the following three methods: 'inheritance', 'purchase' and 'transfer from the state'. This concept of 'owned land' is therefore different from modern property rights. 'Exploited land,' is the sum of parcels directly managed by the household, calculated by adding borrowed parcels to the 'owned land', and deducting lent parcels from it.[18] Although the official agricultural statistics say nothing about borrowing and lending land, they play an important role in agricultural management (See Table 5-6). According to the methodological explication of the agricultural statistics (République Rwandaise 1992: 8), the figures for cultivated lands in Table 5-3 represent what we have called 'exploited land'. The figures for cultivated land in Table 5-3 and for 'exploited land' in Tables 5-4 and 5-5 are not very different.[19]

Drawing on both the official statistics and our field surveys, we can observe some characteristics of Rwanda's rural society. First, it is clear that the land tenure of rural households is generally very small, but the differences between them are important, as the high Gini coefficients indicate. Rural households are clearly not the same; the great majority has only tiny lots, but a few households have relatively large land holdings. Second, although land availability is very limited in general, landless farmers are rare. The majority of rural households manage to survive by borrowing some parcels of land and working in others' fields.[20]

Comparing the Gini coefficients between the two sites, we note that difference in the sizes of land holdings among the canvassed households are greater in Kibingo than in Rukara.[21] This difference can to a large extent be attributed to the division of land between the Old Case and New Case returnees, which occurred often in Rukara. This point will be discussed in detail, but for the moment note that in Kibingo, where the typical land holding is smaller than in Rukara, many households cultivate only tiny fields: in 2002 for instance, out of 21 households, 11 claimed less than 0.3 ha of 'exploited land'.

Table 5-6. Proportions of borrowed land to total exploited land (%)

	1999	2000	2001	2002	2003
Kibingo	7	8	14	10	10
Rukara	14	16	23	19	13

Source: Survey data.

In addition to their dissimilar geographic and socio-economic characteristics, the inhabitants in the two research sites experienced the civil war differently. After the recurrence of the civil war on 6 April 1994, the RPF quickly took control of Umutara Prefecture. According to our interviewees, the research site in Rukara District appeared to be under RPF control by the end of April. Fearing the violent conflict, almost all of the inhabitants fled to Tanzania through the National Park, and took up residence in the refugee camps there. After the new government was established in July, an enormous number of the Old Case refugees returned to the eastern part of Rwanda, especially Umutara and Kibungo Prefecture. Several factors interlink to explain this inflow of Old Case returnees to the eastern part of the country. First, being relatively less densely populated than other areas, and nearer to the borders with Uganda and Tanzania, it was relatively easy for the Old Case returnees to travel to and stay in the area.

Population density and proximity alone, however, are not sufficient to explain this phenomenon. The Old Case returnees were also encouraged by the local authorities to settle there. Although we do not have sufficient information to determine whether this policy was explicitly adopted by the central government, it is at least certain that the measure was in accordance with the intentions of the new government.

The Arusha peace accord between the RPF and the Habyarimana government stipulated that 'refugees who left the country more than ten years ago should not claim their properties if they were occupied by another. In compensation, the government will give them land and help them to resettle'.[22] Under the new political regime, local authorities encouraged the Old Case returnees to occupy any vacant land that they could find rather than returning to their natal place. With the extremely high population densities of western and central Rwanda, the properties of the Old Case returnees had undoubtedly already been occupied by others. Considering the huge number of returnees, their claims for land might give rise to considerable conflicts in these densely populated areas. Locating the Old Case returnees in the eastern part of the country was therefore preferable for the new government, which wanted to minimize the instability that might follow the massive influx of returnees and conflicts over land.

When the Old Case returnees flowed into the eastern part of Rwanda, the majority of the inhabitants of Umutara and Kibungo Prefectures had already fled the country. These New Case refugees, stayed in refugee camps in Tanzania for a period, and then began to return home in late 1996.

It was therefore quite easy for the Old Case returnees to find 'vacant' lands when they arrived in the area in 1994. Two or three years later, when the New Case refugees returned to their homeland, they were faced with the Old Case returnees occupying their houses and lands. The local authorities then directed that houses should be returned to their New Case owners, but the lands should be equally divided between the two. In accordance with this policy, there was a widespread division of land between the Old Case and the New Case returnees in Rukara.

In the Butare area, in contrast, the RPF did not achieve control until July 1994, just before the war ended. Strongly encouraged by the political leaders of the Habyarimana regime to flee, a great majority of Kibingo District inhabitants poured into a camp for internally displaced persons in Gikongoro Prefecture (the Kibeho camp). The leaders themselves, accompanied by a huge number of civilians, continued their way up to the DR Congo, but others remained in the camp. Furthermore, compared to the eastern part of the country, the number of the Old Case returnees that flowed into the Butare area after the war ended was not very large. More specifically, compared to Rukara, few Old Case returnees lived in the rural areas of Kibingo, and they tended to dwell in government provided housing (*imidugudu*). In the period immediately following the civil war, then, the impact of returnees on rural societies was not as significant in Butare as in Umutara.

The different experiences of war in the two regions can be interpreted from the processes of land acquisition. Tables 5-7 and 5-8 present the means of land acquisition among the canvassed households in the two research sites. Based on our interviews, the acquisitions were classified into four categories: 'inheritance', 'purchase', 'transfer from the state', and 'borrowing'.[23] The proportions of 'inheritance' and 'transfer from the state' in the two tables are clearly different. An overwhelming proportion of the land holdings in Kibingo were acquired by 'inheritance', while a considerable proportion of the land in Rukara was 'transferred from the state'. The land 'transferred from the state' in Kibingo was almost exclusively wetlands (*bas-fonds*) between hills. In Rukara, as mentioned, land parcels were often divided between the Old Case and the New Case returnees. Land acquired through this division is included in the category 'transfer from the state' in Table 5-8.[24] As the land was divided under the local authorities' initiative, the Old Case returnees did not consider the land to have been acquired from the New Case returnees, but as donations from the state.

Table 5-7. Means of land acquisition—Kibingo (%)

	1999	2000	2001	2002	2003
Inheritance	76	75	74	73	73
Purchase	15	15	16	17	18
Transfer from the state	9	10	10	10	9
Total owned land	100	100	100	100	100

Source: Survey data.
Note: N = 21.

Table 5-8. Means of land acquisition—Rukara (%)

	1999	2000	2001	2002	2003
Inheritance	45	42	40	39	35
Purchase	15	18	26	27	30
Transfer from the state	40	40	34	34	35
Total owned land	100	100	100	100	100

Source: Survey data.
Note: N = 22.

Division of land between the two sets of 'returnees': The case of Rukara

As discussed, the Umutara area experienced huge outflows and inflows of refugees after the civil war. Among 104 households canvassed in the course of our rural survey in 1999, 32 heads were Old Case returnees, who had returned from Uganda or Tanzania after 1994.[25] Although we cannot calculate their proportions with any precision, it is certain that a considerable number of the Old Case returnees moved into the Umutara area after the war. Hence, land was commonly divided between the Old and New Case returnees in Rukara. Among the 26 households included in our interview and land measurement sample, 12 were headed by Old Case returnees, 11 by New Case returnees, and three were Tutsis who managed to survive the massacre (called 'survivors').[26] All but two of the Old Case returnee households, had acquired their land through division with New Case returnees. The heads of the two households that had not acquired land by division had relatives—one a wife, the other a cousin—who were born in the area and acquired family land from their relatives.

Of the New Case returnees included in our survey, 6 of the 11 households had divided their family land with Old Case returnees. Table 5-9 shows the New Case households of our interviewees having divided their family land

Table 5-9. The New Case returnee households that divided their lands with Old Case returnee households

'New Case' households	'Old Case' households	Division and transfer
R60	R52	Transfer of half of inherited land
R63	n.d.	Transfer of half of inherited land
R71	n.d.	Transfer of all inherited land
R74	n.d.	Transfer of a part of his father's land
R86, R97	R91	Transfer of one third of their father's land

Source: Survey data.

with Old Case returnees. If the Old Case returnees who divided with them were included in our sample, they are also indicated in the table. A detailed discussion of three cases will suffice to illustrate these relationships.

Case Studies

The case of R60

R60, a Hutu born in 1965, lived with his wife (born in 1978), two children (daughters born in 1999 and 2000) and a son of his sister. He was a member of the Gendarme (military police) before the civil war. After stints at Kigali and Ruhengeri, he was posted to Gisenyi in early 1994. In July, informed that the RPF had taken control of the capital, he crossed the border, without fighting, and escaped into the DR Congo. He returned to Rukara in December 1996. Arriving in his homeland, he found that his fields, inherited from his grandfather, had been occupied by an Old Case returnee (R52, born in 1941). He was therefore obliged to divide his fields with R52. Among the five parcels that R60 had inherited, he gave half of each of four parcels to R52, keeping the smallest one for himself. As of August 2002, the total area of his exploited lands (identical to his owned lands) amounted to 0.97 ha. Except for a parcel that he purchased in 2002 as a site for a new house (0.06 ha), the size of his property was almost equal to R52's (0.88 ha). The relationship between R60 and R52 was harmonious; the latter had given the former a calf in thanks for the land. In 2001, R52, who had been a widower, married a young cousin of R60, born in 1981.

The case of R86 and R97

R86 (born in 1971) and R97 (born in 1974) are Hutu brothers. When the war recurred in April 1994, their mother was killed by an RPF soldier, and the family fled to Tanzania in fear. After more than two years in a refugee camp, they returned to their homeland in December 1996, where they found their family land occupied by R91. Their father had a second wife, so he divided the land into three equal portions, giving one to R91, and another to the second wife and her seven children. He then divided the final piece into four roughly equal parcels for his three children (including R86 and R97) and himself. The father and his late first wife had a fourth son who was still in Tanzania as of August 2003. If he returns to Rukara, they will have to divide the land once again. Figure 5-2 depicts the family relations.

R91, a Tutsi born in 1964 in Uganda, belongs to the second generation of the Old Case refugees. He returned in 1994 with his father, born in

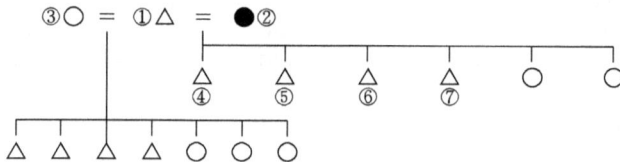

Source: Survey data.
Note: ① Their father (born in 1945), ② First wife of the father, their mother (died in 1994), ③ Second wife (born in 1974) with seven small children, ④ Their elder brother (born in 1968, staying in Tanzania), ⑤ R86 (born in 1971), ⑥ R97 (born in 1974), ⑦ Their younger brother (born in 1983).

Figure 5-2. Kinship diagram for R86 and R97

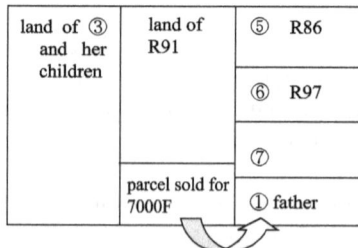

Source: Survey data.
Note 1: Numbers in Figure 5-3 correspond to those in Figure 5-2.
Note 2: The father (①) possessed all of the land before the civil war.
Note 3: This is a conceptual figure. The father's parcel is bigger than that sold by R91.

Figure 5-3. The land division concerning R86, R97 and R91

Butare in 1925. Having been persuaded by the local authorities not to return to Butare, they decided to settle in Rukara. The father acquired his land by division from a New Case returnee. Using a sewing machine he had recently purchased, R91 could earn some income from tailoring. He therefore decided to sell part of his field (0.09ha) to the father of R86 and R97 for 7,000 Frw. Figure 5-3 illustrates this division of land. As of August 2003, that is, after the sale, R91 still owned 0.53 ha of land, in contrast to R86 whose parcel was a mere 0.29 ha and R97 at 0.26 ha. With such small parcels of their own, the two brothers had to borrow other fields to support themselves and their families.

The case of R71
This is a rather peculiar case, because this New Case returnee lost all of his land property after the war. R71 (Hutu, born in 1974) came to settle in Rukara District in 1985, when his father purchased a parcel which was situated near the National Park. He fled to Kigali in April 1994 when the civil war broke out. When he returned in July 1996, he found that a ranch managed by a former RPF officer had enclosed the fields he had inherited from his father. The former officer had been officially granted the use of the land by the local administration, who considered it to be vacant. When R71 took his grievance to the local administration, he was given a substitute lot of 0.44 ha within the area of our research site. However, he had to give-up these fields in 2000, when the previous landowner, who had also taken refuge, returned. The local administration gave him another lot of 0.74 ha in the same area. But a year later, he was once again obliged to abandon his fields because of the return of the previous owner. He could not divide either piece of land with the returnees, as Old Case returnees had done, explaining that this was impossible for a New Case returnee.[27] In early 2002, he travelled to Uganda alone to work, leaving his wife and baby in Rukara. As of August 2003, his wife was using a small parcel inside the ranch to cultivate some food crops for herself, at the invitation of the former officer. He also permitted others who had lived in the area now comprising his ranch before the war to use land, but without giving them ownership.

Instability of land rights
Because of the huge influx of Old Case returnees to the Rukara District, many of the original inhabitants were compelled to divide their land. Although this process could have serious repercussions, the local authorities were very optimistic about it. We systematically asked the local authorities (a Sector-chief and four Cell-chiefs) what they thought about the division of land. All replied that it had not caused serious disputes. In

their opinions, the peasants understood very well the necessity of the land division for peaceful coexistence with the Old Case returnees.

The canvassed households concur that no apparent conflict has broken out in response to the division of land. But the local authorities' claims must nevertheless be read as an official discourse. We will discuss the various reasons for their particular replies shortly. But in our interviews with ordinary people, tensions over the land division were apparent. Although there certainly were harmonious relationships, such as the case of R60 and R52, we should nevertheless not draw general conclusions on this basis. For one thing, of the Old Case returnees who had acquired land by division, some expressed anxiety about the discontent of New Case returnees.

For example, R1 (Tutsi born in 1969) admitted that the man who had divided the land for him was unhappy about it. R1 returned from Uganda in 1994 and acquired a piece of land (0.53 ha) by division. Managing a small shop near the market, he had been relatively successful in business. He could therefore purchase another lot of 0.81 ha for 72,000 Frw in 2000. When we interviewed him shortly after the purchase, he insisted that he intended to return the field that he had acquired by division to its previous owner, but he had not done so as of August 2003. The more unpredictable life is, the more important land property becomes as a means of production. Thus even though he was aware that the former landowner, his neighbor, was discontent, it was not easy to part with the field.

The previously discussed case of R91, who sold part of his land, can be interpreted in the same way. R91's standard of living was, by all appearances, better than his neighbors', because in addition to his own land, his father, who had returned from Uganda with him, had acquired divided parcels from another family. Although no open conflict had yet broken out, this apparent inequality seemed dangerous—in the sense that it could easily stimulate jealousy and dissatisfaction among his poorer neighbors, who had given up land for him. At the same time, his success as a tailor gave him relative independence from agriculture. The latter point seems to be the principal reason for R91 to have sold part of his land back to the former owner. In 2002, he began to build a new house on a lot near the market, which would also serve as his tailor's shop. Clearly, he was trying to shift the weight of economic activity from agriculture to tailoring, a shift which appears to at least in part have been motivated by the potential conflict with his New Case returnee neighbors.

These examples from Rukara illustrate the instability of land rights. On the one hand, the land rights of the New Case returnees were clearly unstable after the war, as they were often obliged to divide their property with Old Case returnees. The New Case returnees may understandably regard this as a violation of their legitimate rights. At the same time, while the Old Case returnees could acquire land through such divisions, their rights were not stable either, ensured only by the legitimacy (or force) of the present political regime. Rwanda's recent history clearly shows that their land rights could easily be lost by political changes at the national level.

Increase of land disputes: The case of Kibingo

In contrast to Rukara, we heard numerous reports of land disputes during our research in Kibingo. We conducted systematic interviews about land disputes in 2002. Among the 25 interviewees, 12 households admitted to having been involved in a dispute over land since 1999. The 12 households and the nature of the disputes are indicated in Table 5-10. Two categories of dispute are distinguishable: those within a family and those with Old Case returnees. Land disputes within families have been generally observed for many years. For example, in the case of K63, a divorced sister returned to her homeland and claimed land rights. Although K63 gave her a parcel, the sister was not satisfied and demanded more. This kind of land dispute is not directly related to political change, but may nevertheless increase in number or intensity as a result of political change. For instance, K66, an old widow born in 1945, recently had to hand over a considerable part of her land to one of her family members who had taken refuge in the DR Congo and then returned.

Land disputes with Old Case returnees, however, are inextricably related to the recent civil war, as the following three case studies reveal:

Case studies

The case of K97
K97, a Hutu, was born in 1934 in the southern part of Butare Prefecture, near the border with Burundi. He moved to the research site in 1961 and had lived there ever since. When he had first moved into the area, the *Bourgmestre* (chief of the Commune) had authorized him to occupy a piece of land. He had even purchased a land certificate for 50 Frw. However, the parcel that the local authority had given him had previously belonged to a family who had fled in 1959. When the family returned to Kibingo in 2000, they asked K97 to give the land back to them. Having resided in Kibingo for so long, K97 could not claim any land in his birthplace. He finally decided to divide his land, giving half of it back to the Old Case

Table 5-10.   Households admitting to having land disputes in Kibingo
              (investigation in 2002)

Household number	Ethnicity of household head	Outbreak of dispute (year)	Type of dispute
1. Land dispute with family members			
K3	Tutsi	2000	Division of an inherited parcel for three female relatives: an aunt, a cousin and a sister.
K4	Hutu	2000	Division of an inherited parcel for the second wife of his grandfather.
K63	Hutu	2002	Dispute with a sister who claimed to be given a bigger parcel.
K65	Hutu	2002	Claim of land by the second wife of the late husband.
K66	Hutu	2002	Division of an inherited parcel, as a family member returned from the DR Congo.
2. Land dispute concerning refugee return			
K1	Hutu	2001	Dispute with an Old Case returnee who claimed his rights in a purchased parcel.
K3	Tutsi	2000	Dispute with an Old Case returnee who claimed his rights in an inherited parcel.
K26	Hutu	2002	Dispute with an Old Case returnee who claimed his right in a parcel inherited from his father, who had been given it by the local authority.
K55	Hutu	1986	Deprivation of a purchased parcel during a long absence (see the text).
K56	Tutsi	2002	Dispute with an Old Case returnee who claimed his right in a parcel that the husband had purchased (see the text).
K97	Hutu	2000	Division of a parcel transferred from the local authority for an Old Case returnee (see the text).
3. Other reasons			
K20	Hutu	2000	Deprivation of a borrowed parcel despite payment.

Source: Survey data.

returnees. As of 2003, a field of 0.11 ha and a small parcel of woodland
(0.24 ha) were his total property, with which to feed his family.

The case of K56

K56 (born in 1966) is a Tutsi woman who survived the genocide. Before
the war, her husband (a Hutu) earned money from agriculture, tailoring,
the production of folk crafts, and running a bar (selling banana beer and

sorghum beer). During the genocide, her husband had hidden her behind a wall of the bar. While hiding there, she had heard the voices of visitors beyond the wall, boasting of horrible acts of killing and looting. In July 1994, she fled with her family to the Kibeho camp. After returning to Kibingo, her husband was arrested and jailed in Butare in May 1996 on suspicion of genocide. As her own father and brothers had been killed during the genocide, she inherited their fields (2.76 ha) in an adjoining Sector, making her the largest landowner among the 25 canvassed households in Kibingo. Lending the majority of this inherited land to others, her exploited land was only 0.80 ha in 2002, of which 0.21 ha was her husband's family land, 0.28 ha was her own inherited land, 0.25 ha had been purchased by her husband, and a 0.06 ha parcel of wetland was transferred by the local administration. Of these, a dispute broke out with an Old Case returnee over 0.03 ha that her husband had purchased. This parcel had originally belonged to the Old Case returnee, who had fled the country in 1960. After he had fled, the land was confiscated by the local administration and reallocated to another peasant, who had sold it to K56's husband in 1989. K56 had requested the intervention of the District administrator when the Old Case returnee occupied the entire parcel of land, demanding compensation, either monetary or in kind (i.e., another parcel of land).

The case of K55

Among the canvassed households in Kibingo, only K55 (born in 1927) had been a refugee of the Social Revolution. In spite of his Hutu ethnic affiliation, he had been a sympathizer of the UNAR (Union Nationale Rwandaise), a party loyal to the king and supported mainly by the Tutsi. When the PARMEHUTU (Parti du Mouvement de l'Emancipation Hutu), a republican party supported mainly by the Hutu, took power immediately before independence, its supporters began to persecute the other parties' sympathizers. In August 1961, K55 was obliged to flee to Tanzania in fear for his life. Life in Tanzania had been stable, but he returned to Kibingo in 1986 to take care of his mother who was living there alone. Upon his return, he found that a parcel of land he had purchased before his flight had been occupied by an unfamiliar inhabitant. He requested that the authorities return the parcel, but the Sector-chief rejected the request and threatened to put him in jail, on the grounds of having been in exile for a long period. After the war ended in 1994, he asked the new Sector-chief to settle the dispute and was finally permitted to recover the majority of the parcel in 2003.

Political change and land problems

These cases reveal several characteristics of the land disputes with Old Case returnees in Kibingo. First, it is clear that the root cause of these conflicts can be traced to the political turmoil around the time of independence (i.e. the Social Revolution), which forced the Old Case returnees to flee their homeland. These accounts of land disputes reveal that in the aftermath of the Social Revolution, the land abandoned by the Old Case was confiscated by the local authority and reallocated. These parcels were thus officially granted to their new owners, who therefore felt that they had done nothing wrong.[28] Second, the rights to land were further complicated by sales and inheritances. In the case of K56, for example, the disputed land had been sold to her husband by a man who had acquired it from the local authority. Clearly such complications increase the difficulty of settling the dispute to anyone's satisfaction. Third, ethnic relationships in Rwanda are so complex that framing an interpretation of the land disputes through the dichotomy between Tutsi and Hutu is quite misleading. There has been a tendency since the genocide to interpret every social phenomena in Rwanda through this ethnic framework. On the surface, this seems to be an obvious approach, since the Old Case returnees are mainly Tutsi and the New Case returnees are mainly Hutu, but the situation is far more complex. We can begin to discern these complexities when we consider that K3 and K56 are both Tutsi, whose land disputes were with Old Case returnees; or that K55, a Hutu, was a refugee from the Social Revolution, and his confiscated land was not returned to him.

Land problems and local authority

Although there are land problems in both Rukara and Kibingo, the responses of the local authorities to these problems were quite different. On one hand, local authorities in Rukara tended to down-play the seriousness of the tensions caused by returnees, many even denying that such tensions existed between the Old and New Case returnees. On the other hand, the local authorities in Kibingo were quite forthcoming about the frequency and seriousness of land disputes. How do we explain the different attitudes of these local authorities?

Two factors have already been mentioned: the socio-economic conditions and the timing of the returns. The local authorities in Kibingo seemed to be greatly concerned that a huge influx of Old Case refugees demanding land would have a negative impact on already difficult living conditions. As discussed, the land holdings are generally small and the standard of living low in Kibingo. Compared to Rukara District, the situation in Kibingo was therefore more vulnerable to the impact of Old Case returnees. Our examples clearly illustrate this situation. Only 0.11 ha of cultivated land was left for K97 after having divided land with an Old Case returnee. In another case, K26 was directed to return his small family plot (0.13 ha). Although it did not receive as many Old Case returnees as Rukara, their arrival nevertheless appears to have seriously affected Kibingo.

The timing also appears to be an important factor for explaining the different attitudes of the local authorities. The sharp increase in the number of land disputes with the Old Case in Kibingo has only occurred quite recently. In Rukara, where the Old Case returnees had occupied the land of the New Case returnees during their absence, the majority of the land divisions were completed in 1996 and 1997, when the latter returned from the refugee camps. In Kibingo District, however, there was a time-lag between the end of the civil war and the largest waves of Old Case returnees. The latter's demand for land in the area therefore only began to increase recently. The very new-ness of the phenomenon is perhaps the most significant reason why the local authorities in Kibingo emphasized the frequency of land disputes when interviewed; but this still requires further explanation.

The time lag between the land disputes in the two research sites high-lights another important problem. As mentioned, during the massive return of the Old Case refugees in 1994, local administrations directed them to occupy whatever vacant land they could find in the border areas. Rwandan policy makers appear to have been trying to contain the influence of massive returns to those prefectures where the land was relatively abundant. The recent increase in land disputes with Old Case returnees in Kibingo, however, might signify the limitations of that policy. In many cases, the Old Case returnees now claiming land rights in Kibingo did not return there directly: rather, upon their return they first settled in other places, such as Umutara or Kibungo Prefecture. Only later did they decide to re-turn to their birth places, where they might claim legitimate land rights. This second relocation was not infrequently motivated by trouble with their neighbors in the first resettlement. That is, many of them chose to return to their homeland after serious disputes with their neighbors made life uncomfortable, if not dangerous.[29] Although there was no overt con-flict among the canvassed households in Rukara, the increasing number of land disputes in Kibingo indirectly reveals the frictions between the Old and New Case returnees in other areas.

The life histories of the local authorities can also provide some insight into their attitudes. Table 5-11 lists some features of the local authorities and clearly reveals differences between the two research sites. Four of the five local administrators in Rukara at the time were Old Case returnees. In the election of March 2002, the Sector-chief was replaced by 'Cell-chief 2', a 'survivor', but his previous post of Cell-chief was filled by another Old Case returnee. In this area, the Old Case returnees occupy a considerable proportion of important administrative posts. Under these circumstances, then, it might be difficult to express grievances about the division of land. In contrast, there were no Old Case returnees occupying any post of the local authority in Kibingo during the same period. As Table 5-11 indicates, the Sector-chief was a 'survivor', and of the four Cell-chiefs, three were Hutu and one was a 'survivor'. The administrators in Kibingo are also more or less compliant with the political direction of the government. Nevertheless, since they are not Old Case returnees themselves, they might be more sensitive to the problems caused by the return of the Old Case refugees, and more frank in their discussion of these problems than their colleagues in Rukara.

Concluding remarks

After the civil war ended in 1994, following the establishment of the new RPF-led regime, a tremendous number of Rwandan refugees returned to their home country in a very short period. Settling in areas where the population density was generally low, they succeeded in acquiring land by division. The land division was overseen by the local authorities in order to assure new land for the Old Case returnees. Although we do not have sufficient information to ascertain the extent to which the new government detailed or supported this policy, it is unlikely that these measures were implemented without its approval. For the newly established government, minimizing the turmoil that would accompany the mass return of Old Case refugees was imperative. The policy of dividing the land between the Old and New Case returnees seems to have been part of a strategy to contain the impact of mass returns within relatively limited geographical areas, thus curbing the potential for turmoil.

Land division is a risky approach to providing land to returnees, because of its potential for creating strong friction between the new and

Table 5-11. Local authorities in two research site (1999–March 2002)

	No.	Year of birth	Sex	Ethnicity	Dwelling Before the war	Just after the war	Old Case returnee
Rukara							
Sector-chief	R3	1955	M	Tutsi	Uganda	Rukara	yes
Cell-chief 1	R29	1949	M	Tutsi	Uganda	Rukara	yes
Cell-chief 2	R105	1960	M	Tutsi	Rukara	camp in Tanzania	
Cell-chief 3	R106	1947	M	Tutsi	Uganda	Rukara	yes
Cell-chief 4	R107	1963	M	Tutsi	Tanzania	Rukara	yes
Kibingo							
Sector-chief	K108	1970	M	Tutsi	Kibingo	camp in Burundi	
Cell-chief 1	K1	1943	M	Hutu	Kibingo	camp in Gikongoro	
Cell-chief 2	K105	1957	M	Tutsi	Kibingo	camp in Burundi	
Cell-chief 3	K106	1963	M	Hutu	Kibingo	camp in Gikongoro	
Cell-chief 4	K107	1971	M	Hutu	Burundi	Burundi	

Source: Survey data.

original habitants. Two factors seem to stand out for explaining how such measures could be relatively successfully implemented in Rwanda. First, the Old Case returnees' strong influence in the local administration was crucial to implementing the policy. Especially in Rukara, where Old Case returnees occupied many posts in the local administration, they played very important roles in implementing the policy and controlling grievances. Second, the RPF's victory in the civil war and the new regime they established were pivotal factors. The government and RPF made it clear that they favored the transfer of land to the Old Case returnees, thus providing strong support for the policy, even though there were not many Old Case returnees in local administrative posts.

There has been no significant violence over land disputes in Rwanda since the end of the civil war. This is somewhat surprising when we consider that more than 500,000 Old Case refugees returned in a short time-frame and that many of them acquired land by division. The relative peacefulness of this process perhaps indicates that the new RPF-led administration has been successful in establishing a new political order in post-conflict Rwanda.

However, it is as yet too early to judge whether the new government has successfully dealt with the land distribution problems caused by the mass return of refugees. The two types of land problems we have examined in this chapter are clearly closely related phenomena. Considering that many Old Case returnees recently claiming land in Kibingo had initially settled elsewhere upon their return to Rwanda, the increasing number of land disputes in the area may indicate that tensions about land divisions are increasing in the regions where these returnees initially settled. The government appears to be facing an increasingly difficult challenge in managing discontent about land distribution all over the country.

This examination of land problems at two research sites makes it clear that such problems originate from national level political changes: i.e. power shifts by the Social Revolution around independence and by the civil war in the 1990s. Following the RPF's victory in 1994, the Old Case returnees were able to acquire land under the strong influence of the government. At the same time, the present political situation is the only guarantee for these property rights. If the political situation once again becomes unstable, the land tenure of the Old Case returnees may be called into question in both Rukara and Kibingo.

Rwanda's modern history is marked by repeated power shifts which have highly politicized already scarce land. As a result, land rights in Rwanda have often been dependent upon the legitimacy of the national government. Any analysis of Rwanda's land problems must take this into account.

Notes

1 See the 1951 Convention Relating to the Status of Refugees, Article 1.
2 In this paper, the terms 'refugee' and 'refugee problem' are used in the broader sense that includes victims of armed conflict, not in the narrow sense defined by the 1951 UN Refugee Convention.
3 In this paper, 'Africa' refers to Sub-Saharan Africa.
4 Land problems are of course not the only problems which returnees have to face. For example, Cernea (2000) indicates eight principal risks for displaced populations: landlessness, joblessness, homelessness, marginalization, food insecurity, increased morbidity, loss of access to common property resources, and community disarticulation. Considering that the overwhelming majority of returnees are farmers, the importance of land is obvious; landlessness often lies at the heart of several other disadvantages, such as joblessness, homelessness, food insecurity, and increased morbidity.
5 The few exceptions are studies about the problem of 'villagisation'; see for example Hilhorst and van Leeuwen (1999; 2000); van Leeuwen (2001).
6 Limitations of space prevent us from defining Rwanda's ethnic groups. We must limit ourselves to a few important points. Three ethnic groups,

Hutu, Tutsi and Twa, compose the Rwandan population; Hutu is the most numerous, comprising more than 80%, while Tutsi is about 14% and Twa is about 1%. All three groups share the same language and live in mixture. Their ethnic consciousness was elevated under the colonial administration. For the historical formation of Tutsi and Hutu, see Newbury (1988) and Vansina (2001).

7   Rwanda's political process around the independence was described in detail in Lemarchand (1970) and Reyntjens (1985).

8   Lemarchand estimates the number at the end of 1963 as about 130,000 (1970: 172); Lugan about 200,000–300,000 (1997: 436); Reyntjens about 300,000 (1985: 455). The number in the year of 1964 was estimated by the UNHCR as 336,000, of which 200,000 were in Burundi, 78,000 in Uganda, 36,000 in Tanzania, and 22,000 in the DR Congo (Prunier 1995).

9   Rwanda's population in 1959—before the exodus—was about 2.6 million. About 14% was Tutsi, making the number of Rwandan Tutsi 344,000. It was said that between 40 and 70% of Tutsi, therefore between 137,600 and 240,800, fled from the country between 1959 and 1964. As Rwandan Hutu also fled the country, we can estimate that between 150,000 and 250,000 Rwandan flowed out as refugees at that time. This calculation is based mainly on Mamdani (2001: 319, n.6).

10   The Commune was a unit of local administration, later reorganized into 'Districts' in 2001. See n.14.

11   Another period of internal and external political instability pushed refugees out in 1973. In Burundi, more than 100,000 civilians, mainly Hutu, were massacred in 1972 after an attempted coup d'état. The incident fueled tensions in Rwanda, and thus increased the instability of the Kaybanda regime, which had already weakened. In February 1973, the regime, looking for scapegoats, started to organize a campaign to purge Tutsi from urban areas. As a result, many highly educated Tutsi, including workers in the formal sector (such as government administration and important private companies) and university students, fled the country. In July, Defense Minister Juvenal Habyarimana, a Hutu elite like Kaybanda, overthrew the regime on the pretext of controlling the turmoil and saving Tutsi. Once he had power, Habyarimana refused to permit the return of Rwandan refugees because, he claimed, of the shortage of land.

12   Participating in armed struggle of the National Resistance Movement led by Museveni, Rwandan refugees played an important role in the process of establishing the new Ugandan regime in 1986. Ugandan policy on Rwandan refugees varied from government to government. The Obote

administration purged them in the late 1960s. The Amin administration, on the contrary, recruited them into the army and secret police. This motivated the Obote II administration to repress Rwandan refugees, which in turn led to the refugees supporting Museveni's anti-government movement (Mamdani 2001: Chapter 6).

13 We should be cautious about using the figures in Table 5-1. Although the table is useful for understanding the approximate sizes of the two refugee returns and the time lag between them, the figures are disputable, especially for 1994. The UNHCR estimated the number of Rwandan refugees in 1993 as 447,900 (UNHCR 2000: 250), which could be considered as the number of the Old Case refugees at that time. Estimating from the fact that the population of Rwanda roughly tripled between 1960 and 1994, if 200,000 flowed out by the early 1960s, their number would be about 600,000 in 1994. In any case, the figure in Table 5-1 (900,000) seems to be overestimated.

14 The largest unit of local administration in Rwanda is a 'Prefecture,' which generally has several hundred thousand inhabitants, and is composed of several 'Districts,' the second largest unit with a population of tens of thousands. A 'District' is composed of several 'Sectors' with a population of several thousand, and the smallest administrative unit is a 'Cell' with several hundred inhabitants.

15 For results of the survey, see Takeuchi and Marara 2000.

16 In this survey, the poverty line was fixed at 64,000 Rwandan francs (Frw). Calculated at the August 2001 exchange rate, this was approximately the equivalent of US$150.

17 To ensure the continuity of data, the data sets for Tables 5-4 and 5-5 contain only the households we had been interviewing since 1999 (22 in Rukara, 21 in Kibingo).

18 Concerning the acquisition of land, we distinguish the following concepts. 'Inheritance' is a transfer of family lands. 'Purchase' is an acquisition of lands by paying money. 'Transfer from the state' is an allocation of lands by the local administration. 'Borrow' and 'lend' mean using land temporarily, either with or without payment.

19 The land areas that we measured include cultivated land (owned and borrowed parcels), as well as fallow and woodland. Fallow is generally scarce and difficult to discern from other fields. Among the canvassed households, only two (K97 and R4) have woodland. While K97 possessed a small lot (0.24 ha) from the beginning of our research, R4 acquired a significant parcel (2.64 ha) in February 2003. This is the main reason for the Gini coefficients in Rukara to abruptly increase in that year. If we

exclude R4's woodland and recalculate it, the Gini coefficients for both exploited land and owned land in Rukara in 2003 decrease to 0.33.

20 In Tables 5-4 and 5-5, the minimum size of exploited land was zero in several years. These are households whose heads are either dead, have disappeared, or left the rural area to seek employment in town.

21 According to our survey, the average area of 'owned land' was larger than the 'exploited land' in Kibingo, while the latter was larger than the former in Rukara. As more households borrow parcels than lend them, the 'exploited land' were generally larger than the 'owned land.' The peculiarity of our data in Kibingo can be attributed to one household, whose female head inherited large fields after her father and brothers were killed during the genocide, and lent them to others (the case of K56, we will discuss later). This is a special case, but the tendency that the gap among the holding area of the 'exploited land' is smaller than that among the 'owned land' is correctly indicated in the figures of Gini coefficients in Tables 5-4 and 5-5.

22 Agreement on Refugees of 9 June 1993, Article 4 (our translation from French text).

23 Among four categories, 'inheritance' and 'borrowing' were in some cases difficult to distinguish. Borrowings without rent between family members or friends were common, and a 'borrowing' can become an 'inheritance' in the long term. Thus, although the classification was in principle based on the interview, it ultimately relies our judgment.

24 In Kibingo, no one among the canvassed households had acquired land by such a division.

25 Here, a 'head' of household means the person who principally supported the household. In the case of a couple, the husband was regarded as the head, in principle. Among 32 heads, 30 had returned from Uganda, and two from Tanzania.

26 It is common in Rwanda to use the word 'survivor' (or 'réscapé' in French) to indicate those Tutsis who managed to survive the genocide.

27 When we asked the Sector chief if R71's explanation was true, he denied it, informing us that everyone who needed land could apply to the local administration for a division. We have not yet verified the official regulations on this point, but considering the general scarcity of land, the time-lag (almost all land divisions were completed immediately after the return of the New Case refugees, i.e. during 1996 and 1997), and his status as a New Case returnee, it is easy to imagine that acquiring such a division would be very difficult for R71 (in our survey, we did not find any cases in which a New Case returnee acquired land by division).

28 Although the Arusha agreement stipulated that refugees who had stayed
    abroad for more than ten years had lost their land rights in Rwanda, as
    we have seen, some Old Case returnees recovered their land in Kibingo.
    In fact, people generally consider that if an Old Case returnee makes a
    claim to prior land rights, it is difficult to ignore it. A Sector-chief in
    Kibingo explained three principles of land division: (1) The total of the
    claimed land would be returned to the Old Case returnee, if the current
    owner does not reside there and has other land property; (2) If the current
    landowner resides on the claimed land but owns other parcels, all of the
    land property except the house would be returned to the returnee; (3)
    If the current landowner resides on the claimed land and owns no other
    parcels, the land would be divided into two equal part for each (interview
    16 August 2002). The parcels of K97 had been divided according to the
    third principle.
29 During his research into 'villagisation (*imidugudu*)', Jean Marara
    interviewed returnees in Kibingo, where he found several similar
    cases.

References

Adriaenssens, J. (1962) *Le droit foncier au Rwanda*, mimeo.

André, Catherine and Philippe Lavigne Delville (1998) 'Changements fanciers
    et dynamiques agraires: le Rwanda, 1900–1990', in Philippe Lavigne
    Delville (Dir.), *Quelles politiques foncières pour l'Afrique rurale?*
    Réconcilier pratiques, légitimité et légalité. Paris: Kartala.

Bart, François (1993) *Montagnes d'Afrique, terres paysannes: le cas du*
    Rwanda. Talence: Presses Universitaires de Bordeaux.

Cernea, Michael M. (2000) 'Risks, safeguards, and reconstruction: A model
    for population displacement and resettlement', in Michael M. Cernea and
    Christopher McDowell (eds), *Risks and Reconstruction: Experiences of*
    Resettlers and Refugees. Washington DC: World Bank.

Crisp, Jeff (2000) 'Africa's refugees: Patterns, problems and policy challenges',
    Journal of Contemporary African Studies, 18(3), pp. 157–78.

Hilhorst, Dorothea and Mathijs van Leeuwen (2000) 'Emergency and
    development: The case of *imidugudu*, villagization in Rwanda', *Journal*
    of Refugee Studies, 13(3), pp. 264–80.

——— (1999) *Imidugudu, Villagisation in Rwanda: A Case Study of*
    Emergency Development. Wageningen Disaster Studies, Disaster
    Sites, No. 2.

Lemarchand, René (1970) *Rwanda and Burundi.* London: Pall Mall Press.

Lugan, Bernard (1997) *Histoire du Rwanda: De la préhistoire à nos jours.* Courtry: Bartillat.

Mamdani, Marmood (2001) *When Victims Become Killers: Colonialism, Nativism, and the Genocide in Rwanda.* Princeton: Princeton University Press.

Newbury, Catharine (1988) *The Cohesion of Oppression: Clientship and Ethnicity in Rwanda, 1860–1960.* New York: Columbia University Press.

Office of United Nations Resident Coordinator for Rwanda (2000) *Common Country Assessment Papers, No. 3 (Resettlement & Reintegration).* Kigali.

Prunier, Gerard (1995) *The Rwanda Crisis, 1959–1994; History of a Genocide.* London: Hurst & Company.

République Rwandaise, Ministère de l'Agriculture et de l'Élevage (1992) *Enquête nationale agricole 1990: Production, superficie, rendement, élevage et leur évolution 1984–1990.* Kigali.

République Rwandaise, Ministère des Finances et de la Planification Économique (2002) *Rapport final, Enquête intégrale sur les conditions de vie des ménages au Rwanda (2000–2001).* Kigali.

République Rwandaise, Service National de Recensement (2003) *Recensement général de la population et de l'habitat, Rwanda: 16–30 août 2002.* Kigali.

Reyntjens, Filip (1985) *Pouvoir et droit au Rwanda; Droit public et évolution politique, 1916–1973.* Tervuren: Musée Royal de l'Afrique Centrale.

Takeuchi, Shin'ichi and Jean Marara (2000) *Agriculture and Peasants in Rwanda: A Preliminary Report.* Tokyo: Institute of Developing Economies, Joint Research Series No. 127.

UNHCR (2000) *The State of World's Refugees: Fifty Years of Humanitarian Action.* Oxford: Oxford University Press.

van Leeuwen, Mathijs (2001) 'Rwanda's Imidugudu programme and earlier experiences with villagisation and resettlement in East Africa', *Journal of Modern African Studies*, 39(4), pp. 623–4.

Vansina, Jan (2001) *Le Rwanda ancien: Le royaume nyiginya.* Paris: Karthala.

Part 2
Development- and Conservation-Induced Displacement

6
Concept and Method: Applying the IRR Model in Africa to Resettlement and Poverty

Michael M. Cernea

Introduction

Forced population displacement is a painful social pathology, regardless of whether it is caused by justified development programs, or by atrocious conflicts such as civil wars, inter-state wars, or violent ethnic persecution. *Development-induced* forced displacements and *war/conflict-caused* forced displacements, although emerging from different causes, share profound similarities, as well as important differences. The African continent has experienced, and continues to experience, both types of population displacements and their severe consequences.

This chapter examines the *impoverishment processes* in forced displacements, common in both types of displacements mentioned above. Risk analysis is the methodological and content perspective through which this study is conducted. My purpose is to examine the extent to which potential poverty risks materialize into actual impoverishment during displace-ment and resettlement, and how such risks can be avoided.

Africa is in the crucible of multiple strategies that aim at reducing African chronic poverty, which by many measurements is the most severe in the world today. But in addition to what we may name the '*existing old poverty*', which is the target of all poverty-reducing development programs, we cannot help but notice the emergence of a '*new poverty*' as well. This new poverty appears as a 'side-effect' of some of the same development programs and is directly linked to the forced displacement caused by some of these projects.

Therefore, I think that some important questions must be raised and answered: what has social science in Africa found in recent years about the specific risks of impoverishment through development-caused

displacements? And with better knowledge about such impoverishment
risks, can they be preempted or reduced?

To explore these questions, I propose to bring into discussion, and to
rely upon, the work of a number of social scientists who have carried
out recent research on a vast spectrum of Africa's displacement cases.
This study will analyze their methodology, and highlight their empirical
findings and conclusions.

Conditions of research

In selecting the primary resettlement studies for my analysis, I set three
limiting conditions:

1. that the primary resettlement studies themselves directly focus on
   risks;
2. that the social scientists who authored them explicitly employ in their
   research the Impoverishment Risks and Reconstruction (IRR) model
   as analytical methodology, or discuss the IRR model conceptually
   with reference to its validity for Africa's resettlement experiences; and
3. that their research has been carried out in the last 6–8 years, and
   reflects the current state-of-the-art in the resettlement literature.

Since these conditions, particularly (2) and (3), impose stringent selectivity
regarding the IRR methodology employed and a limited time-span, I did
not expect to find a large number of primary studies meeting them. To my
surprise, however, the sheer number of studies that I did find employing
the IRR model greatly exceeded my expectations.[1] Already in 2001 it
was publically estimated that *'the risks and reconstruction model...has
probably become the dominant model used to approach involuntary
resettlement within the context of large-scale projects'* (Koenig, 2001:1).
Indeed, this conceptual framework has been received with strong and wide
interest within the international community of resettlement researchers and
many have internalized and followed it in their field studies, publications,
and teaching.

Since 2001, the use of the IRR framework has expanded much further.
It is being used both in development-induced displacement studies and
in analyzing other types of displacements. It is therefore appropriate to
take stock and examine what such research applications have generated as
results, new ideas and findings. The Kyoto conference (see p. xiv) and the
present volume on multidimensional risks appeared therefore as a good
opportunity to undertake such analytical stock-taking on resettlement
research on the African continent.

It is important to note that the breadth of social science research on
resettlement has grown visibly in Africa, encompassing sectors in which

forced population displacement, although frequent, have not until recently come under the lens of research. One example is the displacement caused by the mining industries sector, discussed further in this chapter. Another significant characteristic is that this notable research-expansion is due not only to academic scholars, but quite largely to applied researchers, responding to the growth in effective demand coming from planned developments and entrepreneurial interventions in the public or private sectors. In fact, academic research (in Africa and elsewhere) is being criticized, justifiably in my view, both from the outside and from within, for still showing insufficient interest in the study of development-induced resettlement and its effects.

The majority of research studies analyzed in this chapter deal with development-induced displacement and resettlement (DIDR), but some empirical studies and theoretical contributions refer directly to war and conflict-caused displacements. Moreover, their richness of substance is impressive, and it has made the task I took on more complex,[2] by pushing this analysis towards domains I did not anticipate initially.

Altogether, undertaking this exploration has proven scientifically rewarding in several respects: it has yielded a vast panorama of expanding resettlement processes in Africa; it is demonstrating the centrality and grim seriousness of displacement's impoverishment consequences; and, most important, it points to major imperatives regarding needed policies and formal legislation to regulate processes now rife with human rights abuses and counter-development impacts. These research outcomes are both relevant and timely for current practice, right now, given the trends towards accelerating development investments in Africa, including investments in infrastructure construction, with their entailed resettlements.

Structure of the study

Along these lines, the present study is divided into eleven sections. The first section will briefly outline the relationship between development and forced-population displacement and resettlement. The general typology of forced population displacement processes (Cernea 2004) distinguishes four broad causal categories of displacement, and the research discussed here falls into three of these four categories. The prospects of Africa's accelerating development rhythms in the coming years—given increasing public and private capital flows to and within Africa—will also bring, however, the likelihood of many new instances of forced population resettlements of large and small scale.

The second section of the paper will highlight the recent ascent of the *concept of risk* in social science theory, methodology and research.

In this context, the paper describes succinctly a conceptual framework for applying risk analysis to forced displacement and resettlement processes: this is the Impoverishment Risks and Reconstruction (IRR) model for resettling displaced populations, highlighting its functions and constitutive elements. The adequacy and uses of the IRR model in research in Africa will then be examined in the following sections.

Further, the core of this paper consists of eight sections in which I analyze the corpus of resettlement studies that I have identified to date, studies that have examined displacement in Africa by using the IRR model in various ways: either as methodology to guide and structure their investigation (for case-based in-depth analyses, or for sector-wide cumulative syntheses), or as a theoretical framework for interpreting the content of DIDR processes.

Section III summarizes the main topics dealt with in the risk-oriented studies which will be reviewed further. Sections IV and V discuss sectoral specificities: first the specific features and growing extent of displacements caused by Africa's expanding mining industries, both in themselves and in comparison with the global mining sector. In turn, the presence of impoverishment risks and their specific forms are investigated in the urban sector, including displacement from shanty towns and the peri-urban displacements triggered by expanding cities; here the resettlement of war-displaced people into urban contexts is also addressed.

Section VI reviews the theoretical issues and empirical findings of studies devoted to one of the most pernicious impoverishment risks: the loss of access to common property natural resources and the unraveling of customary ownership patterns.

Section VII is devoted to resettlement studies in Ethiopia, a country in which resettlement processes have been dominated not by displacement caused by development investment projects, but rather by state-initiated programs of population transfers in which movements have been mixed— both voluntary and compulsory. Considerable emphasis in the Ethiopian resettlement research is placed on the relationships between resettlers and hosts populations and on social re-articulation of community patterns after relocation.

Section VIII addresses the important issue of using the IRR model not only for analyzing development induced displacements, but also for studying war- and conflict-induced displacement. The section presents the theoretical discussion among scholars on the use of the IRR framework in this type of displacement and outlines how actual research using the

IRR has been carried out on civil war refugees and conflict-IDPs in some African countries.

Section IX moves the discussion to conservation programs in Africa and their relation to forced displacements and poverty reduction or creation issues. It examines the displacement of resident people from Africa's parks, highlighting their impoverishment. Displacement is defined according to international standards (see World Bank 2001: 3b) not only as inhabitants' physical relocation but also as restriction of access to natural resources. This research, as this section will show, has led to an explicit argument for changing policies predicated on physical displacement as a strategy for park creation.

Section X is devoted to IRR analysis in dam-caused forced resettlement. It discusses, among studies by several authors, the findings of an uniquely illuminating synthesis carried out by Thayer Scudder based on impact data from 50 large hydroelectric dams, along the lines of the IRR model and the stage model. Africa's hydropower dams represent 25% of the dams analyzed in this study.

Altogether, the above group of eight sections offers a broad view on a large research front in Africa, in multiple sectors of the economy, and in both rural and urban areas. This overview testifies to the creative, innovative ways in which many social scientists, working at a distance from each other and independent of each other, have used the same IRR methodology. Their research innovations are highlighted, together with their contribution in revealing not only the general risk-characteristics of such processes, but also the specific, idiosyncratic risks encountered in different context-related circumstances.

Finally, section XI rounds up this extensive analysis by distilling its main conclusions. These refer to the commonalities in empirical findings evidenced in resettlements across the African continent, to the general theory of forced displacements, and to the methodological opportunities, difficulties and benefits that surface in carrying out impoverishment risk analyses. This section also points out research directions worth pursuing in Africa's future development.

I. Africa's accelerating development and displacements

To understand displacement-related risks, it is first necessary to place forced displacement and resettlement processes on the broader canvas of Africa's development.

Typology of state-initiated displacements

Many public sector programs—particularly, but not only, in infrastructure—require land and cause forced population displacements[3] of various
magnitudes. I suggest the following causal typology to help distinguish
the most important types within the large variety of displacement processes:

1. *Displacements by development programs* (in infrastructure, public
   utilities, highways, etc.);
2. *Displacements by environmental conservation programs* (e.g., the
   establishment of national parks, game reserves, game corridors, etc.;
   often these conservation projects are treated under the rubric of
   development, although they are distinct in content and outcome);
3. *Displacement by military programs* for constructing military training
   and testing facilities. These forced displacements are unpublicized,
   but nevertheless very real. They definitely are not development
   projects, but are defined to be in the public interest and the state is
   their initiating and enforcing agent;
4. *Displacement by population-transfer programs*, initiated by governments, under either a development rationale or a disaster-avoidance
   rationale. Such programs often are a mixture of forced and voluntary
   resettlement.[4]

Further in this paper, I will deal with displacements under sub-types (1),
(2), and (4).[5] Africa has experienced many large displacements belonging
to all these types. It is obvious that forthcoming development programs
and investment flows will also cause such displacements. Therefore, an
increase is to be expected in development-caused forced displacements
in Africa, even if other internal displacements (caused by wars, civil
conflicts) do not increase, or decrease.

Moreover, the public sector is not the only 'agent' in development and
forced resettlements in Africa, and projects of private-sector agents that
require 'right of way' and cause displacement are multiplying. However,
studies of resettlements by non-state agents in Africa are still scarce,
and this is one of the persisting gaps in the social science research on
displacements.

In theory, development projects undertaken by private sector corporations are not supposed to displace people coercively by invoking
the eminent domain principle. Yet in practice (through arrangements
reached with governments) this often occurs, compounding the numbers
of development-displaced people.[6]

Table 6-1. Public and private capital flows to Africa (1980–2002)

Year	Sub-Saharan Africa		North Africa	
	Concessional aid flows (proportion of GDP)	Foreign direct investment (in US$)	Concessional aid flows (proportion of GDP)	Foreign direct investment (in US$)
1980	4.8%	763 mil	1.7%	78 mil
1985	6.1%	938 mil	1.6%	384 mil
1995	8.2%	1,459 mil	1.8%	1,350 mil
2000	5.9%	4,223 mil	1.0%	2,886 mil
2001	6.0%	5,533 mil	0.9%	5,519 mil
2002	6.2%	5,733 mil	0.8%	4,365 mil

Source: Based on data from Global Coalition for Africa (2004) *African Social and Economic Trends: Annual report 2003/2004*. Washington, DC, pp. 68 and 70. Data on Sub-Saharan Africa in this table are exclusive of South Africa and Nigeria.

Premises of accelerated development in Africa

Recent trends in public and private capital flows to Africa reveal a substantial increase of such flows between 1980 and 2002, particularly in the last decade. This sets the stage for likely increases in programs that require land acquisition, changes in land and water-use patterns, and entailed relocation of populations inhabiting these lands.

Table 6-1 shows that aid flows to Sub-Saharan Africa increased between 1980–2002 as a share of recipient country GDP (General Domestic Product) from 4.8% to 6.2%. The increase in absolute terms is spectacular. But foreign capital investments, mostly private, have increased more than 800% over the same period! For the North African countries, these trends are even stronger: while the concessional aid has decreased by 50%, foreign direct investments have increased over 55 times!

Foretelling new development in Africa, the continuation and possible acceleration of these investment trends in the coming years brings us back to examining the risks of development-caused displacements and the aggravated poverty embedded in them.

II. The impoverishment risks and reconstruction model

The concept of risk has gained much prominence in social science during the last two decades. For research on development especially, risk analysis has proven to be a magnifying lens, able to render visible unfolding causal mechanisms that otherwise may remain obscure. It helps reveal trends, trade-offs, and contradictions in development, and it focuses attention on actors, either as *risk-generators* or as *risk bearers*, and on their social behaviors. The conference organized at Kyoto University on the 'multidimensionality of risks in Africa', which prompted the work for preparing this study and the present volume altogether, reflected precisely this propensity of recent social research toward illuminating the risks at the genesis of any development.

It is in this vein as well that the present paper attempts to analyze how one specific research area in Africa—the research on forced population displacements and resettlement—has shifted markedly to the use of risk-centered methods of inquiry and analysis of risks' content. The research on forced resettlement in Africa has a history of several decades and has produced enduring knowledge. But never before has it manifested as strong an interest in revealing risks and in risk-conceptualizations as the cohort of studies recently published on resettlement (including studies in this volume) demonstrates.

The deceptively simple proposition that 'social risks are multidimensional' is not only an ontological statement: it is also a methodological guide. It prompts social analysis to unveil the complexities of risks and their multiple effects, to enable societies to deal in practice with them. Forced displacement processes are, in Robert Merton's classic expression, an optimal 'strategic research site' for risk analysis.

To define the main social risks in forced displacement and the main ways for counteracting them, we developed during the 1990s a theoretical model: the *'Impoverishment Risks and Reconstruction Model'* (Cernea 1990; 1997a; 2000). The IRR model reveals the content of displacement, de-constructing the overall impoverishment of those displaced in eight distinct components of impoverishment and illuminating their interconnection. Impoverishment processes are *potential* risks in displacement, not necessarily inevitabilities, but most often these risks materialize into actual, real processes of impoverishment because they are not preempted or reduced through up-front counter-risk strategies and reconstruction plans, before displacement even begins.

It is precisely the analysis of how these potential risks are arrested and preempted, or of how they sharpen and materialize into real negative impacts, that is the subject of research through the IRR framework. As an analytical tool, the IRR illuminates the patterns of de-capitalization, marginalization, and social disarticulation to which those displaced are subjected through expropriation and dislocation.

Numerous social scientists who research displacement processes in Africa have found the IRR to be a useful analytical instrument and over the last decade have employed it either in studying development projects, or in theoretical conceptualizations. Such studies are included in this volume as well (see Gebre; Kibreab; Schmidt-Soltau; de Wet). The use of the IRR methodology for conducting field research has generated risk findings and knowledge that are comparable and that we will examine in the next sections. Before that, I will briefly summarize the IRR framework for the purposes of this paper.[7]

Functions

The IRR model is built upon three fundamental concepts: risk, impoverishment, and reconstruction. These 'building blocks' are further split into sets of specifying notions, each reflecting another dimension or variable, either of impoverishment or of reconstruction (e.g., landlessness, marginalization, social disarticulation, social inclusion, etc.). This set of interlinked concepts refines the theoretical discourse on displacement and resettlement processes, helping to illuminate better their nature, effects, and socioeconomic remedies. In this way, the IRR model captures the dialectic between *potential* risks and actuality, and it remains open to analyzing whether or not the risks fully materialize in a given development context. The IRR framework posits that all forced displacements are subject to major socioeconomic risks, *but are not fatally condemned to succumb to them.*

The IRR framework can help in the following four functions:

1. *A predictive function*, to anticipate risks to be expected in programs entailing displacement and resettlement;
2. *A diagnostic function in the field*, to guide operational research on assessing the local presence and (different) severity of each specific impoverishment risk;
3. *A problem resolution and planning function*, to help include project measures commensurate with each identified risk, for prevention or mitigation; and
4. *A research methodology function*, to inform scientific research in organizing the study of displacement, in generating hypotheses, and in conceptualizing and interpreting the findings.

Risks of impoverishment

The cognitive and analytical advantage of the IRR model results from the information about past processes 'stored' and synthesized in the model.

Employing the model saves time and efforts by obviating the need for starting anew the general risk analysis in each project from 'square one', and instead offering ex-ante a well-tested starting point: the matrix of eight basic impoverishment risks which, in light of historical experience, are predictable in most forced displacement situations. It directs analysts towards measuring impoverishment not only in terms of income, but also in terms of employment opportunities, health care, nutrition and food security, access to common natural resources, shelter, or social capital. Indeed, the eight most common impoverishment risks captured in the IRR model are:

1. landlessness;
2. joblessness;
3. homelessness;
4. marginalization;
5. increased morbidity and mortality;
6. food insecurity;
7. loss of access to common resources and services;
8. social (community) disarticulation.

A detailed discussion of each risk is contained in the papers on the IRR model (Cernea 1997a; 2000) and a concise description of the main risks is attached in Appendix 1 of this article.

Orientations in reconstruction

The second part of the IRR framework turns the risks matrix on its head and outlines counter-risk strategies to be translated into targeted operational project provisions. Indeed, before displacement actually begins, the social and economic risks of impoverishment are only potentialities, likely processes. The concept of risk is about processes that are not yet actual, that may happen but also that may NOT happen—if adequate counter-risk measures are taken. But if preventative counteractions are not initiated, these potential hazards convert into actual, materialized impoverishment. Therefore, for overcoming impoverishment, the internal logic of the IRR as an analytical and problem-resolution tool prescribes attacking the risks preemptively, early on. Similar to the way in which its risk analysis de-constructs displacement processes into distinct risks, the IRR also deconstructs risk-reversals into a set of reconstructive, pro-poor support activities,[8] potentially able to lead:

1. from landlessness to land-based resettlement;
2. from joblessness to reemployment;

3. from homelessness to house reconstruction;
4. from marginalization to social inclusion;
5. from increased morbidity to improved health care;
6. from food insecurity to adequate nutrition;
7. from loss of access to restoration of community assets and services; and
8. from social disarticulation to rebuilding networks and communities.

The research question, however, remains equally major and sharp: do these preemptive or reconstructive processes occur? Are the coping responses of those displaced, and the mitigation actions by the displacement's agents and sponsors, effective in averting impoverishment?

The strategic orientations towards reconstruction indicate that the IRR model is not just a predictor of inescapable pauperization: on the contrary, it maps the road for restoring the livelihoods of the displaced. Analyzing whether, or how, the roads towards containing impoverishment are followed in actual projects is a task that might be achieved through reconstruction-focused resettlement research.

III. Risk-oriented resettlement research in Africa

Precisely such risk-focused impoverishment research has been fast-growing in Africa during the last decades, a growth to which the spread and use of the IRR methodology might have strongly contributed. This research is carried out both by African scientists and by researchers from other countries. Risk-oriented studies have stepped into sectors and processes not examined in the past. We can review in this paper only some of these studies and parts of their findings.[9] Overall, the general literature now coming out on resettlement in Africa is definitely larger.[10]

In addition to their geographic focus on Africa (exclusively, or as part of world-wide syntheses) the research works discussed below have in common either an interest in exploring the IRR and its concepts theoretically, or in using it as methodology for empirical investigations, or both. As stated earlier, my own purpose is three-fold: (a) to assess, even in part, what can be achieved cognitively by employing the IRR model; (b) to examine how the model has fared through the tests of practical application, and its critiques; and (c) to bring the findings of other researchers in support of this book's attempt to identify the multifaceted risks of displacement in Africa, their causes and remedies.

The topics on which I found that the IRR-informed studies offer substantive new insights and findings are:
- displacement risks at project level, including in-depth analyses of distinct risks or counter-risk responses (e.g., landlessness, social disarticulation, loss of commons);
- characteristics of sector-level displacement risks in industrial sectors (mining industry and dam construction, in particular);
- specifics of impoverishment risks in urban displacements;
- creation of parks for nature conservation, game reserves, etc. in Africa by using population displacement approaches, and the needed policy-changes;
- risk-characteristics of population redistribution and transfer programs, with particular focus on social cohesion variables and resettler-host relations; and
- theoretical risk conceptualizations and the inherent complexity of DIDR.

The primary test to which all studies have submitted the IRR model was: are the basic risks it identifies evidenced by new empirical research on displacement in Africa? This question was asked by Sonnenberg and Münster (2001) and Downing (2002) regarding displacement risks in mining sector projects; by Scudder (forthcoming), de Wet (2004), Kassahun (2004), Modi (2003), and others for displacements by hydropower dam projects; by Dinku (2004), Faure (2004), Feleke (2004) for urban and peri-urban projects; by Schmidt-Soltau (2000, 2003) and Rudd (2004) for conservation park programs; by Gebre (2003, 2004), Wolde-Selassie (2000, 2004b) and others for population transfer programs.

The test resulted in a general empirical validation. Perhaps the broadest comprehensive assessment was formulated by de Wet, who writes:

> The ethnography of dam-induced resettlement in Africa provides plentiful evidence to support Cernea's now well-established impoverishment risks schema of: landlessness, joblessness, homelessness, marginalization, loss of food security, loss of access to common property resources, increased morbidity and mortality, and community disarticulation becoming actualized at the individual, household and community levels (de Wet, this volume).

Findings that signal certain sectoral or area differences in the severity, intensity or manifestations of one or another of these risks are also notable; there are of course variations from one sector to another, or between locations; for instance, in the park-conservation displacement operations in Central Africa, Schmidt-Soltau (2000) found that the 'food insecurity risk' tends to be much less frequent than in other contexts.

Further, the contrast between risks that materialize and the reconstruction that does *not* is shocking. While the basic poverty risks are reported to be virtually similar, recurrent, and widespread, the reconstruction processes towards which the 'risks and reconstruction model' calls, on the contrary, are reported to occur much less frequently. Therefore, together with de Wet,

> one is left asking why it is that in Africa, as elsewhere in the world, so many of the attempts to counter...Cernea's impoverishment risks, continue to meet such limited success (de Wet in this volume).

This is a valid and fundamental question, of course, which we are also asking, and to which we'll return further in this paper.

Consistent with the IRR approach, in addition to the model's basic risks most researchers tend to explore the presence of various other risks specific, in their view, to one or another local context. Among these are risks stemming from losses in the structures for institutional services, weak as these may be to begin with, particularly in school services for the group. Displacement and resettlement processes are 'inherently problematic institutional processes' (de Wet in this volume); risks related to defective institutions range on a broad spectrum,[11] inherently complicating (or 'complexifying') through inadequate management what are already very painful social pathologies that are difficult to keep in check. The general idea emerging from multiple studies is that the risk-focused perspective is fertile not only in analytical and theoretical ways for knowledge generation, but also in terms of generating policy guidance towards preemption.

IV. Sector specificities: Displacement by the mining industry

While in the 1960s and '70s the early literature on Africa's development-displacements centered on hydropower dams (Kariba Dam, Akosombo Dam, Aswan Dam, Kpong Dam and others), during the past 5–6 years we have witnessed the entrance into research limelight of a sector very little studied in Africa in the past: the extractive mining industry and its accompanying mining-induced displacement and resettlement.[12] The expansion of these extractive industries is accelerating now, but

in fact began decades ago, and has caused many displacements, largely
unreported in research (e.g., the long development of Nigeria's vast oil
extraction industry). Indeed, social science studies on mining-induced
displacement and resettlement (MIDR), for as yet unexplained reasons,
have generally not been conducted until quite recently.[13]

Africa's expanding mining sector

Two major syntheses are available on mining-caused displacements in
Africa and both explicitly adopted the IRR model as their methodological
and conceptual framework: the Sonnenberg and Münster (2001) study focuses on a mineral-rich region encompassing 10 states in Southern Africa
(Angola, Botswana, Malawi, Zimbabwe, Lesotho, Swaziland, Namibia,
Mozambique, and Tanzania).[14] Downing (2002), in contrast, addresses
African mining-caused displacements as part of his world-wide synthesis
on this sector. All three authors centrally focus on impoverishment processes. However, while Sonnenberg and Münster primarily explore economic aspects, Downing takes a more holistic anthropological approach,
stressing cultural as well as material impoverishment.

Sonnenberg and Münster (2001) selected the IRR model as their
research-lens

> because it provides a comprehensive framework with which to approach
> resettlement projects, [and] is current, and relatively widely accepted as an
> improvement over previous models. Because it is generic, it can be tailored to
> the specific needs of industrial programs…(p. 5) The IRR model calls for the
> correction of three entrenched flaws that account for the current neglect of
> the risks of impoverishment: flaws in conventional risk methodology, flaws in
> cost-benefit analysis, and lack of genuine community participation (pp. 8–9).

Downing, in turn, explains his choice of the IRR by writing that:

> development-induced displacement unleashes widespread social, economic,
> and environmental changes that follow well established patterns…A frequently
> used model for organizing these risks patterns is the impoverishment risks and
> reconstruction model. Worldwide academic research has confirmed this model,
> expanding its scope…(Downing 2002: 8).

A third, more limited, study on mining in Africa (Sinkala 2002), comments
that the eight impoverishment risks in displacement identified by the model
causally lead to an overall 'loss of socio-economic security' by affected
populations. Sinkala points out that insecurity caused by displacement

backfires and, in turn, 'weakens the mining and minerals sector's contributions to Africa development' (pp. 1, 14).

What have these studies of the mining-industry found? Sonnenberg and Münster (2001) included both *brownfields*[15] and *greenfields*[16] among the projects studied. The data available for each case was limited,[17] because the companies were not forthcoming about the displacement that resulted from their projects. Sonnenberg and Münster's study therefore only counted about 37,000 people displaced, an obviously understated number. Yet, the overall image pieced together by the authors is appalling; displacement in the mining sector resorts to primitive means compared to sectors were both scientific research and civil society concerns have been present. The 'shortcomings of existing legislation...' for instance, regarding land acquisition and lack of assistance '...are not specifically addressed as issues in their own rights' (p. 28), and compensation 'is not adequately addressed'[18] leaving plenty of room for arbitrariness. The result, as the authors conclude, is that responsibilities for resettlement—vital to the avoidance of further impoverishment—'are not clearly defined and are subsequently reflected to the detriment of the displaced and host communities' (pp. 28–9).

The Sonnenberg-Münster study goes further to identifying some of the specific characteristics of the South African mining sector,[19] grouping features under relevant rubrics such as 'institutional frameworks' in the sector, 'attitudes' and mind-sets, planning patterns that result in people becoming poorer and worse off than they were previously. They signal critically important shortcomings in the mining industry, not monitored effectively. Some of these features and issues, in the authors' strong words, are:

- 'Southern African States are not equipped with the right legal/policy frameworks to guide involuntary resettlement'.
- 'Legislation on resettlement, when present, protects the state, not the displaced'.
- 'Civil servants implementing resettlement are ill equipped or disinterested'.
- 'Mining companies externalize the cost of resettlement squarely on the shoulders of affected communities'.
- 'Mining companies regard involuntary resettlement as a nuisance or impediment to core business'.
- 'Local development opportunities are either non-existent or not factored into resettlement planning'.
- 'Planning excludes the development livelihood needs of the people and focuses on the physical infrastructure requirements, which are tangible'.

- 'Mining companies regard involuntary resettlement programmes as housing projects'.
- 'Mining companies regard participation and consultation as a 'necessary evil''.
- 'Mining companies disregard diversity within communities'.
- 'Exclusion of community from the actual planning of the mine'.
- 'Exclusion from planning of land-users who may not live on the land, e.g. people who use land to graze cattle'.
- 'Internal company politics weaken efforts to conduct thorough resettlement planning and implementation'.
- 'The rights of the displaced are ignored, the displaced do not know their rights...and thus are open to abuse'.
- 'Little support for host communities...Host communities do not cope with (the impact of) resettlement'.

(Sonnenberg and Münster, 2001: 38–41)

Overall, the combined findings of research on Southern Africa's developing mining industry reveals what can only be characterized as primitive displacement and resettlement practice, far behind our time and age. This industry compares poorly to practices in development projects co-financed in Africa by international agencies, although those are also often conducted at low standards and fall below the respective agencies' policies. They impoverish affected populations materially and grossly violate their human rights.

Comparison with the global mining sector

These conclusions are reinforced by Downing's study. Downing analyzes mining-induced displacement in Africa within the context of the global mining sector, building his global analysis also within the IRR framework and methodology, and applying it, risk after risk, to the global data available. The larger scale of Downing's synthesis highlights the international scope of the issues, and projects MIDRs impoverishing effects onto the map of the developing world, although with inevitable gaps in data. The study warns ominously that the rapid expansion of the sector in coming years will make forced displacements an even more significant issue.[20]

The paradox of impoverishing outcomes resulting from mining gold, oil, platinum or coal is particularly unacceptable on equity and social justice grounds. These projects extract natural resources of extraordinarily rich value, sufficient, among other things, to secure much better, and sustainable, livelihoods for the populations out of whose lands these riches are extracted.

Taking advantage of his macro-sectoral analysis of displacement, Downing also brings up important elements of the broader risks-in-displacement theory. One of these is the 'definition of liability', to which the assessment of impoverishment risks logically leads. He distinguishes between 'acknowledged liabilities', 'possible liabilities', and 'probable liabilities', and puts forward an original idea of instituting a 'displacement insurance'. This certainly is an idea worthy of further operational elaboration.[21] All these concepts have special significance not only for our discussion of mining, but also for the broader displacement theory and policy issues.

In this vein, Downing re-aligns the discussion around a basic argument we developed (Cernea 1999) in support of the IRR model—its conceptualization, timeliness, and suitability for policy, practice, and public discourse. The core of the argument is stressing the sharp causal distinction between what we called 'old poverty' and 'new poverty'. We argued explicitly that the sociological theory of forced displacement and resettlement (as well as the advocacy for improving resettlers livelihood) stands to gain in scope and impact from linking displacement analyses to the paradigm of poverty reduction that justifies essentially all development work today. The contradiction between the paradigmatic objective and displacement's real outcomes is total. The mass-scale on which 'new poverty' is created through miserably handled displacements conflicts with, and subtracts from, the overall struggle to reduce 'old poverty' (Cernea 2000). Downing has forcefully reiterated this reasoning, being the strongest among the few voices in the community of resettlement scholars who has picked up and continued this key argument:

Failure to mitigate or avoid impoverishment risks may generate 'new poverty'... poor people become even poorer...Measured in terms of long-term impacts, mining-induced displacements significantly truncates social and individual chances for sustainable development...[He continues] It may be argued, that profiting from a mining endeavor without paying the costs of rehabilitation of newly created local poverty is morally indefensible. In such a situation the poor are in effect taxed to benefit those who profit financially from the mine...Costs...transferred to third parties are coercive, especially when the costs are transferred without their consent...Governments might also be indifferent to the plight of the displaced; in such a case, mining interests and their financiers

are considered willing accomplices to what may be judged by others to be an
unethical business transaction (Downing 2002: 8–9, 16–17).

V. Urban resettlement: Can risk analysis highlight successes?

A common problem looms large on all African governments' agendas:
coping with urban growth. Massive rural-urban migration during the
last half century and rapid urbanization have produced giant conurba-
tions, lacking master-planning, with haphazardly located and meager
infrastructure, shocking roads, countless squatters and slums, and more
environmental problems than can be listed here. Re-ordering city spaces
to construct wider roads, public and private modern buildings, improved
transportation, new drinking-water and sewage evacuation systems, will
require wide restructuring of urban land uses.

Inevitably, this will entail compulsory intra-urban relocation processes
of a cumulated magnitude, that, we predict, will become larger in Africa
than population displacements in any other single sector, dam-building
included. Against this imminent trend, the paucity of urban relocation
studies in Africa's mega- and medium-size cities is hard to explain.

Among the existing studies, most tell dire stories. In the present
analysis, we can reflect on three recent case studies in Africa which
analyzed urban resettlement in the IRR perspective. They were carried
out, respectively, by Faure (2004) in Mauritania, and Feleke (2004) and
Dinku (2004) in Ethiopia.

Shantytown renewal and resettlement

Faure's research stands out for reporting the case of a *successful* urban
resettlement, in Nouakchott. She reached her findings not by circumventing
the hard questions of impoverishment, but by positing them head-on in a
project evaluation context. She explicitly placed her study within the IRR
framework, and her research methodology aimed to ascertain, risk after
basic risk, whether impoverishment trends set in or whether they were
prevented or mitigated. The relocation affected one of the many *Kebbe*
(shantytowns, or *'bidonvilles'* of the capital city) named Kebbe El Mina,
situated near Nouakchott's center, whose land area (128 ha.) was needed
for infrastructure construction. According to the 2000 census, the Kebbe
El Mina population counted about 30,000 people grouped in some 4800
households. Seventy percent of the household heads had resided in the
Kebbe El Mina for about 10 years and the reminder for about 20 years.

Were the shantytown's displaced dwellers, asked Faure, deprived even more of their precarious residential security, through displacement? '*The operation was very delicate ... At the beginning, the inhabitants were more than skeptical, fearing that they will be forced to move far away. They also doubted the promise of land allocation extended to them*' (Faure 2004: 2). But the new area was gradually equipped under their eyes with water services, school, health center, latrines, market, transportation, etc. and phase I of the relocation was completed in 2003. Legal entitlements over house-plots (120 m² per recipient family) were formalized, with built-in safeguards against reselling the new plots and against return to the Kebbe area, coupled with long-term security for the new residence. Faure's survey found that the affected population perceived its situation as having improved. In short, she wrote, the risks of impoverishment through 'landlessness' and 'homelessness' were in this case preempted.

Similarly, the risk of employment loss around the old site was mitigated and prevented. A cash payment equal to two month's average wages was paid for loss of productive time during relocation and readjustment. Those with stable jobs in the formal or informal sectors in Nouakchott kept them (regular workers, fishermen, drivers, port laborers, etc.). The self employed artisans and food-stall keepers received a two-month payment to help with their relocation and the growth of a new pool of customers. The massive population move itself created transport-work for many people, paid immediately, and new employment was created by the sudden boom in the construction of private dwellings at the new site, replacing the mostly wooden barracks of the old site.[22]

Faure's risk-by-risk analysis paints a nuanced picture: it concluded that the food insecurity risk of the IRR template did not appear here and documented how the marginalization risk was successfully prevented. However, it also estimates that the new system of individual house-latrines, requiring weekly emptying by families unaccustomed to this practice, may generate new and serious morbidity risks.[23] Social disarticulation was prevented with the help of NGOs work and also to a significant extent through the community's collective participation in negotiating relocation with authorities. But the relocation process itself, wrote Faure, fostered change in the community's social stratification.

In our view, this urban relocation study brings up data[24] and issues worthy of comparative examination. Findings from other sites, which we described elsewhere, show that in urban contexts disastrous displacements are far more frequent and typical in Africa than successful ones (e.g., see Cernea 1993, describing the case of urban displacement in Sudan's capital,

Khartoum, where about 500,000 people, mostly refugees and squatters, were brutally removed by government decision).[25] Yet what Faure's study demonstrates from the view point of the present paper is an aspect of the versatility of the IRR model as an analytical framework. Those who fear even the mention of risks in development falsely believe that risks-analysis would necessarily lead to findings undercutting the development enterprise. This belief is both naïve and mistaken. The IRR and risk analysis, as such, are not announcements of unavoidable and foreordained gloom, but are tools apt to make development sounder, more beneficial, by anticipating and preventing risks. And, as shown in the Faure case study, IRR is a tool also apt to reveal with precision that (and how) risks can be overcome even in complex settings.

Most probably, Faure did not aim to demonstrate this general point about risk analysis or about the IRR model. But the study itself proves the point. And this key point—about the general need, acceptability, and benefits from risk analysis—is more important than any specific analytical risk instrument itself, because it applies to all modalities of timely focusing on risks for predicting and improving outcomes.

War refugees: Coping in new urban contexts

The complex texture of often unpredicted outcomes from displacement risks is richly reflected also in the two studies in Addis Ababa on diverse urban population groups. The study by Dinku (2004) brings in a group of refugees displaced by the Ethiopia–Eritrea war in 1991 and relocated in the country's capital city: it explores the coping experiences of 'tefenakkai' ('the uprooted') in the Mekanissa neighborhood, the largest among 16 other similar neighborhoods of conflict-IDPs relocated in the city of Addis Ababa. In turn, Feleke (2004) studied the less researched peri-urban communities surrounding Addis Ababa.

In studying refugees, Dinku opted to focus on 'the risk of social disarticulation' in Mekanissa and its cultural dimensions. Contrary to what some think, this risk is far from 'elusive' and its multiple expressions are measurable. Dinku reports employing several research techniques in support of his IRR perspective (focus groups, general surveys, school surveys, etc.) to identify 'the major manifestations of social disarticulation among the displaced'. He found, among others: 'the evasion of customary obligations towards widows and orphans as an example of disintegration caused by impoverishment'; the emergence of 'streetism' defined as an increase 'in the number of street children of alarming proportions'; various kinds of 'community conflicts'; and that 'the most important social control mechanism is not internalized values and norms, but the threat of superior power' (pp. 374–85). The social tensions between previous urban residents and resettled refugees have telescoped to the younger generation, as Dinku learned due to a special investigation in two of the local schools:

> about 80% of the conflicts that occurred in the school compounds during the last five years were ones that took place between the displaced students and the non-displaced ones…The conflicts usually arise from certain kinds of inferiority complex predominantly suffered by the displaced community (p. 383).

Yet, the picture is not homogeneous: the same researcher looked for and revealed, in parallel, emerging indicators of social re-articulation, new patterns of mutual help in fetching water, of new solidarities, of coping and of life adjustments to the new circumstances…His nuanced conclusion deserves quotation:

> The characterization of socio-cultural displacement as a condition of disintegration does not imply that the displaced are unable to give meaning to their existence and suffering as the capacity to draw on social or religious ideals, and on co-operative efforts and solidarity, can bolster psychological and physical defense in even the most extreme situations. Nevertheless, their coping responses mask uncertainty, anxiety, and stress; the most important social control mechanic is not internalized values and norms but the threat of the superior government power (p. 385).

Peri-urban displacement

Less researched than the urban areas, but at even higher exposure to the pressures of displacement, are the peri-urban zones. Expanding cities covet peri-urban land either for locating new industries close-by, or for new residential quarters.

How should research approach the double economic nature, agricultural and urban, of the peri-urban households subject to displacement? Feleke (2004) confronted this problem when he studied the inhabitants of the Yeka Taffo peri-urban area of Addis Ababa, where the municipality earmarked 2.4 million m^2 for expropriation and new housing construction. Feleke clearly defined three research topics 'in light of the IRR model':

> …first, finding out how the typical peri-urban sources of livelihood are at risk, or fully lost;

...second, finding out the key social impoverishment variables in addition
to the economic ones; and
...third, finding out the factors accounting for possible individual gain, not
only loss, from displacement (Feleke 2004: 484).

But Feleke also considered critically that the IRR framework 'overlooked
to relate the impact that development projects bring on migration' and
therefore he added to his analysis 'four elements for (securing) livelihood:
agricultural intensification, crop livestock integration, livelihood
diversification, and migration' (p. 503).

What were the actual findings?

The principal loss to the 172 evicted-household was the farming and
grazing land adjacent to their dwelling (between 1–10ha/family). As a
result, the peri-urban peasants 'have now become landless and stopped
farming', which is the local form of 'farmers' joblessness' (p. 496). The
cash compensation is used for buying food supplies, but the families
'are not certain about their future' and feel 'seriously insecure with the
potential threat of a second wave of displacement' (p. 497). Grazing
and livestock in the peri-urban area have decreased and it is most likely
that 'most households would face food insecurity in the future' (p. 501).
Employment in the project construction work, notes the author, has
different effects, bringing gains to the young households, but not to the old
ones, who in practice could neither 'intensify agriculture', nor 'diversify'
their livelihood sources'.[26]

Many other reported findings[27] validate Feleke's adjusted use of the
risk and reconstruction model. He concluded that the

> model of risk assessment is found useful to analyze the threats that are facing the
> people of Yeka Taffo: it is important to note that all variables are very interdepend-
> ent...For instance, the dispossession of land directly affects food security, the lack
> of common resources and style of off-favor activities, and vice-versa. Including
> the 'migration' variable among the variables will broaden the analysis (p. 508).

The 'closing' of this insightful study does what every good study should
do. Relying on his many findings, the researcher then proceeds to make
a considerable number of constructive recommendations to Addis Ababa
City Council, whose

> urban planning methodologies should be strengthened with social engineering
> skills—that would analyze the effects of displacement at different project cycles
> and in multi-variable manners (p. 502).

VI. Personal and common property losses in displacement

There are many options in analyzing risks with the IRR methodology, among which researchers are making their choice: for instance, the choice between either studying the *full system* of risks in a certain resettlement process, or *focusing on one* of the displacement risks, distinctly, in detailed depth, and the responses to that particular risk.

A good number of studies have indeed chosen to focus on a single displacement risk. The researchers have done so in order to either (a) gain analytical depth through focus (e.g., Kibreab 2000 and Koenig and Diarra 2000 on common property losses; Wolde-Selassie 2000 on social disarticulation); (b) to adopt a comparative perspective (Lassailly-Jacob 2000); (c) in order to test a hypothesis related to a specific risk; or finally (d) because a certain operational need urgently dictated a single-issue analysis (Wolde-Selassie 2004b on food insecurity).

This approach markedly differs from the one taken in the studies discussed in the previous sections, where most authors carried out a multiple-risks analysis of given displacement processes.[28] Yet, both approaches are epistemologically valid and cognitively fertile. The quality and findings of the studies confirm it. Of course, because of the interconnectedness of the risks, the analysis of one or another risk taken in itself should never be strictly insular: implicitly or explicitly, it should be linked to the full risk-pattern embedded in forced dislocations.

Landlessness

Consider, for instance, the loss of land and the risk of impoverishment through potential landlessness. The in-depth study of the risk to land-entitlements in African countries (Lassailly-Jacob 2000) reveals not only the material impoverishment, but also its cultural dimensions, the related psycho-social stress, and the deeper effects of land-loss on cultural and ethnic identities. In fact, this analysis is linked by Lassailly-Jacob with her prior studies on Africa's large-scale voluntary land settlement programs, and enables her to do what is still rare and coveted in forced displacement research: a comparative analysis between the *coerciveness* of land expropriation in development-caused displacements and the *voluntariness* of those land resettlement programs which were predicated on free land endowments to resettling families, without the expropriation of previously owned assets.

The risk of landlessness is probably the most analyzed and highlighted impoverishment risk in the African context, and the vast majority of researchers document it and reveal its implications. On the continent with the lowest population density and the highest ratio of land per capita in the world, this is particularly significant. Be it from mining expansion, or from dam and reservoir construction, loss of land still looms as a fundamental risk among the multiple causes of impoverishment afflicting Africa's poor.

Customary ownership and dispossession

The loss of land, however, is not only a case of *personal* property dispossession, but also—most frequently in Africa—a loss of *group* property over land and forest resources. The IRR identified the loss of access to group (common) property resources as one of the most pernicious risks of impoverishing populations that vitally depend on such customarily owned resources. In development programs, such losses are very frequent.

Knowledge generated by researchers of resettlement processes is often relevant far beyond the issues of displacement, strictly speaking. The variables at stake in displacement are engaged by many other societal processes as well. Several topical areas that are 'plowed' in-depth by displacement studies are also under social inquiry for other issues, and knowledge generated by displacement studies serves those other issues as well.

One such topical area is the system (or rather systems) of customary common property over natural resources in Africa. A number of researchers have set their task to study and explain the impoverishment risks involved in dismantling these customary systems as a result of development-induced forced dislocations (see Kibreab 2000, 2003, focused on Ethiopia, Eritrea, Sudan, and his study in this volume; also, Koenig and Diarra 2000, on Mali). However, in so doing, they have generated analyses of these systems useful for other concerns—e.g., for the concerns about the management of natural resources under common property regimes.[29]

Kibreab's historical theory of common property rules and rights, for instance, has gained scholarly stature, as it helps 'read' the African social systems in general and, in addition, explains the enduring disruption that dispossession inflicts on those displaced. A good example is Kibreab's explanation of what 'belonging' means in a cultural/psychological sense, different from 'ownership' and 'owning' he highlights the *actors' own* perspective on 'territorial belonging', as a relationship between physical place and cultural identity. Planners and planning theories typically only think about land as a commodity that 'belongs' to people, but never also that in turn, culturally, people can by self-definition 'belong' to specific lands. Many populations perceive themselves in this way—as 'belonging' to a specific place—and so define their identity. In forced displacement, common lands and assets are taken away without consideration for either the loss in cultural identity or the loss in material livelihoods. Kibreab suggests that the proper way of responding to this major risk, when it cannot be prevented, is to reconstruct a pool of common property resources at the place of relocation and to reestablish formal and informal institutions that regulate group assets. By not doing so, he argues, development projects that confiscate customary property resources for right of way without making good the loss, inevitably set in motion a process of impoverishment and increased powerlessness (Kibreab 2000).

Drawing on their research in Mali on loss of access to common property in the Manantali Dam displacement, Koenig and Diarra (2000) stress in turn the political dimension of access to CPR (common property resources). Such losses may cause sharp political conflicts between displacees and host communities, when resettlement leads to competing claims on the same common property resources. Addressing this point in discussing the IRR model, Koenig (2003) observes, critically, that the IRR only 'minimally discusses political aspects' (p. 3) although it 'specifically notes that social disarticulation can worsen powerlessness, dependency, and vulnerability.' Therefore, Koenig recommends, with good justification in my view, a stronger recognition of the political variables in the analysis of displacement risks.

VII. Poverty risks to hosts: Population transfers in Ethiopia

Much social research has been invested over the last 30–40 years in one of Africa's largest resettlement processes—the state-initiated population redistribution in Ethiopia. From 1965 to the present these processes have crossed several distinct phases, under a succession of different political regimes, with changes in their causes, goals, content and outcomes.

An important recent book produced by Addis Ababa University (Pankhurst and Piguet 2004a)[30] contains a set of seven insightful studies which analyze with the help of the IRR methodology and conceptual apparatus several segments of Ethiopia's resettlement processes: in the Metekel area (Yntiso Gebre 2004 and, separately, Wolde-Selassie 2004a), at the Gilgel Gibe Hydroelectric Dam (Kassahun 2004), in the urban

context of Addis Ababa (Dinku 2004), among the peri-urban and rural
communities surrounding Addis Ababa (Feleke 2004), or assessing the
risk of food insecurity also as a cause of resettlement (rather than as
effect, as this risk is usually treated) (Wolde-Selassie 2004b). The seventh
study discusses theoretical issues regarding the IRR framework (de Wet
2004).

The complementarities between all these studies create the possibility
of comparing and integrating findings obtained with the same methodology—a study in itself, which may await its author.

Resettlers and hosts

As a group, the Ethiopian studies strongly display the researchers'
common interests in the processes of social disarticulation and re-
articulation.[31] This probably reflects the general concern in Ethiopia with
the wide upheavals and changes in social organization patterns within
the nation, caused by massive and repeated transfers of population from
one part of the country to anther.

Yntiso Gebre addresses, along this line, one of the least treated issues in
the worldwide resettlement literature:[32] the relationship between the host
populations and the incoming resettlers, analyzing this relationship in the
perspective of the IRR. In fact, he asks a broad and pertinent question: to
what extent the host populations are prone to the same or to a comparable
set of impoverishment risks, by dent of arrival of a substantial population
within its midst? (see Gebre 2002a, 2002b, 2003, 2004 and the study in
this volume).

Among his studies on resettlement in the Metekel area of Ethiopia, one
has an ominous title: 'Why did it fail?' In Metekel, the ratio of incoming
resettlers to the host population was more than 1.1:1, which overwhelmed
the hosts: some 82,000 resettlers moved into an area already inhabited
by 72,000 Gumz shifting cultivators. The sheer demography imbalance
was compounded by profound cultural differences, ethnic differences,
and differences in agricultural practices between the groups of natives
and incomers.

The IRR model that I elaborated explicitly indicates that hosts do incur
the risks of adverse impacts from resettlement. It also emphasizes that
policies, project decision making, and project planning must be aware
of and recognize the distinct risks to the established host population
resulting from the sudden demographic increase caused by resettlement
and its multisided effects. But I also wrote that 'risks to host are not

identical with the risks to displacees, in substance or intensity, but are related to them and may also result in impoverishment implications' (Cernea 2000: 32). However, in light of Gebre's empirical analysis, my cautious wording appears to be an understatement, and must be corrected. Ethiopia's Metekel situation may not be very common, but Gebre demonstrates that under certain circumstances the potential for very severe impoverishment risks, some similar in substance, does exist. The impoverishment risks to hosts may be exacerbated by flawed planning and, contrary to my earlier statement, in some situations they may be comparable 'in substance or intensity' to those of the displaced and incoming population.

Gebre starts by observing that no special 'conceptual framework has been developed to explain what happens to hosts' (2003: 51) and proceeds to test whether the IRR is adequate for this as well. He designed a sophisticated research program, including comparative matrices and intensive interviews with two groups—settlers and hosts—which were cross-referenced with findings from a sample survey of 368 households in 16 of the 45 villages with resettlers in the area. Gebre's study, in his words,

> compares and contrasts the gravity of displacement risks for the new settlers and for the host population in light of the impoverishment risks and reconstruction (IRR) model. It is true that the experience of forced settlers has different dynamics than that of hosts...The lesson from Metekel reveals that massive resettlement could disrupt the livelihood of the original inhabitants the way dams, national parks, and other development projects do to displacees.

For this purpose, Gebre also constructed a *comparative risk chart* that evaluates how the same set of impoverishing risks affected the two different groups: this kind of comparative chart is indeed a type of instrument that many other researchers could use beneficially.

The empirical findings are described in Gebre's studies in detail, and are compounded by a chronological description of how the tensions between hosts and resettlers escalated into deadly conflicts and bloodshed. Many people were killed and wounded on each side. The clashes, in the given cultural context, triggered in turn spate after spate of revenge killings. The competition for scarce natural resources was the economic underpinning of the intense inter-ethnic clashes. When ad-hoc militias were created by both hosts and resettlers, the intervention of the army became necessary.

To a large extent, although not fully, these were the consequences of ill-preparation for resettlement and of the authorities' un-awareness or non-anticipation of impoverishment risks for both groups.

What are the findings, in terms of the IRR model's methodological validity? Gebre sums up the outcomes of his detailed empirical risks analysis showing that

> five of the IRR variables—landlessness, homelessness, loss of access to common property assets, marginalization, and food insecurity—undoubtedly apply to the Gumz hosts' situation. Two other variables—increased morbidity/ mortality and social disarticulation—may also be related to the experiences of the hosts (2003: 52).

Reflecting the severity of the ensuing conflicts, he also defines the 'security risk to life' as a contextually specific and distinct risk, which is not part of the general IRR framework but is present and relevant locally.

Overall, Yntiso Gebre derives two main conclusions from his analyses. First, that

> Cernea's model is also relevant to host populations such as the Gumz, as most of the variables identified by the model are also manifested in their experience...The methodological tool developed to analyze the situation of the displacees can be employed to examine that of the hosts. The 1980s resettlement in Ethiopia resulted in land dispossession, loss of life, home destruction, decline of access to common resources, marginalization, erosion of customary laws, and periodic food insecurity for the Gumz. These variables strikingly correspond with the components of the displacement process delineated in Michael Cernea's IRR model, which demonstrates that hosts encounter serious risks of impoverishment (2003: 60).

The second main conclusion is of a policy, operational, and applied research nature, and is addressed, among others, to social scientists. Gebre writes militantly:

> Researchers should document risks encountered by hosts, communicate research results to the wider public and those who can influence policy, give briefing to governments and donor agencies, generate policy ideas, and collaborate with those embracing the host cause (2003: 60).

I find this study's analysis and recommendations both creative and convincing. Beyond testing, validating and expanding the application of the IRR framework, the study is a most pertinent argument for the need to recognize the impoverishment risks to which hosts are also potentially exposed in all situations—with the degree varying according to context—risks that must be preempted through economically, technically, and morally sound resettlement planning.

Social disarticulation and community rearticulation
A 'study in contrast' to the above case is reported by Abutte Wolde-Selassie (2000a) from the Belles Valley resettlement area (another name for the same Metekel zone) at a later point in time, which he studied as part of his PhD thesis. In more than one way, Gebre's and Wolde-Selassie's studies complement each other in that not only the losses and disarticulation caused by displacement are revealed, but also that the dynamics of reconstruction post-displacement begin to emerge after a certain time.

Wolde-Selassie examined the patterns of social organization along the displacement-resettlement time-continuum, and explores both the 'risks components' and the 'reconstruction components' of the IRR framework. He shows that the onset of various social disarticulation syndromes started at the departure site and continued also at the arrival site. 'Partners abandoned spouses at the very initial stage...Resettlement brought about the breakup of many families' (Wolde-Selassie 2004a: 42). Many other indicators converged into a multi-variable image of social disorganization and loss of pre-existing precious social capital.[33]

But then, after the initial phase of emergencies, conflicts, illnesses, and transition, adaptation slowly started. 'Entrepreneurial activities,' Wolde-Selassie writes, 'such as trade and market exchange were, in my own view, one of the best and effective adaptive strategies...Marriages strengthened ...affinal kin groups began to develop...' among the resettlers (2000: 422–4). Other indications followed, and are reported in turn, based on the researcher's field observations. 'The role of elders regained importance in village life'; 'The rebirth of religious associations...' followed. 'Resettlers managed to revitalize the *idir*', the strongest traditional mutual assoc-iation within village communities, and a 'reemergence of labor exchanges' began. At the community level, the author documents 'the articulation of farmers production' support organizations, re-born in the new context but maintaining their vernacular names from the place of origin.

Wolde-Selassie's analysis is relevant not only sociologically, but also in terms of the lessons it derives for the operational delivery of post-relocation assistance. This assistance ought to not be limited to technical 'inputs'—food, tools, medicine, etc.—but should also nurture and facilitate local capacity building. The researcher concludes:

> Providing the conditions necessary to facilitate rather than hinder people's own initiatives and the development of community associations and institutions is vital in the social re-articulation of a disrupted community. This process is central also for the entire economic reestablishment process...the risks and reconstruction conceptual framework—in identifying key risks and pointing to strategies for reconstruction—is a relevant analytical and guiding framework (2000: 430).

Questioning project design: Dam-building in Ethiopia

While population transfer programs swept the country, major dams were not built and the displacement effects of dams have not been the subject of much research in Ethiopia. Therefore, Kassahun's thesis and published study (2004) on the Gilgel Gibe hydroelectric dam displacements are seen as among 'the first of their kind' in Ethiopia. In organizing his research, Kassahun explicitly considered choices between several theoretical models and opted for 'the model which marked a shift from stages-ridden archetypes to packages of risks in development-induced displacement' (2004: 445).

Distinct from many other case-studies on dams, and therefore interesting in a different way, Kassahun started the application of the risks model by asking whether and how the World Bank-assisted Gilgel Gibe project took into account all of the impoverishment risks during project design and preparation. He found the World Bank's preparation process to have been unsatisfactory on this ground and convincingly criticizes the project's design because it did not adequately prevent the landlessness risk. It secured only insufficient land per resettled family in a typical area of swidden agriculture, 'making fallow unthinkable'. He also faulted the underestimation during project preparation of the loss of common property pastures which contributed to severe reduction in livestock ownership after relocation and caused a 'traction-power deficiency' in agricultural work. In this context, Kassahun also criticized the IRR model for 'mostly neglecting part-farming in its prescription about land for farming' (p. 457).

Many other insightful observations resulted from considering whether or not, and how, the other basic risks, such as loss of employment, food insecurity, house-loss and social disarticulation—were handled during project implementation. The rich texture of the study's findings confirmed to the researcher the promise of the risk-based methodology in field research.

This study also validates convincingly, in my view, another premise of the IRR methodology: namely, that risk intensities are always non-uniform and context-specific. When empirical research does not treat risk-outcomes wholesale but instead explores the 'differential impacts' of risks on various population segments and includes risk-intensity indicators, it stands a much better chance of capturing the complexity inherent in DIDR processes.[34] Kassahun followed this recommendation and selected four variables for assessing risk intensities and impacts: age, gender, position in the domestic cycle, and wealth. The study reports distinct findings on the young, on children, the elderly, on women and men, etc. With this finely grained assessment, the author concludes that the Gilgel Gibe displacement outcome 'scenario remains differential impact (rather) than wholesale impoverishment.' It is worth pointing out that the Gilgel Gibe study shows one of the ways in which nuanced risk analysis can respond to this requirement.

Expanding the application of the IRR framework
Beyond their individual findings, the set of Ethiopian studies discussed above have another key methodological significance. Taken together, they embody an important expansion in the analytical use of the IRR model beyond the category of development-displacements to the category of state programs for population territorial transfer and redistribution. We know the important causal and contextual differences between these two types of displacement. Nonetheless, the model's analytical use is not hampered when done carefully, rather than mechanically, and when the differences are kept in view.

We have also examined already (see section VII above) the extension of the IRR framework to the study of host populations' conditions. Together, these extensions confirm the cognitive versatility of the framework, in that it lends itself to flexible adaptation, facilitates comparability of findings through the identification of both similarities and differences, and allows integration of results. Thus, it creates new premises for incremental knowledge and for theoretical generalizations on causes and widespread processes of impoverishment.

VIII. War-caused displacements and the IRR model

Along the same lines, another area of extended IRR applicability arises in the context of certain displacements caused by conflicts, with appropriate caveats. Real life processes have brought up this question and highly reputed scholars have developed the argument for using the IRR framework in studying this category of displacements, caused not by development programs but by violent conflicts—war, civil wars, or violent ethnic persecution. Indeed, there are not only substantive similarities in impacts, but also causal and substantive differences between these categories in the options for their resolution, yet the differences are well known and can be factored-in. Of crucial interest is the *theoretical argument* for such an expanded application, with due awareness of its limits.

Theoretically, the strong argument for applying the IRR model to researching conflict displaced populations was first made by Gaim Kibreab (2000), based on his extensive studies on refugees and IDPs and on Africa's overall socio-political experiences with refugees. His argument is rooted in the centrality and generality of impoverishment risks in both conflict-displacements and development-displacements and in the imperative of reforming approaches used in refugee assistance. Kibreab argues as follows:

> Any government or agency concerned with the welfare and viable reconstruction of sustainable livelihoods among displaced communities—the cause of displacement notwithstanding—could gain pivotal insights and inspiration from the risk model. The problems faced by refugees and relocatees in re-settlement schemes are more or less the same as those embodied in the risk model. The major problems facing refugees in resettlement schemes are landlessness, unemployment or underemployment, especially during trough seasons, overcrowding, marginalization, increased morbidity and mortality, food insecurity, lack of access to CPRs as compounded by lack of communal tenurial security, and social disintegration. It is true that in the case of refugees, most of these losses are suffered in connection with flight, but this is immaterial because the declared aim of any refugee resettlement scheme is to rectify these losses and to avoid risks of further impoverishment rather than to consolidate and exacerbate such detrimental processes. Instead, failed refugee resettlement schemes have resulted in reinforcing the losses and the risks of impoverishment (Kibreab 2000: 323).

Kibreab supports his reasoning with the historical record of refugee resettlement schemes analyzed in his many studies, a record replete with examples of dismal failures: in fact, failure seems to be the rule rather than the exception with respect to refugee resettlement schemes. Between 1962 and 1985, about 155 refugee resettlement schemes were established in Africa and only a few have been able to achieve the minimum goal of self-sufficiency...This bleak situation would undoubtedly have been avoided, or at least mitigated, if host-government policies and donor responses were to be informed by the risk model (pp. 323–4).

In turn, other scholars of displacement, like Voutira and Harrell-Bond (2000), have also stressed the need of 'arriving at a theoretical model of resettlement that applies to different situations of forced migration—those resulting from impoverishment, civil strife or 'development' projects that uproot populations' (p. 56). Voutira and Harrell-Bond regard the elaboration of such a theoretical model as a 'major challenge' facing researchers. Discussing the options for, or limits to, applying the IRR also to conflict caused displacements, they agreed with Cernea that impoverishment is a 'consequence of virtually all types of displacement' and that methodologically [impoverishment] allows for a common denominator in refugee and 'oustee experience' (p. 56). But they saw difficulties in that causes are different and that 'definitions of 'success' are not the same' in the two categories of displacement (p. 57).

Sure enough, there are indisputable differences between displacement types, those mentioned by Harrell-Bond and Voutira, and others too. But the response to the question of tool-usability, in my view, is to respect the methodological requirement of not taking a conceptual framework and mechanically 'appling' or transposing it *tale quale* elsewhere, on another category of processes. 'There is considerable potential for this extension, if mechanical application of the model is avoided' (Cernea 2000: 18). The challenge is to explore the investigative advantages offered by this analytical tool by adjusting it to studying refugee displacements as well and probe the value-added knowledge benefits.

Gaim Kibreab also addressed the epistemological question of whether differences between these type of displacements preempt the use of the IRR model. Breaking stereotypes, he turned the question around, arguing that not only the similarities, but the differences as well justify comparative analysis within the IRR framework. Kibreab readily recognizes

...the differences that may at first glance appear to have a bearing on the immediate relevance of the risk model as applied to resettlement of refugees...Yet, in spite of the ostensible dissimilarities between oustees' and refugees' situations, a closer examination of the issues reveals that the so-called

differences do not limit the scope of the model, but rather, make it compellingly
relevant (2000: 325).

Kibreab substantiates his argument by proceeding methodically to
consider one by one the specific differences. Among these are: the
'planned [development-displacements] versus sudden [conflict] events';
'the permanent [development-displacement] versus temporary [conflict]
displacement'; the 'nationals versus aliens' difference and its effects on
attitudes and practices of access to natural resources under common
property regimes; and the differences in institutional responsibilities and
mandates for refugees and development displacees.[35] Based on the very
content of these real differences, Kibreab then argues why they cannot
and should not be construed as obstacles to applying a risk-oriented
analysis and to pursuing reconstructive strategies, instead of simple relief
assistance. The awareness of partial differences must not deter from the
use of a certain research tool, it only dictates to factor the knowledge about
the differences into the research. Thus, the recognition and thoughtful
examination of differences enables Kibreab to conclude powerfully:

> It is noteworthy to state here, however, that this does not in any way limit the
> pertinence of the risk model in the formulation of refugee resettlement policies.
> Its *raison d'être* is to stimulate development of strategies designed to fill
> existing policy or organizational vacuums. The model warns governments, inter-
> governmental organizations, and nongovernmental organizations of the dangers
> involved in the failure to develop policies and organizational structures that
> allow them to plan ahead and to implement corrective measures that counteract
> or rectify negative consequences. With regard to resettlement of refugees, if the
> model is embraced, it could stimulate fresh and innovative conceptualization,
> which could, over time, shift the frontier of the existing deficient approaches to
> refugee resettlements (Kibreab 2000: 330).

In research practice, in fact, the impoverishment risk-analysis has
already been innovatively employed by some conflict-researchers both
in Africa and elsewhere, for instance in Latin America (Muggah 2000),[36]
demonstrating partial but extensive applicability. Some of IRR research
in Ethiopia (see earlier, and Dinku 2004) covered war-displacees as well;
more recent research on conflict-refugees in West-Africa is discussed
below.

IRR analysis of refugees at country level: Sierra Leone
Ten years of civil war, several coups, and interventions of foreign military

have caused wave after wave of forced displacements in Sierra Leone. A research project undertaken by Damien Mama (2003)[37] in Sierra Leone deliberately aimed to test the investigative and cognitive adequacy of the IRR for conflict-displacements, offering four explicit reasons for his test.[38]

The methodological apparatus of this study has particular relevance for the discussion on applying risk analysis to conflict IDPs. Mama deliberately avoided a 'mechanical application' by taking into account what in the phases of displacement is *specific to conflict* and by considering the UN guiding principles on IDPs and 'protection regimes', all the time aware of differences from development-displacement situations. He also points out that conflict-refugees are exposed to different risks in the different phases of their ordeal: for instance, when fleeing conflict, the risks are different from the risks experienced upon return. Accordingly, he made adjustments in the IRR model's definition of risk-reversal behavior and strategies.

Damien Mama's field methods, in turn, strive to identify local 'problems faced by resettled populations'. 'Respondents were given the opportunity to answer in their own words' (p. 17) and content analysis methods were applied to answers collected from interviews (p. 18). His effort was to adjust the general risk framework to the particular circumstances of post-conflict resettlement in Sierra Leone by identifying 'the impoverishment risks in some selected resettled communities and cross them also with responses provided by the policy of the Sierra Leone government, of international organizations, and local partners' (p. 16). Further, his analysis took into account 'the 5 major phases of resettlement in Sierra Leone and made a comparative analysis of IDP case-loads that fall under different phases'.

In 'testing the main components of the IRR model', Damien Mama found 'important similarities with predicted risks' (p. 49), but not full identity with the general description of the risks in the IRR model. Some risks, like landlessness, proved in Sierra Leone to be only temporary for these resettlers, rather than becoming chronic and definitive land-losses. The researcher found that in this case '*the houses and lands that were occupied in rebel held areas were vacated without resistance by occupants*' (p. 50) when those displaced returned.[39] Post-conflict marginalization and stigma were not faced either, and IDPs were welcomed upon return by community members, '*increasing their feeling of belongingness despite the economic challenges encountered*'. Other risks, however, such as food insecurity and community disarticulation materialized in an enduring way, exacting a heavy toll after return: 'loss of (mobile) property', 'lack of access to cultural resources' and of 'access to education'. The research, therefore, finds fault with the premature discontinuation of official resettlement assistance. It identifies inconsistencies between the publicly declared resettlement strategy and the measures actually implemented, as well as non-concordance and gaps between the assistance delivered and the actual needs of the returned resettlers.

We can thus observe how Mama's approach employed the IRR model simultaneously as a theoretical research paradigm and a set of testable hypotheses. His approach paid off. It enabled him to construct a theory-led image of the displacement by conflict and particularly of the post-conflict resettlement as experienced by IDPs in Sierra Leone. The specific cluster of risks, or the 'Sierra Leone risks-pattern' that resulted from his research differs in several respects from the general risk-pattern of the IRR risk-model, and this is a gain in knowledge. The research 'specified' the general model in a particular context and the knowledge so gained is apt to inform specific policy and operational responses. As to the test of the IRR model, Mama's thesis concluded:

> The hypothesis of this thesis is verified. In brief, this research has contributed to understanding some dynamic that characterize resettlement in a post-conflict setting. Besides, this research showed that the IRR model primarily developed for development-induced displacement also provides useful tools for problem analysis and policy planning in conflict-induced displacement (2003: 60–1).

The Sierra Leone study indeed embodies a valuable experience of using and interpreting the risk and reconstruction framework in ways that account for the specifics of *post-conflict* situations and the socio-political particularities of the country context.

The research on conflict-caused displacements will continue, most probably, to test this framework, employ its cognitive advantages and explore the scope for its uses. The framework has proven its capacity to illuminate the life experiences of those displaced, their own risk-perceptions and risk-responses. Moreover, the research shift towards such human experiences, and away from overemphasis on assistance agencies, is prone to generate new and indispensable knowledge.

I expect each new study to develop new modalities of using and enriching this framework, in ways tailored to particular objectives and contexts. Integration of findings with comparable findings from development-caused displacements will facilitate broader theoretical generalizations and increase the public impacts of resettlement research. Keeping the research focus on conflict-refugees' and IDPs' impoverishment, rights and livelihood reconstruction, is not only desirable, it is of paramount importance.

IX. Displacements from African parks: The poverty argument for changing park-creation policies

Another topic most relevant for Africa, in which the use of the IRR model has led to recommendations for changing long practiced policies, are the demographic and social variables of conservation park programs. Indeed, important new studies of impoverishment through displacement from Central and East African parks feed critical empirical evidence into the current sharp international debate (see Adams et al. 2004) around the approaches of IUCN, WWF and other major NGOs on the need to re-balance biodiversity conservation policy with poverty reduction policy.

The establishment of natural parks across Africa for conserving areas with precious biosphere resources has been for decades predicated on the forced removal of the populations long inhabiting those areas. Not in every case have such displacements been imposed, but in numerous cases they were the very premise of park creation and had terrible socio-economic effects on the livelihood of the locally affected populations. It is a matter of record that the displacements initiated in order to create parks, game reserves, or corridors for wildlife passage have often involved the brutal violation by the state of the populations' basic human and customary rights. Yet while each new park was hailed as a conservation triumph, the forced human removals and their dire effects have been much less advertised publicly. Case by case anthropological studies on such removal processes have been sporadic and individualized; although they did signal the issues, they didn't offer a comprehensive, macro-image of the destructive social processes set in motion. Biodiversity sustainability is surely a paramount objective, essential for global and national reasons, but park creation itself cannot be a success if predicated locally on *socially* un-sustainable and morally unacceptable conditions. The establishment of conservation parks must also include *sustainable* alternative livelihood for the indigenous people of the areas made into parks and natural reserves.

From case narratives to systematic synthesis

Starting from 1999, an original research on displacement and resettlement triggered by the establishment of parks in several countries of Central Africa has been carried out by Kai Schmidt-Soltau. He was the first to systematically apply the IRR model to analyzing the population displacement effects in the national parks of several countries: Republic of Congo, Gabon, Cameroon, Equatorial Guinea, Central African Republic and Nigeria. What is original about Schmidt-Soltau's research methodology is the application of the IRR model to the analysis of displacement and resettlement processes of *a cohort* of parks considered together, rather than independently, all located in a contiguous region of Central Africa, in order *to distinguish the general characteristics* of such processes.

The benefits of methodology and synthesis became immediately obvious: instead of the case-by-case narratives, customary in the anthropological literature, Schmidt-Soltau has constructed with the help of the IRR model an integrated image of what is *typical about a class of processes*—the processes set in motion for establishing large natural conservation parks and protected areas. The IRR methodology enabled him to produce not only a narrative account, but also generalizing propositions about the characteristics of population displacement out of Africa's new parks.

Schmidt-Soltau (2000, 2003) has found that despite Central Africa's low population densities and despite the large territories to which the affected groups usually had access previously, the displaced groups were suddenly rendered landless. The states and agencies which uprooted them did not provide, in exchange, land entitlements elsewhere. Marginalization and social disarticulation materialized in severe forms. Conflicts and competition with populations resident at the relocation sites escalated and the impoverishment of both populations (that already had low living standards previously) aggravated further.

Risk analysis, however, can be nuanced and can deconstruct syncretic processes. Thus, Schmidt-Soltau found that under the local Central African circumstances not all the risks of the IRR framework surfaced with equal intensity. Homelessness, for instance, didn't prove to be a severe impoverishment risk, because the simplicity of local housing enabled the relocated people to rebuild relatively easily, and materials were plentiful. Similarly, during displacement the risk of food insecurity did not materialize either. With differences carefully considered, the generalized picture of impoverishment through displacement built along the IRR framework provides what is probably the most comprehensive synthesis of such processes in Africa to date.

Emerging policy recommendations
The empirical findings about multisided impoverishment risks and real-life outcomes, analyzed from the perspective of conservation and development, led further also to policy recommendations. In subsequent studies, produced jointly with the writer of the present paper, the authors

relied on the IRR framework to critically re-place in discussion *the current strategy itself* of park creation: namely, the strategy and practice of forcibly removing the areas' previous inhabitants without effective counter-impoverishment safeguards and compensations (see Cernea and Schmidt-Soltau 2003). These studies strongly argue the need to ensure *'double sustainability'*—that is, both the sustainability of biosphere resources and the social sustainability of people's livelihoods. Since brutal displacement practices have demonstrably worsened livelihoods, approaches predicated on forced displacement of people must be discontinued (Cernea and Schmidt-Soltau 2003a, 2003b).

The 'power-base' of this recommendation is, in our view, the con-solidated empirical analysis of several cases carried out with *the same methodology* in various countries. The aggregation of pauperization indicators, and the similarity of findings across a cohort of cases, lent added force to this argument,[40] and its empirical basis has been further broadened in another study (Cernea and Schmidt-Soltau forthcoming) and by the findings of other researchers of park-displacements in East Africa (Risby 2002; Rudd 2004). In sum, the understanding of poverty risks and of the actual pauperization inflicted on local people must be taken as a premise for avoiding them and for seeking alternative, socially sustainable solutions.

Confirmation in East Africa

An independent and most interesting replication of the study in Central African parks comes from East Africa, through the research carried out in Southwest Uganda's Bwindi Impenetrable Park on the Batwa population by Kristina Rudd (2004). Unrelated to Schmidt-Soltau's study, Rudd did a virtually similar 'year-long research project exploring the situation of the Batwa, using the IRR model as a theoretical base' and as 'the most helpful theoretical model for understanding displacement and impoverishment'.[41] The Batwa are a pigmy indigenous ethnic group, displaced from Bwindi Park in 1991 and uncompensated for their loss of land. Over 80% of the group remained landless six years after their displacement, squatting without security on land owned either by private individuals (66%), by the government (8%) or by churches (8%) (Rudd 2004).

This risk by risk analysis confirmed all eight risk categories, and Rudd generated significant new data particularly on health, demonstrating the Batwa's *'decreased access to health care'*. Given that the Batwa have, in most cases, moved physically closer to health clinics, this finding may

appear counter-intuitive. But the researcher convincingly argues, based
on field-studies in seven Batwa settlements, that the 'interconnectedness'
of all the other materialized risks, along with other factors, 'has resulted
in a decrease in access to health care which is one of the root causes of
increased morbidity and mortality in their community.' For instance, the
Batwa have infant and child mortality rates up to four times higher than
other ethnic groups in the same region. Rudd writes:

> I found that the child mortality rate in these villages was 47.7 percent. This means
> that nearly half of the children who are born to Batwa women die before the age
> of five years. This figure is much higher than Uganda's national average of 14.1
> percent (according to World Bank 2004 data), but is similar to Kellermann's
> (2003) values of 40 percent and 41 percent (2004: 101).

Resettlement has indeed changed the Batwa group's terms of access to
inputs affecting health conditions, including access to both traditional
and Western medicine: because of marginalization and discrimination,
their access remains 'unequal to that of their non-Batwa peers', and, in
addition, they now have lost the prior access to their traditional medicinal
plant resources.

Based on this analysis, Rudd reformulates the 'increased morbidity
and mortality' risk of the IRR model and proposes to replace or define
it differently as the risk of 'inadequate access to health care' which in
turn leads to increased illness and mortality. Overall, the researcher
concluded that the impoverishment risks model 'is affirmed by the case
of the Batwa, and can be used to analyze their situation of displacement,
as well as to predict, and hopefully prevent, impoverishment secondary to
conservation projects in the future' (2004: 13). The risks, she observed,
'are deeply interconnected, and cannot be analyzed outside of the context
of the full model.'

Rudd conducted her risk study with a view to facilitating social
improvements, and therefore turned the analysis into a set of

> proposed recommendations for the Batwa, including: ways to address the issues
> of marginalization and landlessness; changes in international conservation
> ideology and policy; and an increase in indigenous rights legislation in
> multilateral, bilateral, and non-governmental institutions (2004: 2).

If anything, the findings from Bwindi Park reinforce the conclusion
derived from the Central African park research about 'just development

and conservation strategies', that is—about the need to renounce forced displacement as an approach to park creation, because of its unmitigated impoverishment effects. The debate, of course, is still open. But new research is continuously surging on this subject in Africa. A recent paper by Brockington and Schmidt-Soltau (2004) calls in again the IRR methodology argument and findings, and outlines a larger scale research program on the poverty and parks issues. Several other convergent research projects revolving around the same theme were announced at the IUCN's World Conservation Congress in November 2004, likely to further expand the empirical evidence.

Although the forced displacement strategy for park establishment is being now increasingly discredited by the evidence of its impoverishing effects and human rights violations, so far no formal change in official park strategies of the involved governments or international agencies have been placed on record. But risk-analysis has demonstrated the ability to reveal the pervasiveness of the induced impoverishment processes, has built a powerful poverty case against forced displacements, and has helped elevate the reasoning and the debate to the higher level of policy-changing arguments. I expect that, on its own multiple merits—developmental, conservationist, and moral, considered together—this argument will eventually win.

X. Major dams: Scudder's IRR analysis of displacement's impoverishing effects

To conclude this analysis, I will discuss some of the most recent research carried out on dams and resettlement by Renu Modi (India) and by Thayer Scudder (USA), with the IRR methodology (see also dam building in Ethiopia, earlier in this paper).

Comparing findings on women in large scale resettlements

Africa's dam-caused major displacements in the '1960s–70s, studied early, became the cornerstone of academic scholarship about forced resettlement worldwide—particularly the Kariba dam's resettlement analyzed in Colson's (1971) and Scudder's (1993)[42] landmark studies, and in Chambers' and Butcher's book (1969) on the Akosombo dam on the Volta river. The comparison of these early processes in Africa and today's dam-caused resettlements is aptly made by several studies contrasting the 1960s Kariba with the 1990s Sardar Sarovar dam on the Narmada

river in India. Among them, I'll highlight in particular the monograph by
Renu Modi (2003) assessing resettlement processes at these two big dams
several decades apart.

Modi explains that she used *'the impoverishment risk and reconstruction (IRR) model as a theoretical framework for (my) analysis'* and applied it, retroactively, to data on Kariba in Africa, comparing them with
recent data on Sardar Sarovar in Gujarat, India. Her comparison focuses
on a major group at risk—the women—'seeking *to study the gendered
impact of relocation on women and family with the IRR model'*. For this,
she *regrouped* the original Kariba data along the model's risks of impoverishment (landlessness, homelessness, food insecurity, marginalization,
common property etc.), and her own field data, to inquire whether the 40
years that passed between building the two dams have brought changes in
how women's needs are recognized in resettlement practice. In the case
of land, for instance, Modi notes that the displaced women, both among
the Hindu tribes or casts and among the Gwembe Tonga, did not have land
ownership rights, but had usufruct rights over land and thereby access
to it. But she found that women have lost out on access, and virtually
little has changed in this respect,except for the worse. *'Following relocation,'* Modi says, *'women also lost out on access to common property
resources.'*

Based on her systematic analysis of risk variable after risk variable,
Modi observes:

> In the case of the Gwembe Tonga women and women displaced by the SSP we can
> surmise that displacement has had an injurious impact on their economic, social
> and cultural capital or they were further impoverished. When the resettlement
> of the Kariba Dam took place, concerns for equity and justice in the social or
> gendered context did not inform the discourse on DIDR. But such concerns did
> exist at the time of the SSP resettlement (2003).

Nevertheless, the change in discourse didn't go far enough to result in real
change.[43] Despite the World Bank policy on involuntary resettlement, the
distributional impact in the social or gendered context remained skewed
against women. Modi repeatedly emphasizes *'the transformational
potential that large dams can have, and the positive changes they can
bring about if the actual project planning and implementation are sensitive
to the gendered aspects'*. Therefore, she concludes her analysis with the
strong recommendation that general policies, however indispensable, are

not enough: they need to be specified with respect to distinct groups at risk, such as women, and must give guidance on women's options in resettlement in more detail:

> Equity or a better distributional impact of large dams can be achieved only if resettlement policies and implementation are gender sensitive and are accompanied with a vision of women's empowerment in the economic, social and cultural context (2003).

A comparative synthesis on 50 hydropower dams

A comprehensive study on development-caused displacement by hydro-electric dams was carried out by Thayer Scudder, and is reported in a forthcoming book.[44] Scudder speaks with great authority on this topic, since his body of research and writings on dam-caused displacement has made a seminal contribution to what is scientifically known today about forced resettlement.

The 50 dams synthesis undertaken by Scudder, the first of its kind, is relevant for our analysis in the present paper for obvious reasons. First, it includes Africa and reflects a vast amount of resettlement research on the continent, part of it done and published by Scudder over the years, and part carried out and published by many other well known scholars, such as Adu Arie, Brokensha, Butcher, Chambers, Colson, Fahim, Fernea, Horowitz, Kalitzi, Koenig, Salem-Murdock, Sorbo, and others. Second, it makes conceptual and methodological use of the IRR model as an essential analytical tool. The sample of 50 dams includes 12 dams in Africa, and out of the 29 countries included 10 are African countries: Egypt, Ghana, Kenya, Ivory Coast, Lesotho, Mali, Mozambique, Nigeria, Togo, Zambia. The aim of the study is to sum up essential aspects of the 'global experience in resettlement' in terms of the impacts of dams on the welfare of the populations displaced and resettled.

Attempting to construct comparative matrices of resettlement impacts from hydroelectric dams, Scudder employed both the IRR framework to interpret and organize his main findings and the four-stage model that he developed with Colson (Scudder and Colson 1982). Scudder took an interesting road to using the IRR model: he painstakingly collected socio-economic impact data from studies on 50 large dams, organized them along the poverty risks indicators of the IRR paradigm, and subjected them to secondary analysis and generalized interpretation. The research questions he posits are: what has resettlement achieved regarding displaced people's livelihood? Have prior living standards been improved? Restored? Have the displacees ended up worse off?

To answer these questions factually but in a generalized form, Scudder 'interrogates' the collected data about whether or not the impoverishment defined in the IRR model has materialized in the set of 50 large dam cases examined. The findings are relevant both from the perspective of distilling development lessons and from an epistemological perspective, confirming the ability of the IRR methodology to produce generalizations through the secondary analysis of primary research data.

Scudder found sufficient data for analysis of seven of the IRR's eight impoverishment risks, verifying once again their generality.[45]

> While the IRR's impoverishment risks were especially important in explaining failure, [Scudder writes,] the frequency with which the most important occur is itself a condemnation of the nature of resettlement outcomes in connection with the 50 dams sample.

To generate a quantified image, Scudder constructed a 'well being index' of the resettled populations by combining five of the IRR model's impoverishment risks. Both the consolidated index itself and each of its five components were found *'to have a significant relationship to outcome'*, with a small standard deviation. For instance, the landlessness risk materialized into reality in 86% of Scudder's cases, and the joblessness risk—in 80%. 'Looking to the future', he writes, 'the importance [of landlessness] can be expected to rise as an increasing proportion of dams are constructed in the tropics'.

Equally relevant results came out about the other risks: food security surfaced as a grim reality in 79% of the cases; loss of access to common property resources materialized as an impoverishing loss of both natural capital, community power and social organization; and *'marginalization, as Scudder wrote, had the highest association with an adverse outcome of any of Cernea's impoverishment risks'*. As to social disarticulation, in analyzing the primary data Scudder coded it mainly as an outcome of the 'inability or unwillingness of project authorities to resettle people in communities and social units of their choice': in this somehow narrow interpretation, it still scored as a problem for a majority of resettlers in 34% of cases. My own definition of social disorganization, however, is considerably broader, since it results from intrinsic complex changes in displacement beyond what project authorities are willing to do, and therefore social disarticulation effects are likely to be more widespread.

Finally, Scudder found that

least problematic of Cernea's impoverishment risks was homelessness, provision of housing being the most successful resettlement component worldwide. Housing was considered adequate in 81 percent of 47 cases and inadequate in none.

Indeed, this risk is confirmed by many researchers as being largely preempted, due largely to the strong aspiration of poor resettlers to acquire a better dwelling, for which they mobilise their own resources as well.

Positive outcomes in resettlement from dams have also occurred, but in a small number of cases. Their analysis, in turn, illustrates what is required to enable a majority of a resettling population to become not victims but rather beneficiaries of resettlement. For that to happen, reconstruction post displacement must reverse risks and follow a full fledged multisided strategy.

Whether or not the social results achieved so far demonstrate that dams are inherently unsustainable projects, or that they can be sustainable and beneficial at both national and local levels, appears to depend primarily on implementing policy norms and allocated means, and on better handling the social complexities of resettlement. Despite my full agreement and appreciation of Scudder's own IRR analysis of outcomes in the 50 dams sample, and despite our common assessment that the current planning and execution of many hydropower projects 'continues to be seriously flawed', I cannot share his position when he writes that *'I'm convinced that large dams do not constitute sustainable development'* (Scudder 2004). The hugely positive contributions of hydroelectric dams to generating clean, non-polluting energy, to irrigation in agriculture, to flood control, and to drinking water can be made sustainable and enduring, provided that sound policies, adequate investments and equitable profit sharing with those adversely affected are implemented as well. It is precisely the virtue and due of the IRR analysis to reveal what *can and must be done early on to preempt de-capitalization risks and, with political will, to allocate commensurate financial and institutional resources for implementing realistic counter-risk action*, at satisfactory social, economic, and equity standards.

XI. Brief conclusions

At the end of this analysis several main conclusions virtually impose themselves. Yet it may be proper to state that the vast material examined is much too rich to be summarized simply. It can be best looked at as a vast platform of knowledge for further reflection, analysis, scientific and public discussion, and mostly, for policy and practical action.

First and foremost, we must conclude that the study of risks in forced resettlement has hugely expanded in Africa. The social science research on resettlement is today more divesified, gaining more breadth and sharper depth. It has entered sectors in which forced displacements have happened before as well, but have not been explored previously. The 'classic' knowledge on resettlement in Africa is being used, built upon, compared with new experiences, developed further, enriched. Surely, the overall resettlement research field and literature in Africa are much larger than the risk-related research analyzed here, but it is clear that this new and expanding interest in risk studies is moving the frontier further and is broadening the entire domain. New cohorts of researchers have joined the ranks of resettlement scholars. Tribute must be paid to the growing numbers of social scientists whose endeavor has produced this vast research panorama on the risks of displacement/resettlement processes embedded in the fabric of today's struggle for Africa's development.

The most important overall finding of the present analysis is the *indisputable link* between forced displacements and new poverty processes. The aggregate analyses of recent social research glaringly reveal and factually document that *new* impoverishment is now taking place in Africa. This must be recognized as the biggest paradox, and the most unacceptable, in induced development: the fact that some development programs, although launched, financed, and designed to reduce poverty, end up causing more poverty to a segment of their populations. And nonetheless, this paradoxical outcome is ineptly and immorally tolerated, and it occurs again and again. It is predictable, and yet it is not preempted. Impoverishment from displacement becomes a strange and routine outcome of most projects that displace a number of people, but do not provide effective safeguards to protect their livelihood. The risks to livelihoods can be avoided or much mitigated. But investments in safeguard measures are not made and the risks of pauperization materialize again and again into disastrous actual impacts.

Impoverishment through displacement, moreover, occurs in most cases—and the risk analyses discussed above revealed this aptly—as a process of *multidimensional* pauperization. Such impoverishment is not just an 'economic' or 'cash poverty' matter, it is a political one as well; it also causes asset poverty, health poverty, nutritional poverty; it is also power poverty and disempowerment. The findings of many researchers on the risks of poverty have produced a multidimensional picture of impoverishment stemming from now ongoing forced displacements in Africa, inadequately carried out when induced by development interventions ungoverned by sound resettlement policy.

This broad picture sends a loud signal. Governments and international agencies must genuinely listen to and hear this loud signal; and they must re-adjust both their policy content and policy discourse about poverty reduction accordingly. It is not only the old, inherited poverty, that must be reduced and eliminated. 'New poverty' emerges surreptitiously while the 'old poverty' is being fought. Yet the scourge of this new poverty is not pre-ordained: it is man-made. Some of it comes, unacceptably, on the wings of development programs that are needed, but are incomplete or one-sidedly designed. But precisely because this new poverty is man-made, it is not inevitable. It can be preempted when potential/incipient risks of poverty are arrested before they grow, proliferate, and materialize into actual poverty impacts.

Unfortunately, however, while displacement by development projects is expanding at a fast clip in Africa, with severe impoverishing effects, the regulation of displacement processes in Africa through formal state policies is almost nil. Such policy regulation in Africa lags behind the policy advances made in all other continents. This *policy-vacuum* should be a matter of high concern to all governments interested in promoting faster development in Africa.

Throughout numerous recent studies analyzed above, the Impoverishment Risks and Reconstruction Model has been tested and proven, due to the efforts of many independent researchers, as a robust scientific tool capable to predict, diagnose, and incisively deconstruct the anatomy of impoverishment risks. It appears that in a short period the analytical applications of the IRR have grown rapidly and have considerably fertilized resettlement research.

The explicit use of the IRR methodology and conceptual apparatus has empowered resettlement research in Africa to focus—stronger than ever before—on risks indicators and poverty's measurable dimensions. Bridges are being built, linking resettlement research to the dominant paradigm in development today—the paradigm of poverty reduction—thus gaining important strategic space for a forceful argument in international development: the argument that forced displacement and resettlement, when it is absolutely unavoidable, must be done much better, sounder, to become itself one of the roads upon which those affected could step towards poverty reduction is writ large.

As evident from the studies discussed in this paper, during its use the IRR methodology was not only 'applied', it was also enriched and diversified, adjusted and improved, by the scholars and researchers who have used it, through their precious contributions. With adequate adjustments and caveats, its application has been advanced and ex-panded creatively beyond development-investment projects to other types of displacements, such as population transfer and territorial redistribution programs, conflict-caused forced displacements, and conservation-park programs. It has also been tested and used for analyzing the impoverish-ment risks affecting host populations as well, not only resettlers.

A good number of research techniques, indexes, scales, matrices, indicators, etc. have been devised inventively in support of employing the IRR effectively, with due consideration to local contexts and to different research goals. Much creative use of the IRR methodology and concepts has also been done beyond Africa by many researchers on other continents, particularly in Asia, upon which the present paper did not dwell. The robustness of the IRR has been greatly enhanced through all these contributions from several continents.

Beyond these advances, however, there also are as yet un-explored research territories in risk analysis. The programs of further research on resettlement risks and their ramifications must be outlined collectively by the resettlement research community. The expansion of research on risks and counter-risk activities in resettlement still has gaps to fill, in my view, in terms of 'scaling up', to analyze the state's social policies and public expenditure patterns, and the private sector's practices. The IRR methodology is also apt to strategically guide planning and reconstruction programs, but in the present analysis I found much less current research in Africa on how state policies are or are not framed, on how reconstruction is being pursued, and how reparation of harm and losses is or is not carried out, when they are identified and recognized. Institutional constraints and contradictions in managing displacement's risk have specificities not encountered in, so-to-say, 'normal' development work. Yet the well established domain of *risk management* research, although highly respected in the 'social protection' sector, has yet to include the social protection from imposed displacement risks.

There is much un-traveled research territory also in the opposite direction, in 'scaling-down', to explore deeper the strategies of those displaced themselves: this needs to include not only research on coping and adaptation-to-risk strategies, but also research on resisting displacement risks through political action (a topic still virtually absent in African resettlement research). The IRR framework also calls for expanding the practices of risk-communication, yet quite often the risk-generating development actors tend to hide the risks from the risk-bearers. There is as well, in my view, a rich agenda to be ploughed by research on risk-information and communication of responses to risks, but such research is still lacking. Also, the more intimate human and cultural-psychological aspects, the perceptions and traumas of displacement stress and the fear of risks are frequently recognized declaratively but not systematically examined. Computing the aggregate numbers of for-cibly displaced people, however important, only seems to tell the full story of displacement's proportions, but the full story is larger, because the micro-dimensions of forcible displacement at the individual human level, at the level of what men and women, the elderly and the children, actually experience in displacement, constitute an entire universe, with its own proportions.

The facts on poverty revealed by the many IRR studies on which this paper relies are deeply painful, and deeply true. Beyond numbers and percentages of risks and losses are countless real families and human beings which suffer these losses as tragic setbacks in their daily existence and in their aspiration for a better life. The obligation to prevent and reduce these risks of further impoverishment is a developmental and ethical high commandment.

I'd like therefore to conclude these thoughts by affirming that doing research on impoverishment risks gives the social researcher a great privilege: the privilege of, hopefully, being useful to many people deeply affected, vulnerable and exposed to losing very much of the very little they posses. This privilege and duty, together, are a tall order for what must be engaged scholarship, and deserves the most committed response.

Appendix 1: The IRR—Impoverishment risks summary

1. *Landlessness*. Loss of land removes the main foundation on which many people build their agricultural productive systems or com-mercial activities. The land lost is often only partially replaced (only rarely fully replaced), and often replaced with land of poorer quality. Compensation in cash is usually insufficient to buy back land of same quantity or quality. Loss of land, in full or in part, is the main form of

de-capitalization and impoverishment of the people displaced. Both natural capital and man-made capital are lost.

2. *Joblessness*. Loss of paid employment occurs both in rural and urban displacement. People losing jobs may be landless agricultural laborers, service workers, or artisans. The unemployment or underemployment among resettlers may last long after physical relocation. Creating new jobs for resettlers is difficult: it requires substantial investment and general area development to absorb those who lost old jobs.

3. *Homelessness*. Loss of house may be temporary for many people, but in some situations it remains a long-term condition. Loss of home is perceived also as loss of identity and cultural impoverishment. Loss of house tends to have negative consequences on family cohesion and on mutual help networks, when neighboring households become scattered. Relocation of related people and neighbors as groups is preferable instead of dispersed relocation. Compensation of lost houses at replacement cost can reduce this impoverishment risk more than the risk of landlessness or joblessness.

4. *Marginalization*. Marginalization occurs when relocated families lose economic power and slide down towards lesser socio-economic positions: middle income farm-households become small land-holders; small shopkeepers and artisans lose business and fall below poverty thresholds, and so on. Human capital (skills) may become unusable, obsolete. Economic marginalization is often accompanied by social and psychological marginalization. This is expressed in a drop in social status, in resettlers' loss of confidence in themselves and in society, in a feeling of injustice and vulnerability

5. *Increased morbidity and mortality*. The exposure of the poorest people to illness is increased by forced relocation, because it causes increased stress, psychological traumas, and often the outbreak of parasitic or vector-born diseases. Decreases in health levels may result from unsafe water supply and bad sewage systems that proliferate epidemic infections, diarrhea, dysentery, etc.

6. *Food insecurity*. Food insecurity is defined as levels of calories and protein intake which are below the minimum necessary for normal healthy growth and work. Forced displacement diminishes self-sufficiency in food, often dismantling local arrangements for food supply. It increases the risk that people, particularly children, will fall into chronic malnutrition and food insecurity.

7. *Loss of access to common property natural resources*. Poor farmers suffer a loss of access to the common property goods belonging to

communities that are displaced (for instance, loss of access to forests and forest products, to water bodies, to grazing lands, etc.), as well as to some common services. This is a form of income loss and livelihood impoverishment that is typically overlooked by planners and remains often uncompensated.

8. *Social dis-articulation (community dis-organization).* The dismantling of community social structures, the dispersion of informal and formal networks, local associations, etc. is a massive loss of social capital. Such disarticulation undermines livelihoods in ways usually not recognized and not measured by planners. It is a major cause of disempowerment and impoverishment.

Differences in impoverishment risks

The general impoverishment risks express themselves differently in different contexts, and differently affect each category of people: rural and urban, indigenous or non-indigenous populations, tribal and non-tribal groups, children and the elderly. For instance, research findings in different contexts show constantly that women suffer displacement impacts more severely than men.

Host populations living in the areas where the resettlers are relocated also suffer negative impacts in their livelihood, especially when resources at arrival sites are scarce. Often hosts are impoverished also. The impoverishment risks to hosts must also be mitigated by development projects

Notes

1 Although the number of such studies is important, as will be seen further, most probably there are many others works discussing or employing the IRR framework, of which I regret to not yet have learned. My analysis is therefore restricted, by force, to those risk-oriented studies from Africa that have come to my attention (and I would welcome signals about any other such studies).

2 Clearly, not all issues raised in the studies analyzed could be addressed in this paper: I'm giving priority here to highlighting the empirical and methodological dimensions, while discussing some theoretical aspects as well. This discussion will certainly continue.

3 In addition to the concept of 'forced displacement', another term—'forced migration'— has gained circulation in the literature. It designates more

or less the same category of processes. However, considerable reservation has been expressed about the term 'forced migration' (see Turton 2004; Cernea 2004; and others) as being somehow a contradiction in terms and inviting confusion between coerced (no-choice) displacement, on the one hand, and regular migration, which involves a voluntarily taken and deliberate decision of those who migrate, on the other hand. In this paper, I will consistently use 'forced displacement'.

4 Examples of such projects are the large scale villagization program in Tanzania in the 1970s, or the resettlement programs undertaken in Ethiopia under a disaster-avoidance rationale. Usually, such state programs are introduced as voluntary resettlement programs and—if this were consistently the case—they would not have a place in our typology of *forced* displacement. In practice, however, such programs often turn coercive, forcing some population groups to move against their will. The degrees of coercion and freedom vary from program to program, from region to region, and sometimes from period to period within the same program. It is therefore difficult to reduce such programs to just one type or another; instead, it may be often more adequate to recognize their mixed nature, on a case by case analysis. The balance of the mixture tends to tilt definitively toward coercion in the case of programs which also pursue a government's goal of introducing tighter political controls over certain populations.

5 Of course, within the large category of development-displaced people, other subtypes and groupings can be distinguished based on objective features and differences, such as sector-based criteria (Cernea 2004). These may entail vast differences, in content and effects, between urban displacements and displacements caused by water-resource projects, or by mining projects.

6 Since private sector corporations undertake their projects for private profit, these cannot be defined in the same way as state-sponsored development projects, which are regarded as being of *compelling* and *overriding public interest* and thus carry out population displacement justified under the legal principle of eminent domain. When a private sector development project needs a site, the land should be purchased through a *willing buyer-willing seller* market transaction, that protects the land owner against imposed expropriation and enables price negotiation. If the price is satisfactory to the seller, his relocation becomes voluntary rather than forced. However, recent practice in some developing countries indicate that private sector agents attempt to avoid the market and to use the state as an instrument for acquiring land at state-imposed prices.

7 For a fuller presentation of the IRR model, see also Cernea (1999; 2000)
   see also the discussion of the IRR model by other authors, in Asia as well
   (Mahapatra 1999; Pandey et al. 1998; Mathur 1999; Koenig 2001; Robinson 2003; de Wet 2004 and in this volume; Scudder forthcoming).

8 Asian Development Bank (ADB) (1999) *Fighting Poverty in Asia and the
   Pacific. The Poverty Reduction Strategy of the Asian Development Bank.*
   Manila.

9 The numerous studies which we found refer to three out of the four
   DIDR types distinguished earlier in the typology proposed in section II
   of this paper: (a), (b), and (d). Somehow unexpected to me, a considerable
   number of these risk-oriented studies are those analyzing population
   redistribution and transfer programs of the kind undertaken in Ethiopia,
   either examining such programs retroactively, or zeroing in on current
   programs (see for example Gebre in this volume).

10 Of course, many valuable studies have also been produced by scholars
   who have not employed the IRR framework, contributing in various
   other ways to the body of knowledge on resettlement in Africa. Given
   the conditions set for this study (see Introduction), those studies are not
   examined here.

11 Still at this time, unfortunately, the vast majority of African countries have
   not yet adopted explicit policies and laws on state-induced displacement;
   nor have they created institutional capacities to manage such processes
   when they occur.

12 This broad sector encompasses coal and all other mining extractive
   industries (aluminum, oil, gas, iron ore, etc.), the thermal plants with
   their large footprints, LNG plants, pipelines crossing long distances to
   the sea-shore, etc. This sector's industries require considerable expanses
   of land to extract and process natural resources, as well as lands for
   ancillary structures and protection zones.

13 It is worth noting that a similar rapid escalation in studying mining-induced displacement has taken place over the last decade in Asia, particularly in India, where numerous researchers also explicitly employ the
   IRR model. This has created an opportunity for undertaking comparative
   secondary analyses of findings along similar risk variables (for India, see
   studies by Agarwal 2000; Mahapatra 1999; Mathur and Marsden 1998;
   Mathur forthcoming and others).

14 This African sub-region is one of the richest mineral zones on the planet
   (and its population one of the poorest). The region's states derive, on
   average, about 10% of their GDP from mining and 40% of their foreign
   exchange from mineral exports.

15 Projects that expand existing facilities causing less displacement, like the Konkola mine in Zambia.

16 Projects that construct new extractive industries where none existed, causing larger land-takes, like the Bulyanhulu project in Tanzania.

17 Additional projects included the Mozal plant in Mozambique, the Kwale project in Kenya, etc., plus three mining projects in West Africa (the Tarkwa gold fields in Ghana, and the Yatela Gold Mining and Sadiola Hill projects in Mali).

18 Ironically, the projects analyzed were still among those with better practices, since some had resettlement plans or social development plans, claiming to follow certain international guidelines. This prompted the authors to conclude: 'It is fair to expect that many unrecorded cases of resettlement have taken place that have not followed...guidelines. It is *impossible* to estimate the number of people resettled as a result of mining' (Sonnenberg and Münster 2001: 30, emphasis added).

19 The identification of sector-wide features of displacement practice is, in my view, a main contribution of this study, providing the empirical case for the institutionalization of compelling sector-wide policy guidelines.

20 Downing writes:

> The likelihood that MIDR will be a significant issue increases as several factors converge. Rich mineral deposits are found in areas with relatively low land acquisition costs (in the global market) that are being exploited with open-cast mining and are located in regions of high population density—especially on fertile and urban lands—with poor definitions of land tenure and politically weak and powerless populations, especially indigenous people...Displacement can be expected to increase as national mining policies are liberalized as companies opt for open-cast mining, and as rural population density increases (Downing 2002: 6–7).

21 A comparable recommendation was made independently by Ravi Kanbur in an exchange with Cernea (2002). Tracing the history of the compensation principle in economic thinking, Kanbur concluded that given the inefficiencies of compensation, the introduction of some kind of 'general safety net' might be warranted in the practice of development-induced forced displacements (Kanbur 2002). Yet, Kanbur has not detailed and operationalized his proposal either. Whether what Kanbur terms 'general safety net' is akin to Downing's 'displacement insurance' must be examined, to produce practicable and actionable policy measures.

22 Faure notes: 'After re-establishment, the remarkable phenomenon of constructing new dwellings with solid materials (*'en dur'*) created

employment for males (brick layers, painters, carpenters, etc.) and new gainful opportunities (stone collection, sand quarrying, cart transportation, etc.) for the local population. Some could become professional construction workers in a capital city whose demand of such skills grows constantly' (2004: 6).

23 'The sanitary problems have not been yet resolved in the relocation area and there are growing risks of mismanaging the latrines and the refuse' (p. 11).

24 The study reports on many relevant findings and issues that we cannot visit here.

25 A report published at the time described that displacement in Khartoum as follows:

> Mile after mile of houses have been summarily razed by government bulldozers under an urban renewal plan that has forced nearly a half-million people from their homes over the past years. The new urban refugees are being relocated in ill-equipped camps outside the city, mostly without adequate water, food or shelter, creating what foreign aid officials describe as a new—and unnecessary—humanitarian crisis...(*Washington Post*, March 7, 1993).

26 Feleke writes: 'Elderly people who had land before have become landless and their chances of getting employment at the project have been minimal...Landless young and adult households are among the previous marginalized groups who '*gained*' from the project, while the elderly who had land are the ones who 'lost' their economic resources and became marginalized due to landlessness and limited access to the employment opportunities' (2004: 502).

27 Given that this displacement was caused by a housing project, it would have also been of interest to know who could afford the new dwellings. Feleke does not tell us, however, why the evicted 172 households were not relocated by the municipality within the new 6250 housing units being built on their former lands, as it is practiced in some other countries. In China, for instance, vast numbers of displaced urban families are re-housed in this way.

28 Such studies will also be discussed further, in sections IX and X.

29 This observation is based not only on research in Africa. A wide corpus of research dedicated to the assault on common property systems because of development-caused displacements has been generated in Asian countries.

30 Pankhurst and Piguet, the editors of this remarkable volume, offer a comprehensive and nuanced overview of Ethiopia's many resettlements

and their structural causes. They propose a periodization, discuss several types of sectoral displacements, and examine highly controversial questions about the extent of voluntary versus involuntary resettlement in Ethiopia's population transfers. On this last point, the authors write:

> Most studies have focused on abuse of human rights and the numerous injustices of the involuntary resettlement. However, what needs explaining is the voluntary end of the spectrum which has tended to be overlooked in highlighting the coercions and impositions...The limited options for access to land by the younger generation, therefore no doubt contributed to their 'willingness' to resettle, and can be considered an underlying structural factor. Whatever the overt and covert motives, the overall verdict is that the experiment was a clear disaster in political, economic, social, cultural and environmental terms (Pankhurst and Piguet: 2004b).

31 It is remarkable that even when the immediate focus of one or another study is a different displacement risk or context, the analysis links it to the general state and fabric of social relationships within the nation.

32 Among the few other empirical investigation of the host-resettlers relationship is one carried out some 12 years earlier by Salem-Murdock (1989), also in Africa, among the Aswan resettlers and their Nubian hosts.

33 Wolde-Selassie offers the following comprehensive and compelling image:

> During the initial phase, resettlers did not have proper community village institutions, such as *idir* and other religious or secular mutual associations. The observation of religious holidays was constrained. Long-established kinship ties that had performed multipurpose functions were altered in the new location, and there existed no kinship-based leadership. The complex web of social networks which had previously formed the interhousehold and group relationships in communities, no longer functioned. In other words, from the early days of resettlement, the various communities close bonds and webs of relationships along several lines—such as neighborhood, kinship, religious beliefs, work groups, land exchange, bond-friendship, fictive and godparenting—were either lost or in abeyance. The new villages were, in Cernea's terms, socially disarticulated (2000: 420).

34 The importance of recognizing and capturing the extreme complexity 'inherent' in resettlement was adequately and strongly emphasized by de Wet (2004) in the same volume.

35 For a detailed and very interesting discussion of these differences, the interested readers, and particularly those who study conflict-caused

displacement, are encouraged to review Kibreab's full argument on these points in his original study (2000).

36 A remarkable study on the chronic civil-war-caused displacements in Colombia was carried out by Robert Muggah (2000) explicitly applying the IRR framework. Columbia's forced displacements had been analyzed by numerous researchers in many other previous studies, and Muggah's research accomplishment was to open new perspectives by studying this specific set of conflict-caused displacements as a series of unfolding impoverishment processes.

37 Working for his graduate research thesis under the guidance of the Ruhr Universität, Bochum, Germany.

38 The reasons given by Damien Mama follow:

The theoretical framework of the present research is drawn from the Impoverishment, Risk and Reconstruction model developed by Cernea (2000). This model is used for the following reasons. First, although developed for development-induced resettlement, the model offers useful tools applicable for conflict-induced resettlement as most of the problems raised are common to both groups of displaced people. Second, there is no other theory on resettlement which can be used for problem diagnosis and policy analysis as it is intended in this master thesis. The UN guiding principles on resettlement are more a framework for legal protection needs of the IDPs than a decision-making tool for resettlement and reintegration. Third, the model has yet to be broadly tested in the post-conflict situations...Finally, the impoverishment angle through which the model was developed offers useful tools to analyze the situation of the resettled population in Sierra Leone that is one of the poorest countries in the world (2003: 12–13).

39 Damien Mama concluded that land problems turned out to not be acute because

mediation and (the) involvement of former fighters in reintegration opportunity programs for their economic self reliance have contributed to curb potential problems and settled major disputes (2003: 50).

40 At the World Park Congress, held in Durban, South Africa, the debates around these findings on impoverishment were intense and generated considerable support, but also entrenched resistance from some conservation practitioners. Forced displacement as a park creation strategy in developing countries profoundly conflicts with poverty reduction. After decades of experiences with the population displacement approach, the argument is that this strategy has exhausted both its potential and its

credibility. It has produced great damage, has not fulfilled expectations, and is compromising the reputation of the efforts for biodiversity parks conservation by inflicting aggravated poverty on resident people.

41 Rudd writes:

> The impact of Bwindi Impenetrable National Park on the Batwa can best be analyzed through the framework of Cernea's Impoverishment Risks and Reconstruction (IRR) model. I understand the Batwa's situation as one of absolute poverty—a poverty that extends far beyond monetary terms to encompass a broader social struggle—that is effectively outlined in the eight risks of the IRR model. While all of the risks are applicable in analyzing the Batwa's relationship to the park, they have impacted the community to varying degrees. Using this model as an analytical framework allows us to better evaluate the impact of Bwindi on the Batwa people, and to apply those findings to the formulation of more effective and just development and conservation strategies (2004: 54).

42 The 1993 paper is a synthesis of Scudder's several papers on this case.

43 Modi (2003) criticizes the policy of the World Bank for not being strong enough on women's entitlements, and India's Governmental authorities responsible for project implementation for the same weaknesses. It is also noteworthy that, in the case of the Sardar Sarovar Project, when the World Bank following the Morse Commission Report made exacting formal requests that India's Government adheres rigorously to policy, India's Government responded by asking for the Bank's withdrawal from overseeing and financing this project, even though India had to forgo over US$100 million in as yet unused Bank project financing.

44 Thanks are expressed to the author for permission to quote some of the data from the book's manuscript.

45 For the 8th risk of the IRR framework—increased morbidity and mortality—Scudder reports that he has found insufficient research data in the primary dam impact studies to allow statistically valid processing.

References

Adams, William M., R. Aveling, D. Brockington, B. Dickson, J. Elliott, J. Hutton, R. Dilys, B. Vira and W. Wolmer (2004) 'Biodiversity conservation and the eradication of poverty', *Science*, 306(5699), pp. 1146–9.

Agrawal, Dinesh (2000) *Restoring Livelihood and the Consequences of Social*

Risks. Paper presented at the Xth World Congress of Rural Sociology, Rio de Janeiro.

Brockington, Dan and Kai Schmidt-Soltau (2004) 'The social and environmental impacts of wildernesss and development', *Oryx*, 38(2), pp. 140–142.

Cernea, Michael M. (1990), *Poverty Risks from Population Displacement in Water Resources Development*. Harvard University, HIID, Cambridge, MA: Harvard Univ.

———— (1993) *The Urban Environment and Population Relocation*. World Bank Discussion Paper No. 152. Washington DC: World Bank.

————(1995) *Social Organization and Development Anthropology*. The 1995 Malinowski Award Lecture, Washington DC: World Bank.

———— (1997a) 'The risks and reconstruction model for resettling displaced populations', *World Development*, 25(10), pp. 1569–88.

———— (1997b) *African Involuntary Population Resettlement in a Global Context*. Washington, DC: World Bank.

————(1999) 'The need for economic analysis of resettlement: A sociologist's view', in M. M. Cernea (ed.), *The Economics of Involuntary Resettlement: Questions and Challenges*. Washington, DC: World Bank.

———— (2000) 'Impoverishment risks and reconstruction: A model for population displacement and resettlement', in M. M. Cernea and C. McDowell (eds), *Risks and Reconstruction: Experiences of Resettlers and Refugees*. Washington, DC: World Bank.

———— (2003) 'For a new economics of resettlement: A sociological critique of the compensation principle', *International Social Science Journal*, 175, pp. 37–43.

————(2004) *The Typology of Development-Induced Displacements: Field of Research, Concepts, Gaps and Bridges*. Paper presented at the workshop on Typologies of Relevance in Forced Migration, US National Academy of Sciences, Washington, September.

Cernea, Michael M. and Kai Schmidt-Soltau (2003) 'The end of forcible displacement? Conservation must not impoverish people', *Policy Matters*, Geneva: IUCN.

———— (forthcoming) 'National parks and poverty risks: Policy issues in conservation and resettlement'.

Cernea, Michael M., Scott Guggenheim, Warren van Wicklin and Dan Aronson (1994) *Resettlement and Development: Report on the Bank-Wide Review of Projects Involving Involuntary Resettlement*. Washington, DC: World Bank.

Chambers, Robert and David Butcher (1969) *The Volta Resettlement Experience*. New York: Praeger.

Colson, Elizabeth (1971) *The Social Consequences of Resettlement*. Manchester: Manchester University Press.

Cook, Cynthia C. and Aleki Mukendi (1993) 'Involuntary resettlement in bank-financed projects: Lessons from experience in Sub-Saharan Africa', in C. Cook (ed.), *Involuntary Resettlement in Africa*. Washington DC: World Bank.

de Wet, Chris (2004) 'Why do things often go wrong in resettlement projects?', in Alula Pankhurst and Francois Piguet (eds), *People, Space, and the State: Migration, Resettlement and Displacement in Ethiopia*. Addis Ababa: Addis Ababa University, pp. 50–70.

Dinku, Lamessa (2004) 'Socio-cultural dimensions of conflict-induced displacement: The case of displaced persons in Addis Ababa', in Alula Pankhurst and Francois Piguet (eds), *People, Space, and the State: Migration, Resettlement and Displacement in Ethiopia*. Addis Ababa: Addis Ababa University, pp. 371–86

Downing, Theodore E. (2002) *Avoiding New Poverty: Mining-Induced Displacement and Resettlement*. IIED and World Business Council for Sustainable Development. (*www.iied.org*)

Faure, Armelle (2004) *L'analyse de l'operation de reinstallation de populations deplacees du bidonville d'El Mina a Nouakchott-Mauritanie*. Paper prepared for the sourcebook of the World Bank assisted project: Mauritania Urban Development Program. Cr.3574. Processed.

Feleke, Tadele (2004) 'Urban development and the displacement of rural communities around Addis Ababa', in Alula Pankhurst and Francois Piguet (eds), *People, Space, and the State: Migration, Resettlement and Displacement in Ethiopia*. Addis Ababa: Addis Ababa University.

Gebre, Yntiso (2002a) 'Differential reestablishment of voluntary and involuntary migrants: The case of Metekel settlers in Ethiopia', *African Study Monographs*, 23(1), pp. 31–46.

———— (2002b) 'Contextual determination of migration behaviors: The Ethiopian resettlement in the light of conceptual constructs', *Journal of Refugee Studies*, 15(3), pp. 265–82.

———— (2003) 'Resettlement and the unnoticed losers: Impoverishment disasters among the Gumz hosts in Ethiopia', *Human Organization*, 62(1), pp. 50–61.

———— (2004) 'The Metekel resettlement in Ethiopia: Why did it fail?', in Alula Pankhurst and Francois Piguet (eds), *People, Space, and the State:*

Migration, Resettlement and Displacement in Ethiopia. Addis Ababa: Addis Ababa University, pp. 92–111.

Kanbur, Ravi (2002) 'Development economics and the compensation principle', in M. Cernea and R. Kanbur, *An Exchange on the Compensation Principle in Resettlement*. Working Paper 2002–33, Cornell University, Department of Applied Economics and Management, Icatha, New York.

Kassahun, Kebede (2004) 'The social dimensions of development-induced resettlement: The case of the Gigel Gibe hydroelectric dam in Ethiopia', in Alula Pankhurst and Francois Piguet (eds), *People, Space, and the State: Migration, Resettlement and Displacement in Ethiopia*. Addis Ababa: Addis Ababa University.

Kibreab, Gaim (2000) 'Common property resources and resettlement', in M. Cernea and C. McDowell (eds), *Risks and Reconstruction: Experiences of Resettlers and Refugees*. Washington, DC: World Bank.

———(2003) 'Displacement, host governments' policies, and constraints on construction of sustainable livelihoods', *International Social Science Journal*, 175. Paris: UNESCO, Blackwell.

Koenig, Dolores (2001) *Diversity in Practice: Multiple Contributions to Improving Involuntary Resettlement*. Paper presented at the Annual Meetings of the American Anthropological Association, Washington, DC, November.

——— (2003) *Toward Local Development and Mitigating Impoverishment in Development-Induced Displacement and Resettlement*. http://www.rsc.ox.ac.uk/PDFs/rrtowardlocal01.pdf.

Koenig, Dolores and Tieman Diarra (2000) 'The effects of resettlement on access to common property resources', in M. Cernea and C. McDowell (eds), *Risks and Reconstruction: Experiences of Resettlers and Refugees*. Washington, DC: World Bank.

Lassailly-Jacob, Veronique (2000) 'Reconstructing livelihoods through land settlement schemes: Comparative reflections on refugees and oustees in Africa', in M. Cernea and C. McDowell (eds), *Risks and Reconstruction: Experiences of Resettlers and Refugees*. Washington, DC: World Bank.

Mahapatra, Lakshman K. (1999) *Resettlement, Impoverishment and Reconstruction in India: Development for the Deprived*. New Delhi: Vikas Publishing House PVT Ltd.

Mama, Damien (2003) *Partnerships for Post-Conflict Recovery: An Analysis of Resettlement and Reintegration of IDPs in Sierra Leone*. Thesis submitted for Master's Degree at Ruhr Universität-Bochum, Germany.

Mathur, Hari Mohan (1999) 'The impoverishment potential of development projects: Resettlement requires risk analysis', *Development and Cooperation*, 6, Frankfurt: Deutsche Schiftung für Internationale Entwicklung.

———— (forthcoming) 'Mining coal, undermining people: Compensation policies and practices of the Coal India Limited', in M. Cernea and H. M. Mathur (eds), *The Compensation Dilemma*. Delhi: Oxford University Press.

Mathur, Hari Mohan and David Marsden (1998) *Development Projects and Impoverishment Risks: Resettling Project-Affected People in India*. Oxford: Oxford University Press.

Modi, Renu (2003) 'Gender and development-induced displacement: Case studies from Zambia and India', in C. Brun and Nina M. Birkeland (eds), *Researching Internal Displacement: State of the Art*. Acta Geographica Series A, No. 6, NTNU, Norway, Trondheim.

Muggah, Robert (2000), Through the developmentalist's looking glass: Conflict-induced displacement and involuntary resettlement in Colombia', *Journal of Refugee Studies*, 13(2), pp. 133–64.

Pandey, Balaji (1998) *Depriving the Underpriviledged by Development*. Bhubaneshwar: ISED.

Pankhurst, Alula and Francois Piguet (eds) (2004a) *People, Space, and the State: Migration, Resettlement and Displacement in Ethiopia*. Addis Ababa: Addis Ababa University.

———— (2004b) 'Conceptualizing migration, resettlement and displacement in Ethiopia', in Alula Pankhurst and Francois Piguet (eds), *People, Space, and the State: Migration, Resettlement and Displacement in Ethiopia*. Addis Ababa: Addis Ababa University.

Risby, Lee .A. (2002) *Defining Landscapes Power and Participation: An Examination of a National Park Planning Process for Queen Elizabeth National Park, Uganda*. PhD Thesis, Cambridge University.

Robinson, W. Courtland (2003) *Risks and Rights: The Causes, Consequences, and Challenges of Development-Induced Displacement*. Washington, DC: Brookings Institution.

Rudd, Kristina E. (2004) *'Death is Following Us': The Impoverishment of the Ugandan Batwa Associated with Bwindi Impenetrable National Park*. Middlebury College, Vermont.

Salem-Murdock, Muneera (1989) *Arabs and Nubians in New Halfa: A Study of Settlement and Irrigation*. Salt Lake City: University of Utah Press

Schmidt-Soltau, Kai (2000) *Conservation and Resettlement in the Central African Rainforest.* Paper presented at the World Congress of Rural Sociology (IRSA) in Rio de Janeiro.

——— (2003), 'Conservation-related resettlement in Central Africa: Environmental and social risks', *Development and Change*, 34(3), pp. 525–51.

——— (2004) *Safeguards for Sustainability: Learning from the Mistakes of Conservation and Development Induced Involuntary Displacement in Central Africa.* Paper presented at the international conference on displacement and resettlement in Asia and Africa in Hyderabad, November.

Scudder, Thayer (1993) 'Development-induced relocation and refugee studies: 37 years of change and continuity among Zambia's Gwembe Tonga', *Journal of Refugee Studies*, 6(3), pp. 123–52.

——— (2004) *Global Experiences in Resettlement.* Paper prepared for the workshop on impacts of large dams, Istanbul, Turkey, October 25–27, 2004.

——— (forthcoming) *The Future of Large Dams: Dealing with Social, Environmental, Institutional and Political Costs.* Earthscan.

Scudder, Thayer and Elizabeth Colson (1982), 'From welfare to development: A conceptual framework for the analysis of dislocated people', in Art Hansen and Anthony Oliver-Smith (eds), *Involuntary Migration and Resettlement*, Westview: Boulder.

Sinkala, Thomson (2002) 'The mining and mineral sector: Factors weakening its contribution to African development', *Industry and Environment*, January–March, pp. 14–17.

Sonnenberg, Dan and Frauke Münster (2001) *Mining Minerals: Sustainable Development in Southern Africa and Involuntary Resettlement.* African Institute of Corporate Citizenship (www.iied.org).

Turton, David (2004) 'Refugees, forced resettlers, and "other forced migrants": Towards a unitary study of forced migration', in Alula Pankhurst and Francois Piguet (eds), *People, Space, and the State: Migration, Resettlement and Displacement in Ethiopia.* Addis Ababa: Addis Ababa University, pp. 34–49.

Voutira, Eftihia and Barbara Harrell-Bond (2000) 'Successful refugee settlement: Are post experiences relevant?', in M. M. Cernea and C. McDowell (eds), *Risks and Reconstruction: Experiences of Resettlers and Refugees.* Washington, DC: World Bank, pp. 56–76.

Wolde-Selassie, Abutte (2000) 'Social re-articulation after resettlement:

Observing the Belles Valley in Ethiopia', in M. M. Cernea and C. McDowell (eds), *Risks and Reconstruction: Experiences of Resettlers and Refugees*. Washington, DC: World Bank, pp. 412–30.

————— (2004a) 'Impact of resettlement in Beles Valley, Metekel', in Alula Pankhurst and Francois Piguet (eds), *People, Space, and the State: Migration, Resettlement and Displacement in Ethiopia*. Addis Ababa: Addis Ababa University.

————— (2004b) 'Resettlement as a response to food insecurity', in Alula Pankhurst and Francois Piguet (eds), *People, Space, and the State: Migration, Resettlement and Displacement in Ethiopia*. Addis Ababa: Addis Ababa University.

World Bank (2001) *Operational Policy 4.12: Involuntary Resettlement*. Washington, DC: World Bank.

7
Some Socio-Economic Risks and Opportunities Relating to Dam-Induced Resettlement in Africa

Chris de Wet

Introduction:
A brief overview of dam-induced resettlement in Africa

Over 400,000 people have been resettled as a direct result of dam construction in Africa—although many more have also been negatively affected, such as those people living downstream whose flood cultivation regimes have been disrupted by the dams. The major instances are represented in Table 7-1.

The ethnography of dam-induced resettlement in Africa provides plentiful evidence to support Cernea's now well-established impoverishment risks schema of: landlessness, joblessness, homelessness, marginalization, loss of food security, loss of access to common property resources, increased morbidity and mortality, and community disarticulation (Cernea 2000) becoming actualized at the individual, household and community levels. There is also some positive evidence of agricultural recovery (a successful pilot irrigation scheme) at Kpong and at Manantali ('fertile soils, adequate rainfall and a very modest host population density'; Horowitz et al., 1993), and of successful income restoration—although more through the settlers' initiative and capitalizing on unexpected opportunities than through scheme planning—at Kainji, Kariba and the New Halfa scheme in Sudan. In the case of the Kom Ombo scheme in Egypt and the related development of Aswan City, and the Kpong scheme in Ghana, new job opportunities have arisen, from which resettlers have benefited. For the most part, however, the record is one of diminished access to land and resources, and increased socio-economic impoverishment.

Table 7-1. Major instances of dam-induced resettlement in Africa

Name of scheme	Numbers resettled	Date of move	Source
Aswan High Dam (Egypt/Sudan)	100,000	1963–1969	Cernea 1990: 331; Fahim 1983: 45; Sorbo 1985: 104
Cabora-Bassa (Mozambique)	25,000	± 1974	Lassailly-Jacob 1996: 189
Kainji (Nigeria)	44,000	1967–1968	Ayeni et al. 1992: 111; Roder 1994: 124
Kariba (Zambia/Zimbabwe)	57,000	1958	Scudder 1973: 206
Kossou (Ivory Coast)	75,000	1970	Lassailly-Jacob 1996: 189
Manantali (Mali)	10,000	1986–1987	Koenig and Horowitz 1988: 2; Grimm 1991: Ch.4
Nangbeto (Togo/Benin)	10,600	1987	World Bank 1998: i, 2
Selingue (Mali)	15,000	± 1980	Lassailly-Jacob 1996: 189
Volta a) Akosombo (Ghana) b) Kpong (Ghana)	80,000 6,000	1963ff 1978–1981	Adu-Aryee 1993:133; Lumsden 1973: 119; World Bank 1993: 5

A framework for locating the sources of risks and opportunities relating to dam-induced resettlement in Africa

One is left asking why it is that in Africa, as elsewhere in the world, so many of the attempts to counter the negative effects of resettlement, including the specific attempts to counter Cernea's impoverishment risks, continue to meet such limited success. My argument is that a significant part of the answer lies in risks which are located at a different level than the individual or community, namely, at the level of the resettlement process itself—a problematic institutional process—and, linked to this, risks at the national level that impact upon the resettlement process. I submit that these risks perpetuate the conditions that actualize Cernea's impoverishment risks, and I attempt to provide the outlines of a framework to spell out some of these 'higher level' risks.

Risks relating to the resettlement process as an inherently problematic institutional process

The resettlement process has a number of characteristics which, in combination, serve to make it an inherently problematic process that operates in such a way that it often does not achieve its stated goals, and serves to impoverish those it resettles. These characteristics include:

1. Rew et al. (2000) argue that policy is fundamentally transformed in the very process of being implemented. This is because it is usually political in nature, and therefore a negotiated instrument, subject to further negotiation during implementation. Negotiation takes place in a context of limited staff and resources, and poor communication and coordination, in which local level officials have considerable de facto discretionary powers as to what actually happens.

2. Countries that need infrastructure projects are usually lacking in the very things needed to make resettlement work, such as money, manpower, skills, and experience—which, when combined, make for mistakes and insufficient time, with resettlement being rushed, poorly planned and messed up.

3. Resettlement is often seen as of secondary importance to the infrastructure project. So, as a 'necessary evil' of sorts, resettlement is usually poorly budgeted for (budgets are often less than 10% of the overall project costs; Scudder 1997: 688–9) and its staff are often poorly trained and motivated.

4. Accordingly, resettlement projects are all too often planned as mere relocation exercises, rather than as development undertakings.

5. Not surprisingly, resettlement projects are typically characterized by inadequate consultation with and participation of the affected people.

6. Because they are often poorly planned, funded and staffed, when resettlement happens, everything happens at once. Cernea (2000: 31) argues that the impoverishment risks he identifies hit affected people all at once, and 'they must deal with these risks virtually simultaneously...The result is a crisis'. Similarly, resettlement officials have to handle a range of problems of different orders at the same time—creating a crisis for them as well. Thus, for both the affected people and officials, the result is ad hoc crisis management, with rational planning and actions becoming increasingly unlikely.

7. Resettlement projects tend to involve competing visions of what development should be about, and how it should be implemented, with outside implementers and local communities often at odds on this score, and with local communities also often divided among themselves.

8. Most resettlement projects are involuntary, in the sense that the people have to move whether they want to or not—and they usually do not. It is very difficult to launch a successful development project,

the logic of which involves an action to which the affected people
are bitterly opposed.

In combination, these factors result in the absence of the proper consultation, planning, provision and follow-through required to offset
Cernea's impoverishment risks.

Risks operating at the national level which impact upon resettlement projects

Two sets of risk factors that operate at the national level and impact upon
the way in which resettlement projects unfold, will now be outlined.

Dams as nationalistic projects

Large dams were built principally for the provision of hydro-electricity
for industrial purposes and urban growth, and for the supply of irrigation
for agricultural development. However, they were also seen as cornerstones of national, and often nationalistic, projects. Thus, the Aswan
High Dam was conceived in the context of Nassers' vision of agrarian
reform and 'the abolishment of feudalism' (Fahim 1981: 15). Nkrumah
saw the Volta River Project as a 'scheme which transcends any political
consideration, and which is, in the truest sense, an expression of our
national unity and of our national purpose and aspirations' (Nkrumah,
quoted in Lumsden 1973: 117). The Lesotho Highlands Water Project was
to be a springboard for national development through the sale of water to
South Africa and the generation of hydropower for import substitution
(Maema and Reynolds 1995: 1, 3). The Orange River Project reflected
decolonization of a different kind: in the wake of South Africa's departure
from the Commonwealth, and the political upheaval and capital flight
after the Sharpeville shootings in 1960, South Africa was concerned
to utilize a large project such as the Orange River Project to rebuild
confidence in the country, both nationally and internationally (World
Commission on Dams, 1998: 5).

Nationalistic agendas introduce potentially irrational elements to large
dam projects. The project—as well as any accompanying resettlement—
must accommodate itself to political goals and timing, whether these are
compatible with sound planning, financing and implementation, or not.

Lack of an enabling institutional context

Many countries in which resettlement occurs lack adequate legal and
policy frameworks at the national level, as well as the necessary political

will, commitment, fiscal restraint, and functional co-ordination between the various departments or agencies responsible for different aspects of resettlement. This creates the direct risk of resettlement not being properly planned, funded or implemented. The wider context within which a scheme is situated is often characterized by political and economic weakness and instability—which creates the risks: not only that the scheme will not be effectively integrated into its wider setting, but also that the wider context will function in a manner that is actually disabling for the scheme. Furthermore, the state is both player and referee, in as much as it implements resettlement and it is also the source and supposed upholder of the laws that are to protect people from being unfairly resettled in the first place (Barutciski 2000). All of these factors impact upon the way a resettlement project is implemented.

Some specific risks and opportunities operating in the context of dam-induced resettlement in Africa

Risks and opportunities relating to planning and participation
The participation of resettlers and other affected people in the planning of and preparations for resettlement has varied quite significantly on African dam projects, not least because participation and consultation have over time become more firmly entrenched as standard parts of the resettlement process. Perhaps the starkest example of non-participation is one of the earliest dam projects—Kariba. In 1958, a headman and his village refused to move. The authorities attempted to arrest them. There were riots, resulting in the fatal shooting of eight Gwembe Tonga people, and the end of the resistance (Colson 1971: 41). It is, however, not only those on the wrong end of the power relationship that have been denied participation. In the case of the Orange River Project, farmers who were members of the powerful white South African agricultural lobby were not consulted about the dam or the impending move, and had no part in the planning of projects that affected them (World Commission on Dams 1998: 24).

At the other end of the spectrum, Nangbeto serves as a successful instance of participation. Villages formed committees to supervise their own resettlement, and the resettlers 'participated in designing the program, constructing the resettlement houses, and selecting village sites and household plots within the village' (World Bank 1998: 16). The Lesotho

Highlands Water Project designed a 'People's Involvement Programme' to emphasize the importance of local committees in negotiating favorable resettlement conditions (LHWP June 1996: ii).

Manantali perhaps better reflects what has been occurring more generally, where a greater degree of participation was achieved in planning, but less in implementation, because of the tight time frames that were involved (Koenig and Horowitz 1988: 9–10).

The problem of time frames has dogged the planning of resettlement in Africa, perhaps nowhere more dramatically than at Akosombo, where the formation of Lake Volta began more than a year ahead of plan—putting tremendous pressure on the planning and preparation for resettlement (Lumsden 1973: 119). The lack of time is a constant refrain in the first major volume on the Volta River Project (Chambers ed. 1970). The effect was that because issues around evacuation and relocation had to be prioritized, other, longer-term, development-focused issues had to be delayed or abandoned (Chambers 1970b: 262).

This contrasted with the more participatory planning at Nangbeto (discussed above), where planners had three years before the reservoir was due to fill (World Bank 1998: 3) and at Akosombo's successor—Kpong—where resettlement surveys were completed in time to allow their findings to be applied in the planning process (Adu-Aryee 1993: 150).

Most schemes have been characterized by a serious lack of participation. Where there has been positive participation, it has been more successful at the planning than the implementation stages, because of tight time frames. Key to whether participation is compromised is the time available, and this is directly related to the degree to which the resettlement planning and physical infrastructure schedules are/not coordinated.

Risks relating to placing too much emphasis on relocation and infrastructure, at the cost of longer-term development planning

In a number of instances, the actual relocation was carried out fairly successfully. People participated in its preparation, were allowed to move as communities, in a number of cases houses were ready before the move (the first relocation campaigns at Aswan and at Manantali, however, did not go quite so smoothly, as the houses were not all ready in time; Grimm 1991: 136; Fahim 1983: 44). At Kainji, there was 'Only minimum necessary pressure' to move (Ayeni et al. 1992: 112) and at Nangbeto 'Disturbance was minimal' (World Bank 1998: 21). Basic services were available in the new settlements.

However, there does not appear to have been the same commitment to longer-term development planning. At Akosombo, pressured schedules meant that there was competition between housing and agricultural programmes for construction equipment, with the result that fields were not cleared by the time the resettlers arrived in the new areas (Chambers 1970b: 262). But in a number of other cases, time constraints do not appear to have been the major problem. At Nangbeto (where there was plenty of time for planning), there was simply no provision made for rehabilitation. 'There was no income restoration beyond re-creating the previous farm economy' (World Bank 1998: 21). Manantali lacked a coherent development plan for the region. 'A fatal flaw of the entire project [was that] it lacked an emphasis on the need for income-generating actions' (Grimm 1991: 113). The first major academic study of Kainji warned that there was a looming crisis with regard to matters such as the provision of water, sanitation and housing (Oyedipe 1973: 45). The reports of the Panel of Experts for the Lesotho Highlands Water Project repeatedly complained that relocation plans were not synchronised with development strategies, and that there were problematic delays in the supply of basic services such as water and sanitation (LHWP April 1995: i; November 1996: x)—as at Kainji.

In spite of the actual relocation having been carried out fairly well in a number of cases, African resettlement schemes have been characterized by a serious lack of longer-term development planning. This cannot simply be explained in terms of time constraints, as in some instances there was plenty of time for planning, e.g. at Nangbeto. Resettlement seems to have been reduced to relocation in officials' minds, operating on the idea that, once the people had been moved, the job was done (World Bank 1988: 13).

Risks and opportunities relating to compensation issues

Central to any attempt to achieve resettlement with development is the manner in which compensation is handled. Problems in this area often reflect broader problems within the resettlement project itself. It is broadly acknowledged that straight cash compensation for displacement is unsatisfactory in most cases, as once the money has been spent, people are typically left much worse off than before. One of the worst cases of this occurred with the Akosombo scheme. People were given the choice of minimum compensation and resettling themselves elsewhere, or being resettled in official resettlement areas, with housing provided. The majority opted for official resettlement (Chambers 1970a: 28). However, the 'Gone Elsewheres', as those who opted for cash and self-settlement were known, had to wait something like five years for their money (Hart 1980: 82). In a somewhat atypical case, that of the Gariep and van der Kloof Dams on the Orange River, commercial farmers had to move out of the way of the dams, and were paid cash compensation at market-based rates. Their farm workers were not compensated, however, and had little choice but to either move with the farmer, or strike out on their own (World Commission on Dams 1998: 14).

Some schemes have opted to combine cash and kind, with compensation for houses being in two parts: a new house on the scheme, and a cash payment to enable relocatees to improve their houses as they choose. This applied in Aswan (Fahim 1983: 37) and at Nangbeto (World Bank 1998: 8), although in the latter case the people had to wait for three years after resettlement for payment. In Manantali, people were supplied with a new house and paid cash for other lost property, such as granaries, kitchens, trees—with the problem of how that cash is used coming to the fore again, as people spent it on, *inter alia*, investments in marriages (Grimm 1991: 294). At Kainji, the policy of cash and self-settlement was abandoned in favour of scheme-built housing in an effort to avoid the problems and choices made in Akosombo's cash-based compensatory scheme.

While people have generally received compensation for crops in their old fields, compensation for land has been problematic, and has raised questions concerning customary tenure and compensation. In the case of Aswan at New Halfa, for instance, the government did not compensate the Arab pastoralists coming on to the scheme (other than giving them a tenancy on the scheme) as their lands had not been individually registered (Salem-Murdock 1989: 60)—and by implication were state property—and it thus felt that it did not owe them anything. By contrast, the Nubians coming onto the scheme, who had owned freehold land before resettlement, were not only given houses and tenancies on scheme, but double the hectarage they had previously held (Salem-Murdock 1989: 6). Nubian landowners also received larger tenancies than former labourers (Fahim 1983: 37). In these ways, compensation policies may serve to reinforce existing patterns of differentiation.

At Nangbeto, there was no direct compensation for available land, as land was held to belong to the state. A rather ad hoc notion of replacement operated, as people were allowed to choose farm sites, depending on availability. They had to clear the fields themselves, but the project agency backed away from its commitment to pay them for their labour (World Bank 1998: 9).

The host communities into which resettlers move often do not receive compensation for the land they have to relinquish. At Akosombo, there seems to have been uncertainty as to the state's domain over the land. Local inhabitants regarded land as something to be bought and sold, whereas the state had more of a customary tenure type of perspective, not compensating the former owners for their loss. The latter therefore still regarded the land as their own, which led to disputes over who had rights to the land (Hart 1980: 80).

Whatever policy approach has been adopted, there have usually been delays in providing compensation. At Aswan, by 1979 (15 years after relocation) only 60% of resettlers had received available land (Fahim 1981: 37)—and as of 1998, Nubians still did not have title to their land or houses (Fernea 1998: 7). At Manantali (Grimm 1991: 136) and the Lesotho Highlands Water Project (LHWP August 1994: 31) there were delays in the provision of housing. At Nangbeto (World Bank 1998: 8–9) people waited three years for the final cash payments for their houses, and are still waiting for compensation for trees lost to the dam. Such delays impact negatively upon attempts to achieve resettlement with development, affecting initiatives aimed at agricultural production, income generation and community formation.

In several cases, schemes have changed their compensation policies in midstream, with sometimes positive and sometimes negative effects. Thus at Kainji, the change was made from cash compensation to the provision of scheme housing, to deal with various problems, including a growing time pressure (Roder 1994: 124). At Nangbeto, it was first decided that the scheme would clear fields for the resettlers. It was then decided that the resettlers would be paid to do the work, but in the end, they were not paid for the task. It was similarly decided to pay resettlers cash for lost trees, which was then changed to provision of seedlings—with compensation still outstanding after ten years. Such vacillation and non-delivery has made for dissatisfaction and mistrust among the resettlers (World Bank 1998: 9–10).

Compensation policy changes have had a positive effect in the Lesotho Highlands Water Project, where the experiences acquired during Phase 1A were put to good effect in Phase 1B. Policy has been expanded to provide a range of options to meet the various circumstances of different resettlers, some of whom may choose to move to urban, rather than rural areas. Options include annuities, lump sum cash payments, land for land, and grain provision for a number of years. People were also given the option of whether to have the scheme authority build their house for them, or to be granted the money and make their own building arrangements. This allows for greater flexibility, as well as linking compensation to development and income-generating initiatives (LHWP June 1996: iv, 5, 9).

Compensation has for the most part been problematic, and a source of impoverishment in African dam situations. Cash compensation has typically been delayed in being paid, and has often been spent on shorter term considerations, such as weddings, rather than invested. Compensation for lost land has been problematic, with people typically finding themselves with less, or inferior land, which they have to clear themselves, and pastoralists and people with customary tenure rights sometimes finding themselves with no compensation at all. Host populations, who have not actually moved, have not been compensated for lands they have had to give up to people moving into the area, either. At times, schemes have changed their compensation policies after the project was in motion—a positive adaptation at Kainji, and leading to confusion and non-delivery in the case of Nangbeto. Where compensation policy seems to have worked best, is where it has provided resettlers with a range of options, as in the case of the Lesotho Highlands Water Project.

Risks and opportunities relating to agricultural production
While agricultural development has been one of the goals of resettlement schemes in Africa, whether by irrigation or intensification through mechanization, the result has for the most part not been impressive, serving to increase rather than decrease dependence upon scheme structures.

Arising out of poor planning and provision, both of which relate to problems inherent in the resettlement process as an institutional process, this failure occurred for the usual and therefore predictable range of reasons. These include: lack of cleared land; lack of time, resources, supplies, marketing links, managerial capacity; poor water distribution; focus on irrigation rather than attempting to intensify dry land production; over-reliance on costly, heavy maintenance technology, top-down structures which were opaque and very costly. The focus on large, technology-loaded schemes at the cost of strategies to boost existing production systems would seem to relate at least in part to the nationalistic aspects of many of these schemes, with the resulting need for high-tech, high-visibility projects, which result in financial and managerial demands that cannot be sustained. Large schemes do not exist in isolation from their environment, and a downward turn in the regional or national economy can make such schemes unsustainable. Akosombo and Nangbeto are clear cases of resettlement agriculture falling foul of such downturns. Another national factor that impacts upon resettlement agriculture is changing political priorities in relation to rural development. For example, Nkrumah had seen resettlement as a special project, with its communities serving as 'bridgeheads of modernization' (Diaw and Schmidt-Kallert 1990: 200). His successor, Busia, was concerned with rural upliftment in general, through organizing the poor, rather than through specific state interventions, such as the Volta River Project. The result was that resettlers no longer received any special attention, and hence resettlement with development was not a possibility, with the inevitable deterioration of conditions (Diaw and Schmidt-Kallert 1990: 201).

Not all such efforts, however, have been dismal failures. At Kpong, a conscious attempt was made to avoid the mistakes made at Akosombo. Planners sought wherever possible to retain resettled communities within their traditional lands, with land, where necessary, being cleared in stages, on demand. Settlers for the most part worked their plots, and a successful pilot irrigation scheme was established (Adu-Aryee 1993: 141–7). There are, however, different interpretations of and sources of information about Kpong. While Adu-Aryee (1993) takes a fairly positive view, the World Bank (1993) report is much more negative, suggesting that incomes have not been restored, and that agriculture at Kpong has undergone a policy change towards intensification and is saddled with many of the same problems as Akosombo. It is not immediately clear how to reconcile these analyses. At Manantali, where the new area has 'fertile soils, adequate rainfall, and a very modest host population density' (Horowitz et al. 1993: 237), agricultural production has been satisfactory, and is 'driving the expansion of marketing in the resettlement area' (ibid: 241).

While initially struggling with the usual problems confronting irrigation agriculture, the situation at Aswan seems to have improved considerably, with new lands having become productive and tenants cultivating more extensively, using irrigated tenancies to produce crops for own consumption as well as for sale (Fernea 1998: 4, 8).

At Kainji, there has been agricultural success related to the dam, but more by virtue of local initiatives than from any specific scheme undertaking. People are using small petrol-powered pumps to irrigate areas above the dam's water level, and are using the drawdown area for livestock forage (Roder 1994: 57). In a similar fashion, resettlers for a number of years were able to benefit from the dam at Kariba, boosting agricultural and livestock production. For the first five years after the dam was completed, a scheme-initiated fishing enterprise flourished, with people using the earnings from this to diversify into the cash crop production of cotton, and to boost their livestock numbers and sales (Scudder 1985: 29).

With the exception of the more recent positive developments at Aswan, Roder's (1994: 162) pessimistic view of the viability of large schemes seems valid, and it seems that whatever benefits have come, have been through local peasant initiative, utilizing available opportunities resulting from the dam.

Increased agricultural production has been the goal of many govern-ments in Africa, and has typically been one of the justifications for reset-tlement schemes in the first place. With few exceptions (e.g., Kpong and Manantali) and cases of resettlers capitalizing on essentially unplanned opportunities arising out of the schemes (Kainji, Kariba and New Halfa), the agricultural record on African resettlement schemes has been dis-mal—for all too predicable reasons, such as: lack of cleared land; lack of time; lack of managerial capacity; poor water distribution; over-reliance on irrigation and costly technology, and top-down structures. While these factors exist mainly at the project level, agricultural projects are also vulnerable to the risk of changes in national policy and the regional economy. Akosombo and Nangbeto are two cases where such changes impacted negatively upon the viability of resettlement agriculture in the longer term.

Risks and opportunities relating to the diversification of incomes
The above kinds of initiatives suggest that we should not evaluate the success or failure of a resettlement scheme purely in terms of its own goals. In such narrow terms, most schemes would count as failures. However, schemes create new opportunities for resettlers and other affected people to diversify their incomes, thereby both spreading risks and enhancing incomes.

Perhaps the clearest case of this is the New Halfa scheme, which is part of the Aswan High Dam project. Arab pastoralists were brought onto the scheme and given tenancies. Agriculturally, this was not successful. However, these pastoralists continued to maintain their herds off-scheme, while cultivating on scheme, as well as bringing their animals onto the scheme, thus deriving additional grazing benefits from the scheme. Indeed, their off-scheme activities have kept a number of tenant households viable (Sorbo 1985: 15), and played a significant role in averting the collapse of the scheme. 'Through mutual transfers and conversions between animal husbandry and agriculture, a large number of Shukriya [i.e. Arab] pastoralists are able to continue a (more or less) settled existence on the Scheme, thus also benefiting from improved commercial, social and educational services' (Sorbo 1985: 17).

The agricultural scheme itself is a source of job-creation and income-generation (Salem-Murdock 1989: 86), as is the Kom Ombo Scheme and the city of Aswan for Egyptian Nubians (Fahim 1981: 108ff). In addition, a number of Nubians also continue their pre-resettlement tradition of working as labour migrants in Egyptian towns, while sub-contracting out their tenancies on the scheme (Fahim 1981: 63). Residents of the resettlement areas of the Kpong scheme in Ghana benefit in similar fashion from the employment opportunities at the nearby factories and industries that have arisen in response to the hydro-electricity generated by the dam (Adu-Aryee 1993: 149). As at Kariba, the fishing industry has also had a multiplier effect.

The construction of dam-related infrastructure gives rise to a number of temporary income-generating opportunities. Thus, at Manantali, only locals were employed in these jobs, greatly contributing to the cash flowing into villages, and not unlike Kariba, contributing to subsequent economic development (Grimm 1991: 118).

Such diversification of incomes tends to perpetuate existing patterns of differentiation, both across, and within groups. Thus the differentiation between Nubians and pastoralists was accentuated by their differential access to resources on the scheme, and within the Arab group, the gap between wealthy Shukriya, with more off-scheme resources, and influence in obtaining resources within the scheme, and poor Shukriya, has widened (Salem-Murdock 1989: 6, 12).

These benefits of diversification would, as with agricultural success, seem to result from the abilities of entrepreneurial individuals to utilize the benefits that the scheme provides, rather than from any planned income-generation strategies emanating from the scheme itself. It is the absence of such strategies that constitute a 'fatal flaw' in schemes (Grimm 1991: 113 for Manantali), and which have resulted in resettlement accelerating the process of impoverishment, e.g. at Kariba (Scudder 1985: 59) and Nangbeto (World Bank 1998: 12).

Risks and opportunities relating to service provision

Besides access to available land and to additional sources of income, one of the principal benefits of resettlement schemes is—or should be—better access to services. Facilitating service provision is one of the main justifications used to move people into concentrated residential areas.

Settlers on African schemes have for the most part been happy initially—with better access to water, transport, schools, medical care, social services, and marketing links. However, the service design has been faulty at times (as at Kpong; World Bank 1993: 31) and the *maintenance* of services has often been problematic. Thus at Nangbeto, people initially had better access to water via pumps than before resettlement, but the pumps were soon over-worked and began to repeatedly break down, resulting in a water supply that is worse than before resettlement. Similarly, where new clinics have been built, they are often short on staff and supplies (World Bank 1998: 14). Roads initially built at resettlement areas such as Kainji are deteriorating (Ayeni et al. 1992: 117).

Two of the few schemes where services appear to have been maintained and even improved, are Kainji, where there has been progress in the building of new tarred roads (i.e. subsequent to resettlement) and the provision of water and education (Ayeni et al. 1992: 119), and Aswan, in Egypt, where residents of Kom Ombo now have electricity and piped water in their homes (Fernea 1998: 8). The ability to maintain or improve services would seem to relate to administrative and economic capacity at both local and regional level, and to the importance of schemes such as Kom Ombo in their regional political context, as is reflected in the growing political influence of the Nubian population in Egypt. The inability to maintain services appears to be the principal risk in this regard, and would appear to manifest itself, and to be dealt with—or not, as the case may be—at the regional or even national, rather than the project, level.

Risks and opportunities relating to health

While improved income and services should be the best health policy (LHWP September 1993: 7), a number of diseases relate directly to dam construction and the resulting body of water in the lake—and the fact that the planning process, which is part of resettlement, is often not able to deal with the risks related to these diseases.

One of the results of the movement into an area by outsiders who come to work on the dam, and who as a result have disposable income, is an increase in AIDS and STDs (sexually transmitted diseases). These are already showing signs of being 'major problems' in a youngish scheme such as the Lesotho Highlands Water Project (LHWP September 1993: vi, vii).

Lower-lying dams in tropical areas are particularly prone to diseases such as river blindness, bilharzia and malaria. Rates of bilharzia have increased in a number of dams such as Akosombo (Hart 1980: 91) and Kainji (Roder 1994: 145), although less so at Kainji because of the large change in water levels and the corresponding drying out of the draw-down area. At Aswan, rates have gone down because of improvements in piped water supplies (Fahim 1981: 139). While the geographical distribution may have changed, rates of river blindness do not appear to have changed significantly at Akosombo (Hart 1980: 96) where there has been a programme to combat it, or at Kainji, 'where the great variations in flow from the spillway below the dam prevent the breeding of Simulium damnosum' (Roder 1994: 145).

Apart from increases in bilharzia, the incidence of water-related diseases does not appear to have increased significantly.

Dam-resettled populations are thus at risk to two kinds of diseases: sexually transmitted diseases brought into the area by workers on the project with disposable income and water-borne diseases resulting from the new lake, such as bilharzia (although at Aswan, rates have declined because of piped water). Paradoxically, many people find themselves further from potable water than before the dam was built.

Risks and opportunities relating to ethnic relationships

Two principal types of 'ethnic' relationships pertain to resettlement schemes:
1. between resettlers from formerly different social groups before resettlement;
2. between resettlers and members of the host communities which receive them.

As far as *relationships between heterogenous resettler groups* is concerned, the evidence seems somewhat mixed. Lumsden, working three years after resettlement at Akosombo found that, while there was still conflict between the five former villages brought together into one settlement around matters such as leadership and access to resources, co-operation and cross-cutting ties were beginning to emerge, with ritual and ceremony helping to forge new ties (Lumsden 1973). Some ten years later, he found that 'inter-group conflict...seems much less overt than before' (Lumsden 1980: 14)—which one would expect with the passage of time. However, a study of another Volta settlement, 25 years after relocation, found persisting divisions and suggests that the rivalries present after resettlement have continued 'and relations have worsened over the years. The younger generations have also begun to support and fan the conflicts ... a freeze on intermarriages is an undercurrent' (Diaw and Schmidt-Kallert 1990: 120). These tensions are hindering economic co-operation and progress. The fact that this divided settlement is much more diverse in origin than the one studied by Lumsden may partly explain the difference, as may the fact that 'the resettlement town has not permitted to any appreciable extent fulfillment of the role expectations and aspirations of the sub-groups' (Diaw and Schmidt-Kallert 1990: 120)—the social and economic goods resulting from the Volta River Project are presumably too limited to accommodate such diversity.

The relationship between lack of political and economic resources, and ethnic rivalry, seems to be borne out by material from Kom Ombo, where three ethnically diverse groups of Nubians were brought together in the resettlement area. While some ten years after resettlement, local politics still ran along ethnic lines, and intermarriage was still limited, 'a sense of identification with a common community was emphasized' (Fahim 1983: 99). This move towards community was probably spurred on by the rising importance of local Nubian leaders, and the strategic advantages of co-operation for purposes of patronage, as well as by the fact that as a group, the Nubians received a generous and standardized compensation, and thus did not have to compete among themselves for resources, as did many people at Akosombo.

While they have learned to co-operate out of necessity, for the most part, *relationships between hosts and resettlers* remain tense, because the two groups tend to see themselves as in competition, and in particular, the hosts often feel that they have been unfairly treated in comparison to the incoming strangers. This sense of injustice and of competition relates to matters such as differential compensation and access to services, conflicting interests between pastoralist hosts and resettler cultivators, and the fact that hosts have often not been compensated or paid for the land they gave up and still see themselves as the rightful owners. Obosu-Mensah (1990: 91) suggests that this sort of 'poorly conceived compensation programme', rather than ethnicity, underlies the conflicts and lack of integration in resettlement areas at Akosombo. Such tensions are graphically brought out in the New Halfa scheme, where the pastoralist hosts on the scheme sought to obtain separate political representation on the local council system after the Nubian resettlers had sought to evict them from the scheme (Salem-Murdock 1993: 314, 316).

Resettlement brings people together from different social and ethnic backgrounds. Sometimes they bond over time to form stable new communities, and at other times they do not, remaining factionalized. Whether the opportunity of community or the risk of factionalism will be realized, would seem to depend on two sets of factors: the degree of initial cultural diversity of the various groups coming together, and economic realities, i.e. the nature of the compensation, and the way the economic cake has been cut between the various groups. Tensions continue between hosts and resettlers on the Volta River Project and on the New Halfa Scheme because the host communities feel that they have been differentially, and unfairly, compensated. This relates directly to the way the project was planned and implemented.

Risks and opportunities relating to gender

Colson (1999: 25) notes 'the paucity of data' about the gender dimension in resettlement. What little material there is appears to be rather economic and political in emphasis, looking at the ways in which resettlement creates or limits access to resources, or whether it opens out or limits freedom of movement and opportunities, and at how men and women strategize accordingly. Rather little is said about the qualitative dimension of male-female relationships in the resettlement context.

While resettlement seems to harden men's control over resources to women's detriment (as in Aswan, Kariba, Manantali and Akosombo), the other side of the coin is that resettlement—and the movement of communities out of relative isolation, into wider socio-political contexts— open out social opportunities for women. Thus, Nubian women at Aswan enjoyed greater opportunities for employment, education, participation in community affairs, and travel (Fahim 1983: 54), while at Kariba, young women enjoyed wider exposure to educational opportunities and widening marriage pools (Colson 1999: 37).

Risks and opportunities relating to the long-term viability of the settlement scheme

Does the resettlement area ever become home? This question, which must be answerable in the affirmative if we are to be able to regard resettlement as successful, demonstrates the importance of taking a long-term view of the resettlement process. The Kom Ombo scheme is a stark illustration of the point. More than a decade after moving, Nubians were still suffering from what Fahim (1983: 116) terms 'resettlement illness'—women showed signs of fatigue and depression and people still expressed a desire to return to their old home area. 'The Kom Ombo settlement failed in the eyes of most Nubians to become a community that could provide a promising future' (Fahim 1983: 68). People stopped maintaining their houses and surroundings.

But two to three decades after resettlement, it was hardly recognizable as the same community described by the Ferneas (Fernea and Fernea 1991: Ch. 16, 17; Fernea 1998). Despite not yet having formal title to their houses, which now have piped water and electricity, Nubians have invested time and money in improving their homes, contributing to communal buildings, developing small businesses, and cultivating their land. Part of the reason for the metamorphosis has been the way in which access to land, efficient irrigation, and services have improved over the years.

Improved services may well relate to an increasing ability to pay for them, as disposable incomes have probably risen as a result of the increased job opportunities that follow from improved education and the development of the Kom Ombo scheme and Aswan City. But perhaps more important has been the manner in which a new and more valued Nubian identity has developed in the Egyptian context, and the ways in which that identity has developed out of, and is associated with, the move to Kom Ombo. Through the enhancement of their incomes and living conditions, as well as their political status and influence as a group, the Nubians have developed a collective sense of self-respect that is critically tied up to the Kom Ombo experience, which has led to self-identification in terms of it. Kom Ombo has become 'home'.

The contrast with Akosombo is stark, where 25 years on, it still seems as if nothing works. Services are dilapidated, water supplies provisional, land contestations and struggles for compensation drag on, settlements are still internally divided and successive government policies have led to resettlement areas becoming increasingly marginalized. The result has been an ongoing emigration, as people leave in search of opportunities elsewhere (Diaw and Schmidt-Kallert 1990). Nkrumah's initial vision for Ghana has perished and there is no sense of pride or identity to resonate with the Nubian experience.

While one cannot plan for identity in the same way as one can plan for access to resources and services, no one is readily proud of living in a factionalized rural slum such as many of the Volta resettlements have evidently become—there is very little to identify with. The absence of a long-term vision for social and economic development on the planners' part at the time of resettlement has led many resettlers at schemes such as Akosombo and Nangbeto to pull up their roots again and seek to make a home elsewhere.

If a resettlement scheme is to be regarded as successful, its inhabitants must identify with it, and remain on it, and ideally their children should take over from them. As Akosombo illustrates, there is a very real risk that this will not happen. Kom Ombo, by contrast, has had a turn about, with resettlers identifying strongly with the new area after a difficult first ten years. While this may be the result of a number of factors largely unique to the Aswan experience, one message is clear: without sustainable economic development, there will be no sustainable long-term social development in the resettlement area.

Conclusion: Catering for complexity by keeping options open for as long as possible

Taken in combination, the risks operating at the level of the resettlement project and at the national level suggest that there is a complexity inherent in the phenomenon of resettlement itself, which cannot be resolved simply by 'getting one's inputs all lined up'. Important as they may be, the necessary legal framework, resettlement policy, planning, finance, monitoring, political will, etc—while necessary conditions for successful resettlement—do not by themselves seem able to overcome the seemingly inherent and troublesome complexity in resettlement, and therefore cannot be seen as sufficient conditions for successful resettlement. So, what else is needed? Forced resettlement seems to operate in such a way as to diminish people's choices and options—because it takes away their freedom of movement, because the task is always larger than initially anticipated, and because it is usually in the planners' interests to simplify procedures wherever possible. By robbing people of the complexities inherent in their everyday existence, and imposing its own alien complexities, forced resettlement imposes limits on their adaptability, and hence on their livelihood options.

To deal with this 'clash of complexities' (i.e. the complexities of local people's everyday lives and world views, and the complexities of policy makers' and bureaucrats' culture and modus operandi) brought about by resettlement, we need to find ways to build open-endedness and flexibility into the formulation and implementation of resettlement policies—which have invariably been more concerned with structure and generalisability across cases. We need to find ways to encourage, support and incorporate the creative and entrepreneurial capacities of the resettlers. There will be ongoing trade-offs and lessons, on a case by case basis. Policy reform, like project design, is—or should be—a dynamic process.

We need to find ways of formulating policy that allow for a more open-ended and participatory approach to planning and decision-making, which deals with the implications of the complexities generated by resettlement. Officials may well prefer clearer timelines and budgets for their projects—but experience keeps telling us that this is not the most effective approach. False parameters and economies can be very costly. Unrealistic constraints generate real, and very costly, restraints of their own. Genuine participatory planning evokes local involvement, puts real problems and more viable solutions on the table, encourages realistic budgets, facilitates local capacity and leadership—all of which reduce conflict and enhance local co-operation.

In the end, policy has to be general, to cut across cases. Therein lies both its moral justification, in terms of respecting people at a general level, and its problematic nature, at a case-specific level. The challenge is to try to find equitable ways to ride the universal/ specific line: to find ways of developing criteria and procedures that allow us to keep open people's choices and to cater for complexity and multiplexity in the process, for as long as possible, balancing that with the legitimate claims of more structured frameworks and procedures of policy.

If we are to be honest, we have to admit that how we (i.e. those of us who, in any way, exercise some influence over the resettlement process) draw that line, how we strike that balance, will be a judgment call, which will have to be made in consultation and in conscience, case by case. With great privilege comes great obligation.

Note

The author would like to thank the World Commission of Dams for sponsoring the research on which this paper is based, as well as Teresa Connor and Karen Juul for their help in researching the documentation.

References

Adu-Aryee, V. Q. (1993) 'Resettlement in Ghana: From Akosombo to Kpong', in Michael M. Cernea and S. E. Guggenheim (eds), *Anthropological Approaches to Resettlement: Policy, Practice and Theory.* Boulder: Westview Press, pp. 133–52.

Ayeni, J. S. O., W. Roder and J. O. Ayanda (1992) 'The Kainji Lake experience in Nigeria', in C. C. Cook (ed.), *Involuntary Resettlement in Africa.* Washington, DC: Environmental Division, World Bank, pp. 109–22.

Barutciski, M. (2000) *Addressing Legal Constraints and Improving Outcomes in Development-Induced Resettlement Projects.* Unpublished Report, Refugee Studies Centre, University of Oxford.

Cernea, Michael M. (1990) 'Internal refugee flows and development-induced population displacement', *Journal of Refugee Studies,* 3(4), pp. 319–39.

———(2000) 'Risks, safeguards and reconstruction: A model for population displacement and resettlement', in M. M. Cernea and C. McDowell (eds),

Risks and Reconstruction: Experiences of Resettlers and Refugees. Washington, DC: World Bank, pp. 11–55.

Chambers, R. (ed.) (1970) *The Volta Resettlement Experience.* London: Pall Mall Press.

———(1970a) 'Introduction', in R. Chambers (ed.), *The Volta Resettlement Experience.* London: Pall Mall Press, pp. 10–33.

———(1970b) 'Postscript and discussion', in R. Chambers (ed.), *The Volta Resettlement Experience.* London: Pall Mall Press, pp. 226–69.

Colson, E. (1971) *The Social Consequences of Resettlement.* Manchester: Manchester University Press.

———(1999) 'Gendering those uprooted by "Development"', in D. Indra (ed.), *Engendering Forced Migration.* Oxford: Berghahn Books, pp. 23–39.

Diaw, K. and E. Schmidt-Kallert (1990) *Effects of Volta Lake Resettlement in Ghana: A Reappraisal after 25 Years.* Hamburg: Institute für Afrikakunde.

Fahim, H. M. (1981) *Dams, People and Development: The Aswan High Dam Case.* New York: Pergamon Press.

———(1983) *Egyptian Nubians—Resettlement and Years of Coping.* Salt Lake City: University of Utah Press.

Fernea, E. M. and R. A. Fernea (1991) *Nubian Ethnographies.* Prospect Heights, Illinois: Waveland Press.

Fernea, R. A. (1998) *Including Minorities in Development: The Nubian Case.* Washington, DC: Unpublished report for the World Bank.

Grimm, C. D. (1991) *Turmoil and Transformation: A Study of Population Relocation at Manantali, Mali.* Unpublished PhD thesis, State University of New York at Binghamton.

Hart, D. (1980) *The Volta River Project: A Case-Study in Politics and Technology.* Edinburgh: Edinburgh University Press.

Horowitz, M. M., D. Koenig, C. Grimm and Y. Konate (1993) 'Resettlement at Manantali: Short-term success, long-term problems', in M. M. Cernea and S. E. Guggenheim (eds), *Anthropological Approaches to Resettlement: Policy, Practice and Theory.* Boulder: Westview Press, pp. 229–50.

Koenig, D. and M. M. Horowitz (1988) *Lessons of Manantali: A Preliminary Assessment of Involuntary Relocation in Manantali.* Binghamton (USA): Working Paper No 43, Institute for Development Anthropology.

Lassailly-Jacob, V. (1996) 'Land-based strategies in dam-related resettlement programmes in Africa', in C. McDowell (ed.), *Understanding*

Impoverishment: The Consequences of Development-Induced Displacement. Oxford: Berghahn Books, pp. 187–200.

Lesotho Highlands Water Project (LHWP), *Panel of Experts' Reports*, Maseru (September 1993; August 1994; April 1995; June 1996; November 1996).

Lumsden, D. P. (1973) 'The Volta River project: Village resettlement and attempted rural animation', *Canadian Journal of African Studies*, 7(1), pp. 115–32.

—— (1980) 'Some reflections on restudying the Nchumuru of Krachi District', *Legon Review*, 12(1) (Ghana).

Maema, M. and N. Reynolds (1995) *Lesotho Highlands Water Project-Induced Displacement: Context, Impacts, Rehabilitation Strategies, Implementation Experience and Future Options.* Oxford: Unpublished Paper, Refugee Studies Programme, January 1995.

Obosu-Mensah, K. (1990) *Ghana's Volta Resettlement Scheme: The Long-Term Consequences of Post-Colonial State Planning.* Bethesda, Maryland: International Scholars Publications.

Oyedipe, F. P. A. (1973) 'Problems of socio-economic adjustment of resettlers', in A. L. Mabogunje (ed.), *Kainji: A Nigerian Man-Made Lake. Kainji Lake Studies, Vol 2: Socio-Economic Conditions.* Ibadan University Press, for the Nigerian Institute of Social and Economic Research.

Rew, A., E. Fisher and B. Pandey (2000) *Addressing Policy Constraints and Improving Outcomes in Development-Induced Displacement and Resettlement Projects.* Unpublished Report, Refugee Studies Centre, University of Oxford.

Roder, W. (1994) *Human Adjustments to Kainji Resevoir in Nigeria.* New York, London: University Press of America.

Salem-Murdock, M. (1989) *Arabs and Nubians in New Halfa: A Study of Settlement and Irrigation.* Salt Lake City: University of Utah Press.

—— (1993) 'Involuntary resettlement: A plea for the host population', in M. M. Cernea and S. E. Guggenheim (eds), *Anthropological Approaches to Resettlement: Policy, Practice and Theory.* Boulder: Westview Press, pp. 307–22.

Scudder, T. (1973) 'Ecological bottlenecks and the development of the Kariba Lake Basin', in M. T. Farvar and J. P. Milton (eds) *The Careless Technology.* London: Stacey, pp. 206–35.

—— (1985) *A History of Development in the Twentieth Century: The Zambian Portion of the Middle Zambezi Valley and the Lake Kariba Basin.* Unpublished document.

—— (1997) 'Resettlement', in A. K. Biswas (ed.), *Water Resources:*

Environmental Planning, Management and Development. New York: McGraw-Hill, pp. 667–710.

Sorbo, G. M. (1985) *Tenants and Nomads in Eastern Sudan: A Study of Economic Adaptions in the New Halfa Scheme.* Uppsala: Scandinavian Institute of African Studies.

World Bank (1988) *Recent Experience with Involuntary Resettlement: Togo-Nangbeto.* Washington DC: World Bank, Operations Evaluation Department, Report No. 17543.

————— (1993) *Early Experience with Involuntary Resettlement: Impact Evaluation on Ghana, Kpong Hydroelectric Project (Loan 1380-GH).* Washington: World Bank, Operations Evaluation Department, Report No. 12141

World Commission on Dams (1998) *Orange River Pilot Study: Work in Progress; 111 6—Vol. 1.* Cape Town: World Commission on Dams.

8

The Environmental Risks of Conservation Related Displacements in Central Africa

Kai Schmidt-Soltau

'The forest does not belong to us, we belong to the forest. Mó-bele created it as our home. If we live outside the forest, mó-bele becomes angry because it shows that we do not love mó-bele and his forest.' (Kpokpo—a Baka elder from Bongo: CAR)

Introduction

Biodiversity conservation has long been merged with the concept of protected areas, that are created by governments as wildlife habitats to protect them from the often negative influences of human habitation. But like most concepts, which at first appear to be simple and easy, protected areas have turned out to have quite a number of negative impacts on both humans and the natural environment. While establishing protected areas has been considered to be best practice for more than a lifetime, the consistent findings of numerous case studies have caused human rights activists—especially those working closely with indigenous people—social scientists, development practitioners, politicians and even conservationists to reassess this 'one-size-fits-all' solution.

In September 2003, at the World Parks Congress in Durban, the international conservation community declared its concern 'that many costs of protected areas are born locally—particularly by poor communities—while the benefits accrue globally' (WPC 2003: 2). This consent was achieved on the basis of evidence from hundreds of case studies from all over the world, which have documented that in most cases protected areas caused the impoverishment of rural, indigenous and/or mobile people in poor countries (IIED 1994; Western and Wright 1994; Emerton 2001; Western 2001; Chatty and Colchester 2002; Barrow and Fabricius 2002; Borrini-Feyerabend et al. 2002; Igoe 2003a, 2003b; Schmidt-Soltau 2003; Cernea and Schmidt-Soltau 2003, 2004; Brockington and Schmidt-Soltau 2004; Schmidt-Soltau and Brockington 2004a, 2004b).

This chapter focuses on the most serious social impact of protected areas: the physical and/or economic displacement from the parks. It examines the outcomes and risks of this approach—both social and environmental—and proposes several research-based recommendations for a change of strategy. It responds to the demand of the World Park Congress to 'improve the knowledge and understanding of the impact of protected areas on the livelihoods of the rural poor, negative and positive' (WPC 2003a: R29) and of the Convention on Biological Diversity, which calls for an assessment of 'the economic and socio-cultural costs and impacts arising from the establishment and maintenance of protected areas, particularly for indigenous and local communities, and (an adjustment of) policies to ensure that such costs and impacts—including the cost of livelihood opportunities forgone—are equitably compensated' (CBD 2004).

Method and case study design

Current standards define development-caused displacement as 'the involuntary taking of land resulting in...loss of income sources or means of livelihood, whether or not the affected persons must move to another location' (World Bank 2002). In a sociological and economic sense, displacement occurs not only when land-takings compel physical relocations, but also when a certain development or conservation project introduces 'restriction of access' to cultivatable lands, fishing grounds, or forests, even if the traditional users are not physically relocated, but are administratively prohibited from using the natural resources. This explicitly includes the creation of parks, when—as the World Bank's policy clearly states—'the involuntary restriction of access to legally designated parks and protected areas is resulting in adverse impacts on the livelihoods of the displaced persons' (World Bank 2002).

Between 1996 and 2004, I conducted surveys in twelve protected areas and national parks (listed in Table 8-1) in six countries (listed in Table 8-2). Some visits resulted from consultancy contracts directly related to resettlement, dislocation and questions of landownership, others were official or private project visits.

The fieldwork findings are analyzed through the conceptual lens of the Impoverishment Risks and Reconstruction (IRR) model for resettling displaced populations (Cernea 1997; 1999; 2000), which identifies eight major impoverishment risks embedded in the displacement

Table 8-1. Protected areas in Central Africa analyzed in this article.

Name[a]	Country	Promoter[b]	Total area[c] (km²)	Impact on local populace[d]	Displaced population[e]	Density (people/km²)	Compensation[f]	Success?[g]
Dja Bio. Reserve	Cameroon	ECOFAC	5,260	Expulsion of Pygmy-bands / Expropriation	7,800	1.5^q	No / No	No / No
Korup NP	Cameroon	WWF	1,259	Involuntary resettlement of villages / Expropriation	$1,465^h$	1.16	Yes / No	No / No
Lake Lobeke NP	Cameroon	WWF	2,180	Expulsion of Pygmy-bands / Expropriation	4,000	2.0^i	No / Partly	No / No
Boumba Beck NP	Cameroon	WWF	2,380	Expulsion of Pygmy-bands / Expropriation	4,000	2.0^i	No / Partly	No / No
Dzanga-Ndoki NP	CAR	WWF	1,220	Expulsion of Pygmy-bands / Expropriation	350	0.25^j	No / Partly	No / No
Nsoc NP	Equatorial Guinea	ECOFAC	5,150	Expulsion of settlements / Expropriation	10,000	1.98^k	No / No	No / No
Loango NP	Gabon	WWF	1,550	Expulsion of settlements / Expropriation	2,800	1.8^l	Partly / Partly	No / No
Moukalaba–Doudou NP	Gabon	WWF	4,500	Expulsion of settlements / Expropriation	8,000	1.8^l	Partly / Partly	No / No
Ipassa-Mingouli	Gabon	Brainforest	100	Expulsion of Pygmy-bands / Expropriation	100	1.1^m	No / Partly	No / No
Cross-River Okwangwo Div.	Nigeria	WWF	920	Involuntary resettlement of villages / Expropriation	$2,876^n$	3.13	Yes / No	Has not started
Nouabalé Ndoki NP	Republic of Congo	WCS	3,865	Expulsion of Pygmy-bands / Expropriation	3,000	1.5^o	No / Yes	No / Yes
Odzala NP	Republic of Congo	ECOFAC	13,000	Expulsion of Pygmy-bands / Expropriation	9,800	0.75^p	No / No	No / No
Total			41,384		54,000	Ø 1.3		

Sources and definition:

a = Some of these parks do not have clearly defined names, like Nsoc in the south east of Equatorial Guinea.

b = A 'Promoter' is an organization which appealed to and assisted the national government in the implementation of the specific national park.

c = See Sournia 1998; Schmidt-Soltau 2003.

d = While 'involuntary resettlement' is an organized approach in which the population receives assistance through the national government and/or the promoter, the term 'expulsion' in this paper is used for forced displacement imposed without significant assistance and regulated compensation, in kind and cash, from a village or settlement that is permanently inhabited. 'Expulsion of pygmy-bands' refers to the expulsion of 'pygmies', which do not utilize permanent settlements, from some parts of the forest utilized and inhabited by them on a temporary basis. Dispossession/expropriation refers to cases in which the national government or the promoter did not recognize common law ownership or usufruct rights—such as traditional land use titles—as legal title, and in which the elementary rules of expropriation with compensation and allocation of titled alternative land are not respected.

e = Most data are rough estimates based on published and unpublished data.

f & g = A displacement is considered as success, when all parties involved are satisfied with the outcome of the displacement and the change of land-use patterns. Compensation refers to financial mitigation towards livelihood restoration, which must be offered to the resettlers. A partial compensation refers to compensation for only one or some of the assets taken away or for damage inflicted, but does not offer the full array of assistance.

h = Schmidt-Soltau 1999a: 6.

i = PROFORNAT 2003; Curran & Tshombe 2001; 521, FPP 2003.

j = Noss 2001: 330.

k = Schmidt-Soltau: unpublished data.

l = MDP 1994 and IFORD 2003.

m = MDP 1994 and IFORD 2003.

n = Schmidt-Soltau 2001: 20.

o = PROECO 1997.

p = Joiris and Lia 1995: 41.

q = Abilogo et al. 2002: 10; FPP 2003. While several elements of conservation induced displacement are similar to displacements due to other types of development projects, some significant differences exist. One refers to the fact that when land taken for the project becomes a park and not a reservoir, road or coal mine, etc. it is still accessible for the displaced population. But each entry is now illegal. It can be prosecuted following the forestry laws, and sometimes puts even the life of the intruder at risk. Since it is unacceptable to expect that people base their livelihood on illegal activities, this illegal utilization is a non-solution, as in fact is the basic intention of the park creators. The same is true when some settlements are left in the protected area temporarily, not yet physically uprooted but already dispossessed economically of rightful access to resources, and at risk of being also physically evicted any time. In some of the new parks in Gabon, not all settlements in the parks have been burned down and are still used, but in line with the forestry law, these settlements are illegal and should not be there.

Table 8-2. Deforestation and protection indicators in the Congo basin countries

Country	Total area (km²)	Original tropical forest (km²)	Remaining tropical forest 1992 (km²)	Forest loss (%)	Remaining wildlife habitat 1995 (km²)	Habitat loss (%)	Protected forest 1994 (km²)	Protected forest 2002 (km²)	Protected forest 2002 (% of forest)	Population density 1995 (people/km²)	COMIFAC goal (≥30% of land protected)
Cameroon	475,440	376,900	155,330	59	192,000	59	11,339	26,135	16.8	28.4	46,599
Central African Republic	622,980	324,500	52,236	84	274,000	56	4,335	4,335	8.3	5.3	15,671
Equatorial Guinea	28,050	26,000	17,004	35	13,000	54	3,145	8,295	48.8	14.3	8,295
Gabon	267,670	258,000	227,500	12	174,000	35	17,972	23,972	10.5	5.1	68,250
Nigeria	910,770	421,000	38,620	91	230,000	75	2,162	2,162	5.6	122.7	11,586
Republic of Congo	341,500	341,500	212,400	38	172,000	49	12,106	27,136	12.8	7.6	63,720
Total/Average	2,646,410	1,747,900	703,090	Ø 60	1,055,000	Ø 60	51,056	92,035	13.1	Ø 50.2	214,121

Source: Naughton-Treves and Weber 2001: 31–33; Perrings 2000: 14; Data 2002: COMIFAC 2002. Remote sensing, which is the basis of all estimates on surface areas covered by forests or serving as wildlife habitat, is a quite new approach. Due to the fact that satellite images are only available for the last twenty years, the data on the area covered originally by rainforest is very much in debate. Wilkie and Laporte (2001) document a variation of up to 50% in the estimates of the various organizations working on that subject. In the line of the work of Fairhead and Leach (1996) some scientists even raised the question, if the search for an 'original forest' is not a useless exercise, since the forest is at least to some extent the result of the human utilization of the area.

and resettlement process. These risks are discussed not only within the concept of pro-poor development, but also within the concept of environmental sustainability, which strives to link pro-poor growth and biodiversity conservation.

Before focusing on the various impoverishment risks, it seems necessary to discuss the question of the number of people affected. A significant problem for any assessment of the impacts of existing parks derives from the fact that in most developing countries no baseline data on the economic and social utilization of the land exists. This uncertainty about the pre-park situation was tackled by a full array of data collection methods and strategies:

• Detailed literature reviews of published and unpublished data to find for example old census data (which could be extrapolated), old maps (documenting the number and spatial position of settlements), data on similar areas, regional market data (to examine lost trade following eviction), bio-monitoring and forest inventories (to calculate the lost stumpage value), correspondence of relevant governmental departments (to reconstruct the process of displacement from trip reports etc.), etc.

• Detailed interviews with displaced populations (utilizing the snow-ball sampling method) to establish population lists, land use maps (to identify affected populations and the extent of their land losses), detailed descriptions on the non-monetary social costs (especially risks 4–8 in the IRR model), and assessments of livelihood change based on oral history, local records, and comparison with similar livelihoods in places, which have not experienced displacement.

• While detailed assessments of the economic value of land exist for most parts of the world, the land in the case study areas is not a market good. The costs therefore had to be established via a theoretical assessment of the benefit that the area under research would offer, if used for the most economic utilization (lost stumpage value). These cost-assessments were supported by an evaluation of the costs necessary for acquiring land for that group on which they could practice their livelihoods with similar freedom. It might be true that especially mobile and/or indigenous populations would not, in a no-park-situation, have the chance to capitalize the land utilized by them, but even if it is common to ignore the rights of local people, that does not justify the refusal to assess and/or compensate their losses.

As to be expected hardly any baseline data are available for the twelve parks in the heart of the Congo basin. Only the two parks with an organised resettlement programme (Korup and Cross River) had any data at hand, and even these data turned out to be incorrect. Some of the findings are surprising: The Dzanga-Ndoki National Park, sandwiched between Lake Lobeke National Park and Noubale-Ndoki National Park, has only one-tenth of the population density of its neighbouring areas, while comprising a very similar ecosystem. The reasons for that are unknown and require additional research. Anyway, while conservation projects complain bitterly that my estimates are exaggerated, the rural population and local administration, as well as published materials, suggest that my estimates are very conservative. It becomes clear that, in total, more than 50,000 people have been displaced from the twelve case study areas in Central Africa (Table 8-1).

Beside those people directly displaced by conservation projects, a significant number of people face new impoverishment risks, because they have been forced to 'host' the resettlers. Since all but two of the national parks have expelled the inhabitants without providing new settlement areas, the total number of people acting as hosts against their will is difficult to assess. In 2001/2002 research was conducted on subsistence farming in one of the remotest areas of Cameroon. On the basis of 239 measured farms, we reached the conclusion that on average one individual utilises $14,547\pm10,693$ m^2 for pure subsistence farming (Schmidt-Soltau 2002: 10). Since slash and burning agriculture makes it necessary to allow farms to 'rest' for a certain period, the ratio between this space and the total space utilised per person in the slash and burning circle was surveyed to be $1:5.2\pm2.1$ (Schmidt-Soltau 2002: 11). On the basis of these data, one could assume that on average an individual would need 75,644 m^2 = 7.6 ha = 0.076 km^2 for pure subsistence.[1] But the real figures available (Table 8-3) offer different results. While the absolute minimum of farmland would lead to an average population density of 13.2 people per square kilometre after resettlement, the two sets of data available document a lower population density.

Table 8-3. Available data on pre-post displacement ratio

Name	Total area (km^2)	Displaced population	Density after (people/km^2)	Resettlement area (km^2)	Host population	Resettler host ratio (Resettler = 100%)
Korup National Park	1,259	1,465	3.94[a]	372	1357[a]	92.6
Dzanga-Ndoki NP	1,220	350	2.7[b]	130	200[b]	57.1

Sources: a = Estimate on the basis of the pilot village. b = Noss 2001: 330.

Due to the huge differences it is not possible to extrapolate these data in the scientific sense. If the 54,000 resettlers were to end up with just enough land for subsistence and resettle in an area with similar population densities, they would theoretically 'displace' less than 6000 hosts, which can be regarded as an absolute minimum. It is more likely that the resettler-host ratio varies between 2:1 and 1:1. That would mean that between 27,000 and 54,000 people in the study region have been forced to be hosts, because forced migration does not embody the chance to say no—for either the displaced or the hosts.

And there is no end in sight. While the 2002 WSSD in Johannesburg and the 2003 WPC in Durban maintained the goal that 10% of all land should be protected, in 2002 the heads of states in the Central African sub-region came up with a plan to ensure that in ten years time not less than 30% of the landmass of their countries (see Table 8-2) should be protected (COMIFAC 2002) and the Yaoundé Declaration of 1999, ratified by seven Central African heads of state, reflects a consensus view that the establishment of national parks and other protected areas in this sub-region is the most effective instrument to protect nature (Sommet 1999). It appears then, that displacement from parks is not only a lingering burden from the past, but continues to be a burden for the future of conservation and the livelihoods of the affected populations.

If one extrapolates the findings from the twelve parks—which constitute around 45% of the overall area under protection—based on the assumption that other protected areas in the six countries would have the same average population density, it can be presumed that not less than 120,000 people have already been displaced and that another 170,000 people will be displaced in the near future if nothing is done to stop this policy. On top of the 300,000 people who have been displaced or are facing significant displacement risks, a further 150,000–300,000 people have been or will be forced to become hosts against their will.

In the end, it turns out that conservation induced displacement affects more than half a million people in the poorest and most remote part of the world.

Impoverishment through biodiversity conservation

The following discussion is based on a review of nearly all documented resettlement case studies analyzed through the lens of the eight im-

poverishment risks outlined by Cernea (2000). Cernea's risks of impoverishment are:
- *landlessness* (expropriation of land assets and loss of access to land);
- *joblessness* (even when the resettlement creates some temporary jobs);
- *homelessness* (loss of not merely the physical houses, but of the family and communal home and cultural space, with resulting alienation);
- *marginalisation* (social, psychological and economic downward mobility);
- *food insecurity* (malnourishment, etc.);
- *increased morbidity and mortality*;
- *loss of access to common property* (such as forests, bodies of water, wasteland, cultural sites, customs and traditions); and,
- *social disarticulation.*

The risk of landlessness

Beside its economic value as a source of livelihood, in the Central African rainforest, land embodies a social dimension, but already the economic aspect appears to end all discussions on the feasibility of a conservation induced resettlements. In extreme cases like the Northern Congo, small hunter-gatherer bands hold customary rights over hundreds of square-kilometres of first class primary forest, valued at millions of US dollars. Of course, one must query whether this is its real value or merely a hypothetical estimate. The inhabitants might never have a chance to cash-in on this natural wealth, since all territories that are not utilised for agricultural production or officially demarcated as private property, are—by law—government land. Relying on this legal argument, conservation projects in the region have refused to consider traditional land titles as land ownership and have thereby rejected all claims for a proper resettlement procedure. In contrast, the World Bank recommends a resettlement policy framework for all cases of displacement, which ensure that the displaced persons are
1. informed about their options and rights pertaining to resettlement;
2. consulted on, offered choices among, and provided with technically and economically feasible resettlement alternatives; and
3. provided prompt and effective compensation at full replacement cost for losses of assets attributable directly to the project (World Bank 2002: 3).

These recommendations force one to ask: what are the 'full replacement costs' for land titles that are not recognised? The World Bank, however, has taken this into consideration, stipulating that besides people who have formal landholdings, 'those who do not have formal legal rights to land but have a claim to such land or assets and those who have no recognizable legal right or claim to the land they are occupying' are entitled to receive at least resettlement assistance (World Bank 2002: 6). The Bank recommends that if the displacement of indigenous people cannot feasibly be avoided, preference should be given to land-based resettlement strategies (World Bank 2002: 4). And yet, since there was no unoccupied land in the region before the resettlement became 'necessary', it simply stands to reason that the conservation projects will not be able to provide an adequate piece of land to the displaced persons without affecting the livelihood and land-holdings of others. The research clearly shows that land-based strategies of displacing mobile indigenous people are not working in the sense that resettlers are provided with pieces of land equal to what they have lost. Which still leaves us with the question of how best to estimate the full replacement costs of the land to be reserved for the creation of a park.

Table 8-4 suggests that the land losses in the two cases—the organised resettlement in Korup and the evictions in Dzanga-Ndoki—vary between 70% and 90%. As to be expected the organised resettlement programme of Korup National Park offers more land to the former inhabitants of national parks than the unorganised expulsion of the inhabitants of Dzanga-Ndoki National Park.

One method to estimate the 'full replacement costs', which is considered to be an indispensable element of any successful resettlement, is an assessment of the current values that will not be realised after the creation of a national park. The two values that constitute what economists call opportunity costs are lost stumpage values and lost forest use. The lost forest use will be assessed under the risk of joblessness, since the forest

Table 8-4. Available data on land losses

Name	Land before (km²)	Affected population	Density before (people/km²)	Density after (people/km²)	Increase in density (%)	Land after (km²)	Land loss (km²)	(%)
Korup NP[a]	1,259	1,465	1.16	3.94	339	372	887	70.5
Korup Hosts[a]	791	1,357	1.71	3.24	189	419	372	47.0
Dzanga-Ndoki[b]	1,220	350	0.25	2.7	1080	130	1090	89.4

Sources: a = Estimate on the basis of the pilot village. b = Noss 2001: 330.

Table 8-5. Loss of land and lost stumpage value of this land (in Euro)

Name	Country	Total area (km²)	Value of timber (€)	Loss per capita (€)	GNP per capita (€)
Dja Biodiversity Reserve	Cameroon	5,260	63,120,000	8,000	1,703
Korup National Park	Cameroon	1,259	15,108,000	10,000	1,703
Lake Lobeke National Park	Cameroon	2,180	26,160,000	6,500	1,703
Boumba Beck National Park	Cameroon	2,380	28,560,000	7,000	1,703
Dzanga-Ndoki National Park	CAR	1,220	14,640,000	42,000	1,172
Nsoc National Park	Equ. Guinea	5,150	61,800,000	6,000	15,073
Loango National Park	Gabon	1,550	18,600,000	6,500	6,237
Moukalaba-Doudou National Park	Gabon	4,500	54,000,000	6,700	6,237
Ipassa-Mingouli Biosphere Reserve	Gabon	100	1,200,000	11,000	6,237
Cross-River NP Okwangwo Division	Nigeria	920	11,040,000	4,000	896
Nouabalé Ndoki National Park	Rep. Congo	3,865	46,380,000	8,000	825
Odzala National Park	Rep. Congo	13,000	156,000,000	16,000	825
Total /Average		41,384	496,608,000	Ø 9,100	

Source: To estimate the net standing value of timber in the protected areas of Central Africa one can utilize the current average export prices of lumber products. This is on average Euro 120,-/m³ with non-labour inputs comprising Euro 60,-/m³ to bring the products to the export point (PC Mersmann). Tropical rainforest in this area contains between 80 and 200 m³ per hectare, but the average yield of 'sustainable' commercial logging is around 5 m³/ha = 500 m³/km² (PC Mersmann and Götz). In contrast to the declarations of conservation agencies, land surveys concluded, that the terrain of the case study areas does not lend itself well to commercial logging and that the number of commercial species and the average yield is lower than in commercial logging concessions. A very conservative figure (2 m³/ha = 200 m³/km²) is therefore used for extrapolation. Based on these figures, the lost stumpage value would be Euro 120/ha = 12,000/km². This figure is a very conservative estimate, if one compares it to, e.g., Carolin Tutin, who estimates that the decision of maintaining parks in the forests of the Congo-basin costs US$15,000 per km² per year (Tutin 2002:81); GNP (2000) = UNDP 2002; 1$ = 1 Euro.

is the only source of income and livelihood for the inhabitants of national parks. The lost stumpage value is associated with commercial clearing of timber in an alternative development scenario. Table 8-5 documents the financial losses the rural population is facing due to the establishment of national parks. These losses are somehow shared between the resettlers and their hosts, but in both cases they have been forced upon one of the poorest populations in the world.

The value of the total forest earmarked for protection (214,121 km² valued at Euro 2,559,542,000) is a significant amount of money in one of the poorest areas of the world—equal to or higher than most national budgets in the region. Since the forest is expropriated without any compensation, conservation does not reduce, but increases the poverty of the rural populations in the heart of the rainforest.

The risk of joblessness: Losses of income and sources of subsistence
To establish a pre-conservation picture of the various economic activities, detailed field data from a livelihood survey (1800 households) in one of the remotest areas of the region were used (Schmidt-Soltau 2001). Before discussing the risks in detail, one must focus again on the legal argument. Following the recommendations of international conservation agencies and donors, the Cameroonian forestry law prohibits all hunting, gathering, fishing and logging activities except under government license and for 'subsistence hunting and gathering with traditional methods' (MINEF 1997: 26). It is also 'illegal' to own fire-arms, unless licensed by the appropriate government authorities (MINEF 1997: 29–30). In the un-conserved baseline research area, with a population of almost 15,000, nobody had the necessary 'permission' to make their livelihood from the forest or had applied for a license for their rifles. Of course, it is as unrealistic to expect hunter-gatherers to travel for days to the nearest sub-divisional capital to apply in writing for permission or a license *to survive* as it is to expect that anybody would attempt to make a living today without using cheaper and more effective hunting methods, such as wire traps. The Forestry Law does recognize this, though, including all hunting and fishing with modern methods (wire traps, guns, nets and poison) under its definition of poaching, and all gathering as larceny. The conservation projects in all six countries studied utilize these legal 'absurdities' to circumvent any legal debate about compensation for lost incomes.

The greatest single factor in the depletion of natural communities and wild species has been the desire to use land for more profitable purposes. This has led to extensive clearing of forests and savannas, burning vegetation, and cultivation of previously undisturbed land for crop production. Practices such as farming, gathering leafs, barks, fruits, etc., is typically carried out for subsistence as well as for generating cash-income. It represents the most important source of cash income (33.4%, Schmidt-Soltau 2001: 51) for the inhabitants of primary rainforests; even more important than hunting and fishing, which generates 21% of the overall cash income (Schmidt-Soltau 2001: 51). The relevance of hunting as a source of cash income increases alongside increasing levels of deforestation and conservation, since prices are increasing.

Table 8-6 estimates the loss of income (subsistence and cash). Considering that the inhabitants of the Central African rainforests generate 67% of their total income from the forest (hunting, gathering, fishing, small scale logging) and only 33% from agriculture, labour, formal employment, etc. (Schmidt-Soltau 2001), it becomes clear that these populations are highly vulnerable to any changes that affect their

Table 8-6. Income loss estimates as effects of resettlement

Name	Area (km²)	Displaced population	Estimated annual income loss from hunting and gathering (€)		
			Per capita in cash	In cash	Total[d]
Dja Biodiversity Reserve	5,260	7,800		544,596	956,103
Korup National Park	1,259	1,465	76.02[a]	111,369	195,522
Lake Lobeke National Park	2,180	4,000		279,280	490,309
Boumba Beck National Park	2,380	4,000		279,280	490,309
Dzanga-Ndoki National Park	1,220	350		24,437	42,902
Nsoc National Park	5,150	10,000		698,200	1,225,772
Loango National Park	1,550	2,800		195,496	343,216
Moukalaba-Doudou National Park	4,500	8,000		558,560	980,618
Ipassa-Mingouli	100	100		6,982	12,258
Cross-River NP Okwangwo	920	2,876	158.96[b]	457,169	802,614
Nouabalé Ndoki National Park	3,865	3,000		209,460	367,732
Odzala National Park	13,000	9,800		684,236	1,201,257
Total/Average	41,384	54,000	Extrapolation figure 69.82[c]	4,049,065	7,108,612

Sources: a = Schmidt-Soltau 2000; b = Schmidt-Soltau 2001; c = un-conserved forest in a remote location: Schmidt-Soltau 2001; d = To move from this cash income to total income, one has to include the quantity of game and NTFPs, which are used for subsistence. The ratio between outtake for cash and outtake for subsistence was assessed to be 56.96:43.04 (Schmidt-Soltau 2001, 2002).

access to forests. They are also very poor: the average total production (subsistence and cash), at 161 Euro per capita per year, is less than half of what is required simply to reach the poverty line of US$1.00 per day (Schmidt-Soltau 2001). In fact the people displaced from parks in Africa are among the poorest in the world.

Conservation projects are aware that they have to offer alternative forms of income generation to protect the parks, at least in part because, in contrast to the savannas of East Africa, law enforcement is nearly impossible due to the nature of forests. Thus the idea of compensating the Aka 'pygmies' relocated from the Dzanga-Ndoki National Park and the nearby Dzanga-Sangha Dense Forest Reserve (both Central African Republic)—even without an official resettlement program—for their lost income (incl. the losses in hunting and gathering for subsistence) and loss of land through alternative income generating activities, such as farming, livestock breeding, eco-tourism etc., was well justified in theory (Carroll 1992; Noss 2001). But travellers to Bayanga, cannot help but notice the miserable permanent plots of the Aka settlements, where alcoholism and disease are rife (Sarno 1993). It becomes obvious that a change in lifestyle, to one which took other societies thousands of years to develop, cannot be implemented over night, or even within a single generation.

Besides the problems outlined above, one must also query whether there are any real benefits that the former inhabitants of the new national parks derive from the conservation project itself. One must be quite naïve or a cynic to declare—like the conservator of Korup National Park (Cameroon) —that 'everybody benefits from a national park, which is a place for hiking, camping, game viewing, photography and scientific research' (WWF 1991: 11). How many villagers will enjoy these opportunities? The popular argument on posters and leaflets, that it is important for humankind and future generations to save this or that animal, is not terribly convincing for those affected. And thus, for example, in Equatorial Guinea, the spokesman of a group of unofficially displaced villagers observed that 'the whites and the animals are against us, we have to fight back'. Conservation projects prattle away nineteen to the dozen about the possible benefits from tourism. Jack Ruitenbeek—an internationally well-known consultant—prepared a cost benefit analysis for the Korup National Park, which is still quoted sympathetically in the literature (Perrings 2000: 37). By his account, the benefits of resettlement far outweigh the social and economic costs—but there are significant problems with the 'future gains' that he assumes. Central Africa is not the Serengeti, and almost no-one wants to hike through the rainforest to see—well, what can you see?—trees.[2] In 1988, Ruitenbeek estimated that 1000 tourists would visit Korup National Park each year, each staying on average seven days, totalling 7000 overnight stays per year; and he anticipated a growth rate of 10% per year (Ruitenbeek 1988: 20). To date, Korup National Park has never attracted more than 200 tourists per year or more than 600 overnight stays per annum. And of the numbers of registered overnight guests in the park in 1999, I personally account for 90 of those days—even though the park was paying me to be there. It is clear, then, that protected areas very rarely generate significant income opportunities for the local populations, and thus rarely live-up to the high-flying promises for income generating opportunities through ecotourism, reducing arguments such as Ruitenbeek's to mere rhetoric. 'It is highly unlikely that revenue from wildlife and/or tourism will ever constitute a particularly large source of income for all members of a community at household and individual level' (Sullivan 1999: 10; see also: Patel 1998; van Schaik et al. 2002; Tutin 2002; Wunder 2000; 2003).

To summarize, the protected areas did not contribute to poverty reduction—as promised by policies and consultants—through alternative forms of income generation, but instead increased the already immense poverty of rural populations by nearly 50%.

The risk of homelessness

The concept of 'homelessness' in the research area is quite different to its primary meaning elsewhere. The personal houses of semi-permanent and permanent settlements as well as huts of hunter-gatherers hardly involve any cash investment and can be built with little effort anywhere. In most of the cases surveyed, the people expelled from a new national park erected new houses in the old style on their new plots. But the types of habitation that are suitable for a hunter-gatherer lifestyle are not suitable for resident farmers. This clash of lifestyles results in a decreasing health situation and undermines acceptance of the resettlement process. Thus it is with good reason that the World Bank recommends that new communities of resettlers should receive housing, infrastructure, and social services comparable to those of the host population (Operational Directive 4.12, World Bank 2002).

The Korup National Park (Cameroon) case clearly illustrates that cooperation and discussion between the resettling agencies and the affected people are not well developed. The Korup Project constructed a resettlement site with 63 stone houses to host a village, which formerly occupied 23 mud huts. The new houses had roofing tiles and integrated kitchens, reflecting the European mode of housing; but they are not suited to the life practices of the new inhabitants, who, for example, are now suffering from smoke-related complaints that result from cooking on open fireplaces in their kitchens (Schmidt-Soltau 2000). There is no globally ideal solution to housing construction, and thus only in discussion with the effected populations are planners able to determine which type of construction is suitable for a particular environment and for certain needs. Unfortunately, in none of the cases studied did the project planners demonstrate any strong interest in increasing their understanding of either the needs and interests of the displaced population, or of their wishes for new houses etc.

The risk of marginalisation

The risk of marginalisation is related to the demographics of the new settlement area. When the new neighbours speak a similar language or belong to the same ethnic group, there is a reduced risk that the resettlers will 'spiral on a downward mobility path' (Cernea 2000: 16). Alienation and marginalisation is most prominent in cases where the new resettlers end-up as strangers (without rights) among homogenous neighbours from a distinctly different cultural, social and economic background. Of the studied hunter-gatherer societies that had been expelled from nature reserves, none had previously existed as radically independent groups, but had lived in a strange 'partnership' with their settled Bantu neighbours. Some have interpreted this arrangement as a form of slavery (Turnbull 1962) while others see it as an excellent intercultural partnership (Grinker 1994). This 'partnership' was long-standing, but once the option of 'disappearing' into the forests has been lost, the hunter-gatherers lose important aspects of their economic and spiritual positions.

Another risk of marginalisation arises from the resettlement process itself. In the case of Ekundu-Kundu (Korup National Park), the resettlers were the centre of national and international attention for several years. After the decision to resettle them as pilot village, government officials, ambassadors, scientists, foreigners and project employees visited the village and listened to their opinions, leaving the resettled people with the impression that not only their resettlement, but they themselves were important. Obviously this level of interest and interaction could not last forever, and it was only one year after they had moved that the national park authorities decided that the village was no longer to be 'managed' as *the* resettlement village, but be given equal status as one village among the 187 villages with which the national park cooperates. It was quite a shock for the villagers to lose all of their benefits and attention (Schmidt-Soltau 2000).

In all of the case studies under review, the displacement from parks has generally resulted in something which is perhaps best described by the French word *attentisme*: the people are waiting for outside assistance to manage their daily lives.

The risk of food insecurity

In the short run, fortunately, this risk can be considered to be virtually non-existent for those displaced from national parks in Central Africa. In none of the research areas were the governmental services able to fully enforce their restrictive forestry laws, which prohibit hunting, gathering, logging and/or fishing without difficult to obtain licenses. At the same time, however, it has long been known that hunter-gatherers and incipient horticulturalists are accustomed to much higher dietary diversity than are settled agriculturalists (Fleuret and Fleuret 1980; Dewey 1981; Flowers 1983; Cohen 1989; MacLean-Stearman 2000), which makes resettling hunter-gatherers in a settled agricultural environment unhealthy in the longer-term. Galvin et al. have documented a significantly lower agricultural yield, and a poorer nutritional state, among the rural populations living near protected areas than for others of the same ethnic background (Galvin et al. 1999: 4). In the longer run, the lack of formal land titles and the denial of land use rights (discussed above) may also result in food insecurity for the resettlers, if the forestry laws and laws on individual property of land are implemented one day. The establishment of a legal title to a piece of land—large enough to provide a sustainable livelihood—would help secure a stable food supply and reduce the risks to the environment from overuse.

Another serious problem for farming activities arises from conservation itself. Around the Nouabalé Ndoki National Park the conservation project is forced to provide subsidized foodstuff from outside to the inhabitants of the neighbouring villages, since conservation has led to increasing the elephant population, which in turn undermines efforts to establish farms. This system, which both provides rural populations with food and offers protection to endangered species, seems, at first glance, to be workable. And yet, in the longer-term, it is uncertain, because nobody can guarantee that the food supply goes on forever, while the population is unable to earn their living with their own hands.

The risk of increased morbidity and mortality

A change in environment and exposure to more frequent interaction with urban life always embody multiple health risks (HIV/AIDS, STDs, alcoholism, etc.). Research has also determined that a shift from foraging to farming may be accompanied by a decline in overall health (Cohen and Armelegos 1984).

However, in contrast to other impoverishment risks, in all cases surveyed the new settlements are closer to formal health services and facilities than the original habitat deep in the forest, which is a specific and positive risk reduction factor.

The risk of loss of access to common property

In the central African Rainforest there is hardly any difference between the risk of landlessness and the risk of losing access to common property, since in the broader sense, the forest is their only and common property. Even among resident farmers, the only individually owned (by the 'house' or 'household') user rights are for 'farm plots', while all untransformed land is collectively owned. Thus, relocating resident communities out of the forest and prohibiting them from exploiting the forest deprives them simultaneously of their ownership of the forest and access to its common pool of resources. Such losses go beyond a potential 'risk' of impoverishment, for real impoverishment is almost assured through prohibition of access.

The risk of social disarticulation

The social disarticulation of resettled hunter-gatherer societies is not a risk but a fact. 'When technological change comes too fast and too soon for a society, it makes stable adaptations difficult if not impossible to achieve without severe pain, emotional stress, and conflict' (Coelho and Stein 1980: 22). In all cases studied, the forced changes in lifestyle atomised all existing social connections, both within the band and in relations with others. The high prestige of the elders, derived from their knowledge of the land, was previously the only social stratification. It has disappeared in all cases studied. The leading figures in the bands are now the youth, who have picked up a few words of French or English and are able to express themselves in meetings with project staff. They are also the ones who are prepared to explore their new environment's hunting and gathering opportunities as well as other opportunities in the area, while the elders remain in their new 'homes', complaining about change and the destruction of their old world.

Another problem arises from the complex interaction between the 'pygmies' and the resident Bantu farmers. While, as mentioned, anthro-pologists' have proffered different interpretations of this relation—rang-ing from slavery to equal partnership—it is evident that this relation is fundamentally changed when the 'pygmies' no longer have the option of 'disappearing' into the forest. Thus this longstanding social interaction, based on the exchange of forest products for farm products, has collapsed along with its economic bases.

The biological risk of conservation induced displacement

Conservation aims at protecting 'wildernesses' against the impact of mankind—an objective that is rendered exceedingly difficult, because 'the mythical pristine environment only existed in our imagination' (Pimbert and Pretty 1997: 3). In other words, there is no such thing as a 'pristine' habitat, and research shows that throughout the tropical areas, the rainforests constitute cultural-natural mosaics (Jacorzynski 1999). Evidence from anthropological, human ecology and archaeological studies has also demonstrated that most 'wilderness areas' have been modified or managed by humans at some point in time (Headland 1997; Sponsel et al. 1996). Hence, there is now a growing fear among those who conceive of forests as ecosystems for men and beasts that the biodiversity of the forest might be irrevocably reduced after resettlement precisely because of the removal of the impact of human activity (Prance et al. 1987; Posey and Balée 1989; Nabham et al. 1991; Meggers 1996; Reichel-Dolmatoff 1996).

To force hunter-gatherers to become farmers for the sake of biodiversity
conservation seems to have significant—unintended and unexpected—
negative impacts on biodiversity itself:

- *Increased communication and trade* resolving from the lifestyle in
  permanent settlements in the case study area quite often resulted in
  increased hunting and gathering. Due to the fact that the displaced
  population does not have any traditional/legal access to land outside
  the park, this commercial hunting and gathering, which results in
  off-takes which are between 10 and 20 times higher than before
  the displacement, occurs inside the protected area. This has been
  long known. Galaty documented in detail that 'the expansion of
  national parks, game reserves and protected habitats—freed from
  human presence—has generally been accompanied by a declining
  of wildlife' (Galaty 1999: 1).

- *Increased population density* in the areas around the protected area
  transforms a forest landscape into a forest island in the middle of
  degraded farm land. This is a slow process, which has just begun in
  Central Africa. But for South Africa, Fabricus and de Wet concluded
  that 'the main negative conservation impacts of forced removals from
  protected areas are that they contribute to unsustainable resource
  use outside the protected areas, because of increased pressure on
  natural resources in areas already degraded due to over-population.
  People's expulsion from biodiversity-rich areas led to their attitudes
  to conservation and conservationists becoming increasingly negative,
  with a measurable increase in poaching and unprecedented incidents
  of natural resources being vandalized, often accompanied by land
  invasions' (Fabricius and de Wet 2002: 152).

- *Increased reliance on agriculture* puts an end to the 'traditional
  forms' of land-use in Africa. The problem is that this 'traditional
  land-use' is considered by environmental scientists as sustainable
  (Nabham et al. 1991; Oldfield and Alcorn 1991; McKey et al. 1993;
  Dove and Kammen 1997; Novellino 1998; Albin 1998), while the
  post-resettlement land-use pattern seems, so far at least, to be unsustainable. Even the often-criticised slash and burning agriculture is
  considered in the literature to be a more environmentally sound way
  to produce food in an inhospitable tropical environment than small
  scale agriculture on permanent plots (Conklin 1954; Thrup and Hecht
  1997). 'The typical resettlement scheme introduces a relatively closed
  and mature pattern of cultural ecology. In the place of biotic and
  social diversity, the settlement scheme brings uniformity of product

and uniformity of producer with the instability to be expected from a system of low diversity and a high rate of productivity to biomass' (Palmer 1974: 241).

- *Increased social stratification* in the case study sites has resulted in an increased harvest of forest resources. In a more or less egalitarian society, most people do not utilise the available resources for anything besides their daily needs, but the struggle for cash income results in the capitalisation of forest resources and undermines the forests' capacity to provide a safety net for the rural populations (Oldfield and Alcorn 1991; Fratkin et al. 1999).
- *Breaking down taboos against hunting and gathering certain species and the erosion of traditional hunting and gathering patterns* is a logical result of displacement, since the rural population can see no 'reason' not to hunt key species such as elephants and gorillas, if they are no longer in direct 'spiritual' contact. In Equatorial Guinea, for example, displaced people explained that their increasing involvement in gorilla hunting stemmed from reduced fear that the evil spirit of the killed gorilla would seek revenge at night, because the eviction from the park placed them outside the forest, 'where the spirits can not rule'. This seems to be a general problem for the environment, because resettlement from national parks 'will alienate the local population from conservation objectives and thus require an ever increasing and, in the long run, unsustainable level of investment in policing activities' (Turton 1999: 1). As long as 'wildlife is permitted to contribute meaningfully to their welfare, people will not be able to afford to lose it in their battle for survival. If wildlife does not contribute significantly to their well-being people will not be able to afford to preserve it' (Child 1995: 232). Another factor is the absence of control of areas which do not belong to individuals or groups but to abstract entities such as the state. People who are actively involved in using a certain area for their livelihood are much 'more effective rangers' (Western 2002), but once the people are displaced from their land, they don't have any reason to be concerned about outside hunters entering the parks and hunting on their former land.

In general, it seems as if the resettlement process itself contributes significantly to the degradation of forest ecosystems. This is consistent with publications on the environmental impact of displacements on other ecosystems (Fabricius and de Wet 2002; Black 1998; Kibreab 1996a and b). Whether the unavoidable biological impacts of resettlement have to be considered as tolerable side effects of conservation or as negative impacts

that jeopardize the conservation objectives is difficult to judge without
further research. But research findings from six of the twelve case studies
in Central Africa signal that the consequences of the displacement and
resettlement process itself have had a number of degrading effects on forest
ecosystems, which are more harmful to biodiversity than the biological
impact of allowing the people to remain within the park.

Conclusion/Recommendation

This article has outlined the various risks arising from the resettlement
of inhabitants of national parks in Central Africa. These involuntary displacement processes are, unfortunately, often carried out in accordance
with unacceptable standards. Wherever displacement destroys people's
livelihood and tramples on their human rights—as in all cases surveyed—it
should not be tolerated by national governments, civil society, international donors or even conservationists. The remoteness of the park areas
tends to help camouflage violence and the lack of compensation from
public scrutiny. The silence of some well-intentioned promoters such as
WCS and WWF is very unhelpful, tolerates the intolerable, and must be
replaced by a clear and principled position of opposing forced and violent
displacements. If, in a park situation, it was considered feasible to resettle
the inhabitants while consistently ensuring decent relocation, equitable
compensation and sustainable reconstruction of people's livelihood, this
might be an acceptable practice when other approaches are not available
or the people do not want to remain in the park. But as long as these basic
conditions are not met, and are not likely to be met, it is contrary to stated
donor and NGO policies, to poverty reduction commitments and objectives,
and to ethics per se to continue displacing and impoverishing weak and
vulnerable populations.

'Conservation is about controlling people and their environment. It is
about exercising power over how people use land, and how they change
their land use and how they lobby their government to allow them to
change their practices. There may be powerful ethical reasons to try to
make this process as inexpensive as possible, but it may be a project for
which there are unavoidable expenses to be paid' (Brockington 1999:
20–1). In the end the conservationists may say that the costs arising from
resettling inhabitants of national parks according to the documented best
practice—Operational Directive 4.12 of the World Bank—are too high,

but it is unacceptable by all moral and ethical standards to free ride on the 'underdeveloped', 'underprivileged', 'underrepresented' inhabitants of the Central-African rainforest. For the inhabitants of natural parks the principles of sustainability are not the questions in dispute. Their quite legitimate concern is whether the costs and benefits of conservation are equally shared. The benefits are global, but the costs are mostly local, and in these case studies, if not always, are paid for by the poorest, most vulnerable groups. Besides the indigenous inhabitants of national parks, no other population is forced to change its lifestyles for the 'survival of mankind' and start a new life from scratch. Yet the claim and grievances of those who *are forced to do so*, to equally share the costs and benefits of conservation, remain unsatisfied.

Despite their fundamental right to resist, the possibility of achieving successful and sustainable solutions through resistance is highly questionable. To avoid lose-lose situations it is necessary to secure the well being of both the people and the rainforest ecosystem. Guidelines such as the World Bank Operational Directive for involuntary resettlements and the various procedures for impact assessments might possibly reduce the social and biological costs of individuals and groups while distributing the costs equally among all stakeholders. Whether the benefits of conservation are then still considered to outweigh the costs is then a political decision. The proof of the pudding will be in the eating.

Acknowledgements

I am grateful for the assistance offered by Bryan Curran (Project Manager; WCS Congo Nouabalé-Ndoki Park Project), Clement Ebin (General Manager; Nigeria Cross River National Park), Albert Kembong (Conservator; Cameroon Korup National Park), Klaus Mersmann (Coordinator, GTZ Environmental and Forestry Programme for Central Africa), Christoph Oertle and Daniela Renner (Project Adviser, Central Africa Rep., Dzanga-Sangha Dense Forest Reserve), and my research assistants: Gabriel Agba, James Atibile, Christol Fombad Foncham, Fuh Divine Fuh, Valere Akpakoua Ndjéma, Jacques Ngang, Hélène Aye Mondo, Martin Kejuo, Julius Kekong, Eyong Charles Takoyoh, Primus Mbeanwoah Tazanu, Cletus Temah Temah. Financial assistance for field work from GTZ, WWF and EU is gratefully appreciated as well as useful comments from Michael M. Cernea, Chris de Wet, Yntiso Gebre, Itaru

Ohta, and Mitsuo Ichikawa. The views expressed in this paper should neither be attributed to the institutions with which the author is associated nor to the persons mentioned above.

Earlier versions of this paper were presented at the International Symposium on Resettlement and Social Development (Hohai University, Nanjing, P. R. China) May 12–14, 2002 and the International Symposium on Multidimensionality of Displacement Risks in Africa (Kyoto University, Kyoto, Japan) November 2–3, 2002.

Notes

1 Toledo (1995) has calculated that an average peasant family in a rainforest area needs about 10 ha for subsistence.

2 Beside the fact that tourism in the rainforests is unlikely to be as successful as tourism on the open planes of East Africa, the absence of any infrastructure, from hotels and roads to trained staff and security, is a major hindrance to establishing tourism as a direct income generating benefit of conservation activities. Political instability in the region further contributes to the international tourism industry's disinterest in investing in the region, because 'investments in tourism typically take 25 to 30 years to realise returns' (Fabricius and de Wet 2002: 158; see also Magome et al. 1999).

References

Abilogo, E., H. Aye Mondo, P. Bigombe Logo and S. A. Nguiffo (2002) *The ECOFAC Project and the Baka Pygmies of the Eastern Border of the Dja Biosphere Reserve.* Brussels.

Albin, R. (1998) 'Plantations: Village development threatens the survival of indigenous Dayak communities in Sarawak', *Indigenous People*, 4, pp. 15–23.

Barrow, E. and C. Fabricius (2002) 'Do rural people really benefit from protected areas? Rhetoric or reality?', *Parks,* 12, pp. 67–79.

Black, R. (1998) *Refugees, Environment and Development.* London: Addison Wesley Publishing Company.

Borrini-Feyerabend, G., T. Banuri, T. Farvar, K. Miller and A. Phillips (2002) 'Indigenous and local communities and protected areas: Rethinking the relationship', *Parks,* 12, pp. 5–15.

Brockington, D. and K. Schmidt-Soltau (2004) 'The social and environmental impacts of wilderness and development', *Oryx*, 38, pp. 140–2.

Brockington, D. (1999) *The Cost of Conservation: Monitoring Economic Change as a Consequence of Conservation Policy at Mkomazi Game Reserve*. Paper presented at the conference: Displacement, Forced Settlement and Conservation. Oxford: St. Anne's College.

Carroll, R. W. (1992) *The Development, Protection and Management of the Dzangha-Sangha Dense Forest Special Reserve and Dzangha-Ndoki National Park in Southwestern Central African Republic*. Bangui: WWF Press.

CBD (Convention on Biological Diversity, 2004) *Governance, Participation, Equity and Benefit Sharing*. http://www.biodiv.org/doc/meetings/cop/cop-07/official/cop-07-l-32-en.doc.

Cernea, M. M. (1997) *African Involuntary Population Resettlement in a Global Context*. Washington, DC: World Bank, Environment Department Papers, Social Assessment Series 45.

—— (ed.) (1999) *The Economics of Involuntary Resettlement: Questions and Challenges*. Washington, DC: World Bank.

—— (2000) 'Risk, safeguards and reconstruction: A model for population displacement and resettlement', in M. Cernea and C. McDowell (eds), *Risk and Reconstruction: Experiences of Resettlers and Refugees*. Washington, DC: World Bank.

Cernea, M. M. and K. Schmidt-Soltau (2003) 'The end of forced resettlements for conservation: Conservation must not impoverish people', *Policy Matters*, 12, pp. 42–51.

—— (2004) *Biodiversity Conservation and Poverty Risks: Is Population Resettlement the Solution?* Hamburg/London: Lit-Verlag.

Chatty, D. and M. Colchester (eds) (2002) *Displacement, Forced Settlement and Sustainable Development*. Oxford: Berghahn.

Child, G. (1995) *Wildlife and People: The Zimbabwean Success*. Harare: Wisdom Foundation.

Coelho, G. V. and J. J. Stein (1980) 'Change, vulnerability, and coping: Stress of uprooting and overcrowding', in G. V. Coelho and P. I. Amed (eds), *Uprooting and Development*. New York: Plenium Press.

Cohen, M. N. and G. Armelegos (eds) (1984) *Paleopathology and the Origins of Agriculture*. Orlando: Academic Press.

Cohen, M. N. (1989) *Health and the Rise of Civilisation*. New Haven & London: Yale University Press.

COMIFAC (Conférence des Ministres en charge des Forêts de l'Afrique Centrale) (2002) *Position commune des Ministres de la sous-région*

Afrique Centrale pour RIO + 10. Yaoundé: unpublished declaration.

Conklin, H. C. (1954) 'An ethno-ecological approach to shifting agriculture', *Transactions of the New York Academy of Science*, 17, pp. 125–41.

Curran, B. K. and R. K. Tshombe (2001) 'Integrating local communities into the management of protected areas: Lessons from DR Congo and Cameroon', in W. Weber, L. J. T. White, A. Vedder and L. Naughton-Treves (eds), *African Rain Forest: Ecology + Conservation—An Interdisciplinary Perspective.* New Haven: New University Press, pp. 321–45.

Dewey, K. G. (1981) 'Nutritional consequences of the transformation from subsistence to commercial agriculture in Tabasco, Mexico', *Human Ecology*, 9, pp. 157–81.

Dove, M. and D. M. Kammen (1997) 'The epistemology of sustainable resource use: Managing forest products, swiddens, and high-yielding variety crops', *Human Organisation*, 69(1), pp. 91–101.

Emerton, L. (2001) 'The nature of benefits and the benefits of nature: Why wildlife conservation has not economically benefited communities in Africa', in D. Hulme and M. Murphree (eds), *African Wildlife and Livelihoods.* Portsmouth: Heinemann, pp. 220–43.

Fabricius, C. and C. de Wet (2002) 'The influence of forced removals and land restitutions on conservation in South Africa', in D. Chatty and M. Colchester (eds), *Displacement, Forced Settlement and Sustainable Development.* Oxford: Berghahn, pp. 149–63.

Fairhead, J. and M. Leach (1996) *Misreading the African Landscape: Society and Ecology in a Forest-Savannah Mosaic.* Cambridge: Cambridge University Press.

Fleuret, P. and A. Fleuret (1980) 'Nutrition, consumption, and agricultural change', *Human Organisation*, 39, pp. 250–60.

Flowers, M. N. (1983) 'Seasonal factors in subsistence, nutrition, and child growth in central Brazilian Indian community', in R. Hames and W. Vickers (eds), *Adaptive Responses of Native Amazonians.* New York: Academic Press, pp. 56–72.

FPP (Forest Peoples Project, 2003) 'Indigenous people and protected areas in Africa', *Forest People Project Report.* Moreton-in-Marsh.

Fratkin E. M., E. A. Roth and M. A. Nathan (1999) 'When nomads settle: The effects of commercialisation, nutritional change and formal education on Ariaal and Rendille pastoralists', *Current Anthropology*, 40(5), pp. 729–35.

Galaty, J. G. (1999) *Unsettling Realities: Pastoral Land Rights and Conservation in East Africa.* Paper presented at the conference:

Displacement, Forced Settlement and Conservation. Oxford: St. Anne's College.

Galvin, K. A., J. Ellis, R. B. Boone, A. Magennis, M. Smith and S. J. Lynn (1999) *Compatibility of Pastoralism and Conservation? A Test Case Using Integrated Assessment in the Ngorongoro Conservation Area (Tanzania)*. Paper presented at the conference: Displacement, Forced Settlement and Conservation. Oxford: St. Anne's College.

Grinker, R. R. (1994) *Houses in the Rainforest: Ethnicity and Inequality among Farmers and Foragers in Central Africa*. Berkeley: University of California Press.

Headland, T. (1997) 'Revisionism in ecological anthropology', *Current Anthropology*, 38(4), pp. 605–30.

IFORD (Institut de formation et de recherché démographiques, 2003) *Base de données Gabon*. Yaoundé.

Igoe, J. (2003a) *Conservation and Globalisation: A Study of National Parks and Indigenous Communities from East Africa to South Dakota*. Belmont, CA: Wadsworth/Thomson Learning.

———— (2003b), 'Scaling up civil society: Donor money, NGOs and the pastoralist land rights movement in Tanzania', *Development and Change*, 34, pp.863–85.

IIED (1994) *Whose Eden? An Overview of Community Approaches to Wildlife Management*. London: International Institute for Environment and Development.

Jacorzynski, W. R. (1999) *People and Nature: The Myth of Conservation and Its Victims in Southern Mexico*. Paper presented at the conference: Displacement, Forced Settlement and Conservation. Oxford: St. Anne's College.

Joiris, D. V. and C. Lia (1995) *Etude du milieu humain du Parc National d'Odzala*. Brazzaville.

Kibreab, G. (1996a) *People on the Edge in the Horn: Displacement, Land-use and the Environment*. London: James Currey.

———— (1996b) *Common Property Resources and Involuntary Resettlement*. Paper presented at the workshop: Reconstructing livelihoods: Towards new approaches to resettlement. Oxford: Queen Elizabeth House.

MacLean-Stearman, A. (2000) 'A pound of flesh: Social change and modernisation as factors in hunting sustainability among neotropical indigenous societies', in J. G. Robinson and E. L. Bennett (eds), *Hunting for Sustainability in Tropical Forests*. New York: Colombia University Press, pp. 73–84.

Magome, H., D. Grossman, S. Fakir and Y. Stowell (1999) *Partnership* in Conservation: The State, Private Sector and the Community at Madikwe Game Reserve (North-West Province, South Africa). London: International Institute for Environment & Development.

McKey, D., O. F. Linares, C. R. Clement and C. M. Hladik (1993) 'Evolution and history of tropical forests in relation to food availability: Background', in C. M. Hladik, A. Hladik, O. F. Linares, H. Pagezy, A. Semple and M. Hadley (eds), Tropical Forests, People and Food: Biocultural Interactions and Applications to Development. Paris: UNESCO, pp. 603–30.

MDP (Ministère de la planification du Gabon, 1994) Base de données sur la population. Libreville.

Meggers, B.J. (1996) Amazonia: Man and Culture in a Counterfeit Paradise. Washington, DC: Smithsonian.

MINEF (Ministry of the Environment and Forestry, 1997) A Compendium of Official Instruments on Forest and Wildlife Management in Cameroon. Yaoundé: MINEF Press.

Nabham, G., D. House, D. Suzan, H. Hodgson and L. Hernandez (1991) 'Conservation and the use of rare plants by traditional cultures', in M. Oldfield and J. Alcorn (eds), Biodiversity: Culture, Conservation and Ecodevelopment. Boulder: Westview, pp. 27–36.

Naughton-Treves, L. and W. Weber (2001) 'Human dimensions of the African rain forest', in W. Weber, L. J. T. White, A. Vedder and L. Naughton-Treves (eds), African Rain Forest: Ecology + Conservation—An Interdisciplinary Perspective. New Haven: Yale University Press, pp. 101–22.

Noss, A. J. (2001) 'Conservation, development and the "forest people": The Aka of the Central African Republic', in W. Weber, L. J. T. White, A. Vedder and L. Naughton-Treves (eds), African Rain Forest: Ecology + Conservation—An Interdisciplinary Perspective. New Haven: Yale University Press, pp. 123–34.

Novellino, D. (1998) 'Sacrificing people for the trees: The cultural cost of forest conservation on Palawan island', Indigenous Affairs, 4, pp. 4–14.

Oldfield, M. and J. Alcorn (eds) (1991) Biodiversity: Culture, Conservation and Eco-Development. Boulder: Westview.

Palmer, G. (1974) 'The ecology of resettlement schemes', Human Organisation, 33(3), pp. 239–50.

Patel, H. (1998) Sustainable Utilisation and African Wildlife Policy: The Case of Zimbabwe's Communal Areas Management Programme for Indigenous Resources (CAMPFIRE). Cambridge: Indigenous Environmental Policy Centre.

Perrings, C. (ed.) (2000) *The Economics of Biodiversity Conservation in Sub-Saharan Africa: Mending the Ark.* Cheltenham: Elgar.

Pimbert, M. and J. N. Pretty (1997) 'Parks, people and professionals: Putting 'participation' into protected area management', in K. B. Ghimire and M. P. Pimbert (eds), *Social Change and Conservation: Environmental Politics and Impacts of National Park and Protected Areas.* London: Earthscan, pp. 63–78.

Posey, D. A. and W. Balée (1989) *Resource Management in Amazonia: Indigenous and Folk Strategies: Advances in Economic Botany.* New York: New York Botanical Garden.

Prance, G. T., W. Balée, B. M. Boom and R. L. Carneiro (1987) 'Quantitative ethnobotany and the case for conservation in Amazonia', *Conservation Biology*, 1(14), pp. 296–310.

PROECO Gis, O. I., Lewis, J. (1997) 'Carte des villages de l'axe Belandjokou', in Projet PROECO, *Etude socioéconomique et cartographique des populations rurales au Nord Congo.* GTZ.

PROFORNAT (2003) *Base de données sur la population au sud-est Cameroun.* Yokadouma: MINEF-GTZ-WWF.

Reichel-Dolmatoff, G. (1996) *The Forest Within: The World-View of the Tukano Amazonian Indians.* London: Themis.

Ruitenbeek, J. H. (1988) *Social Cost-Benefit Analysis of the KORUP Project: Cameroon.* London: WWF-Consultancy Report 3206/14.2.1.

Sarno, L. (1993) *Song from the Forest: My Life among the Ba-Banjelli Pygmies.* London: Bantam Press.

Schmidt-Soltau, K. (2000) *Conservation and Resettlement in the Central African Rainforest.* Paper presented at the resettlement workshop of the 10th World Congress of Rural Sociology, Rio de Janeiro.

——— (2001) *Human Activities in and around the Takamanda Forest Reserve: Socio-economic Baseline Survey.* GTZ-Consultancy report.

——— (2002) *The Surface Area of Agricultural Production in and around the Takamanda Forest Reserve: Findings from Surface Area Measurement of Individual Farmland and from Participatory Cartography on Village Level.* GTZ-Consultancy report.

——— (2003) 'Conservation-related resettlement in Central Africa: Environmental and social risks', *Development and Change*, 34, pp. 525–51.

Schmidt-Soltau K. and D. Brockington (2004a) 'The social impacts of protected areas', http://www.social-impact-of-conservation.net.

——— (2004b) *Resettlement as Conservation Tool: Risk and Resistances.* Paper presented at the XIth World Congress of Rural Sociology, Trondheim, Norway, 25–30 July.

Sommet (1999), *Sommet des chefs d'état d'Afrique centrale sur la conservation et la gestion durable des forets tropicales: Déclaration de Yaoundé*. Yaoundé: WWF-Press.

Sournia, G. (ed.) (1998) *Les aires protégées d'Afrique francophone*. Paris: ACCT Edition Jean-Pierre de Monza.

Sponsel, L., T. Headland and R. Bailey (1996) *Tropical Deforestation: The Human Dimension*. New York: Columbia University Press.

Sullivan, S. (1999) *How Sustainable is the Communalising Discourse of New Conservation? The Masking of Difference, Inequality and Aspiration in the Fledgling Conservancies of Namibia*, Paper presented at the conference: Displacement, Forced Settlement and Conservation. Oxford: St. Anne's College.

Thrup, L. A. and S. Hecht (1997) *The Diversity and Dynamics of Shifting Cultivation: Myths, Realities and Policy Implications*. Washington, DC: World Resource Institute.

Toledo, V. M. (1995) *Peasantry, Agroindustriality, Sustainability: The Ecological and Historical Basis of Rural Development*. Mexico-City: Interamerican Council for Sustainable Agriculture.

Turnbull, C. M. (1962) *The Forest People*. New York: Simon & Schuster.

Turton, D. (1999) *The Mursi and the Elephant Question*. Paper presented at the conference: Displacement, Forced Settlement and Conservation. Oxford: St. Anne's College.

Tutin, C. E. G. (2002) 'Parks in the Congo basin: Can conservation and development be reconciled?', in J. Terborgh, C. van Schaik, L. Davenport and M. Rao (eds), *Making Parks Work: Strategies for Preserving Tropical Nature*. Washington, DC: Island, pp. 76–85.

UNDP (2002) *Human Development Report: Deepening Democracy in a Fragmented World*. New York: Oxford University Press.

van Schaik, C., J. Terborgh, L. Davenport and M. Rao (2002) 'Making parks work: Past present and future', in J. Terborgh, C. van Schaik, L. Davenport and M. Rao (eds), *Making Parks Work: Strategies for Preserving Tropical Nature*. Washington, DC: Island, pp. 468–81.

Western, D. (2001) 'Taking the broad view of conservation: A response to Adams and Hulme', *Oryx*, 35, pp. 201–3.

——— (2002) *In the Dust of Kilimanjaro*. Washington, DC: Island Press.

Western, D. and R. M. Wright (1994) *Natural Connections: Perspectives in Community-based Conservation*. Washington DC: Island Press.

Wilkie, D.S. and N. Laporte (2001) 'Forest area and deforestation in Central Africa: Current knowledge and future direction', in W. Weber, L. J. T. White, A. Vedder, and L. Naughton-Treves (eds), *African Rain Forest:*

Ecology + Conservation: An Interdisciplinary Perspective. New Haven: Yale University Press, pp. 55–68.

World Bank (2002) *Operational Policy 4.12: Involuntary Resettlement.* Washington, DC: World Bank.

WPC (World Park Congress) (2003) Recommendations (R 1–32) at: http://www. iucn.org/themes/wcpa/wpc2003/english/outputs/recommendations.htm

Wunder, S. (2000) 'Ecotourism and economic incentives: An empirical approach', *Ecological Economics*, 32(3) pp. 546–79.

———— (2003) 'Native tourism, natural forests and local incomes on Ilha Grande, Brazil', in S. Gossling (ed.), *Tourism and Development in Tropical Islands: A Political Ecology Perspective.* Northhampton, MA: Edward Elgar, pp. 13–28.

WWF (1991) *Report of the Workshop on the Resettlement of KORUP National Park Villages.* Mundemba: Document.

Part 3
Implications of In-migration for
Host Populations

9
Multiple Socio-Economic Relationships Improvised between the Turkana and Refugees in Kakuma Area, Northwestern Kenya

Itaru Ohta

Introduction

Refugee studies have concentrated on the refugee population as their first concern and focus, and there has been little academic research about the host populations, although the need for such research has been long recognized (Harrell-Bond 1986; Chambers 1986). Some analysts have argued that this lack of attention to the host populations is unsatisfactory, not only because it is unfair, but because it may well undermine efforts at project management (e.g., Lassailly-Jacob 1994).

Refugee camps exert profound impacts on the host population, in many and various aspects of their lives (e.g., Chisholm 1996; Whitaker 1999; Waters 1999). Some scholars assume that refugees represent a problem or a burden for the host community, rather than an opportunity. However, others claim that refugees can also benefit their hosts—by providing cheap labor, attracting foreign aid to improve infrastructure, etc. (e.g., Callamard 1994). It is also important to recognize that the impact of refugees on the hosts vary according to the gender, class, region and generational characteristics of the host community. Thus it is necessary to conduct concrete research to ascertain precisely who benefits, who loses, and why (Callamard 1994; Lassailly-Jacob 1994; Whitaker 1999).

How can we measure the costs and benefits? We might be able to identify the different kinds of opportunities that open to the hosts after the establishment of a refugee camp and what resources are depleted. However, even where a resource or an opportunity exists, its utility and value rest with the perceptions and actions of the social actors themselves. People are not passive beneficiaries or losers, but actively work upon their environments to make their lives better. There have been few empirical studies of host populations from this perspective. In this chapter, then, I aim to provide an alternative representation of the hosts, who have typically been depicted as either shrewd exploiters or wretched losers.

The Turkana who live in the Kakuma area in northwestern Kenya provide the ethnographic data for this research. They received a refugee population of more than 80,000 people, and coped with the abrupt emergence of the refugee camp. This chapter begins with an outline of the history and characteristics of the Kakuma refugee camp. Then, the multiple relationships that have developed between the Turkana and refugees will be described and examined from socio-cultural and economic viewpoints. Finally, I will discuss how the Turkana and refugees spontaneously improvised mutually beneficial conditions, which humanitarian interventions have never anticipated. I will also discuss how this process may have been significantly assisted by the Turkana's cultural background of extroversion.

I commenced my initial anthropological research in the northwestern Turkana District in 1978, and continued to visit there every 1–2 years. The Kakuma refugee camp was established in 1992, adjacent to the village of my host family. Although my focus since has been on other topics of research, I have followed the developments between the Turkana and refugees through daily conversations with the Turkana. In 2001, 2002 and 2003, I conducted field research, about three weeks each year, focusing on their relationships. The data presented here are based on these experiences.

Background

History of Kakuma refugee camp
The majority of refugees at Kakuma camp are Sudanese. In Sudan, there was armed conflict between the North and the South before its independence in 1956. They made peace in 1972, but it proved to be temporary, as civil war started again in 1983, and continues today.[1] In May 1991, the socialist government in Ethiopia collapsed, and the Ethiopian People's Revolutionary Democratic Front (EPRDF)—which had a cooperative relationship with Khartoum—came into political power. Groups opposed to the Sudanese government (e.g., Sudan People's Liberation Army: SPLA) that had been operating in Ethiopia were driven out, together with 150,000 refugees who had been living in the Gambela area of southwestern Ethiopia. In March 1992, the Sudanese government's

army found an opportunity to attack the SPLA in southeastern Sudan and in July 1992 the SPLA lost its base in Torit.

In May and June 1992, Sudanese refugees who had fled from Gambela and walked more than 400 km began to arrive in the border town, Lokichoggio, in the northwestern corner of Kenya. The UNHCR, with the aid of the Lutheran World Federation (LWF), immediately established a camp at Kakuma, to which they transferred the refugees from Lokichoggio. Ethiopian refugees also poured into northern Kenya in response to the political changes there. At about the same time, in January 1991, military forces had overthrown the former government of Somalia, and many Somalis also took refuge in Kenya, mostly in the northeastern and coastal areas.

Figure 9-1. Refugee camps in Kenya (UNHCR 1998, modified)

The UNHCR established 17 refugee camps in Kenya in the early 1990s (Figure 9-1). But they have been closed one-by-one, and now only two camps remain: Kakuma, the focus of this paper, and Dadaab, which comprises three neighboring camps that are typically regarded as one. Kakuma camp is located in the northwestern corner of Kenya, while Dadaab is in the eastern part. Both of them are situated in dry and remote areas, where population density is low and the land is not privately owned. The Kenyan government built refugee camps in order to control refugee movements, and located these camps in remote, less densely populated areas for the same reason. Another reason to select these areas was to minimize the resistance of the host communities.

As the camps were closed, some of the refugees went back to their countries of origin, but others were transferred to Kakuma. Figure 9-2 shows the changes of refugee population in Kenya. In 1993, there were nearly 400,000 refugees. However, the numbers were drastically reduced in 1995, and have been relatively stable ever since. The refugee population in Dadaab was quite stable, but the population in Kakuma continued to increase each year, as some of the refugees from each camp that was closed have been transferred to it. The Kenyan government has been eager to close other refugee camps because, among other things,

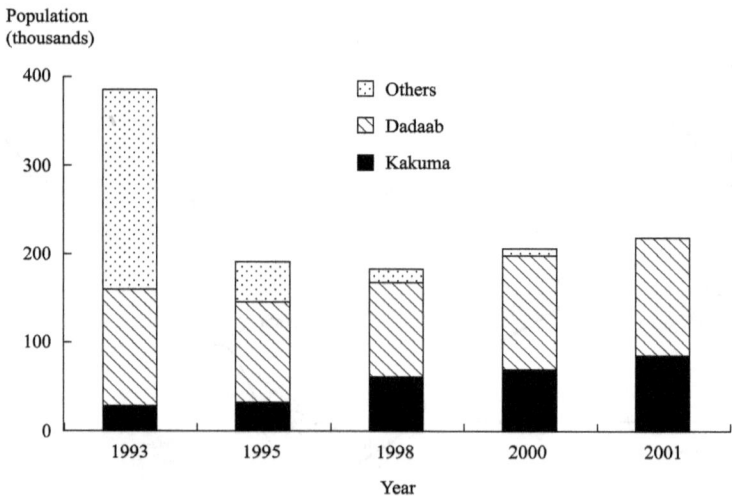

Source: UNHCR, 1993; 1995; 1998; 2001; 2002.

Figure 9-2. Changes of refugee population in Kenya

the refugees (mostly Somalis) had quickly become involved and begun to dominate the local economy, creating tensions with the local population (Verdirame 1999).

Characteristics of the Kakuma refugee camp

Table 9-1 shows the refugee population of the Kakuma camp in August 2001, by their countries of origin. It has a population of more than 80,000 people from nine countries, making it more than four times larger than the UNHCR's recommendation to avoid camps of more than 20,000 people wherever possible (UNHCR n.d.). Almost 80% of Kakuma's refugees are Sudanese, but few of them had any contact with the Turkana prior to the camp's establishment. Somalis are the second largest group at Kakuma (15%), followed by the Ethiopians (3%). It is also clear from Table 9-1 that the male population far exceeds the female. The camp occupies an area of about 2 km x 5 km (Figure 9-3), divided into eight zones for administrative purposes. It is not fenced. Refugees can leave the camp, and the Turkana can enter the camp freely.

The majority of the refugees had never had any contact with the Turkana before they arrived in Kakuma. That is, the refugees and their Turkana hosts commenced their relationship as absolute strangers, sharing no linguistic, social or cultural backgrounds. In contrast, most of the refugee camps that were located near international borders in Africa have been populated by refugees who had already had close relationships with their hosts before the camps were established. They occasionally belonged to the same ethnic group and spoke the same language. They also shared the same cultural background and, through kinship relationships, maintained close social relationships with each other (Hansen 1993; Leach 1992; Lassailly-Jacobs 1994; Kok 1989; Merkx 2000; Horst 2001). In this respect, Kakuma refugee camp is unique.

The camp is not simply a refugee settlement, but a 'town' (De Montclos and Kagwanja 2000; Kurimoto 2001). It has significant infrastructure, such as a hospital, clinics, schools, vocational centers, churches, and mosques. Its shopping centers comprise many kiosks, butcheries, restaurants, bars, satellite TV and video theatres, etc. Bicycle taxis busily pass through the camp, carrying customers on their back seat. It is very economically active, and as we shall see, provides various cash-income generating opportunities for the Turkana. With the population exceeding 80,000, passers-by in the streets and shops are strangers to one another. This sort of economic and social situation was entirely foreign to the Turkana before the refugees began to arrive.

Table 9-1. Population of refugees in Kakuma by nationality, gender and age
           groups (28 August 2001)

Ctry of origin	Sex	0–4 yrs	5–17 yrs	18–59 yrs	≥ 60 yrs	Total	%
Sudan	F	4,169	9,539	10,508	418	24,634	30.7
	M	4,764	15,597	19,153	332	39,846	49.6
	T	8,933	25,136	29,661	750	64,480	80.3
Somalia	F	796	1,826	2,819	110	5,551	6.9
	M	964	2,119	3,557	71	6,711	8.4
	T	1,760	3,945	6,376	181	12,262	15.3
Ethiopia	F	83	171	342	8	604	0.8
	M	104	242	1,436	9	1,791	2.2
	T	187	413	1,778	17	2,395	3.0
Uganda	F	38	51	56	0	145	0.2
	M	27	56	114	2	199	0.2
	T	65	107	170	2	344	0.4
DR Congo	F	18	38	44	1	101	0.1
	M	18	35	141	1	195	0.2
	T	36	73	185	2	296	0.4
Rwanda	F	14	29	41	1	85	0.1
	M	15	36	79	1	131	0.2
	T	29	65	120	2	216	0.3
Burundi	F	2	14	23	1	40	0.0
	M	14	15	54	2	85	0.1
	T	16	29	77	3	125	0.2
Eritrea	F	0	1	5	0	6	0.0
	M	2	1	21	0	24	0.0
	T	2	2	26	0	30	0.0
Liberia	F	0	0	1	0	1	0.0
	M	0	0	1	0	1	0.0
	T	0	0	2	0	2	0.0
Stateless	F	0	15	37	0	52	0.1
	M	6	14	35	1	56	0.1
	T	6	29	72	1	108	0.1
Grand totals	F	5,120	11,684	13,876	539	31,219	38.9
	M	5,914	18,115	24,591	419	49,039	61.1
	T	11,034	29,799	38,467	958	80,258	100
%		13.7	37.1	47.9	1.2	100	

Source UNHCR Sub-Office Kakuma (modified)
F: Female, M: Male, T: Total

The Turkana

About 350,000 Eastern-Nilotic speaking Turkana (Gregersen 1977) live in
northwestern Kenya, mostly in the Turkana District. The average annual
rainfall at Lodwar, the center of the District, is about 200 mm, but we must

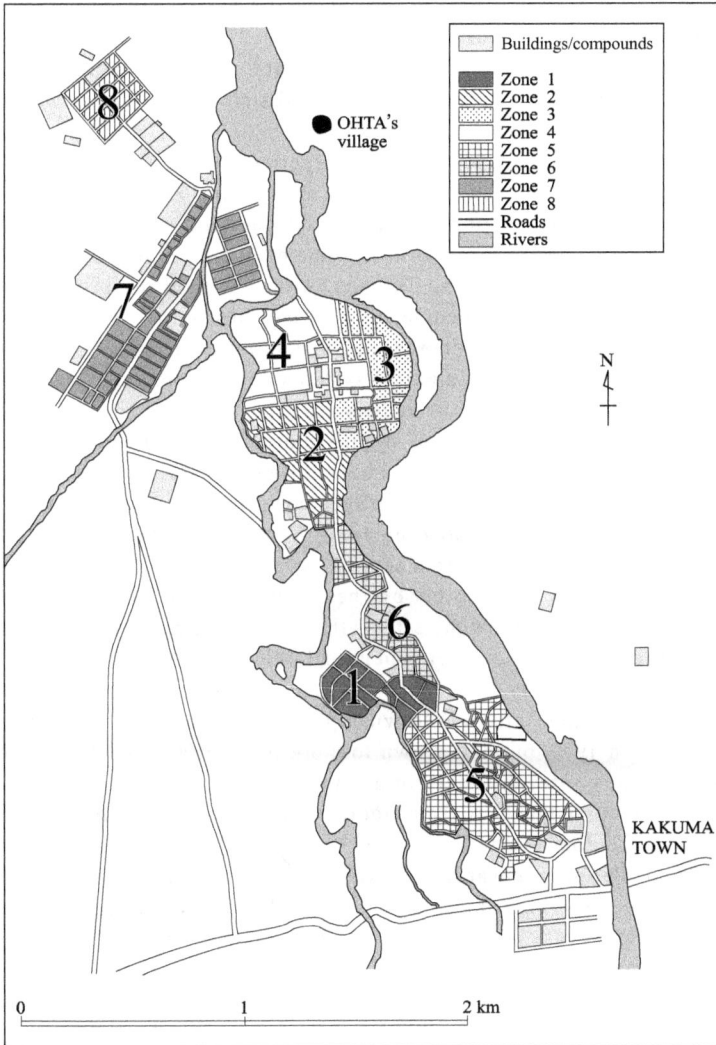

Source: UNHCR Sub-Office Kakuma, modified

Figure 9-3. Kakuma refugee camp

note that Lodwar is located in the most arid part of the area. Because of its dryness, agriculture is not extensively practiced. Most of the people keep five species of livestock—cattle, camels, goats, sheep, and donkeys—and lead a nomadic lifestyle, depending on the distribution of both water and the plants on which livestock feed.

However, the Turkana are currently experiencing rapid social changes. To the best of my knowledge, the severe drought in 1979–80 had the first large-scale and drastic impact. Emergency food aid was extended, and various developmental projects have since been carried out, all of which had a profound impact on the Turkana. A tarmac road reached Kakuma in 1988, and the traffic in people and commodities, as well as channels of information, subsequently increased considerably. The market economy, formal education, modern medical systems and national administration have since infiltrated Turkana society.

Kakuma was a small town of slightly more than 2,000 people in 1989, before the refugees arrived (Government of Kenya 1994). But its population increased significantly after the refugee camp was established, reaching more than 9,000 in 1999 (Government of Kenya 2001). Many traders, for example, came to Kakuma from central parts of Kenya and opened kiosks and restaurants, or sought other business opportunities.

In order to comprehend the effects that aid activities for refugees have had on the Turkana, the development of Lokichoggio town also needs to be taken into consideration. This was also previously a small town, not even achieving the status of a 'township' when the population census was conducted in 1989, but had grown to more than 13,000 by 1999, largely because many international aid agencies established offices there to oversee their assistance programs for the refugees and internally displaced persons in southern Sudan.

The population in and around Kakuma and Lokichoggio increased again during 1999–2000. During this period, the Turkana once again suffered from a very severe drought, as well as increasing rates of livestock raiding, and many became destitute. Although emergency food aid began to be distributed throughout the District in 1999, many Turkana swarmed around Kakuma, sometimes traveling more than 100 km, and settled on the peripheries of the town and refugee camp.

It is difficult to estimate what proportion of the Turkana population were, to a greater or lesser extent, directly or indirectly influenced by the refugee-aid activities. According to UNHCR, the local Turkana population in Kakuma urban area was estimated to be 35,145 in 2001 (Silva 2002). More broadly, the Turkana District is divided into three constituencies

Table 9-2. Population of Turkana North constituency

Division	Male	Female	Total
Kakuma	13,401	15,674	29,075
Oropoi	7,055	9,808	16,863
Lokichoggio	14,458	16,999	31,457
Total	34,914	42,481	77,395

Source: LWF Food Supply Project (July 2001)

(North, Central and South), and we can assume that people in the Turkana North constituency—with a population of about 77,000 in 2001 (Table 9-2)—were touched by the aid activities.

Multiple relationships between the Turkana and refugees

Socio-cultural relationship

Insecurity and conflicts
When the camp was established in 1992, some of the Turkana were obliged to move their homesteads. Several perfunctory meetings were held to explain to the local Turkana some of the details of the construction of the refugee camp. UNHCR and Kenyan administrative officers (District officers and Turkana chiefs) emphasized that the establishment of the camp was approved by the Kenyan government, and that the local people would also benefit from the camp because the infrastructure such as clinics and boreholes would become available to them. Most of the Turkana men present at these meetings did not express any clear or strong objection to the plan, although some of them personally expressed to me anxiety about the arrival of strangers. Because the Turkana, as a pastoral people, do not claim exclusive territorial rights, they did not think that the refugee camp had confiscated their land, or that they should be compensated for the land.

However, the refugee camp undermined public security of this area (Crisp 2000). There were many violent conflicts, not only among the refugees themselves, but also between the refugees and the local Turkana, especially in the first few years after the camp was established.

As mentioned, the Kakuma camp had many of the characteristics of a large town, in which people regularly encountered strangers. The local

Turkana have never before had this experience. Furthermore, the refugees were complete 'cultural others' to the Turkana. Although the Turkana did already have experience in associating with other ethnic groups, this was mostly with the neighboring peoples, whose cultures and languages were more or less similar. But the arrival of the refugees was the first time that the Turkana had close and regular contact with complete strangers, with completely different cultures, on a large scale.

The sources of conflict were multiple. The Turkana informed me that the refugees have cut trees that were vital for the Turkana, that they have beaten Turkana children, that they have stolen the Turkana's livestock, and that they have killed many of the Turkana's donkeys that roamed into the camp, etc. The Turkana are very prideful and sometimes take a confrontational stance even among themselves. For example, when I was walking in the camp with Turkana friends of mine, they sometimes spoke abusively to the refugees, calling them thieves or similar. Likewise, I was walking in the camp with some Turkana women one day when they told me that we should stay in a cohesive group because they were afraid of the refugees.

Many Turkana men have had violent encounters with the refugees. I came across two cases in which Turkana killed refugees. The first occurred around November 1993, and came to my attention when a local Turkana youth got sick. He complained that he had lost all of the strength in his body and could not even stand up. He explained that about a month earlier, he was walking with several Turkana men when he encountered a refugee man in the bush. According to the youth, the refugee was fighting with a Turkana child. The group intervened to rescue the child, and in the struggle the Turkana men had beaten the refugee with sticks and killed him. The youth who had become ill had been the first person to grapple with the refugee and had thrown him to the ground. Turkana occasionally commit murders while raiding the livestock of neighboring ethnic groups. When this occurs, the murderers typically fall ill like the above-mentioned youth, and must conduct a special purifying ritual. Once the youth had performed this ritual, he recovered. The Turkana explained that his sickness was really caused by the murder of the refugee.

The other case occurred in October 1994. When a young man in his twenties was herding goats, three refugees came and tried to steal one, according to the Turkana. The Turkana youth fought with them and struck a severe blow with a stick to one's head. The injured person was quickly taken to Lokichoggio hospital. The Turkana youth was identified and arrested by the Kenyan police, but the case was settled locally. Several meetings were held by Turkana elders and representatives of refugees, and the Turkana youth's family paid 60 goats for compensation.[2]

Trafficking in small arms, such as AK-47s, became easy and prevalent, which enhanced insecurity. Many Sudanese refugees were soldiers of SPLA (the male population of the camp is far greater than the female, see Table 9-1) and they sold small arms to the Turkana in exchange for livestock. Some of them allegedly engaged in livestock raiding with the Turkana.[3] Violent incidents between the Turkana and refugees, as well as among refugees themselves, caused social unrest among the Turkana, which hastened the moral decline. Social insecurity was one of the most serious problems caused by the establishment of the Kakuma refugee camp. Some of the Turkana distanced themselves from the Kakuma area to avoid the insecurity, although many remained because of the economic advantages of the refugee camp, which I will discuss shortly.

Intermarriage and bond-friendship
On the contrary, some Turkana and refugees developed close social relationship. As the Turkana started interacting with the refugees, they began to learn other languages, and became multi-lingual. They learned not only Swahili, a public language in Kenya and in the camp, but also Arabic dialect, a common language in southern Sudan. The girls were the first to develop these language skills, because they had more opportunities to visit the refugee camp to sell firewood, charcoal, building materials, and milk.

There have been some marriages between Turkana and refugees. In most cases, Turkana women married refugee men. I know only three reverse cases, in which a Turkana man married a Sudanese woman. The majority of these marriages were without any bridewealth transaction, and were therefore not formal marriages for the Turkana. Even among the Turkana themselves, it is very common for girls to have sexual relationships without bridewealth transaction. When a girl gets pregnant, the baby's biological father should pay a fixed amount of livestock to the girl's patrilineal family, and the baby belongs to this family.[4]

When Turkana women became pregnant by refugees, the Turkana demanded this payment from the refugees. However, some refugees regarded this custom as unfair and unacceptable because the girl's partner would receive nothing after paying the compensation. There were many conflicts over this issue, sometimes involving physical violence, between the women's families and their refugee partners.

When such troubles occurred, most refugees sought advice from the UNHCR protection officers, sometimes in genuine fear that the Turkana would take strong measures. When the parties concerned could not reach agreement about the payment, they sought arbitration from the local

Turkana chiefs. Both parties were called to the administrative office in Kakuma town to attend an inquiry. After several meetings, a judgment was made.

For example, I attended a series of meetings in September 2002, which were called by the Turkana chief of Kakuma Division. A Turkana girl had delivered a baby boy, allegedly with an Ethiopian refugee, in 1999. At the meetings, the girl, her parents, and a male relative of the parents attended from the girl's side, and the Ethiopian attended with his friends and a UNHCR protection officer. The Division chief, a sub-location chief, and several elder Turkana men acted as mediators. At the meetings, the protection officer tried to understand the Turkana way of settling disputes, and recommended that the Ethiopian comply with the custom. In the end, the Ethiopian paid 30,000 Kenyan Shillings to the girl's parents, which was regarded as a payment of 30 goats.

One might question how far these marriage-like relationships might endure, in the context of a refugee camp that is not permanent but provisional. This is a difficult question with both positive and negative implications. Some of the refugees established enduring social relationships both with other refugees and with the Turkana. But others felt that life in the refugee camp was transient, and approached affairs with Turkana women as such. Some of the Turkana women living in Kakuma town had sexual relationships with several men, and were thus tainted by accusations of prostitution. Although this phenomenon cannot be attributed wholly to the refugees, as it was also a product of the growing urban lifestyle in Kakuma, the presence of the refugee camp undoubtedly amplified this trend.

Another form of sociable relationship that has developed between the Turkana and refugees was 'bond-friendship'. This is also a customary practice among the Turkana, in which two individuals, together with family members of both sides, establish a close social relationship through the exchange of gifts. Starting with small gift-giving, such as tobacco, both parties repeatedly visit the partner's homestead, getting the partner to slaughter a goat or sheep, which is a typical way of giving a cordial reception. Going through this process, they eventually build up an interdependent relationship, which is very important for the Turkana (Gulliver 1951, 1953).

The Turkana seemed to have no difficulties extending this practice to the refugees. Most of these relationships were initiated by Turkana women or youth who regularly visit the refugee camp to sell things such as milk, firewood and goats. They repeatedly encountered and conversed with specific refugees, and exchanged small gifts. Eventually they took their husbands or elders to the camp to introduce to their refugee friends. Then, they repeatedly visited each other's home and gave some gifts. The Turkana offered goats and sheep, as well as firewood and milk, to the refugees, and in return, the refugees gave rations, blankets, and cooking pots, etc. Some of the refugees helped their Turkana partners to access the benefits within the camp, such as arranging to visit the clinics or hospital, or to buy commodities.

Economic relationship

Livestock trade and herding 'contracts'

Prices of livestock went up, especially in the early stage of the camp. For example, the price of goats rose threefold between June 1992 and October 1993. After 1995, when Somali refugees were transferred from other camps in Kenya to Kakuma, demand for camel meat increased, and the price of camels escalated.[5] The creation of the refugee camp proved to be a significant opportunity for the local Turkana to sell their livestock.

Some of the Turkana started to enter 'contracts' with refugees to look after the latter's livestock. Formally the refugees were prohibited from keeping livestock, but some Sudanese, Somali, and Ethiopian refugees had them anyway. The Kenyan police and administration officers turned a blind eye to it. The refugees' purpose in owning livestock was not to multiply the herd; they purchased livestock from a Turkana, contracted its care to another for some period, and then sold it to the butcheries in the camp. In short, they were brokers.

The relationship between the Turkana herdsmen and refugee brokers could be termed a 'contract'. The Turkana herdsmen's duty was as follows: they kept the animals, and when animals needed to be slaughtered, they took them to the slaughtering place in the camp, slaughtered and skinned the animals. They were not paid in cash for their efforts, but were given the hide of the animals that they had been keeping, and certain parts of the meat. They could sell the hide after drying it.[6] Although it has long been the practice that destitute Turkana sometimes put themselves under the protection of relatives or friends and worked as herders, it is the personal social relationship that makes this state possible. The herder might be given some animals at some stage, but there is no fixed payment and, if given, the animals are gifts. On the contrary, the Turkana got a fixed return for taking care of refugees' livestock. The Turkana complained to me, however, that their refugee partners were stingy. This relationship of herding 'contract' was a quite new phenomenon for the Turkana.

Many young Turkana men entered the livestock trade, trying to take advantage of the sudden rise in livestock prices. They bought commodities such as beads, adornments and clothes, and took them to remote areas to exchange for livestock. Then, they brought the livestock back and sold it in the refugee camp, earning the balance of the trade. The more successful men, although they were few, maintained a herd consisting of only male goats and sheep near the camp, and sold them when the prices were attractive.

The refugee camp opened up a range of opportunities for selling livestock, introducing not only the market economy, but also the commoditization of livestock among the Turkana. They once sold livestock only when they needed cash to pay hospital bills and school fees, to buy tobacco, maize flour, sugar, tea leaves, beads, ornaments, etc. But like other East African pastoralists, their livestock were not a simple commodity for the Turkana—they were symbolic and inalienable assets of social and religious importance (Broch-Due 1999; Ohta 2001). The emergence of the refugee camp has considerably accelerated the commoditization of livestock in the area.

Wage labor
The refugee camp provided employment opportunities for the Turkana. Some Turkana with higher formal education were employed by the offices of the UNHCR and its implementing partners (IPs), such as LWF, Don-Bosco, International Rescue Committee, World Vision, etc. Others got various jobs, as drivers, night watchmen, gatekeepers, and part time construction workers, etc. However, the job market was not large enough to fulfill the expectations of young Turkana who had higher formal education, and they complained that they were discriminated against by the members of other ethnic groups who favored their fellows to fill vacancies.

I have no quantitative data on how the Turkana spent their salary. Some of the Turkana whom I know well got jobs as night watchmen and construction workers. They were paid about 140 Kenyan Shillings per day in 2000, which was quite a good salary.[7] One of them, in his middle thirties, worked for six months. He bought 15 goats and sheep spending about 15,000 Shillings, which were equivalent to 60% of his total salary. Some of the remaining money was given to relatives and friends, and some was spent on food, tobacco, clothes, etc., and drinking alcohol.

In addition to the UNHCR and its IPs, the refugees themselves also employed the Turkana. Many refugees from Somalia and Ethiopia had enough money to start various businesses in the camp. Some opened kiosks selling miscellaneous goods; others started vegetable shops, butcheries, restaurants and bars. Kakuma refugee camp turned out to be the biggest town in the area, and offered the local Turkana opportunities to be employed to do physical labor. However, most of them were paid very little and, thus, found it difficult to save money to invest in goats and sheep.

Some Turkana, primarily young boys and girls, were hired as house-keepers. Their tasks included cleaning the compound, fetching water, bringing firewood, cooking, watering trees, building fences and houses, etc. Most lived in their employers' houses, and some were registered as members of their employers' families, and thus got free rations. For their work, they were given food, and paid as little as 150 Kenyan Shillings per month.

I do not have any statistical data, but the local chief of Kakuma Division confirmed the refugees' reports that about 10% of Sudanese households and more than 90% of households from other countries employed this kind of housekeepers. If we make a simple calculation, assuming that one household consisted of five persons, and each household employed one Turkana, it follows that about 4,000 Turkana children were employed as live-in housekeepers. The number could have been higher, however, because, when a boy or girl was employed and stayed with the refugees, his/her siblings often visited and worked with them.

This exploitation of child labor attracted the attention of the local Kenyan administrators. The chief declared that it was illegal to employ children, and that children should be sent back to school. However, it was difficult to enforce this decision, because it required great effort to make a house-by-house search of the refugee camp. If this situation continues, though, it may well have considerable influence on the development of these children, and consequently on the Turkana culture, although the precise nature and extent of these effects cannot be predicted.

Petty trade by women
Turkana women took firewood, branches of trees for building materials, charcoal, sun-dried bricks and milk to sell in the refugee camp. Although the range of items that they traded in was limited, this trade had become very important for the livelihood of their families.

To secure the supply of firewood, UNHCR and its IPs invited tenders and then entered contracts with the successful bidder. Traveling through the northwestern part of the Turkana District, one could see firewood

piled along the roads here and there, which had been collected by local
Turkana, and was awaiting the contractor's lorries. Since the beginning of
2000, however, this system has begun to atrophy. Turkana politicians and
young elites formed an organization, named TERA (Turkana Environment
and Resource Association), and demanded that all tendering and bidding
of firewood should be channeled through them. They argued that if the
UNHCR regulations, which requested an open and competitive bidding
process were strictly applied, suppliers from outside of the Turkana
District could also tender. They insisted that tendering and bidding should
be open only to the Turkana, because the materials (firewood) were locally
sourced in Turkana District. When the UNHCR subsequently awarded a
firewood contract to non-members of TERA, some members of TERA
tried to block the contractors' lorries, and a Turkana woman died when
Kenyan police interfered on 12 July 2002.[8]

The UNHCR's supply of firewood to the refugees was not sufficient
even before this trouble started, with the refugees having to buy some
of it from the Turkana. After the tender system hit turmoil, though, the
distribution of firewood came to a standstill within the camp, creating a
highly profitable situation for the local Turkana women to sell firewood
to individual refugees.[9]

Cutting live trees was strictly prohibited around the refugee camp, and it
was very difficult for refugees to collect firewood. Turkana women living
near Kakuma sometimes had to walk more than 10 km to bring firewood.
Others began digging up the stumps and roots of trees that had died long
ago. Once they got the timber out of the ground, they cut it into pieces and
took them to the camp to sell. The majority of Turkana women had their
regular customers, to whom they took firewood directly. Others sold their
firewood to refugee traders, who divided it into smaller units and sold it
on to the refugees.

Typically, a woman could carry a bundle of firewood that she could sell
for about 50 Kenyan Shillings in August 2003. At that time, according to
the local Turkana, they never failed to sell their firewood. With this money,
a woman could buy, for example, about 5 kg of maize flour, which could
satisfy about 15 people. I witnessed many Turkana women buying food,
tobacco etc., in the refugee camp after selling firewood.

According to RESCUE (Rational Energy Supply, Conservation,
Utilization and Education, a UNHCR/GTZ household energy project in
Dadaab area in Kenya), firewood consumption is 0.7 kg per capita per
day (Hoerz 1995). On this basis, the Kakuma camp of 80,000 people
consumed about 56.0 metric tons of firewood every day. Another simple

calculation, assuming that all necessary firewood in the camp was brought in by Turkana women, and that each woman sold 10 kg of firewood a day,[10] it follows that more than 5,500 women sold firewood daily in the camp. As of August 2003, the Turkana said that it was easy to make a living by selling firewood.

In the early years of the camp, some of the refugees' firewood had been brought from outside the Turkana District by the UNHCR. But in 2004 it was all procured locally. Moreover, trees had been cut to provide building materials for the refugees, and to supply charcoal to refugees and town dwellers. The vegetation around the camp has obviously been devastated,[11] contributing to the Turkana's antagonistic feeling towards the refugees, despite the inconsistency of the fact that they were themselves deriving a profit by selling firewood, charcoal and building materials to the refugees.

Concluding remarks

Multiple and contradictory relationships between the Turkana and the refugees

In studies of the host population of refugees or those displaced by development projects, the kinds of benefits and/or losses that the hosts encounter have become a central issue. In order to understand the hosts' experience, it is necessary to first identify the range of resources and opportunities available from an external perspective, and their decline, because the local people cannot utilize what is not present. For example, vegetation cover around Kakuma has obviously been destroyed, and it is important to objectively assess this ecological problem, no matter how locals perceive or deal with the state of affairs. The same can be said of assessments of the economic and social environments.

From the outsiders' perspective, e.g. the aid agencies, the Turkana are generally seen as failures because the majority of those living near the refugee camp are heavily dependent on the unreliable refugee camp for their livelihood and on emergency food aid in times of drought. Some might see them as losers because their land and its vegetation has seriously deteriorated since the creation of the refugee camp, and the Turkana themselves, as well as the refugees, were major contributors to the destruction.

However, to understand how people cope with uncertain and changing circumstances, it is essential to try to understand the 'insiders' perspectives and strategies, upon which decisions are based and measures taken to deal with the situation at hand. Only then might we understand how they are utilizing their resources and opportunities. The Turkana perceived and understood their situation differently to outsiders. As far as I can tell, the Turkana did not consider themselves to be failures or losers. Facing new opportunities, people repeatedly made decisions, selecting what was profitable, utilizing whatever lay ready at hand, according to their necessity and priority.

As we have seen, the Turkana's attitude towards the refugee camp was ambiguous and contradictory. They were apparently aware of the benefits, mostly economic, which they were exploiting. However at the same time, they complained loudly about the insecurity and environmental destruction caused by the camp. Their relationships with the refugees were also multiple, and seemingly contradictory. On the one hand, they were bitterly antagonistic to each other, even to the extent of the occasional murders. On the other hand, however, they have fostered close relationships. Some of them were employers and employees, partners in petty trade, and others have cultivated bond-friendships through exchanging gifts, as well as marriage-like relations.

This pattern of complicated relationships is similar to the Turkana's relationships with neighboring ethnic groups. They have a history which has alternated between periods of alliance and periods of opposition, and in which livestock raiding was repeatedly a factor in the changes. For the Turkana, a neighboring group may represent a deadly enemy for a time, but when a peace proposal is accepted, they stop fighting each other—and then not uncommonly cooperate to attack a third group. But even when the overall relationship is hostile, the individual members of different ethnic groups maintain social relationships as affines and friends, visiting each other and trusting livestock to one another. They do not find it contradictory to sustain overall hostility while individual close relationships are kept intact. Moreover, ethnic affiliations are not rigidly fixed. The boundaries between ethnic groups are commonly transgressed. When one has moved to the area of a neighboring group, speaking its language and observing its customs, s/he might be incorporated to the group.

Self-assuredness of the Turkana

In the development of personal and positive relationships with the refugees, the Turkana have a certain unique style—an important element of Turkana culture—that plays a vital role. That is, they have a propensity of tirelessly working on others, so to speak, in face-to-face communication (Kitamura 1997). They are relatively free of the nervousness and hesitation that we usually feel when interacting with 'cultural others'. The Turkana are self-assured and carry their way of doing things throughout; this is often perceived by outsiders as arrogance.

For example, they demanded that I should behave just as they did from the very first day of my research. They spoke to me tirelessly in Turkana language, which I didn't understand, in the manner of someone who has never imagined that somebody does not know their language. Evans-Pritchard evocatively described a similar experience in the introduction to his book, *The Nuer,* explaining how the attitude of the Nuer was different from that of the Azande: 'Among Azande I was compelled to live outside the community; among Nuer I was compelled to be a member of it. Azande treated me as a superior; Nuer as an equal' (Evans-Pritchard 1940: 15). The latter aptly describes my experiences among the Turkana.

They are self-confident and straightforward when engaged in face-to-face interactions. It is this unique attitude of self-assuredness that makes it easy for them to approach and associate with strangers, and thus enables many Turkana boys and girls to be employed as live-in housekeepers, and for Turkana women to 'marry' refugees.

Another element of the Turkana culture that provides a key to understanding their relationships with the refugees is their propensity for territorial and social expansion. In the 25 years since I first visited the Turkana, they have been continually expanding their territory east and southeast. They have not only enlarged the space for livestock herding and habitation, but have also settled in and on the peripheries of towns and private ranches. They do not hesitate to intrude themselves upon others' territories, and settle there. On the peripheries of towns, they earn a living by selling firewood, charcoal, etc., and by engaging in physical labors. They are not reluctant to work on private ranches to do miscellaneous odd jobs, such as housekeepers, watchmen, herders, etc., which people of other ethnic groups sometimes disdain. It seems that such jobs do not affect the Turkana's pride at all.

The Turkana's self-assuredness, combined with their inclination towards expansion, has greatly contributed to building personal relationships with the refugees. But of course these relationships are not grounded only in the Turkana's extrovert attitude, but through their repeated mutual interactions. Further research is necessary to explore this process.

Acknowledgments

This research was financed by the Ministry of Education, Culture and Science, Japan (Grant-in-Aid for Overseas Research Nos. 12372005,

11410084, and 15251010), MEXT 21st Century COE Program 'Aiming for COE of Integrated Studies' (No. 14219101), and the Toyota Foundation (Research Grant No. D01-B2-020). The staff and graduate students of the Center for African Area Studies, Kyoto University encouraged this study. Numerous Turkana people offered me friendship. To these people and institutions, I make grateful acknowledgments.

Notes

1 Sudan's government and the Sudan People's Liberation Movement/Army (SPLM/A) signed a memorandum of understanding on 19 November 2004 in Nairobi, in which they agreed to conclude a final peace deal by the end of the year 2004.
2 Traditionally, the murderer's family pays a blood-price in livestock, called *ngibaren-lu-a-ekwori* (lit. livestock of contention [trouble, hostility, collision]) to the family of the victim. The amount of this payment is decided in an elders' meeting that considers the solvency of the wrongdoer's family. However, the Turkana do not pay this compensation when they kill humans whom they regard to belong to other ethnic groups. However, in this case, they had little choice but to pay, because the Turkana youth was arrested by the police, which approved a local way of problem resolution. The Turkana disliked and avoided taking the case through formal channels because they knew that policemen were sometimes very brutal to prisoners.
3 Livestock rustling causes serious insecurity. In earlier times, when people raided livestock they would take the animals home and add them to their flock. Any weapons used then were not very destructive. But since the collapse of Idi Amin's government in Uganda in 1979, there has been an influx of small arms on a large scale in northwestern Kenya, and the flow increased tremendously in the 1990s, fueled by civil wars and political instability in Sudan, Ethiopia, Somalia and Uganda. Livestock raiding has changed into mere robbery, and plundered animals are taken directly to urban areas to sell (see Hendrickson et. al. 1996; 1998).
4 Traditionally, for the first child, the genitor's family should pay 10 big animals (cattle, donkeys and camels) and 20 small animals (goats and sheep) to the girl's family. For the second and thereafter, 1 big animal and 10 small animals should be paid. However, today it is possible to give small animals in place of big ones. When the genitor maintains close social relationships with the girl and her family members, this payment can be postponed for quite a long time. I know one Turkana

man who had six children with a woman out of formal marriage, but had only finished paying for the first born and about half of the animals for the second.

5 For example, the price of the largest castrated goat rose from 500 Kenyan Shillings in 1992 to 1,500 in 1993. The price of a castrated camel was about 10,000 in 1994, and rose to 25,000 in August 2004. 1US$=80 Kenyan Shillings approximately.

6 The price of a goat skin was 100–120, while that of cattle was 500–700 Kenyan Shillings in August 2004.

7 This was equivalent of 4,200 Shillings per month. The monthly salary of a primary school teacher could be between 2,250–8,000 Shillings at the same time.

8 After the general election in December 2002, when the former ruling party, KANU, lost office, TERA began to lose the support of the Turkana people and became inactive.

9 According to the chief of Kakuma Division, the County Council of Kakuma Division began to charge 5–10 Shillings on each firewood sale from around July 2004. A market place was established in the refugee camp where Turkana women should take and sell their firewood, but many women evaded this supervision (and thus the tax) and continued to sell firewood individually.

10 The firewood bundle that a woman carries at a time was roughly 10kg, and most women went and sold the firewood once a day.

11 A joint project to assess the environmental destruction of the vegetation destruction around the Kakuma, utilizing GIS and RS, was in progress at the time of writing (Tachiiri and Ohta 2004).

References

Broch-Due, V. (1999) 'Remembered cattle, forgotten people: The morality of exchange and the exclusion of the Turkana poor', in D. M. Anderson and V. Broch-Due (eds), *The Poor Are Not Us: Poverty and Pastoralism in Eastern Africa*. Oxford: James Currey, pp. 50–88.

Callamard, A. (1994) 'Refugees and local hosts: A study of the trading interactions between Mozambican refugees and Malawian villagers in the District of Mwanza', *Journal of Refugee Studies*, 7(1), pp. 39–62.

Chambers, R. (1986) 'Hidden losers? The impact of rural refugees and refugee programs on poorer hosts', *International Migration Review*, 20(2), pp. 245–63.

Chisholm, C. L. (1996) *Refugee Settlements are an Economic Magnet to Host*

Populations: A Case Study of Meheba Refugee Settlement, Northwest Province, Zambia. (mimeo).

Crisp, J. (2000) 'A state of insecurity: The political economy of violence in Kenya's refugee camps', *African Affairs*, 99, pp. 601–32.

De Montclos, M-A. P. and P. M. Kagwanja (2000) 'Refugee camps or cities? The socio-economic dynamics of the Dadaab and Kakuma Camps in northern Kenya', *Journal of Refugee Studies*, 13(2), pp. 205–22.

Evans-Pritchard, E. E. (1940) *The Nuer.* New York: Oxford University Press.

Government of Kenya (1994) *Kenya Population Census, 1989, Vol. 2.* Nairobi: Central Bureau of Statistics, Government Printer.

——— (2001) *1999 Population and Housing Census, Vol. 1.* Nairobi: Central Bureau of Statistics, Government Printer.

Gregersen, E. A. (1977) *Language in Africa.* New York: Gordon and Beach.

Gulliver, P. H. (1951) *Preliminary Survey of the Turkana.* Cape Town: Cape Town University.

——— (1953) *Family Herds.* London: Routledge Kegan and Paul.

Hansen, A. (1993) 'Long-term consequences of two African refugee settlement strategies', in P. W. Van Arsdate (ed.), *Refugee Empowerment and Organizational Change.* Arlington: American Anthropological Association, pp. 140–54.

Harrell-Bond, B. (1986) *Imposing Aid: Emergency Assistance to Refugees.* New York: Oxford University Press.

Hendrickson, D., R. Mearns, and J. Armon (1996) 'Livestock raiding among the pastoral Turkana of Kenya', *IDS Bulletin*, 27(3), pp. 17–30.

Hendrickson, D., J. Armon and R. Mearns (1998) 'The changing nature of conflict and famine vulnerability: The case of livestock raiding in Turkana District, Kenya', *Disasters*, 22(3), pp. 185–99.

Hoerz, T. (1995) 'The environment of refugee camps: A challenge for refugees, local populations and aid agencies', in RPN 18 *Burning Issues (Environmental Issues)*, Refugee Participation Network (http://www.fmreview.org/rpn185.htm, accessed on 29 August 2004).

Horst, C. (2001) *Vital Links in Social Security: Somali Refugees in the Dadaab Camps, Kenya.* New Issues in Refugee Research, Working Paper No. 38, UNHCR.

Kitamura, K. (1997) 'Communication for "negotiation" among the Turkana', *African Study Monographs*, 18(3–4), pp. 241–56.

Kok, W. (1989) 'Self-settled refugees and the socio-economic impact of their presence on Kassala, eastern Sudan', *Journal of Refugee Studies*, 2(4), pp. 419–40.

Kurimoto, E. (2001) *Reconstructing Social Space among the Pari Refugees in Kakuma.* (mimeo).

Leach, M. (1992) *Dealing with Displacement: Refugee-Host Relations, Food and Forest Resources in Sierra Leonean Mende Communities during the Liberian Influx, 1990–91.* England: IDS Research Report No. 22. Institute of Development Studies.

Lassailly-Jacob, V. (1994) *Planners' Role in Refugee-Host Relationships: A Field Report from the Ukwimi Mozambican Refugee Settlement, Zambia.* Paper presented at the 4th International Research and Advisory Panel Conference. Oxford: Comerville College, 5–9 January 1994.

Merkx, J. (2000) *Refugee Identities and Relief in an African Borderland: A Study of Northern Uganda and Southern Sudan.* New Issues in Refugee Research, Working Paper No. 19. Geneva: UNHCR.

Ohta, I. (2001) 'Motivations, negotiations, and animal individuality: Livestock exchange of the Turkana in northwestern Kenya', *Nilo-Ethiopian Studies,* No. 7, pp. 45–61.

Silva, Maria de Conceicao das Neves (2002) *Impact of Kakuma Refugee Camp on Turkana Women and Girls.* UNIFEM (mimeo).

Tachiiri, K. and I. Ohta (2004) 'Assessing impact of a large-sized refugee camp on the local vegetation condition using remote sensing: A case study of Kakuma, Kenya', in *Proceedings of the 2004 IEEE International Geoscience and Remote Sensing Symposium, III,* pp. 1547–50.

UNHCR (n.d.) *Handbook for Emergencies,* Second Edition.

———— (1993) *Information Bulletin,* June.

———— (1995) *Information Bulletin,* April.

———— (1998) *Information Bulletin,* July.

———— (2001) *Provisional Statistics of Refugees and Others of Concern to UNHCR for the Year 2000.* Geneva: Population Data Unit (11 April 2001), UNHCR.

———— (2002) *2001 UNHCR Population Statistics (Provisional).* Geneva: Population Data Unit (10 June 2002), UNHCR.

Verdirame, G. (1999) 'Human rights and refugees: The case of Kenya', *Journal of Refugee Studies,* 12(1), pp. 54–77.

Waters, T. (1999) 'Assessing the impact of the Rwandan refugee crisis on development planning in rural Tanzania, 1994–1996', *Human Organization,* 58(2), pp. 142–52.

Whitaker, B. E. (1999) *Changing Opportunities: Refugees and Host Communities in Western Tanzania.* New Issues in Refugee Research, Working Paper No. 11. Geneva: UNHCR.

10
Multidimensional Impact of Refugees and Settlers in the Gambela Region, Western Ethiopia

Eisei Kurimoto

Introduction

The influx and settlement of involuntarily displaced people has a significant impact on the host population. This is particularly so when the
newcomers are huge in number, culturally different from the hosts, their
settlement is planned without any consultation with or consent from the
hosts, and there is inadequate coordination and mediation between the
two groups. Quite often, the results of such settlement are disastrous. The
Gambela (Gambella) region of western Ethiopia provides such a case.[1]
During the 1980s some 50,000–65,000 settlers from the Ethiopian highlands were relocated to the area, along with approximately 366,000 refugees[2] from South Sudan who settled in two camps in Gambela. The local
population had previously been between 100,000–150,000.[3] From these
figures we can imagine how great the impact must have been. Indeed,
Gambela appears to be an extreme case. The landscape was completely
changed and there were tremendous impacts on the host population in
environmental, economic, social and political terms. It was not only
disastrous for the host population, but for the settlers and refugees as
well. The aim of this chapter is to examine the extent of the disaster, and
to assess how and why it happened. I argue that there were five fundamental contributing factors. First, settlers and refugees arrived with no
prior consultation and certainly without the consent of the local hosts.
Second, the size of the settler and refugee population was disproportionate to the host population. Third, settlers and refugees were more able
to adapt to the newly created market and cash economy than the hosts,
who were primarily engaged in a subsistence economy. Fourth, by local
standards, the refugees were overly privileged; provided with much better
resources and facilities than those available to the hosts. Finally, there

was no forum where problems between hosts and settlers/refugees could be openly discussed and resolutions sought.

The relations between hosts and settlers/refugees are very complex, with local, national and international factors at work. To explain this, I will focus on the policies of the socialist state regime (Derg), the 'Sudanese factor', i.e. the influence of the civil war and the relation between the Sudan People's Liberation Movement/Sudan People's Liberation Army (SPLM/SPLA, hereafter SPLA) and the Ethiopian government, inter-ethnic relations between the local hosts and new settlers, and the local hosts' perception of the situation.

Gambela is a frontier region bordering with the Upper Nile province of Sudan, and one of the most remote regions in Ethiopia (Figure 10-1).[4] Until 1991, under both the Imperial and the socialist regimes (Derg, 1974–1991), it was administratively an *awraja* (district) of Illubabor Province.[5] A substantial proportion of the region is savannah woodland and grassland, although the eastern parts are covered with dense forests that extend from the escarpments of the Ethiopian highlands. It is sparsely populated with a density of less than ten people per square kilometer. The two main indigenous peoples are the Nilotic speaking Anywaa (Anuak) and the Nuer, both of whom are fundamentally different linguistically, culturally and physically from the majority of Ethiopians, who are Semitic, like the Amhara, and Cushitic, like the Oromo.

Nuer and Anywaa are 'black', tall and slender, while Amhara and Oromo are 'red' or reddish brown. This classificatory system is recognized and accepted by both sides. The 'black' peoples who inhabit the lowlands on the peripheries of the modern Ethiopian empire and the present Ethiopian state are looked down upon by the 'highlanders'—particularly by the 'Abyssinians', i.e., the Semitic speaking Tigrayan and Amhara. Being black had derogatory connotations: uncivilized and primitive. In Amharic black peoples used to be called 'shankilla', which at the time was a synonym for 'slave' (*baria*). Although these derogatory terms were banned during the Derg regime, which had embraced progressive and revolutionary ideology and advocated equality for all of the peoples ('nationalities') of Ethiopia, the sense of difference seems to linger in the minds of some people. In the old Ethiopian ethnic/racial stratification, the Cushitic and Omotic speaking peoples were ranked between the top ('Abyssinians') and the bottom ('black' peoples in the lowlands) (cf. Donham 1986). But for Anywaa, this internal difference among the highlanders does not make much sense, for they see the Oromo and the Omotic peoples as well as the Amhara and Tigrayan, as *gaale* (sing. *gaala*), that is, 'people of red skin'.

Figure 10-1. Map of the Gambela Region

According to the 1994 national census the total population of Gambela state was 162,397. Its ethnic composition was: Nuer 64,473 (39.7%), Anywaa 44,581 (27.5%), Amhara 12,566 (7.7%), Oromo 10,543 (6.5%), Majangir 9,350 (5.8%), Kafa 6,783 (4.2%), Kambata 3,632 (2.2%), Mocha 3,089 (1.9%), Tigrayan 2,596 (1.6%), others 4,784 (2.9%) (Central

Statistical Authority 1995). Of these, only the Nuer, Anywaa and Majangir are indigenous. Other indigenous peoples, such as Komo and Opuo, are too few in number to be separately represented.

The settlers and refugees who arrived in the area were located in Anywaaland, and it was among the Anywaa that I conducted my fieldwork. Hence, in this article the term 'hosts' primarily refers to the Anywaa. From their perspective, Gambela belongs to them, and the recent arrivals from the Ethiopian highlands, as well as the Nuer, are seen as late-comers.

Encroachment of socialist policies

The social and economic changes that occurred among the Anywaa during the Derg era was unprecedented and profound (Kurimoto 1996a, 1997).[6] A variety of 'traditional' customs and institutions were banned on the ground that they were 'feudal', 'reactionary' and 'anti-revolutionary'. Mass associations imposed from above—such as peasant associations, women's and youth associations—'replaced' traditional institutions. All association members were registered and issued with ID cards. Each peasant was obliged to pay taxes on the land s/he cultivated.[7] A significant number of young men were forcibly recruited into the national army and sent to the war fronts in northern Ethiopia, Eritrea and Tigray, all of which are extremely far from their homes. Numerous primary schools were built throughout the region, even in areas so remote that the teachers had to walk for days to reach them. The capacity of secondary schools was also extended, and a Teacher Training College was later opened. The Workers' Party of Ethiopia (WPE), the only political party at the time, established branch offices in the region. Gambela was no exception of the 'project of *encadrement*' implemented so thoroughly by the Derg in the entire Ethiopia (Clapham 2002). Through the schools and adult education programs, socialist and nationalist ideology was propagated at the grassroots level. For the first time in history, I suggest, the Anywaa were fully integrated into the Ethiopian rule.

Numerous development projects were also begun in Gambela during the Derg era, as the regime regarded the region, with its rich water resources and sparse population, as an ideal target for agricultural development. These projects included: a state farm for cultivating cotton, mechanized agricultural schemes using East German made tractors, a dam construction and irrigation project coordinated by a number of USSR experts, and a rice project supported by North Korea. The resettlement program, which is discussed below, can be included on this list as well. To facilitate these projects, and to maintain the refugee camps, the transportation infrastructure was greatly improved. A network of all weather roads was built, connecting Gambela to the other regions of Ethiopia, and Gambela town to other administrative centers, such as Itang, Jikaw, Abwobo (Abobo) and Pinyudo (Fugnido). A bridge, said to be the longest in Ethiopia, was built over the Baro River. Transport by air improved when a new airport was constructed outside of Gambela town. Telephone communication was also improved and the electricity supply in Gambela town became more reliable.

Many Anywaa were employed by these new agricultural extension projects. Others were employed by the various projects of *encadrement*, voluntarily becoming Party cadres, administrators and school teachers. Generally speaking the local people welcomed the development of infrastructure and education, appreciating the fact that they were enjoying more opportunities than ever before.

There were also high levels of resentment, though. High rates of taxation and forcible army recruitment were common complaints. The alienation of their ancestral lands by state projects, settlers and refugees was a significant source of grievances. Although resentment was generally not publicly expressed out of fear of intimidation and arrest, occasionally direct measures were taken against the Derg. For example, in 1979 peasants in Jor district led by deposed traditional leaders revolted against the Derg. They were soon suppressed, and many fled to Sudan. Anywaa dissidents in Khartoum organized the GLF (Gambela Liberation Front) around 1980, which was renamed as the GPLM (Gambela People's Liberation Movement) in 1985. With support from other anti-Derg organizations based in Sudan, they began to broadcast underground radio and launched small scale military operations against the government. Their actions made the situation in Anywaaland more difficult, as the Anywaa were collectively regarded as anti-government.

Resettlement program

The first settlers arrived in Gambela in 1984. Somewhere between 50,000 and 65,000 re-settled in about 30 villages (*mandar*) along the Baro and Giilo rivers and around Abwobo. Ethnically, there were three different groups: Tigrayan from Tigray province, Amhara from Wello province, and Kambata from Kambata and Hadiya province. This resettlement was part of the national level projects that transferred about 600,000 people—mainly from famine stricken Tigray and Wello provinces—to sparsely populated and fertile regions in the west and south. Although the government argued that the projects were for relief and development, for the sake of people and Ethiopia, the projects were widely criticized for the way they were carried out, and because the real purpose was allegedly military: to depopulate the strongholds of the rebel movements. Most of the settlers were forcibly relocated, and given empty promises of agricultural, educational and medical facilities and services (Human Rights Watch 1991; Clay and Holcomb 1986).

Certainly the settlers in Gambela suffered. First of all the natural environment of Gambela's lowlands is radically different to their homes in the highlands. For them, Gambela might as well have been a foreign country. Because it is hot and dry, cultivating their staple crops—such as *tef, ensete*, and barley—was impossible, and they had to rely instead on maize cultivation. Medical and educational facilities were very poor, and mechanization was not to the standards expected. Furthermore, the area is rampant with tropical diseases like malaria, and their local hosts are a kind of 'uncivilized' people that they had never encountered before. It was as if they had been abandoned in the wilderness.[8]

According to the local Anywaa administrators, most of these settlers were not self-sufficient in food production, but had to depend on relief from the RRC (Relief and Rehabilitation Commission), a state organization in charge of famine victims and settlers. I was not able to interview them, because of the language barrier and surveillance by the government, but quite often saw them and on a few occasions visited their villages. They looked quite wretched, both spiritually and physically. I have met a lot of refugees and IDPs in Ethiopia, Sudan, Uganda and Kenya, and am under the impression that these were the most depressed and least well-off. Since relocation, their population has continually declined in numbers. Many have died; many have fled to other areas in Ethiopia; and still others have fled across the border into Sudan. By early 1993, their population was less than 10,000, and many of these were living in small urban centers rather than villages. The population decline is evidence of the total failure of the resettlement projects.

Civil war in Sudan and the influx of refugees

During the first civil war in Sudan (1955–72) Gambela hosted refugees from South Sudan at the Itang refugee camp. When the second war broke out in 1983 and then escalated, a huge number of displaced people began crossing the borders seeking refuge. A refugee camp was set up at Itang again to house the ever increasing number of refugees. In 1988 there were about 200,000 at Itang and another 40,000 at Pinyudo (Fugnido), where a new camp was established that year. By January 1991 the official number had reached 280,000 at Itang and 86,000 at Pinyudo. Itang was by then one of the largest refugee camps in the world. Although the actual numbers may have been about half of the official figures, it was nevertheless extraordinary to house so many refugees in one location.

The ethnic composition of the refugee population was quite diverse. Although the majority were Dinka and Nuer—both of who speak Nilotic languages like Anywaa—from the Upper Nile and Bahr al Ghazal provinces, there were also many other ethnic groups from South Sudan as well as some from North Sudan.

It was common knowledge in Gambela at the time that the official figures were overestimated, perhaps by as much as 100% (Scott-Villers et al. 1993). The discrepancy reveals an important characteristic of the refugees in Gambela. Itang is known as the birth place of the SPLA, one of whose main military bases was adjacent to Itang. There were also a number of other SPLA military bases in Gambela, and all of the newly recruited guerrilla soldiers arriving from Sudan were initially registered as refugees, either at Itang or Pinyudo. There they spent some time resting and recovering from the fatigue of their long journey by foot. New soldiers were also recruited from among the refugees. When these refugee/soldiers were deployed back to Sudan, their registrations as refugees were never cancelled. Having conducted fieldwork in South Sudan intermittently between 1978 and 1986, I once again met a number of old friends in Gambela and Addis Ababa. I could not readily distinguish whether they were genuine refugees or SPLA officers and men—nor could the local Anywaa, for whom refugees and SPLA were almost synonymous. As many of the SPLA officers and refugees were Dinka, who politically dominated both the SPLA and the refugee administration, the Anywaa put both in one category and called them *ajwilli* (sing. *ajwil*, meaning a Dinka), even though they knew that there were many members of other ethnic groups among the SPLA officers, soldiers, and refugees. This is an important factor in the 'ethnicization' of relations between the Anywaa and SPLA/refugees.

Another important aspect of the Sudanese refugees in Gambela was that the SPLA were given a free hand in the refugee camps, as well as in the Gambela region more generally. The SPLA and the Derg cooperated fully with one another, with the latter generously providing logistics and other support to the former. The refugee camps were administered by committees comprised of 'representatives' of the refugees, who were invariably SPLA officers. The committee was in charge of distributing food rations and other relief goods, such as soap and clothing. Thus they could divert resources originally intended for refugees to other purposes. In fact without access to and utilization of relief goods, the SPLA would not have been able to sustain its activities. Moreover, the entire Gambela region was under a sort of informal joint administration of the SPLA and the Derg, under which the SPLA officers and men as well as the refugees enjoyed freedom of movement, while there were strict regulations imposed on ordinary Ethiopians.

In May 1991 when the Derg regime fell, the entire population of SPLA-refugees in Gambela was obliged to withdraw to the Sudan side of the border, as the advancing EPRDF (Ethiopian People's Revolutionary Democratic Front) forces seized power, both in the center and Gambela (because the SPLA was closely allied with the Derg, they were regarded by the EPRDF as an enemy). This was a major disaster for the SPLA, whose officers, men and allied refugees suddenly lost all of the support and privileges they had received under the Derg and UNHCR protection, and became targets of aerial bombardment by the Sudanese army as they were now in Sudanese territory.

Many of the former refugees in Gambela resettled in the refugee camp at Kakuma in north-western Kenya, after a long and tough journey. The SPLA officers and troops eventually redeployed to other places in South Sudan, Kenya and Uganda. I have since met a number of them in various places, who recall their stay in Gambela as the 'good old days', when they were free and food was plentiful. They had enjoyed freedom of movement as well as access to the refugee facilities and resources.[9] For those who relocated to Kakuma, the quantity and quality of food relief makes a great difference, because they consider the food distributed at Kakuma to be extremely poor.

Impact of settlers and refugees

Environmental impact
In 1984, as a part of the national campaign, large numbers of university students, lecturers and administrators were sent to Gambela to construct huts for the new settlers. The forests in the eastern part of the region provided timber for the settlers and refugees. In addition to the building materials extracted from the forests, the amount of firewood consumed

by some 200,000 settlers and refugees was enormous. Although there is no concrete data in this regard, the massive deforestation was quite obvious.

The sudden change to the human environment also had a profound impact on the local wildlife. Hunting had long been an important economic activity for the Anywaa, and the Gambela region was known for its rich abundance of wildlife. After they began to arrive in the area in 1983, the SPLA soldiers hunted wild animals such as elephant, buffalo, giraffe, antelope and gazelle with automatic weapons for their own subsistence. The local Anywaa were soon also hunting with automatic weapons, namely AK-47 rifles that they had either purchased from SPLA soldiers or had been supplied by the government to equip the militia. It was thus not long before the previously rich wildlife was almost exhausted, and the Anywaa lost their primary source of dietary meat.

Economic impact

An enormous amount of relief food was distributed to the settlers and refugees. The amount supplied to the refugees was calculated on the basis of the 'official' figures rather than the actual number of people, and thus there was an enormous surplus of relief supplies. Part of it was sold, and thus flooded the local market. Maize, beans, rice, wheat flour, biscuits, cooking oil, sugar, and various tinned foods became available at very cheap prices. Soap, clothing, blankets, and empty containers (recycled cardboard boxes, tins, plastic bottles, etc.) were also sold. Note that at that time in other regions of Ethiopia, including the capital city Addis Ababa, commodities were scarce, in sharp contrast to the remote Gambela, where commodities brought from foreign countries as relief supplies were abundant and cheap. For instance, in the late 1980s, one gallon of cooking oil was 50birr[10] in Addis Ababa, while in Gambela the Canadian one was 15birr. A Swedish canned corned beef (1kg) was 5birr in Gambela, and was totally unavailable in Addis Ababa. One sack of maize (90kg) was 20–25birr in Gambela town and nearer to the refugee camps was less than 5birr, while the same weight of *tef*, the staple crop for Ethiopians, was more than 100birr.

As it suddenly became more populous, Gambela became a trading center, and the town expanded. Smaller towns in the area, such as Abwobo, Pinyudo and Itang, also expanded as settlers and refugees arrived and settled down. These places had been merely 'posts' for primary school teachers and policemen, but soon developed into small urban centers. In those small towns there were small kiosks, butcheries, tea and coffee shops, bars and restaurants, and hotels of mud walls and corrugated iron roofs. The development of transportation and communication systems, various agricultural projects, and an increasing number of workers from the highlands all contributed to this. The trade network expanded deep into South Sudan. Although the majority of settlers and refugees remained in utter poverty, many became successful small traders, selling goods to refugees, settlers, the local Anywaa and Nuer, and the highlanders. Some of the settlers were successful enough to become the owners of shops, bars, restaurants and milk cows—and hence suppliers of fresh milk in Gambela town.[11]

The Anywaa also rapidly became involved in this flourishing market and cash economy. Taxation, education, transport, and the newly introduced practice of paying bridewealth in cash,[12] all contributed to the need for cash. But they did not produce commodities for sale. Instead, their agricultural productivity declined as they began to buy maize and other food crops; and because the young men, the main labor force, left the villages to go to larger towns, the war fronts, and panning for gold. According to a household survey that I conducted in Cwobo village near Abwobo town in 1989–1990, 62 (37%) of the 168 households surveyed were headed by women; husbands/fathers were absent. Of those 62, the male heads of 33 households were dead, twelve were elsewhere seeking gold, nine were elsewhere working, and three were performing national service (i.e., they were in the army). In the next generation of males, 38 were absent; 16 were panning for gold, 13 were at school, and eight were in the national service. Although I do not have similar data on other villages, my observations in other villages suggest that the rate of female headed households and the total number of absent men—29 husbands and 38 sons out of 168 households—are rather moderate in comparison.

As the system of government expanded and a number of development projects got underway, a good number of Anywaa got jobs as administrators, clerks, teachers and workers. Their numbers, however, were relatively insignificant as a proportion of the total population, and the pay was rather low. The monthly salary for a new primary school teacher was about 200 birr, and for an unskilled laborer less than 100 birr. Before the Revolution, many Anywaa men had migrated as seasonal laborers to Dembidolo and other places in Wellega and Ilubaor provinces during the coffee bean harvest. As the Derg banned the employment of laborers by private farm owners, this practice disappeared and the Anywaa lost a major source of cash income.

For Anywaa men, gold panning provided a potentially far more profitable opportunity. There were two principal gold sites at the time: Runga to the east of Abwobo, and Dambala, which was located in Ilubabor

Province, near Gurafarda town. It took 10 days on foot to reach Dambala
from Gambela town. It is located in a remote area near the Sudanese
border and was not administered by the government. Although both the
journey and staying in Dambala itself was risky, and the labor was hard,[13]
many Anywaa men traveled there to work. Runga is much closer to their
homes, and during 1989–1991 I estimated that more than 1,000 men were
working there at any given time. I was informed that there were many more
men, probably twice as many, working at Dambala. The workers in both
places were exclusively Anywaa, and any Anywaa, whether Ethiopian or
Sudanese, could go there and work. As the government's administration
did not extend into those places, they were also a sanctuary of sorts for
those fleeing from the government: to avoid military service, political
persecution or criminal charges. It was reportedly not too difficult for a
worker to find one gram of gold per day, and the price at Runga was 35 birr
per gram. If one was a bit lucky and worked hard, it was possible to earn
as much as 1,000 birr per month. The price of gold per gram was 50 birr in
Gambela town, and 70 birr at Addis Ababa. Some Anywaa became brokers
who traveled between gold panning places and Addis Ababa. On the way
to Addis Ababa, they would carry a few hundred grams of gold, and
thousands of birr on the way back. Again, this was risky business—there
was always a possibility that the gold or money would be confiscated
by the police, lost in a swindle, or taken by robbers. Nevertheless, some
brokers became extremely rich in cash terms.

But even they, however, much less those engaged in gold panning, had
little success in investing their money in other businesses or trade. To my
knowledge, only one became the owner of a small kiosk and bar. Another
made a joint purchase of a second hand car intended to run an informal taxi
service; but the car soon broke down and the business came to a standstill.
In general, the money earned by gold panning was spent buying expensive
goods such as jeans, sneakers, watches and radio-cassette-players, and
purchasing drinks at the bars in town.

Certainly one of the obstacles to the Anywaa's success in trading was
it was almost entirely monopolized by traders from the highlands. More
importantly, however, very few of them had the entrepreneurial attitude
required to benefit from the market economy. They remained passive
'consumers', while many of the settlers and refugees became 'suppliers',
and this contributed significantly to their impoverishment.

The production and consumption of distilled alcohol (*araki*) can be
directly traced to the settlers' influence. Anywaa had previously drunk
locally brewed beer (*kongo* in Anywaa, *borde* in Amharic), but it was only

drunk by adult men and no other alcoholic drinks were common. During the Derg era everyone began to drink. Those who had money went to bars in town to drink industrially produced beers and spirits. For the rest, *araki* became very popular. The *araki* made by the Kambata settlers was known for its high quality. Anywaa women soon began to distil *araki* themselves, which provided one of the few sources of their income, but also led to heavy drinking which became habitual for many Anywaa. Moreover, as the *araki* and *kongo* produced by Anywaa women were only purchased by other Anywaa, while Anywaa bought alcohol from both Anywaa and others, this enterprise did not increase the total amount of cash circulating within their community.

When I visited a number of Anywaa villages between 1988 and 1991, they looked deserted. Young and middle-aged men were hard to find, and the ones who were there were not seriously engaged in any food producing activities. Old people, women and children were hungry. They were not producing enough food for their own consumption. Alcoholism had become chronic and many were drunk, both men and women. As their traditional political and ritual offices had been abolished by the Derg, the communal aspects of social life had dissipated. Perhaps I was especially sensitized to their feelings of desertion and their low moral, in comparison to the communities of South Eastern Sudan, where I had conducted fieldwork between 1978 and 1986, and where the subsistence economy was strong and communal life was highly cohesive.[14]

Political impact

According to the oral testimonies that I collected, when the settlers and refugees first arrived, the Anywaa had no hostile feelings towards them. Both groups were called *welle* (guests). With the South Sudanese refugees in particular, they recognize cultural and historical ties—in fact, many Anywaa live on the Sudanese side of the border, and new social ties with these refugees eventually developed, including many cases of inter-marriages. However, Anywaa developed very limited social relations with the settlers, although they lived in closer proximity. I did not observe any instance of sustained friendship, nor inter-marriage between the Anywaa and the settlers. Their relations appear to be limited to the economic level.

As the time went by, however, hostility towards the refugees/SPLA grew among the Anywaa. This was partly because some SPLA officers behaved very arrogantly, looting properties and raping women, and partly because the Anywaa became jealous of the general well being of the refugees, who enjoyed more resources—particularly relief food and clothing—and better facilities, such as schools, clinics and scholarship. The hostility came to a head in September 1989 when a group of armed refugees/SPLA attacked the Pinyudo village and razed it to the ground. This was the largest Anywaa village adjacent to the refugee camp. The entire village was burnt down, and at least 120 villagers reportedly died. The attack was apparently triggered by the murder of a refugee. Although the murderer was never identified, the refugees/SPLA concluded that it must have been committed by some Anywaa and decided to take revenge. The Anywaa villagers were taken by surprise. Four days later, the Anywaa militia and refugees/SPLA clashed at Itang, where 20 Anywaa militia members and ten refugees/SPLA were killed. Shops and bars owned by Ethiopian highlanders were destroyed and looted, leaving five highlanders dead as well. Neither the government nor the SPLA took any measures after these deadly incidents. The UNHCR remained silent. The anger and hostility towards the refugees/SPLA subsequently became very strong, but there were no avenues to formally express their grievances, no authority to intervene on their behalf.

In the course of these events, the Anywaa increasingly came to see their situation in ethnic terms. As mentioned, the settlers were called *kambaathe*, as many of them were Kambata. They were also called *gaale*, a more general category referring to Ethiopian highlanders who have 'red' skin. SPLA/refugees were generally called *ajwilli*, which means Dinka. At the time, the most senior posts in the regional administration were all occupied by Nuer.

During the 1980s a number of Nuer migrated to Gambela from Sudan. Some were registered as refugees, but others settled in different places along the Baro River and became Ethiopian citizens. We might regard this as the most recent stage in the historical 'Nuer expansion' to the east, but the Anywaa saw it differently. They believed the arrival of the Sudanese Nuer was part of a deliberate strategy by Ethiopian Nuer leaders to dominate the Anywaa and take over the land. During all of this, an ethnic consciousness was growing out of the notion that the Nuer (*Nuaare*, sing. *Nuaar*), Dinka and Ethiopian highlanders were allied and conspiring against the Anywaa. This 'conspiracy' appears to have been more imagined than real,[15] but for the Anywaa it was both very real and quite threatening. As one old man explained:

> They [*Ajwil*, Dinka] said, '...this government [of the SPLA] is ours. Your name
> is not in it...' They prohibit guns. They said, 'When Anywaa get guns, they

will dominate us.' The policy came from there. They combined themselves with *Gaala* (highlanders) and said, 'Anywaa have no place here'. The one that was given by the people of the world to all people [international relief and aid] was eaten by them [*Ajwil* and *Gaala*]. Anywaa were left outside. It was eaten by *Kambaatha, Gaala, Ajwil* and *Nuaar*. It is those people who took guns. Now our problem is that our land is being invaded. *Nuaar* had no land here. *Ajwil* had no land here. We did not know them before. *Ajwil*, when they were satisfied and became fat, they came and excreted on Anywaa. They killed Anywaa, some were pregnant, some had small children and some were blind. They were thrown into the river and died...[16]

Note that access to international relief and aid is an important source of grievance. The old man asks 'Why did they get it for free, while we were not given anything?' Of course, according to the government and aid agencies, the settlers and refugees were entitled to this aid, but he did not see it that way. Another important grievance is the uneven distribution of 'guns', which is a powerful symbol of 'modernity' as I argued elsewhere (Kurimoto 2001a). Like international relief and aid, it came from outside and was possessed by 'Dinka-Nuer-highlanders', not by Anywaa.

In my experience, it appears that the most profound consequence for the Anywaa from the in-migration of settlers and refugees during this period was a growing sense of territoriality ('Our homeland has been invaded and occupied by outsiders or foreigners'), nationality ('We are Ethiopians, but they are Sudanese') and of autochthony ('We are the first comers'). After 1991 when the Derg was supplanted by the EPRDF, this new consciousness has been growing ever stronger, particularly among the educated Anywaa elite—to the extent that they may now be called 'ethnic nationalists'. Like other nationalists, they recognize their own identity from an essentialist/primordialist point of view and have an exclusive attitude towards other peoples living in Gambela. From another perspective, of course, the Anywaa themselves, like the Nuer, have a history of migration: oral traditions testify that when they reached and settled present day Gambela they encountered aboriginal people who were already settled there, and shifting national identities between Ethiopia and Sudan has been one of their survival strategies for some time. As we have seen, during the Derg era, many Anywaa who were born and raised in Ethiopia registered themselves as refugees in Gambela to enjoy the privileges. But, as elsewhere, these details are largely ignored when reciting one's grievances.

Aftermath: Beginning of ethnicized conflict

At the end of May 1991 the EPRDF forces advanced upon and occupied
Addis Ababa. The socialist regime, Derg, fell. At the same time Gambela
town was also taken by EPRDF forces, after a series of battles with the
SPLA. Then after two weeks the first group of the GPLM arrived there.
This change of power in both the center and Gambela triggered a mass
exodus of some 160,000 SPLA/refugees. With their security no longer
guaranteed under the rule of their enemies, they fled across the Sudanese
borders. They consisted of three different but closely related groups: the
SPLA officers and men with their families, all of the Sudanese refugees,
and Ethiopian Nuer government officials and their families. They
were pursued by GPLM soldiers, Anywaa peasants and former militia
members, who especially targeted the Ethiopian Nuer. The former chief
administrator of Gambela region later informed me, in Nairobi where he
had taken refuge, that more than 30 members of his family were killed
at that time.

One of the more disastrous events that took place during this period
was the massacre of settlers at Ukuuna, east of Abwobo, where some 770
Anywaa and 3,000 settlers lived side by side. When the Anywaa chairman
of the local peasant association was shot dead by fleeing Derg soldiers,
the local Anywaa peasants and militia assaulted the settlers. Although
the Derg's soldiers had gone, the settlers were also *gaala*, and became
the target of revenge. Fire was set to the settlers' huts and the settlers
were indiscriminately killed. It was later estimated that between 1,000
and 2,000 settlers were killed, and numerous villages were completely
devastated. This was a great tragedy. During the Derg era, unlike the
Anywaa's relationships with the Nuer and the refugees, there had been no
open hostility towards the settlers. But their general resentment and hatred
for the highlanders/Derg was now expressed in a brutal fashion. Ukuuna
settlers who were themselves victims of the Derg policies were victimized
again. Under the EPRDF settlers were granted freedom of movement; some
of those who had remained and survived returned to their pre-settlement
homes, while others stayed on in Gambela. The majority left the villages
and moved into towns.

When the situation in Gambela normalized, many of the Ethiopian Nuer
who had fled to Sudan returned. And as the civil war in Sudan continued,
and in fact intensified after the SPLA leadership split in August 1991,
resulting in inter-factional fighting between Nuer and Dinka, there was
a new influx of refugees. New refugee camps were set up in Pinyudo and

Bonga. Today the majority of refugees in Pinyudo are Nuer, with Bonga specifically for Uduk from the Southern Blue Nile. As the boundaries between Gambela Regional State and Southern Regional State were adjusted, the district in which the Dima refugee camp is located was incorporated to Gambela. There are thus now three refugee camps in Gambela.

'Ethnic federalism', the new political structure designed and implemented by the EPRDF regime that created ethnicity-based regional States, has provided an arena for the Anywaa and Nuer elite to compete for resources. The new structure provides an ideal field for the exercise and expression of the ethnic nationalism that emerged during the previous period. While the GPLM who seized power at the regional level was predominantly an Anywaa organization, the Nuer elite organized their own political party, the Gambela People's Democratic Party (GPDP). Instead of seeking power sharing and co-existence, the elites have been struggling for power. Central to the struggle are the issues of territoriality, nationality and autochthony.[17] Anywaa elite insist that the Nuer in Gambela are not Ethiopians but Sudanese, and therefore have no claim to representation in the administrative or legislative bodies at either regional or *wereda* (district) levels. From the other side, the Nuer elite claim that they are Ethiopian citizens and deserve much more representation. In addition to these existing problems, oil resources in Gambela, for which the Federal Government initiated a project of exploitation, became a burning issue in recent years. Anywaa ethnic nationalists claim that the oil belongs to Anywaa, while the Federal Government argues that, according to the constitution, all mineral resources are properties of the Ethiopian state.

These battles have been fought not only in the political arena, but also in very violent conflicts, as people on both sides are instigated and mobilized. During June-August of 1991, there was a series of clashes between armed Nuer and Anywaa GPLM and militia men. In January and July of 1992 there were two major incursions by Nuer from Sudan. The first one was conducted in a highly organized way. The men were in military uniform and armed with guns and weapons. They burnt down 26 Anywaa villages. At that time there was a new faction of the SPLA based in Nasir, just across the border, headed by a Nuer commander, Riek Machar. Anywaa believed that the operation was by order of Riek, strengthening the notion of a Nuer-SPLA conspiracy against the Anywaa. The Anywaa-Nuer armed conflict flared up again in 1998, and once again during 2002–2003.

During 2002 and 2003, inter-ethnic conflict in Gambela entered a new phase. Tension between Anywaa and highlanders grew after some highlanders were murdered by unidentified men. In December 2003 after eight highlanders were killed on the road between Gambela town and Itang, hundreds of Anywaa citizens were killed in Gambela town and in rural areas by outraged highlanders, both civilians and soldiers. This is the worst incident that Anywaa have experienced in modern history.

Discussion

The Gambela case discussed above illuminates how profound and sometimes disastrous are the unintended consequences of resettlement and refugee programs. They deeply affect both the host populations and the settlers/refugees. I am not arguing, of course, that the presence of the settlers/refugees is the sole factor. The problems discussed arose in the specific political space of Gambela, located between Ethiopia and Sudan, and thus political changes in both countries shape the situation. I want to emphasize the essential importance, although mindful that all concerned acknowledge it, of efforts to foresee the unintended consequences of humanitarian aid programs, however difficult it may be. To do this, the specific local, national and international contexts that the space is set in must be fully taken into consideration. Since these contexts are always subject to change, once a program is begun, a constant and critical monitoring and revision is necessary. Another important factor is that the situation may look entirely different from the different perspectives of different participants. In the particular case discussed, the Nuer, Dinka, settlers and highlanders may well each have a radically different view. Moreover, we should not assume that all people of a group speak with the same voice. When trying to develop a comprehensive understanding of the effects of resettlement and refugee programs, these intricate factors need to be considered (cf. Kurimoto 2004).

As noted in my introduction, five fundamental factors can be discerned that contributed to these disasters. First, lack of consent from the local hosts for bringing settlers and refugees; second, disproportionate population of setters/refugees; third, greater economic ability and adaptability of settlers; fourth, more privileged position and greater well-being of refugees relative to the local standard; and fifth, no forum where problems between hosts and settlers-refugees could be openly discussed and solutions sought. If these factors had been taken into consideration by decision makers, namely the Derg, the disasters that happened before 1991, and even disastrous events that have happened since, might have been averted, or at least contained to some extent. It appears that the UNHCR should also be held accountable for the disasters, as it largely ignored what was going on among the refugees and between the refugees and their local hosts. I think these are some of the lessons that we can learn from the case of Gambela.

Notes

1 I conducted fieldwork among the Anywaa in Gambela during 1988–89 and 1989-1991. I subsequently visited the area in 1993, 1995, 1997, 1998, and 1999. For anthropological and ethnographic results of research, see my publications in the bibliography (Kurimoto 1992, 1996a, 1996b, 1997, 2001a, 2001b, 2002, 2004).

2 These are the official figures cited by the UNHCR and the Ethiopian government, which appear to be very high estimates. The real figures seem to have been closer to half of these (Scott-Villers et al. 1993).

3 It is difficult to ascertain the exact number. According to various reports of the Agricultural and Planning Bureau, the population of the region was 106,850 in 1989, 70,718 in 1992, and 110,363 in 1992. The 1994 national census puts it at 162,397. All figures include the settlers.

4 This is not to say that Gambela was completely isolated from the wider world. To the contrary Gambela became a prosperous trading center in the early 20th century, connecting Ethiopia and Sudan, by utilizing river transport. Part of Gambela town was a Sudanese enclave where a British District Commissioner had been stationed. After Sudan's independence in 1956 the DC's office became a Sudanese Consulate. However, the trade through Gambela fell-away after the Djibouti-Addis Ababa railroad was opened, and Gambela became a peripheral region (Johnson 1986; Kurimoto 1992).

5 In 1989 it was upgraded to an 'Administrative Region'. Now under the regime of the Ethiopian People's Revolutionary Democratic Front (EPRDF) it has been granted full status as an autonomous 'Regional State'.

6 For the social transformations in various communities in Ethiopia during the Derg era, see James et al. 2002.

7 The tax was 47 birr per year, about US$23 at the time, according to the official rate.

8 It seems that those resettled in the highlands enjoyed better conditions (cf. Pankhurst 1992).

9 There were also complaints, of course, especially concerning the SPLA's forced recruitment of refugees and the uneven distribution of relief items, food and clothing.
10 At that time 1US$ = 2 birr at the official rate, and 5 birr on the black market.
11 The milk cows were purchased from the local Nuer. It should be noted that before the settlers began trading in it, fresh milk had not been available anywhere in Gambela town, even though the Nuer have long been known as 'people of cattle' and some Anywaa also raise cattle.
12 Bridewealth was customarily paid for with special glass beads (*dimui*), iron hoes and spear heads—all of which were banned by the Derg, who instead introduced a cash payment, which was initially about 200 birr.
13 The work includes digging—sometimes several meters deep—in search of soil containing enough alluvial gold, extracting the soil, and panning with water.
14 It should be noted, however, that a sense of being abandoned, demoralized and powerless was explicitly expressed by the Anywaa themselves, especially by women (see Kurimoto 2002). See also Kurimoto (2001a) to understand how Anywaa conceptualize the status quo, as powerless and impoverished, and how they make sense of it.
15 To date, there is no concrete evidence that any such conspiracy existed. In fact, the relations between the Nuer and Dinka-SPLA were far from cordial and many Nuer had been killed by the SPLA, both in Ethiopia and Sudan, during the first phase of the Sudanese civil war.
16 Uceri Akwer Adora, interviewed 12/8/90. The killing refers to the 'Pinyudo massacre' of September 1989.
17 I owe this part of argument to Dr. Dereje Feyissa who supplied me with new information and his analysis based on fieldwork (see Dereje 2003). He is currently a COE Research Fellow at Osaka University (May 2003 – March 2005).

References

Clapham, C. (2002) 'Controlling space in Ethiopia', in W. James, D. Donham, E. Kurimoto and A. Triulzi (eds), *Remapping Ethiopia*. Oxford: James Currey; Addis Ababa: Addis Ababa University Press; Athens: Ohio University Press, pp. 9–31.
Clay, J. W. and B. K. Holcomb (1986) *Politics and the Ethiopian Famine, 1984–1985* (Cultural Survival Report 20). Cambridge: Cultural Survival.

Central Statistical Authority (1995) *The 1994 Population and Housing Census of Ethiopia, Results for Gambella Region*. Addis Ababa: Central Statistical Authority.

Dereje, Feyissa (2003) *Ethnic Groups and Conflict: The Case of Anywaa-Nuer Relations in the Gambela Region, Western Ethiopia*. PhD dissertation, Martin Luther University and Max Planck Institute of Social Anthropology, Germany.

Donham, D. (1986) 'Old Abyssinia and the new Ethiopian Empire: Themes in social history', in D. Donham and W. James (eds), *The Southern Marches of Imperial Ethiopia: Essays in History and Anthropology*. Cambridge: Cambridge University Press, pp. 3–48.

Human Rights Watch (1991) *Evil Days: 30 Years of War and Famine in Ethiopia*. New York: Human Rights Watch.

James, W., D. Donham, E. Kurimoto and A. Triulzi (eds) (2002) *Remapping Ethiopia: Socialism and After*. Oxford: James Currey; Addis Ababa: Addis Ababa University Press; Athens: Ohio University Press.

Johnson, D. H. (1986) 'On the Nilotic frontier: Imperial Ethiopia in the southern Sudan, 1898–1936', in D. Donham and W. James (eds), *The Southern Marches of Imperial Ethiopia: Essays in History and Anthropology*. Cambridge: Cambridge University Press, pp. 219–45.

Kurimoto, Eisei (1992) 'Natives and outsiders: The historical experience of the Anywaa of western Ethiopia', *Journal of Asian and African Studies*, 43, pp. 1–43.

——(1996a) *Minzoku hunso wo ikiru hitobito* (People living through ethnic conflict). Kyoto: Sekaishisosha.

—— (1996b) 'People of the river: Subsistence economy of the Anywaa (Anuak) of western Ethiopia', in Shun Sato and Eisei Kurimoto (eds), *Essays in Northeast African Studies*. Senri Ethnological Studies, No. 43. Osaka: National Museum of Ethnology, pp. 29–57.

—— (1997) 'Politicisation of ethnicity in Gambella', in Katsuyoshi Fukui, Eisei Kurimoto and Masayoshi Shigeta (eds), *Ethiopia in Broader Perspective. Papers of the XIIIth International Conference of Ethiopian Studies*, vol. 2. Kyoto: Shokado Book Sellers, pp. 798–815.

—— (2001a) 'Capturing modernity among the Anywaa of western Ethiopia', in Eisei Kurimoto (ed.), *Rewriting Africa. Toward a Renaissance or Collapse?* JCAS Symposium Series No. 14. Osaka: The Japan Center for Area Studies, National Museum of Ethnology, pp. 263–80.

—— (2001b) 'Minzoku jichi taisei ka ni okeru minzokukan kankei' (Ethnic relations under ethnic autonomy), in S. Wada (ed.), *Gendai Afurika no minzoku kankei* (Ethnic relations in contemporary Africa). Tokyo: Akashishoten, pp. 92–115.

—— (2002) 'Fear and anger: Female versus male narratives among the Anywaa', in W. James, D. Donham, E. Kurimoto and A. Triulzi (eds), *Remapping Ethiopia*. Oxford: James Currey; Addis Ababa: Addis Ababa University Press; Athens: Ohio University Press, pp. 219–38.

—— (2004) 'Post-conflict peace-building in Africa: The expected and unfilled role by Area Studies', in Masako Ishii and J. A. Siapno (eds), *Between Knowledge and Commitment: Post-Conflict Peace-Building and Reconstruction in Regional Contexts*. JCAS Symposium Series No. 21. Osaka: The Japan Center for Area Studies, National Museum of Ethnology, pp. 21–30.

Pankhurst, Alula (1992) *Resettlement and Famine in Ethiopia: The Villagers' Experience*. Manchester: Manchester University Press.

Scott-Villers, A., P. Scott-Villers and C. P. Dodge (1993) 'Repatriation of 150,000 Sudanese refugees from Ethiopia: The manipulation of civilians in a situation of civil conflict', *Disasters*, 17(3), pp. 202–17.

11
Promises and Predicaments of Resettlement in Ethiopia

Yntiso D. Gebre

Introduction

Lessons from around the globe suggest that population displacement involves risks of impoverishment for the affected people: refugees, internally displaced persons (IDPs), and host communities (Chambers 1986; Scudder 1993; Campbell et al. 1993; Salem-Murdock 1993; Cernea 1996, 2000; Gebre 2003). Traditionally, policymakers, donors, and even displacement researchers focused on migrants, thereby overlooking the concerns of hosts. Elsewhere I forcefully argued that the process of displacement does not necessarily involve geographical mobility, and that the livelihoods of host people are likely to be disrupted by an influx of newcomers (Gebre 2003, 2004b). Based on research[1] conducted in the Metekel (also Pawe, Beles) resettlement area (Figure 11-1), in northwestern Ethiopia, this chapter[2] compares and contrasts resettlement risks for settlers and their hosts in the light of Michael Cernea's impoverishment risks and reconstruction (IRR) model to understand the promises and predicaments of large-scale resettlement in Ethiopia.

In this chapter it is argued that, depending on the magnitude of the impact, both settlers and hosts may experience similar displacement ordeals or benefit from similar recovery measures. The lesson from Metekel reveals that massive resettlements could disrupt the livelihoods of the original inhabitants in the same ways that dams, parks, urban expansion, and other development projects do to displacees. In Metekel, resettlement-induced discord between the settlers and their hosts over resources led to bloody clashes, disruption of livelihoods, the reformulation of inter-ethnic alliances, and administrative complications. Notwithstanding the grave errors of the past, the present government of Ethiopia launched a new resettlement program in the old style. This chapter, thus, explores the differences and similarities between the past and present programs to learn

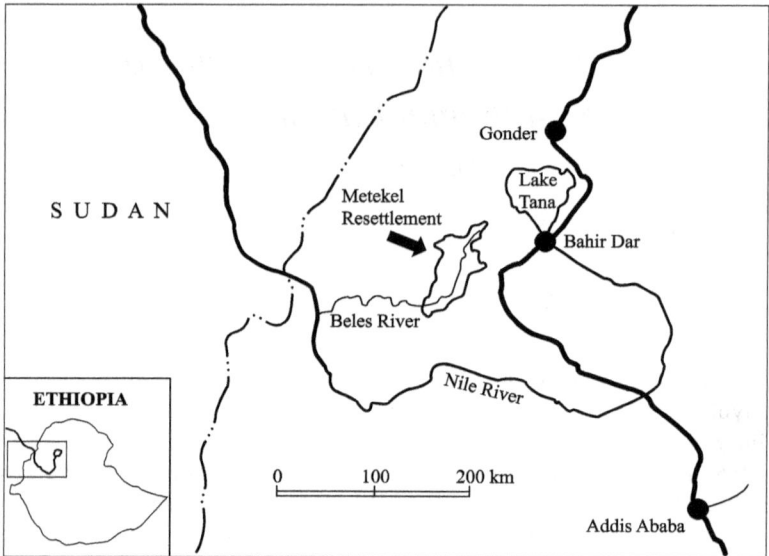

Figure 11-1. Location of Metekel

how resettlement policies and practices have transpired in Ethiopia, i.e., whether the country has learnt from its previous experience.

   Apart from the introductory and the concluding sections, this chapter has four major parts. The introduction is followed by background information on the 1980s resettlement program in Ethiopia. Then, the implications of the program for the settlers and the Gumz people (the hosts) are discussed. A section on resettlement-induced conflicts and the reformulation of inter-ethnic relations, and another on the present resettlement program in Ethiopia precede the conclusion.

Overview of the Ethiopian resettlement

In the 1980s, the Ethiopian government resettled about 600,000 people from drought-affected and over-populated regions of the country to five major resettlement sites (namely, Metekel, Metema, Assosa, Gambella, and Kefa) located in northwestern, western, and southwestern parts of the country. In the process, more than 82,000 people moved to Metekel, a place already occupied by the Gumz shifting cultivators. At the time of the resettlement, the population of the Gumz was estimated at 72,000 (Dessalegn in Agneta et al. 1993: 256–7).

The official objectives of the resettlement program were to prevent famine, reduce demographic pressures in densely populated and highly denuded highlands, and promote agricultural production in sparsely populated lowlands. The Ethiopian government portrayed the resettlement program as a durable solution to the famine problem. Given the slow reaction and/or objections of the international community (in terms of providing food aid) for ideological reasons,[3] resettlement was seen as a way out of a frustrating problem and humiliating dependency on food aid.

The resettlement initiative can be regarded as forced because, in October 1984, the government announced its decision to execute the emergency resettlement plan without the consent of potential settlers. There was a clear determination on the part of the authorities to relocate people, if necessary by force. While those people recruited in late 1984 and early 1985 welcomed the initiative and volunteered to be resettled, those enlisted after mid–1985 tried to resist the resettlement (Gebre 2001, 2002b). Critics questioned not only the sincerity of the government position, but also indicated allegedly hidden motives behind the resettlement program. The government was suspected of suppressing insurgent movements by depopulating their mass base, diluting their ethnic homogeneity (Clay and Holcomb 1986: 29; Keller 1993: 233), using resettlement areas as buffer zones (de Waal 1991: 221), and reorganizing the peasantry into producers' cooperatives (Dawit 1989: 289).

Some writers explained the movement of settlers from northern Ethiopia to southern and western parts of the country as a pattern of state-sponsored north-south migration that began a century ago (Scott 1998: 248; Clay and Holcomb 1986: 28). Dejene (1990: 96–7), who belittled this argument as 'an example of outsiders' superficial understanding of Ethiopian politics,' asserted that the objective of the resettlement was 'to restore the loss of productive land affected by drought and to use the vast amount of land in the fertile southwestern region to increase food production and generate rural income.' According to Kurt Jansson (1990: 65), the allegation that the resettlement aimed at depopulating Tigray Peoples Liberation Front's support base was unfounded as only 15% of the 600,000 settlers came from Tigray. Alula Pankhurst (1992: 79) also noted, 'Recruitment from areas not under central rule was considered unwise.'

Reliable documents about the decision-making processes were lacking to validate the various arguments and counter-arguments. It is difficult to verify whether the resettlement was truly famine-induced, development-induced, politically-motivated, or environmentally warranted. However, there are certain indications that with concerns about the famine being central, the government may have planned for collateral advantages of resettlement (Gebre 2001, 2004b).

Between 1986 and 1990, Italian agencies generously funded the resettlement. The Tana-Beles Project (TBP), a giant program sponsored by the Italian Government, initiated a large-scale development scheme. Apart from relief provision, the project focused on two broad activities: production (mechanized agriculture, forestation, livestock, fishery, agro-industry, and a pipe factory) and general infrastructure (water supplies, roads, bridges, housing, stores, airport, health, education, etc.). The Italians who were running the project withdrew in the early 1990s. The International Committee for the Development of Peoples, an Italian NGO, however, sponsored small-scale multisectoral programs from 1986 to 1999 (with a brief interruption in the early 1990s due to the 1991 change of government in Ethiopia). Neither the giant bilateral cooperation program nor the NGO extended meaningful support to the Gumz villagers.

Resettlement-induced crises

Implication for settlers
The highland settlers were rushed to an undeveloped and physically harsh environment (humid and malaria-ridden) without a feasibility study and proper planning (Gebre 2004a). Since there were no habitable houses, the Metekel migrants were responsible for erecting their own huts. Although the government tried to provide food, the rations were insufficient and so irregular that starvation was inevitable. Moreover, the diets were nutritionally inadequate, as protein and vitamin rich foods were not available. During this initial adaptation period, the incidence of morbidity and mortality was exceptionally high. According to informants, thousands of people perished without receiving any medical attention. Due to the large number of deaths per day, the dead were buried in mass graves. It was rare to find households that had never lost a member(s). The causes of sicknesses and deaths were explained in terms of undernourishment, malaria, tuberculosis, and lack of clean water. Diarrhea was epidemic

throughout the resettlement area. Alex de Waal's (1991: 225–6) report confirmed the high death rates as follows.

> RRC [Relief and Rehabilitation Commission of Ethiopia] figures for recorded deaths during the first year of resettlement indicate heightened death rates: 110 per thousand in Gojjam [Metekel], 68 in Illubabor, 42 in Keffa, 38 in Wollega and 34 in Gonder... The same RRC data indicate that in Pawe resettlement, Gojjam, death rates in the first four weeks of registration were equivalent to 332 per thousand per year—almost 20 times normal.

The settlers relied on meager government relief until the Italian assistance commenced in 1986. As indicated earlier, the Italians generously funded the resettlement program. The huge Italian assistance to the TBP made significant differences in food supply, health provision, basic education, housing, and water supply. However, the projects were unsustainable, as evidenced by the collapse of most of the activities following the withdrawal of the Italians in the early 1990s. Salini Costruttori (1989: 14), the Italian contractor in charge of the TBP, reported that food self-sufficiency was attained in the resettlement area in 1988. Although gross food availability increased in the resettlement area and many lives were saved, thanks to the Italians, the state of undernourishment and malnutrition remained high.

Some informants complained that the quantity and quality of food was inadequate. Over 31% of the sample population (of 368 settlers) reported to have actually starved more than once during the period of Italian operations. About 49% indicated that they did not experience food insecurity, while the remaining 20% found the question not applicable for various reasons (e.g., some arrived after the Italians left). Most residents did not have access to protein and vitamin rich foods. Thus, the state of undernourishment and malnutrition remained significant even during the Italian assistance period. When asked to estimate the frequency with which meat appeared in their diet, many informants answered twice or three times a year. Others, particularly widows and single mothers, indicated that they had not eaten meat for years. Many sarcastically answered that they had long forgotten how meat tasted. Peas, beans, butter, and oil were so expensive that they could not afford them. Vegetables were extremely scarce and inaccessible to the majority of the people. Paolo Antonioli (1992: 387) reported:

> In return for their work...the settlers were given their monthly food rations. These rations consisted basically of cereals...and small amounts of oil

seeds…plus allowances of sugar, salt, and oils. Very clearly an unbalanced diet was being provided, especially as regards protein and particularly vitamin requirements.

The migrants encountered other problems as well. They were forced to join cooperative societies for the socialist transformation of agriculture. Settlers never controlled the fruits of their labor. Instead, they worked as daily laborers for a biweekly ration, distributed according to family size rather than according to work done. This system of distribution discouraged personal responsibility and motivation to work. In 1989, a new distribution method, based on a point system, was initiated to reward devoted workers and raise productivity. A cut-off point of eight was set to measure the participants' daily work performance. Those who worked efficiently for eight hours a day were entitled to eight points. Those who lagged behind in their attendance and performance accumulated lower points, while the points given to individuals exhibiting higher efficiency than average workers exceeded the cut-off point.

Due to lack of clear assessment techniques and qualified personnel to perform an objective evaluation, the overall result was disastrous, as the food income of many households declined and production never increased. In 1990, a combination of food rations, a point system, and a shareholding system was initiated to rectify the problems encountered in previous years. Households were given food rations based on their size; every individual was given Birr 1.95 (US$0.94) for every day he/she spent on the collective farm; and participants were promised distribution of surplus according to their accumulated points. In 1991, with the change of government, the whole program stopped before the efficacy of the new system was tested.

The majority of settlers came from areas characterized by scattered settlement patterns with private farmlands located usually in outlying individual homesteads. In Metekel, however, they were forced to live in compact villages with communal farms located in outlying villages. Apart from the 1000 m² backyard, no private land holding was allowed until the 1990s. Since there was no private accumulation and saving, most settlers remained poor and dependent on the TBP, which was managed by the Italians. This became evident when the foreign expatriates withdrew in 1991—the majority had no assets to fall back on.

The Metekel resettlement had a troubled human rights record. Settlers were denied freedom of movement, religion, holiday, association, ceremonial/ritual performance, and social/public gathering. Movement within the resettled villages as well as outside of the resettlement area required written permission. Multiple checkpoints were established to monitor the movement of the settlers on a regular basis. Until 1989, according to informants, settlers were not allowed to build churches, mosques, and other places of worship. Nor were they permitted to announce their creed in public or engage in any form of religious performance and observance. In an attempt to erode their spiritual integrity and spread Marxist ideology, settlers were forced to work on Sundays and other major holidays. Funeral ceremonies, weddings, and ritual performances were also perceived as 'backward practices' that impeded development. Customary activities associated with birth, marriage, death, planting, and harvesting were prohibited. Settlers were prevented from forming neighborhood associations and conducting meetings.

In 1991, seven years later, the Metekel settlers were not in a position to feed themselves. One informant metaphorically stated, 'The nakedness [emptiness] of our lives was exposed when the Italian aid unexpectedly ended.' Ethiopian authorities assumed responsibility for running the TBP. Budget constraints limited TBP's operations to supporting the project's essential staff. In 1991, the project supplied food to settlers. In the next two production years (1992 and 1993), resettled households were given planted crops to weed and harvest, and were told that the project would never again provide food rations. In 1994 and 1995, the TBP asked settlers to pay for tractor services, fertilizers, and seeds. The introduction of service charges and the inability of most settlers to pay resulted in a production shortfall and the 1994–96 famine in the resettlement area. The relationship between the project and the villagers came to an end in 1995 when the latter failed to pay the service charges. Due to economic hardships and the prevailing political and security concerns discussed later, many settlers left Metekel. The population dropped from 66,091 in 1991 to 26,660 in 1994.

In the mid-1990s, those farmers who had decided to stay in Metekel were left with one alternative: a return to plough agriculture. The challenges and opportunities encountered after this reversal are discussed elsewhere in detail (Gebre 2002a). However, it is important to highlight that the return to the plow and the reinstitution of private production was far from a smooth process. The settlers continued to face a multitude of obstacles, including a shortage of oxen, deadly cattle diseases, scarce farm labor, lack of cash to buy fertilizers, frequent pest attacks, and striga (weed) infestation. It is equally important to note that these challenges were confronted with new resource use strategies, such as expanding and consolidating land holdings, using cows for traction, hiring laborers on family farms, and expanding the production of finger millet as a staple crop.

Unsettling the settled (hosts)

The Metekel Administrative Zone of Benishangul-Gumz Region is largely populated by the Gumz people, who practice shifting cultivation (also horticulture, slash-and-burn agriculture, swidden agriculture). The traditional land tenure systems of the Gumz society combined individual/household use rights with communal control. In Ethiopia, however, the practice of shifting cultivation has not been recognized as a unique socio-economic adaptation that deserves policy attention. This was evidenced by the absence of any legal provisions protecting the land rights of shifting cultivators. In addition, places inhabited by horticulturalists have been misrepresented as unoccupied areas, wastelands, or virgin lands that can be used for settlements and/or large-scale farms (RRC 1981; Salini Costruttori 1989). It was on the basis of this presumption that the decision was made, in the 1980s, to resettle people largely from north Ethiopia to the Metekel lowlands.

The resettlement severely affected the lives of many Gumz communities (Gebre 2003). For instance, the residents of Manjeri village were forced to surrender their farmlands, hunting/gathering grounds, and fishing sites to the resettlement authorities. Many families that had lived on the banks of the Beles and Little Beles Rivers were pushed out and had to find other lands for their agricultural activities. Cultivated and fallow lands that belonged to the local people were allocated for settlers as residential areas and farmlands. Some informants complained that their planted crops were bulldozed to construct roads and build houses for the settlers. Many households were made land poor and landless. The villagers were physically uprooted from their homes three times. An epidemic disease that broke out in one of the resettled villages caused the first displacement in 1986. Two major bloody clashes (in 1991 and 1993) between the settlers and Gumz were responsible for the other two dislocations. The 1993 incident involved confiscation of property and burning the entire Manjeri village to ashes.

Like most other Gumz communities, the residents of Manjeri relied on hunting for their protein supply. However, the game disappeared owing to massive deforestation. When the game disappeared, the Gumz had to switch to the meat of domestic animals. Many households could not afford to buy beef from butcher shops. Nor could they depend on domestic animals due to the prevalence of animal diseases and the lack of cash to buy them. In 1999, beans represented the main source of their protein food. However, it was not sufficient to compensate for the significant decline of animal protein from their diets. The Gumz used to obtain their protein supplement from fish as well. Fishing declined due to security concerns along the riverbanks; the residents of Manjeri refrained from going to the river for fear that the settlers might attack them. It is possible that the reduced amounts of animal protein in their diets may have caused nutritional deficiencies, the levels and consequences of which are yet to be determined through further study.

The Gumz had a long tradition of exploiting plants (shoots, flowers, fruits, leaves, and roots) from the natural environment. In bad years, gathering wild plants represented the most important survival strategy. Certain plants such as bamboo shoots and wild yams were eaten in good years as well. The clearing of forestland reduced the indigenous people's traditional access to wild edible plants. This problem was much more pronounced among the Manjeri people, who were surrounded by five resettled villages encroaching on their land. In Metekel, honey was collected largely from the ground and tree holes. The practice of honey collection had also been impaired by deforestation. In short, the loss of access to common property assets resulted in significant deterioration of food income and livelihood levels. In 1999, most members of Manjeri village were impoverished as evidenced by the lack of assets, reduced food production, reduced access to common property resources, con-sequent food insecurity, and deteriorating housing, clothing, and health conditions.

Comparison of resettlement impacts

The IRR model explains that a forced displacement process involves eight interlinked risks of impoverishment: landlessness, joblessness, homelessness, marginalization, food insecurity, increased mortality and morbidity, loss of access to common property resources, and social disarticulation. More recently, loss of access to education has been added as the ninth variable (Cernea 2002). The IRR model was built to analyze the implications of development-induced resettlement for displacees, rather than for host populations. From the discussion above, however, it is apparent that there are parallels between the types of displacement delineated in the model and the experiences of the host population in Metekel. As indicated in the summary (Table 11-1), the settlers and the Gumz people experienced

Table 11-1. Summary of impacts on settlers and hosts

Risks	Settlers	Gumz (hosts)
Land	Landless until 1994; they worked on project land for food ration	Lost both cultivated and fallow lands; no compensation
Home	Initially, they lived in temporary huts; 2-5 households shared a room	Lost homes & cultural space of homestead when they were forced to evacuate villages
Food	Suffered from food crisis in 1984–6 & 1994–6 and many perished	Some villages (e.g., Manjeri) became food insecure due to loss of food income
Health	Sickness/death increased (malaria, TB); death rate high in the first year	Sickness/death increased (periodic) due to worsening hygiene and increased clashes
CPRs	No data on the past; and now, no CPRs (e.g., forest, grazing field)	Access to forest and rivers lost/ declined due to deforestation and security concerns
Power	No freedom of movement, worship, etc.; were dependent on project	Until 1991, they have been marginalized; neglected; and their rights violated
Security	Many killed; wounded; felt at risk due to deadly conflict with the host	Many killed; wounded; felt at risk due to deadly conflict with the settlers.

Note: CPR stands for common property resource (see Kibreab 2000 for definition)

at least six similar risks that significantly harmed their well-being and security. Increased conflict or security concern has been added as a new risk dimension that characterizes the guest-host relationships. Based on the Metekel experience, it may be argued that in the context of imposed resettlement, settler-host conflict is imminent.

Conflict and inter-ethnic relations

Historical relations
In order to understand the escalation of conflict and recent changes in inter-ethnic alliances in Metekel, it is important to examine the historical relations of the various groups in the area. The old neighbors of the Gumz ethnic group include the Kulsi, the Agaw, the Shinasha, the Oromo (of Wollega region), and the Amhara (of Gojam and Gonder regions). Historically, the Gumz (and the little studied Kulsi), who exhibited distinct cultures and physical appearance from the rest of the ethnic groups in

the area, were subjected to discrimination and subjugation by their more powerful neighbors.

Elderly Gumz informants indicated that their ancestors originally occupied a territory to the east of Metekel up to Lake Tana, the source of the Blue Nile. Over a long period of time, they were pushed towards the Metekel lowlands by the Amhara and Agaw people, supported and encouraged by the state. By their account, slavery, appropriation of property, and violence characterized their relationship with the aggressors. Documentary evidence supports these allegations (Cerulli 1956; James 1986: 119–20; Taddesse 1988: 11–13; Morell 2000: 23). During the reign of Sertse-Dengel (1563–97), the Abyssinian state (old kingdom in present-day northern Ethiopia) made many aggressive attempts to incorporate the Gumz and bring their natural resources under its direct control (Taddesse 1988). Cerulli (1956: 15) wrote that in 1587 Sertse-Dengel went to Belaya and subdued a Gumz tribe called Wambarya. These offensives were reported to have continued during the reigns of Susneyos (1607–32), Fasiledes (1632–67), and Yohannes (1667–83), and it was during the reign of Iyassu the Great (1683–1706) that the state made the final breakthrough among the Gumz (Taddesse 1988).

Later, the region was attached to Greater Ethiopia, Taddesse (1988) noted, through a system of indirect rule where the local leaders of the neighboring groups were assigned as administrators. James Bruce (1790) reported that in the 1770s the Gumz were controlled by Abyssinia. The writer indicated that the residents of Metekel paid tribute in gold, and such payments were effected through the Agaw intermediaries. The indirect rule continued until Hailu Teklehaimanot of Gojam came to power and appointed his own [Amhara] people to control the resources of Metekel (Abdussamad 1988: 238). Until the early 1990s, appointed non-Gumz officials governed Metekel province and its districts. The Amhara rulers had dominated the Agaw, Oromo, and Shinasha as well. However, the Gumz viewed officials from these ethnic groups as agents of the state and the Amhara. Conflict and distrust characterized the historical relationships between the Gumz and these groups.

Resistance and conflicts
The pressure on the Gumz people and their land continued even after they were being pushed to the lowlands. The people had not been passive recipients of the external threats. Members of the Gumz society expressed their objection to encroachment in a variety of ways, including violent confrontation. In the 1960s, for example, the Gumz people resisted the self-initiated resettlement of highlanders in Metekel. They tried to expel

new settlers from Mentawuha, Deq, and other areas. In response, the government sent an army, led by the late Major Lemesa Bedaso and Qegnazmach (old title for warlord) Adamu Bekele to silence Gumz opposition. According to informants, the forces of Major Lemesa and Qegnazmach Adamu destroyed the resistance movement in Dibate and Mandura districts, respectively. The Gumz were disarmed and forced to accommodate the settlers, while the latter were allowed to keep their weapons for self-defense.

The 1980s resettlement program also triggered Gumz resistance and deadly conflict. Initially, alleged Gumz assassins killed settlers on the road, in the forest, in the fields, and even in their homes. The government dispatched militiamen (recruited from among settlers) and police forces to protect the settlers. Continued killings and retaliatory actions triggered direct confrontations between the Gumz, on the one hand, and the settlers and their defenders, on the other. In 1985/6, the first reportedly heavy fighting broke out in Gulbak (also Gublak), one of the early resettlement sites. During this clash, an unknown number of people are said to have died and been wounded on both sides. In 1987, the entirety of eight villages (9520 settlers) in Gulbak were transferred to the main resettlement in Pawe area, partly for security reasons.

According to an internal (unofficial) Tana Beles Project record, on 25 January 1987, settlers in the Pawe scheme[4] clashed with the Gumz near a resettled village called L28. The origin of this incident was explained in relation to conflict over land between the Gumz and two resettled villages, L28 and L29. This clash was reported to have temporarily suspended transportation and project activities in the vicinity of the contested area. After this incident, according to informants, tension escalated and individuals continued to be victimized here, there, and everywhere. Many resettled villagers sharing common boundaries with the Gumz communities reported to have lost members at the hands of their hostile neighbors. Banchamlak Chane of village L131 was gunned down on the road while returning home from a mill shop in Almu town. Tsegaye Negash (herder) and Ahmed Husen (farmer), both from L131, were killed in the woods. In village L2, Habtu Melak was slain in his house during the night; Dagnaw Gebre was killed on his farm; and Beqachew Mengistie was found shot by the riverside. Ayehew Kebkab of village RUS46 and two women from RDS49 were shot dead in the forest.

The Gumz informants, on their part, accused the settlers of killing innocent people. Yigzaw Andarge, a resident of Manjeri village, was brutally beaten to death in village L4. Yigzaw shot dead one of his attackers (a settler) before he was overpowered and killed. A woman from Manjeri was also killed near Almu town while she was heading to the town to sell firewood. Her friend, who narrowly escaped the assault, witnessed that the killers were settlers. A woman from Gitsa village was slain near village L2. An unknown assassin gunned down Dinewa Gas at his home in Aypapa village, a place close to resettled villages called RH101 and RH127. Some unknown number of Gumz men traveling by car were stopped and killed at RDS49. The random slayings culminated in the following series of bloody clashes that left hundreds dead in the early 1990s.

An incident broke out in 1991 on a day many Gumz people gathered for Dinewa Gas' 'kemisha' (memorial service) in Aypapa village. It is said that the family of Dinewa believed that settlers from the neighboring villages had gotten away with the murder. During the memorial service, some participants (relatives) requested that the family of the deceased slaughter animals for the service. The female relatives of Dinewa, who had been expecting vindictive acts, challenged the rightness of the request for meat when the death of their loved one remained unaccounted for. The challenge sensitized young men, who sneaked out of the event to take revenge on settlers without alerting their fellow people. They killed two settlers from the nearby villages. The settlers retaliated by killing four Gumz who were returning from the memorial service (two women from Azarti, a man from Manjeri, and a woman from Deq areas).

In the same year, another incident occurred during Meka Ambra's (Gumz) burial ceremony in Manjeri village. Gumz mourners from different villages attended the funeral. A drunken settler from the neighboring resettled village (L4) unintentionally shot Mekuria Jemos (Gumz) while trying to pass his condolence by firing bullets into the air. The death of Mekuria turned the calm mourners into an angry mob. After killing the gunman, the mob attacked village L4 and massacred some fifty-seven settlers. Moreover, the attackers looted the property of the victims. In terms of legal action, nothing much was done other than indemnifying the victim's relatives (which the Gumz paid in cash) and retrieving some of the goods looted during the raid.

A clash broke out when Gumz men from Gitsa village attempted to attack village L2 to retaliate for the death of their woman who was supposedly killed by a settler. The Gumz occupied one side of the Piza River (also Gilgel Beles) and the settlers fortified the other side. They exchanged gunfire until government soldiers arrived from the settlers' side and pushed the Gumz force back. During the shootout, informants witnessed two government soldiers being killed and another two seriously wounded. No other casualties were reported. Later, the Gumz gave an ultimatum to the residents of L2 that they must either pay an indemnity or await revenge. The tension eased after L2 villagers paid animals and cash as an indemnity for the death of the Gumz woman.

In village L131, fighting took place in July 1993 following the murder of a settler called Ahmed Husen in his field. In retaliation for his death, Ahmed's friends ambushed and fired at Gumz people, who happened to carry guns and fired back. A settler (from Gojam) was seriously wounded during this exchange of gunfire. Police arrived on the scene and cooled down the tension by promising the settlers that the criminal(s) would be caught. On the night of this incident, the wounded settler's friends and relatives from villages L9, L10, and L24 gathered at village L131 to launch a surprise attack on the nearby Gumz village. Hundreds of combatants marched towards their target early in the morning. The Gumz force that controlled strategic positions in anticipation of a possible enemy advance launched a surprise attack and humiliated the settlers. While village L131 lost four people, the casualties sustained by the other three villages and the Gumz remain unknown.

Another violent incident occurred when residents of village L134 attacked a Gumz village called Wendibil to get back grain allegedly taken by the Gumz. The Gumz, who dismissed the accusation, complained that the settlers confiscated their property during the raid. According to the residents of Wendibil, the objective of the settlers' attack was to intimidate the Gumz and retain the farmlands the settlers had acquired illegally. No human casualties were reported. However, the incident created mounting tension until government officials and local mediators intervened to resolve the land dispute. According to the resolution, settlers could not use new lands other than the ones bulldozed during the Italian assistance. Those who acquired new land without permission were ordered to surrender the land to the Gumz. It was also agreed that the Gumz could not claim access to or control over land cleared for the settlers.

The most devastating incident started in September 1993 when unidentified gunmen opened fire in a market place, in broad daylight, and killed twenty-one people. To date, the identities of the gunmen and their motives remain mysterious. Nevertheless, the settlers and the Gumz have been accusing each other of the massacre. Besides denying any connection to this atrocity, each group has made presumptions that would implicate the other group. The settlers believed that Gumz officials and their associates (from Shinasha and Agaw ethnic groups) agitated the ordinary Gumz to rise against the resettled population. They argued that the motivation behind the mass murder of market-goers included controlling political power, driving settlers out of Metekel, and controlling the TBP resources. On the other hand, the Gumz maintained that the leaders of the settlers planned and executed this crime. They believed that the conspirators plotted the crime with the objective of implicating Gumz leaders, impairing the decentralization process that empowered the Gumz, retaining Amhara domination, and controlling TBP resources.

In an alleged retaliation for the market day massacre, organized settlers kidnapped Gumz and Shinasha officials for execution. Some officials tried to save their lives by taking refuge with the Gumz militiamen stationed in the zonal capital—Almu. However, the army of the new government required the militias to surrender their weapons. When the latter defied, electric power and water supplies were cut off for about twenty-four hours in an attempt to force them to surrender. Full scale fighting erupted between the army and the Gumz militiamen. Of an estimated seventy-five militiamen, about fifty were believed to have died during this armed combat. When the militias were subdued, the Gumz officials under their protection were caught by the settlers for another round of execution. Two Gumz officials (Engineer Geremew Flate and Engineer Tigre) and two Shinasha officials (Damtew Gobena and Asefa Aynama) were among victims slain in front of the crowd. The crowd then marched on Manjeri village, crushed the defensive resistance, burned the entire village, and confiscated the property of the residents. Since then, the tension between the settlers and the Gumz has been reduced, if not avoided, by disarming both groups and through reconciliation arbitrated by government officials.

Changing inter-ethnic alliances
Prior to the 1980s, the Gumz were defensive in terms of protecting their territory against Agaw encroachment. They also maintained cautious and measured relations with the Shinasha. The 1980s resettlement, the conflict between the new settlers and the Gumz, and the 1991 change of government in Ethiopia altered inter-ethnic alliances and sentiments in Metekel. In the 1980s and 1990s, the Gumz, the Shinasha, and the Agaw became close allies to an extent that was alarming to many settlers, who then wondered if the associates of the Gumz might have plotted the violent attacks perpetrated against them. The new inter-ethnic alliance created favorable conditions for the old neighbors, particularly the Agaw farmers, to resettle in the vicinity of Gumz villages. In Manjeri, for example, eight Agaw households (forty-eight people) had arrived beginning in 1994, and eight more households were expected to come in 2000. Similar resettlements were taking place in other Gumz villages as well.

The recent ethnic-based regionalization process seemed to facilitate the alliance between the Gumz and their immediate neighbors. Initially, concepts like *balebet* (owners or natives), *newari* (residents), and *sefari* or *metie* (settlers or migrants) have been used in the political discourse to define people's rights to natural resources and self-government. The regionalization process appeared to empower the natives (Gumz) and the permanent residents (Shinasha). For example, members of these groups held key political and administrative positions in Metekel Zone, which consisted of seven districts. The settlers constituted one district and were represented in the zonal council. In terms of sheer size and political power, the representatives of the natives and the residents, who came from the other six districts, obviously overwhelmed the migrants.

The competing groups in Metekel tried to exploit the decentralization policy to protect their rights and promote group interest. The natives and long-staying residents embraced the ethnic-based regionalization principle to ensure economic and political control over Metekel. The Gumz in particular considered the new political development as an opportunity to put an end to the Amhara domination and reverse the course of history. Some even hoped to regain the land they had lost to the settlers in the 1980s. The Agaw and the Shinasha, who had also bitterly resented the previous Ethiopian regimes for marginalizing them, welcomed the new ideals of self-government. The administrative restructuring of Metekel[5] provided the natives and residents an officially sanctioned ground for collaboration.

The settlers, who felt that they were being treated as second-class citizens with restricted rights to live and work in Metekel, demanded that the notion of self-administration should apply to them as well. Some of their leaders are reported to have advocated administrative attachment of the resettlement area to the neighboring Amhara Region, the region from which most of the settlers originated. This agitated the Gumz activists, who then demanded the evacuation of the settlers from Metekel. The extreme positions held by both sides led to tension and the bloodshed described earlier. The compromise reached, through government intervention in 1994, was to recognize the resettlement area as a special district, answerable to the regional government and bypassing the Gumz-dominated Metekel Zone. During the research period, administratively, the district was under the Benishangul-Gumz Region. However, the political party that controlled power in the district was the Amhara National Democratic Movement—an ethnicity-based party operating primarily in the neighboring Amhara Region. In other words, the resettlement area is linked administratively to one region and politically to another. Under conditions of unanimity, some district officials admitted that this dual affiliation has complicated and hampered the business of running the district.

What does it mean for the ordinary Gumz people to welcome the Agaw and resist the resettlement of the Amhara? The legal land rights of the Gumz shifting cultivators were unclear. In the past, authorities considered fallow fields and forest areas as unoccupied lands, and designated them as state farms, resettlement areas, and commercial farms. Strategically, therefore, the Gumz were trying to maintain control over the remaining lands by passing holdings on to people whom they knew and trusted. The Agaw obtained land through sharecropping arrangements or renewable contracts. Out of a total of 97 Gumz households in Manjeri village, 47% reported that they had rented their land. Many informants indicated that this practice would serve as safeguards against arbitrary dispossession by the government or by the Amhara. At the same time, they did not preclude the possibility that their Agaw guests may become permanent residents and claim control over land. Politically, therefore, welcoming the Agaw represented an expression of resistance against the Amhara penetration into their territories. The economic advantage was that the Gumz could generate income to cope with the overall resettlement-induced deterioration of their livelihood. Moreover, some Gumz appeared to be motivated to learn the plough system from the Agaw.

The present resettlement

In 2003, the government of Ethiopia launched a new resettlement scheme that aims at relocating 2,200,000 people in three years with a total budget of US$217 million. An official document shows the following regional breakdown of the program in terms of the total number of people to be resettled: 1,000,000 people in Amhara, 500,000 in Oromia, 500,000 in Southern region, and 200,000 in Tigray (NCFSE 2003). Recent reports reveal that some 326,300 people (about 15% of the target) were resettled in 2004 (Pankhurst and Piguet 2004: 662). The authors further indicated that the figures in June 2004 were 256,000 in Oromia, 30,700 in Tigray, 23,600 in the Southern Region, and 16,000 in Amhara.

The current resettlement is justified as a development response to the recurring crisis of food security. Resettlement as a food security strategy is presented in a document that came to be known as the New Coalition for Food Security in Ethiopia (NCFSE 2003). The document contains critical norms to guide the relocation process. The major principles include: resettlement will be free and voluntary; resettlement will be within the same region; settlers are free to return to their places of origin if they so wish; settlers can regain their land in their places of origin if they return within three years; settlers are expected to share the cost of inputs (e.g., oxen) that will be provided on credit basis; settlers and their hosts are expected to collaborate in building shelters for the former thereby promoting community participation; and government will provide minimum infrastructure to avoid deterioration in service delivery and pressure on host communities.

Many anecdotal and unofficial reports on the implementation of the present program are emerging. Based on available materials, this sub-chapter discusses whether the on-going relocation operation is different from the past, and whether large-scale resettlement is indeed a viable option for attaining food security in Ethiopia.

Resettlement contrast

Similarities

There are outstanding similarities between the current and the 1980s resettlement programs. First, in terms of objectives, both programs aimed at attaining food security, reducing population pressure in vulnerable areas, and rehabilitating environment. Second, in both cases, authorities claimed the abundance of arable land for resettlement without credible evidence of the availability and suitability of land (Dessalegn 1988, 2004; Gebre 2002b). Third, both resettlements were implemented with haste, hence, there was insufficient time for adequate planning, adequate preparation, and proper consultation with the settlers and their hosts (Pankhurst 1992; Hammond and Bezaeit 2004).

Fourth, the two programs started during humanitarian crises and targeted desperate famine victims who are/were receiving relief assistance (Gebre 2002b; Dessalegn 2004). There are reports that relief recipients were told that the famine would be long-lasting or will get worse, and that food aid was not dependable. Fifth, both programs involved different forms of promises and inducements to make resettlements attractive (Pankhurst 1992; Gebre 2002b; Hammond and Bezaeit 2004). The present and previous governments employed quota systems for recruiting settlers, and this raised concerns that the lower level authorities (who are subject to performance evaluation) would employ various means to mobilize settlers to meet the target by the deadline. Sixth, both resettlement programs opted for a large-scale undertaking rather than a modest sized, cost-effective, and easy to manage scheme.

Differences

There are also marked differences between the two resettlement programs. First, the 1980s settlers lost rights to their land and other resources immediately after leaving home. This policy of alienating settlers' land was deliberately perpetrated to discourage attempts to return to homelands. The present settlers can retain rights to their land in their places of origin for three years. This is an important provision that creates a sense of security among the resettled population. Second, the previous settlers were not allowed to leave the resettlement areas. Their freedom of movement was highly restricted, and those who tried to escape risked serious punishment. The current policy provides that settlers can return to their place of origin if they are dissatisfied with the conditions in the resettled villages.

Third, while the previous resettlement was inter-regional, the present program is intra-regional. The principle of resettling people within the same region is adopted, among others, to avoid inter-community conflicts. Given land scarcity and the presence of diverse ethnic groups in many regions, inter-community conflict appears to be imminent. Fourth, the 1980s settlers enjoyed enormous amounts of government support and were expected to become self-sufficient in three years (although the dream did not come true). The current government provides minimum support, but expects the settlers to become not only self-sufficient but also surplus producers in one year. This is an ambitious and unrealistic goal that fails to understand that resettlement is a complex undertaking that requires substantial investment and time. Fifth, the previous government rounded up some of the settlers from their homes, farms, schools, and market places against their will. The present government insists that its program is voluntary, and so far no evidence has emerged to demonstrate the use of force. As indicated above, however, the current program involves inducements to make the resettlement attractive.

Is resettlement a viable option?

In the Ethiopian context, whether massive resettlement is a viable response to food insecurity is debatable. The main concern relates to the availability of suitable land for resettlement. The present government claims that there is about one million hectares of land that has been unoccupied, unused, or underused. If indeed there was unoccupied habitable land, people would have brought it under cultivation long before resettlement was envisaged. Many of the so-called unoccupied areas, currently selected for resettlement, represent inhospitable marginal lands often used by the lowlanders for grazing and shifting cultivation rather than for sedentary agriculture. These areas lie in humid and semi-arid fragile ecologies that are susceptible to environmental degradation. They are characterized by a host of human and animal diseases that impede habitation. The potential of these areas can be realized only with major public investments in health, infrastructure, social services, and water development. With only US$217 million budget, the present government seems to be poorly prepared to develop the resettlement areas.

A large number of settlers have been transferred to already inhabited and agriculturally suitable areas. Worldwide evidence and the Ethiopian experience clearly show that the influx of new settlers to already occupied places tends to (1) unsettle the already settled local people through resource alienation, (2) cause settler-host conflicts over resources that might become ongoing and deadly, and (3) accelerate environmental destruction and disturb the ecosystem. Preliminary reports on the present resettlement reveal the problem of land shortage in the destination areas (Abiy 2004; Wolde-Selassie 2004; Tranquilli 2004), host people's worries about pressure over resources and implications for ecology (Wolde-Selassie 2004), and instances of actual and potential conflicts between settlers and local people (Hammond and Bezaeit 2004; Wolde-Selassie 2004). In a country where farmland is scarce and farm technology simple, moving rural residents from one location to another is not an innovative approach to increase production or bring about sustainable development. In regions where productive resources are scarce, settlers represent a liability rather than an asset for the local community.

Conclusion

The successive Ethiopian governments executed planned resettlements as a strategy for attaining food security without adequate feasibility assessment, planning, preparation, and consultation. The analysis of the 1980s program in light of the IRR model reveals that resettlement has the potential to affect both the settlers and host people in multiple ways that are comparable. Moreover, my research shows that inadequately planned and poorly managed resettlements are likely to involve conflicts between guests and hosts. The comparison of the current resettlement program with that of the 1980s reveals that the past mistakes have been only partially addressed. Therefore, the present program cannot be expected to succeed unless the government revises its plan to resettle modest size, provide sufficient assistance to develop the new areas, and extend the benefits to host communities. The ideal solution to avert impoverishment and social disorder is to avoid disruptive population movements. When resettlements are unavoidable for justified reasons, the following measures should be taken to reduce the adverse effects.

- There should be clear national policy and legal frameworks regarding the rights of people to resources, genuine information, movement, residence, etc.
- Resettlement plans should be based on comprehensive feasibility studies undertaken by qualified researchers with interdisciplinary backgrounds.
- The potential settlers and host populations should be consulted in advance to secure their full consent and active participation in the decision-making.
- The construction of homes, the development of infrastructure and social services, and the commencement of production activities should start before the actual relocation to make the transition smooth and less disruptive.
- Resettlements must be planned with a development approach that transcends mere replacement or restoration of the existing standards of living.
- Donor agencies sponsoring resettlements should study the host areas and ensure that the concerns of the relocatees and the original residents are adequately addressed.

Notes

1 The field research was conducted from September 1998 to December 1999. The major tools used for data collection included intensive interviews, large formal surveys, panel discussions, observations, and a literature review. The Rockefeller Foundation funded the fieldwork. The Center of Excellence Program at Kyoto University and the Japan Society for the Promotion of Science provided a fellowship that enabled me to produce this text. Acknowledgements are due to these institutions

for their assistance. I am also thankful to my informants and several individuals, particularly Drs. Masayoshi Shigeta and Itaru Ohta of Kyoto University, for their support.

2 A preliminary version of this work was published in Gebre 2004b.

3 After the 1974 revolutionary overthrow of the Imperial government in Ethiopia, a military regime that came to be known as the *Derg* assumed power. The *Derg* soon severed relationships with the Western capitalist countries and allied itself with the socialist bloc until its collapse in 1991. Western countries, particularly the USA, the UK, the Federal Republic of Germany, and most other members of the EU were opposed to the resettlement (Jansson 1990).

4 The Metekel resettlement scheme was established on both sides of the Beles River. Each village is identified by a number with L, R, RH, RDS, or RUS as its prefix. All villages on the left hand side of the river course are designated L, while those on the right hand side are designated R. Some of the R villages are further identified with the labels RH (Right Hand), RUS (Right Upside) and RDS (Right Downside) to denote their direction from the main road heading to Guba town, located near the Ethiopia-Sudan border.

5 Prior to 1991, Metekel was a province of Gojam Region. Most of the residents of Gojam are Amhara people. The Gumz, Agaw, Shinasha, and Kulsi are minorities. According to the new administrative structure, Metekel is a zone under Benishangul-Gumz Region. This region is inhabited by several ethnic groups.

References

Abdussamad Ahmend (1988) 'Hunting in Gojam: The case of Metekel 1901–1932', in Taddesse Beyene (ed.), *Proceedings of Eighth International Conference of Ethiopian Studies.* Addis Ababa: Institute of Development Research, pp. 237–44.

Abiy Hailu (2004) 'Dilemmas of mass spontaneous movement seeking government sponsorship, or the rush for "El Dorado": The case of the Mana Angetu internally displaced persons', in Alula Pankhurst and Francois Piguet (eds), *People, Space and the State: Migration, Resettlement and Displacement in Ethiopia.* Addis Ababa: The Ethiopian Society of Sociologists, Social Workers and Anthropologists, pp. 565–74.

Agneta, F., S. Berterame, M. Capirci, L. Magni and M. Tomassoli (1993) 'The dynamics of social and economic adaptation during resettlement: The case of Beles Valley in Ethiopia', in Michael M. Cernea and S.

E. Guggenheim (eds), *Anthropological Approaches to Resettlement: Policy, Practice, and Theory.* Boulder: Westview Press, pp. 251–82.

Antonioli, Paolo (1992) 'The cornerstones of development: Training, private cooperatives, marketing strategies, and handing over', in Paolo Dieci and C. Viezzoli (eds), *Resettlement and Rural Development in Ethiopia, Social and Economic Research, Training and Technical Assistance in the Beles Valley.* Milano: Franco Angeli, pp. 383–96.

Bruce, James (1790) *Travels to Discover the Sources of the Nile.* Edinburgh: J. Ruthven.

Campbell, P. J., Debra Kreisberg-voss, and Joy Sobrepena (1993) 'The UNHCR and the international refugee protection system: Resources and responses', in Peter W. van Arsdale (ed.), *Refugee Empowerment and Organizational Change: A Systems Perspective.* Arlington, VA: American Anthropological Association, pp. 155–80.

Cernea, Michael M. (1996) 'Understanding and preventing impoverishment from displacement: Reflections on the state of knowledge', in Christopher McDowell (ed.), *Understanding Impoverishment: The Consequences of Development-Induced Displacement.* Oxford: Berghahn Books, pp. 13–32.

———(2000) 'Risks, safeguards, and reconstruction: A model for population displacement and resettlement', in M. M. Cernea and C. McDowell (eds), *Risk and Reconstruction: Experiences of Resettlers and Refugees.* Washington, DC: World Bank, pp. 11–55.

———(2002) *Advances in Resettlement Theory and Policy and the Economic Basis of Successful Resettlements.* Paper presented at the International Symposium on Resettlement and Social Development, held at Hohai University, Nanjing, China.

Cerulli, Ernesta (1956) *Peoples of Southwest Ethiopia and Its Borderlands.* London: International African Institute.

Chambers, Robert (1986) 'Hidden losers? The impact of rural refugees and refugee programs on poorer hosts', in D. Gallapher (ed.), *Refugees: Issues and Directions.* A Special Issue, International Migration Review, New York: Center for Migration Studies, pp. 245–63.

Clay, Jason W. and B. K. Holcomb (1986) *Politics and the Ethiopian Famine 1984–1985.* Cambridge: Cultural Survival.

Dawit, Wolde Giorgis (1989) *Red Tears: War, Famine and Revolution in Ethiopia.* Trenton, NJ: The Red Sea Press.

de Waal, Alex (1991) *Evil Days: Thirty Years of War and Famine in Ethiopia.* New York: Human Rights Watch.

Dejene, Alemneh (1990) *Environment, Famine, and Development in Ethiopia.* Boulder: Lynne Rienner.

Dessalegn, Rahmato (1988) 'Some notes on settlement and resettlement in Metekel Awraja (Gojjam Province)', in A. Gromyko (ed.), *Proceedings of the Ninth International Congress of Ethiopian Studies*. USSR Academy of Sciences, Africa Institute, Moscow: Nauka Publishers, pp. 26–9.

———— (2004) *Large-Scale Resettlement in Ethiopia: Is it a Viable Option?* Work in progress (unpublished), Addis Ababa, February.

Gebre, Yntiso (2001) *Population Displacement and Food Insecurity in Ethiopia: Resettlement, Settlers, and Hosts*. PhD Dissertation, Department of Anthropology, University of Florida.

———— (2002a) 'Differential reestablishment of voluntary and involuntary migrants: The case of Metekel settlers in Ethiopia', *African Study Monographs*, 23(1), pp. 31–46.

———— (2002b) 'Contextual determination of migration behaviors: The Ethiopian resettlement in the light of conceptual constructs', *Journal of Refugee Studies*, 15(3), pp. 265–82.

———— (2003) 'Resettlement and the unnoticed losers: Impoverishment disasters among the Gumz hosts in Ethiopia', *Human Organization*, 62(1) pp. 50–61.

———— (2004a) 'The Metekel resettlement in Ethiopia: Why did it fail?' in Alula Pankhurst and Francois Piguet (eds), *People, Space and the State: Migration, Resettlement and Displacement in Ethiopia*. Addis Ababa: The Ethiopian Society of Sociologists, Social Workers and Anthropologists, pp. 92–111.

———— (2004b) 'Resettlement risks and inter-ethnic conflict in Metekel, Ethiopia', *Ethiopian Journal of Social Sciences and Humanities*, 2(1), pp. 47–67.

Hammond, Laura and Bezaeit Dessalegn (2004) 'Evaluation of the 2003 pilot resettlement "Safara" programme', in Alula Pankhurst and Francois Piguet (eds), *People, Space and the State: Migration, Resettlement and Displacement in Ethiopia*. Addis Ababa: The Ethiopian Society of Sociologists, Social Workers and Anthropologists, pp. 623–53.

James, Wendy (1986) 'Lifelines: Exchange marriage among the Gumz', in Donald Donham and Wendy James (eds), *Southern Marches of Imperial Ethiopia: Essays in History and Social Anthropology*. Cambridge: Cambridge University Press, pp. 119–47.

Jansson, Kurt (1990) *The Ethiopian Famine*, revised and updated edition. London: Zed Books.

Keller, E. J. (1993) 'Government politics', in Thomas P. Ofcansky and LaVerle Berry (eds), *Ethiopia: A Country Study*. Federal Research Division, Library of Congress, Washington, DC: US Government Printing Office, pp. 209–66.

Kibreab, Gaim (2000) 'Common property resources and resettlement', in M. M. Cernea and C. McDowell (eds), *Risk and Reconstruction: Experiences of Resettlers and Refugees*. Washington, DC: World Bank, pp. 293–331.

Morell, Virginia (2000) 'The Blue Nile: Ethiopia's sacred waters', *National Geographic*, 198(6), pp. 2–29.

NCFSE (New Coalition for Food Security in Ethiopia) (2003), *Voluntary Resettlement Program*, Volume II. Addis Ababa, November.

Pankhurst, Alula and Francois Piguet (2004) 'Summary and conclusion: Migration, relocation and coexistence in Ethiopia', in Alula Pankhurst and Francois Piguet (eds), *People, Space and the State: Migration, Resettlement and Displacement in Ethiopia*. Addis Ababa: The Ethiopian Society of Sociologists, Social Workers and Anthropologists, pp. 657–88.

Pankhurst, Alula (1992) *Resettlement and Famine in Ethiopia: The Villager's Experience*. Manchester: Manchester University Press.

RRC (Relief and Rehabilitation Commission of Ethiopia) (1981) *Settlement Policy*. Addis Ababa: RRC.

Salem-Murdock, Muneera (1993) 'Involuntary resettlement: A plea for the host population', in M. M. Cernea and S. E. Guggenheim (eds), *Anthropological Approaches to Resettlement: Policy, Practice, and Theory*. Boulder: Westview Press, pp. 307–20.

Salini Costruttori (1989) *The Tana-Beles Project Ethiopia*. Rome: Salini Costruttori.

Scudder, Thayer (1993) 'Development induced relocation and refugee studies: 37 years of change and community among Zambia's Gwambe Tonga', *Journal of Refugee Studies*, 6(2), pp. 123–52.

Scott, James (1998) *Seeing Like a State: How Certain Schemes to Improve the Human Condition Have Failed*. New Haven: Yale University Press.

Taddesse, Tamrat (1988) 'Nilo-Sahara interactions with neighboring highlanders: The case of the Gumz of Gojjam and Wallaga', in *Proceedings of the Workshop on Famine Experience and Resettlement in Ethiopia*. Addis Ababa: Institute of Development Research, pp. 7–15.

Tranquilli, Roberta (2004) 'Resettlement in Amhara and Southern Regions: A comparative assessment of the 2003 programmes', in Alula Pankhurst and Francois Piguet (eds) *People, Space and the State: Migration, Resettlement and Displacement in Ethiopia*. Addis Ababa: The Ethiopian Society of Sociologists, Social Workers and Anthropologists, pp. 595–622.

Wolde-Selassie, Abute (2004) 'Resettlement as a response to food insecurity: The case of Southern Nations, Nationalities and Peoples' Regions

(SNNPR)', in Alula Pankhurst and Francois Piguet (eds) *People, Space and the State: Migration, Resettlement and Displacement in Ethiopia.* Addis Ababa: The Ethiopian Society of Sociologists, Social Workers and Anthropologists, pp. 575–87.

Index

www.ingramcontent.com/pod-product-compliance
Lightning Source LLC
Chambersburg PA
CBHW072043020426
42334CB00017B/1369